CONTRACT NEGOTIATION HANDBOOK
Third Edition

CONTRACT NEGOTIATION HANDBOOK

Third edition

P. D. V. Marsh

Gower

© P. D. V. Marsh 2001

First edition published 1974 by
Gower Press Ltd.
Second edition published 1984 by
Gower Publishing Company Ltd.

This edition published by
Gower Publishing Limited
Gower House
Croft Road
Aldershot
Hampshire GU11 3HR
England

Gower Publishing Company
131 Main Street
Burlington VT 05401–5600 USA

British Library Cataloguing in Publication Data
Marsh, P. D. V. (Peter David Victor), 1926–
   Contract negotiation handbook. – 3rd ed.
   1. Contracts   2. Negotiation in business
   I. Title
   658.7'23

ISBN 0 566 08021 4

Library of Congress Cataloging-in-Publication Data

Marsh, P. D. V.
   Contract negotiation handbook / P.D.V. Marsh. – 3rd ed.
     p. cm.
   ISBN 0-566-08021-4
     1. Negotiation in business. 2. Contracts. I. Title

   HD58.6.M37 2000
   658.7'23–dc21   00-039386

Typeset in Plantin Light by IML Typographers, Chester and printed in Great Britain by MPG Books Ltd. Bodmin.

CONTENTS

PART THREE: Structure and Sequence of the Negotiations

LIST OF FIGURES

INTRODUCTION

Negotiation is a dynamic process of adjustment by which two or more parties, each with their own mutually conflicting objectives, confer together with the intention of reaching an agreement which at least satisfies their minimum needs on a matter of common interest. This definition contains the essential themes which it is the purpose of this book to develop. The chosen field is that of commercial contracts whether for the sale or purchase of goods and services or the construction of engineering works. The area of labour relations is excluded although many of the concepts could be applied there, particularly the strategic and tactical bargaining moves as developed in Part Four.

A dynamic process of adjustment

The process of negotiation takes place within a series of ascending time-scales the nature and significance of which will differ according to the characteristics of the negotiation. Four time-scales have been identified:

1 The period during which the parties prepare for the negotiations and make their initial approach
2 The period during which the parties must reach agreement in order for the common interest to be realized
3 The period during which the agreement which they have negotiated is intended to operate
4 The extended period during which the parties contemplate a continuing business relationship.

The first two short periods will always apply and provide discipline for the negotiators. As Cross has stated 'If it did not matter when the parties agreed it would not matter whether or not they agreed at all.'[1] However, the significance of the second time-scale will clearly differ according to whether the negotiations are concerned with the award of a contract or with the resolution of a contractor's claim for additional payment. In the latter case, while the period may be highly significant to the contractor, who is standing out of his money, it may be of much less interest to the client, who is holding on to the money, unless the dispute is affecting progress or the award of other contracts.

The third period, depending upon its length, will affect the attitudinal structure of the negotiations. If this is a long period, then both sides will be aware of the opportunities which this will provide for a party who considers himself to have been unfairly disadvantaged to recover that to which he believes himself entitled. On other hand, if the third period is short and a one-off deal, then the parties can be expected to take full advantage of whatever negotiating power they possess to extract the maximum benefit to themselves from the deal, regardless of its effect on the other either in terms of economics or human relationship.

The fourth period has always been of significance to major/equipment suppliers or contractors to the government and to the major utilities. Today it has become of much wider significance than in the past because of the acceptance across major sectors of industry of the concept of strategic alliance partnering as a preferred procurement strategy for their high-value business.[2]

In a long-term continuing buyer/seller relationship, it is not just the terms of the bargain which are important but the manner of its negotiation and its impact on the human relationships between the people in both organizations. Partnering is about people and relationships and the culture of working together to achieve common goals. In establishing and developing this relationship, trust is essential. Hard bargaining, conducted in a manner which the other party recognizes as legitimate, will not have an adverse effect. It may even enhance relationships if it adds to the respect which both parties feel for their counterparts. But the use of tactics perceived as illegitimate will destroy the relationship before it can take root.

Each party's objective

A party in setting the objective which he wishes to achieve from a negotiation will do so in relation to a level of aspiration which reflects the economic and social morality of the society within which he operates. 'Society' in this context may mean the particular business area with which the firm is concerned or the wider field of trade in general.

Society does not in general aim to ensure through regulation or religious teaching that commercial dealings are on 'fair terms' or at 'a just price' as was the case in England during the Middle Ages, despite the passing of the somewhat misnamed 'Unfair Contract Terms Act'. There has, however, been a significant strengthening of the protection afforded to consumers in their dealings with business firms through the passing of the Unfair Terms in Consumer Contracts Regulations 1994, the powers given to the Director General of Fair Trading under those Regulations and the legislative control of the contents of contracts with consumers under the Consumer Credit Act 1974. As negotiations between the Director General of Fair Trading and trade associations proceed, it is becoming clear that the expression 'fair', in terms of consumer contracts, is beginning to become a meaningful concept.[3]

Although business firms are basically expected to look after their own interests, there have been a number of cases decided in recent times, either at common law or under the Unfair Contract Terms Act 1974, in which the court has acted to protect a party in circumstances in which he has clearly failed to look after himself.[4]

The conclusion which one can draw from these cases is that the court will tend to look upon some terms as representing a balanced set of norms as between commercial buyer and seller and will refuse to give effect to terms which depart from these.[5] But the cases which come before the courts represent only a tiny fraction of the contracts negotiated and their decisions are of effect only as between the parties and then only on the facts of that particular contract. Lawyers will continue to protect their clients' interests even if this results in 'unfair terms'.[6]

But there are some other signs of change. Within the field of public works or supplies contracts, the European Court of Justice has emphasized the underlying principle of equality of treatment of all bidders.[7] Further, the Council and European Commission have stated that, in relation to tenders to which the Directives apply, and which have been invited under either the Open or Restricted Procedures, negotiations with tenderers on price or any other factor which would distort competition, are not permitted.[8]

In the construction industry, the Latham Report has emphasized the need for contract terms to be fair[9] and the *New Engineering Contract* has been designed along these lines.[10] The use of partnering as a procurement strategy has already resulted in contract terms and attitudes which are less adversarial.[11] The chairman of Birse Construction Ltd apologized in June 1997 that in the face of difficult trading conditions his company had been too adversarial in its approach to both sub-contractors and clients and had caused concern not only to them but also to his own staff, and he promised change. It cannot be coincidental that Birse Construction was one of the contractors whose partnering agreement with Staffordshire County Council was featured prominently in the Construction Industry Board Report 'Partnering the Team', published in the same month.[12]

It is, however, much too early to believe that there is any widespread acceptance of the meaning of 'fair' in relation to contract terms or the negotiation of contracts, let alone an objective definition of what 'fair' means. A glance at some of the contracts prepared for major commercial developments would quickly demonstrate this point. Within the negotiating situation no universal 'practice' exists to which reference can be made in deciding upon whether or not particular acts can be justified: there are no 'constitutive rules' of general application from which one can derive a moral 'ought', although such rules may exist in particular circumstances.

Aside from morality the objective will take account of the economic structure within which the parties do business and the motivation of the individual negotiators. This latter will be directed internally within the party's own organization and externally towards the negotiators of the other side who, in many instances, they will know personally. Just because it is a microactivity, often resolving itself in the ultimate to bargaining between two persons, the process of contract negotiation is necessarily complex and there are three levels upon which the parties will interact. Nevertheless, within the UK at least these are the beginnings of an awareness of what constitutes 'fair' terms or 'fair' practice in certain specific situations. Outside these situations, and particularly when negotiating with companies overseas, the meaning of the concept may well differ or even have no meaning at all.

The structural level

This covers the legal, cultural, technological and economic environments within which the negotiation is to take place. For a particular negotiation, some of these parameters will be fixed. A public authority may be required by regulations only to contract subject to its own legal system or within the European Union to follow the rules of the Procurement Directives.

Negotiators steeped in a particular culture, e.g. the adversarial one of the construction industry, are unlikely to change within the short time-frame of a single negotiation unless compelled to do so by their senior management, e.g. because of their management's recent commitment to partnering, as in the Birse example referred to above.

The range of technologies available which could satisfy the purchaser's requirements is that which presently exists. What perhaps can be changed is the purchaser's perception of which best suits him, often related to the level of risk the seller is willing to accept and the guarantees which the seller is willing to give.

The economic environment covers both the economy of the industry and that of the individual firms concerned. Factually, neither is likely to change within the negotiation's time-scale but the perception by the negotiator's of their economic needs may do so.

THE CORPORATE SOCIAL LEVEL

The extent to which the firm as a matter of policy adopts either an aggressive or a cooperative attitude will clearly affect the setting of the initial objective and of the minimum acceptable terms. It has already been shown that the firm is here not wholly an independent agent but is itself influenced by the cultural norms prevailing in the industry in which it operates and the economic circumstances in which it is placed.

THE PERSONAL SOCIAL LEVEL OF THE NEGOTIATORS

It would simplify our task if we could treat the firm and the individual negotiator as one and the same and ignore the role occupied by the negotiator within the ongoing system of relationships between himself and other members of the firm, predominant among which is the dependent relationship between the negotiator and the dominant power group within the firm.[13] It is to this group which we are really referring when we speak of 'the firm', a point which must never be forgotten otherwise we shall commit the error of reification and assign to the firm as an entity personality characteristics which properly belong only to individuals. References to 'the firm' are only a convenient form of shorthand. The importance of recognizing these relationships is that the attractiveness of any particular bargain is likely to be different for the negotiator and for 'the firm' and it may be expected that the negotiators will bargain not only with each other but additionally with their own firms, even at times to the point of forming informal alliances between themselves, so as to frustrate what they regard as the 'the firm's' unreasonable behaviour.

The negotiators will also react to each other as personalities; they may be attracted or repelled. Personalistic objective setting is strongly influenced by the emotional feelings which one negotiator has towards the other as a person, and this would appear to apply even when such feelings are derived solely from written evidence of the other's personality and the two negotiators have never met![14] Tactics designed to minimize emotional antagonism or indifference, and to provide the environment for constructive problem solving are considered in Part Three.

Mutually satisfying agreement on a matter of common interest

Where the interests of the parties directly conflict, e.g. in the price to be paid, or the risks to be accepted, so that the gain to one will result in less for the other, the bargaining will be referred to as *distributive*.[15] Each party will press for the attainment of its own goal. But some element of cooperation must be present otherwise there will be no agreement at all and the opportunity to take part in the activity will be lost. The dual elements of conflict and cooperation have been described by Siegel and Fouraker in the following terms: 'It is in the mutual interest of the participants to come to *some* agreement and this provides a cooperative aspect; however, given that an agreement will be achieved, the interests of the participants are opposed, and this is a basis for rivalry.[16]

The negotiator is pulled in two directions at the same time; towards holding out for more with the risk of losing all; towards agreeing to the other's demands, and securing the bargain, but in so doing possibly sacrificing the chance of a higher reward.

For each party, there is an upper limit representing the bargain which he believes is the best he could possibly achieve, within the restrictions imposed by the bargaining structure, and a lower limit below which he would prefer not to participate. Provided that the upper limit of one of the parties lies between the upper and lower limits of the other, i.e. there is a degree of overlap between them, then a bargain is feasible. Whether it will be achieved or not, and if so at what point, are questions which will have to be considered (see Chapter 8). They involve the issues of how each party values a series of potential bargains and the process of anticipation and adjustment by which, over a span of time, the negotiators will tend to coordinate. Assuming that finally agreement is reached, the result is compromise; neither is wholly satisfied but both recognize that it is more beneficial to them to agree than to disagree.

Negotiation, however, in the context of contract formation has as its end result the supply of goods/services or the construction of engineering works on a basis profitable to both parties. Merit exists therefore not just in making the bargain but in its proper fulfilment.

This should lead both parties to emphasize the cooperative nature of their relationship and to convert, as far as practicable, the issues dividing them into problems to be solved. By so doing the bargaining process is changed from distributive to integrative. This change completely alters the character of the bargaining process since it admits the possibility, which distributive bargaining does not, of introducing alternatives and of increasing the total benefits.[17]

An example would be negotiation over the period for delivery. The supplier offers say twelve months; the buyer wants the work completed in ten months. Distributive bargaining would lead to a compromise, possibly eleven months, which might or might not be achieved. Integrative bargaining, however, would involve a joint examination of the problem by both parties to ascertain the holding factors, such as long lead items, special test and inspection procedures, etc., and a joint decision between them on these problems aimed at an optimum solution which was at the same time realistic. The finding and implementation of such a solution would be a 'superordinate' goal in Sherif's terminology.[18] The following-out of this concept can have fruitful consequences both for the immediate contract and for the future relationships between the parties, and will be reviewed later.

If the negotiations concern the resolution of a contract dispute, then two situations need to be distinguished according to when the negotiations for the settlement of the dispute take place.

If the dispute arises during the course of carrying out the contract, and it is decided to settle it then rather than wait until the completion of the work, as a result the superordinate goal is the reaching of an agreement which will allow work to continue without disruption to the relationships between the parties. This acts as a powerful incentive to find a genuine solution to what is often a minor issue without allowing it to escalate into a major one.

Deferring settlement until the end of the contract, an occurrence unfortunately only too common in the construction industry, means that, in the absence of any real intent of the parties to do business together again in the near future, there is no superordinate goal. The evil consequences of this will be examined in Chapter 6, p. 23.

Scope of study

It will be evident from this brief examination of the definition of negotiation that the subject encompasses more than one discipline in its total understanding. Economics can provide the basic framework, primarily through its treatment of bilateral monopoly. For the evaluation of a range of possible offers and the establishment of a formal structure for decision taking under risk, the related fields of operational analysis and game theory are examined. Finally, because it is individuals who are involved, psychology is required to provide an insight into the personal motivational drives of the negotiators and the manner in which they will seek to satisfy these. To this is added a behavioural analysis, drawn from practical experience, of the strategies and tactics adopted in the field by negotiators.

Negotiation is treated not as an isolated event but as an integral part of the total business activity. Through the agreements negotiated, the links are established in the chain by which goods are traded, services provided and facilities constructed. In this respect negotiation as a function is subservient to the general commercial interests of the parties involved and is directed towards the achievement of their overall objectives.

Success in negotiation is seen not to be measured therefore in points scored off one's opponent but in the contribution which the negotiation makes to the successful operation of the activity as a whole. This applies also within the negotiation itself. Each participating function must accept the need to modify its own demands as necessary to meet the requirements of the negotiating objective. There is shown to be no room in a negotiating team for the individual who insists on pursuing limited departmental interests to the detriment of his team's overall success.

Plan of study

This study is divided into four parts:

- Part 1, 'The Need to Negotiate', examines the various circumstances under which the need to negotiate arises and identifies the primary characteristics of each.

- Part 2, 'Planning for Negotiations', looks at all the factors which require to be considered in the formulation of the negotiating plan.

- Part 3, 'Structure and Sequence of the Negotiations,' identifies the various phases through which a negotiation proceeds after completion of the planning phase, from the opening to the final recording of the bargain.

- Part 4, 'Negotiation Tactics', discusses the various tactics which negotiators use in practice.

Each part will cover as appropriate both the normative and the psychological aspects of negotiating behaviour. The description of decision techniques, which was in Chapter 2 of the second edition, has been transferred to Appendix 1. Although use will still be made of decision techniques, less emphasis is placed on them than previously.

Notes

1. J. G. Cross, *The Economics of Bargaining* (New York: Basic Books, 1969).
2. Partnership Sourcing Ltd, a non-profit-making company, has been established through collaboration between the CBI and the Department of Trade and Industry to promote the concepts of Partnership Sourcing – see their booklets on the subject with case study examples.
3. See the second Office of Fair Trading Bulleting 1996 and the report on this published in *Croner's Purchasing and Supply Bulletin*, 24 October 1996.
4. See *Interfoto Picture Library* v. *Stiletto Visual Programmes Ltd* 1988, *Lease Management Services Ltd* v. *Purnell Secretarial Services Ltd* 1994, *AEG (UK) Ltd* v. *Logic Resource Ltd* 1995 and *St Albans City and District Council* v. *International Computers Ltd* July 1996.
5. In *Edmund Murray Ltd* v. *BSP International Foundations Ltd* 1992, the Court of Appeal decided that terms under which a seller sought to avoid liability for providing goods as per a detailed performance specification were inherently unfair and unreasonable. At the same time they felt that a term allowing for exclusion of consequential damages would appear to be fair and reasonable.
6. The second annual report of the OFT highlighted a large number of 'unfair' terms in consumer contracts and concluded that 'the use of unfair terms in consumer contracts is widespread and amounts to a serious problem in the UK'. From the examples given it is clear that these terms were drafted by lawyers acting on their clients' instructions to protect their interests. An illuminating view on the approach adopted by lawyers in the drafting of terms and conditions related to their fairness is to be found in Professor Woodruff's letter printed in the magazine *Supply Management* (22 May 1997), from which the following extract is taken: 'Why put a clause in your own terms which limits or even excludes your supplier's liability to you. It's like running down the street knocking yourself over and stealing your own wallet. Leave it to the suppliers to mug you – they will do their best.'

7. In the *Commission* v. *Denmark*, the Storebaelt case, the ECJ based its conclusions on the existence of a principle of equality in the treatment of tenderers underlying the procurement directives.

8. The statement which accompanied the issue of the Utilities and Consolidated Works Directives reads 'The Council and the Commission state that in open and restricted procedures all negotiations with candidates or tenderers on fundamental aspects of contracts, variations of which are likely to distort competition, and in particular on prices shall be ruled out; however discussions with candidates or tenderers may be held but only for the purpose of clarifying or supplementing the content of their tenders or the requirements of the contracting authorities and provided this does not involve discrimination.'

9. The Latham Report, 'Constructing the Team', July 1994, recommended in paragraph 5.18 that amongst provisions the most effective form of contract in modern conditions should include 'a specific duty for all parties to deal fairly with each other and with their sub-contractors, specialists and suppliers in an atmosphere of mutual co-operation'.

10. *The New Engineering Contract*, 2nd edition, issued by the Institute of Civil Engineers, November 1995, but applicable to a wide range of construction contracts, states in its opening paragraph '... the Employer,' the Contractor, the Project Manager and the Supervisor shall act as stated in this contract and in a spirit of mutual trust and co-operation.' Note that under the NEC, there is no traditional engineer or architect.

11. The 1994 Institute of Petroleum report 'Cost reduction and initiative for the new era' (CRINE) recommended limiting the use of liquidated damages to critical cases to provide a risk/reward basis, to keep funding requirements neutral and to eliminate contract terms that encourage adversarial relationships.

12. Partnering in the Team Working Group 12 Report, 'The Tunstall Western Bypass phase 2, where the benefits reported were a £400,000 saving, 20% Programme saving and a £6 million risk averted on a £10 million project.

13. A. Coddington in his *Theory of the Bargaining Process* (London: George Allen and Unwin, 1968), p.6, assumes that the negotiators have as their objective the simple maximization of utility. He also implicitly draws no distinction between the negotiator as an individual and the firm. Thus 'If each party to the bargaining process is an organization rather than a single person we suppose that it acts in a perfectly coordinated way regarding its choice of a demand.'

14. See L. E. Siegel and S. Fouraker, *Bargaining Behaviour* (New York: McGraw Hill, 1963), pp. 65 and 66 for examples of such behaviour.

15. R. E. Walton and R. E. McKersie, *A Behavioral Theory of Labor Relations* (New York: McGraw Hill, 1965), pp. 4, 13.

16. L. E. Siegel and S. Fouraker, *Bargaining Behaviour*, p. 7.

17. R. E. Walton and R. E. McKersie, *A Behavioral Theory of Labor Relations*, pp. 127–28.

18. M. Sherif, *Group Conflict and Cooperation* (London: Routledge and Kegan Paul, 1968), pp. 88 ff.

PART *1*

THE NEED TO NEGOTIATE

1 INTRODUCTION TO PART ONE

No firm wants to pay a higher price or contract on less favourable terms for the goods and services they wish to buy than is necessary, nor does any firm wish to settle a dispute other than on the most favourable basis which they can secure. But how are they to know what are the most favourable terms available? In a purchasing situation certainly not, in general, by relying on competition alone. Other than in certain quite specific circumstances, in which the terms of the initial offer which a firm receives will be the most favourable which they can obtain, the answer is through competition, where feasible, plus negotiation. This is because, those specific cases apart, the purchaser if acting rationally, must assume that the original offer does not represent the last word of the person making it and negotiation is the only way in which the firm can improve the terms of that offer in their favour.

Additionally, the negotiators concerned for both sides have a psychological need to secure a bargain. The satisfaction of the negotiator's drive first for security and then for the earning of the esteem both of himself and others plays a major part in the way that the negotiating process develops.

The purpose of this part of our study is to identify those particular circumstances in which negotiation is not appropriate and then to look at the need for negotiation in other situations both from the rationalistic viewpoint of the firm and the motivational drives of the negotiators themselves.

2 STRICT TENDERING

2.1 Strict tendering

A purchasing situation is one of strict tendering when the purchaser invites sealed bid tenders and states that only firms submitting compliant bids will be considered. It is not necessary that the purchasing authority should have stated their intention to award the contract to the lowest bidder, but it is necessary that they should not have reserved the right to negotiate with one or more tenderers.

Provided that these conditions are met, and the purchasing authority really does regularly carry out in practice its terms of tendering, which fact is known to all the bidders who constitute a small group, then the buyer would be justified in the belief that no bidder had any incentive to submit other than his best offer. It can be shown that in such cases not only is there no need for the purchaser to negotiate with the lowest bidder in an attempt to improve his offer, but that any such attempt would be destructive of good faith and trust between the parties and economically disadvantageous to the purchaser for the future.[1]

It might on the first occasion, if the buyer had sufficient negotiating power, lead either to an initial reduction in price or in an improvement in the contract terms, but with the serious risk of the adoption of a non-cooperative attitude by the supplier during contract implementation which could lead to future increased costs to the purchaser. The more complex the contract, and the longer its time-scale, the greater the opportunity will exist for the supplier to pursue such retaliatory behaviour.

However, even if some advantage does accrue initially to the buyer, which in itself is doubtful, this would be most unlikely to be repeated. The supplier would not make the same mistake twice and the news would also spread fast amongst all the suppliers in the marketplace. This would cause all firms to include negotiating margins in their prices and/or contract terms on the next occasion. In turn this would mean that the purchaser could no longer trust the tendering process on its own to provide him with the best value for money. He would be compelled from then on, if he wished to avoid placing the contract at a price level or on contract terms which included the supplier's negotiating margin, to engage in post tender negotiation, with the associated time and costs involved.[2]

This analysis is valid subject to one important caveat: that it only applies provided that there is genuine competition between the various suppliers.

In practice the circumstances described above only exist in very particular situations. There must be a well-defined market for the goods in which the purchaser is inviting tenders on a regular basis from a fairly limited set of suppliers all of whom are aware of the purchaser's buying practices.

2.2 Cartels

Unfortunately, it is precisely in this situation, which approaches the economist's dream of perfect competition, that the suppliers will be tempted to form a cartel with the object of fixing prices and/or allocating between them shares of the business. Unwittingly, the purchaser's behaviour designed to ensure fair and rigorous competitive tendering has possibly created the very obstacle which will ensure that his objective is frustrated.

Such a cartel, once discovered would almost certainly be held to be void under the Competition Act 1998 which replaced the Restrictive Trade Practices Act 1976, and may leave the suppliers open to a fine under the new Competition Act and an action for substantial damages if the purchaser has suffered a loss through its operation. However, its existence may be difficult for the purchaser to identify even with the assistance of the Office of Fair Trading.[3]

Once the buyer suspects the existence of a cartel then the continuation of a policy of strict competitive tendering would be merely to play into the cartel's hands. Cartels thrive on the predictability of the purchaser's behaviour and, in the absence of legal action, it is only non-predictable behaviour which will disrupt them.

In summary:

- Provided the buyer is satisfied that genuine competition exists, and the above stated conditions as to the market are satisfied, then strict competitive tendering will produce an economic benefit to the buyer which would not be improved by negotiation and avoids the time and costs which negotiation incurs.
- If a cartel is suspected to exist. then the buyer should not follow a policy of strict competitive tendering but should adopt non-predictable purchasing tactics – see Chapter 15, p. 97.
- If the above stated market conditions do not exist, then purchasing simply on a competitive basis without negotiation will not provide the buyer with the optimum bargain which he could obtain.

Notes

1. This point is elaborated and supported by an analysis in game-theory terms in Chapter 15, p. 96.
2. The issue of negotiating time and related costs is discussed in detail in Chapter 16, p. 106 and Appendix 3.
3. The Office of Fair Trading has a Cartels Task Force which relies to a large extent on information from buyers to enable it to act. It is strongly suggested that buyers who believe they have evidence of the existence of a cartel operating should contact that office, telephone or fax number 020 7269 8888.

3 POST TENDER NEGOTIATION

3.1 Post tender negotiation

The Chartered Institute of Purchasing and Supply has defined post tender negotiation (PTN) as

> Negotiations after receipt of formal tenders and before the letting of contracts with the supplier(s)/contractor(s) submitting the lowest acceptable tender(s) with a view to obtaining an improvement in price, delivery or content in circumstances which do not put other tenderers at a disadvantage or affect adversely their confidence or trust in the competitive bidding system.[1]

3.2 Final offer first

It has already been noted that when purchasing is subject to the Public Procurement or Utilities Directives and is conducted under either the Open or Restricted Procedures then PTN is not permitted.[2] Assuming the sellers believe that the buyer will follow the rules, and there is no collusion between them, then this does not matter. All will know that they have only one chance of securing the contract and can be expected to bid accordingly. When discussing negotiating strategy we will refer to this as 'Quick-Kill', otherwise known as 'final offer first'.

3.3 Hold back

In other circumstances, and despite the ethical objections which have been raised from time to time, it is considered, in line with the Government's own views on the matter,[3] that the use of PTN in many buying situations is not only justified but is the only means by which the buyer can secure better value for money.

The need to negotiate after the receipt of tenders lies in the belief held now by the buyer, unlike that which applied in the Strict Tendering situation, that the tenderers will not have offered the lowest price and/or the most onerous contract terms on which they would be willing to accept the contract. They will have held something back, either because they know it is the buyer's policy to negotiate, or they are not certain whether he will do so or not and have therefore played safe. For these reasons, in discussing negotiating strategies we will refer to this practice as 'Hold Back'.

The problem of uncertainty most often arises in practice because the purchase is a one-off, say of capital goods, and there is no established course of dealing between the parties. Neither is therefore likely to be confident of the other's behaviour, the seller of the buyer's propensity to negotiate or the buyer of the seller's policy on pricing or contract terms, and both will assume the worst.

If the buyer is correct in his belief then it follows that if he does not negotiate it is almost certain that he will pay more and/or contract on less favourable terms than the seller would have accepted. How much worse off the buyer will be if he does not negotiate, taking the time and costs of negotiation into account, will depend on the value of the purchase, what the supplier has built into his tender and the probability of the buyer's success in the negotiations, all factors we will discuss later – see Chapter 16.

At the very least, however, the possibility of engaging in PTN is something which the buyer ought to consider – the higher the value of procurement the stronger the argument for his doing so.

However, the analysis of the buyer's need to negotiate by PTN would not be complete if it did not include the buyer's need to provide himself with security or to earn the esteem of others by demonstrating his 'success' as a negotiator. If the culture in which the buyer operates is one which expects him to achieve 'success', and this is known to the seller, then the seller will be only too pleased to provide him with the opportunity of achieving that success by allowing him to earn at least part of that which he seller has included to give away. That may sound like a game – indeed it is often best described as a game or ritual which must be played out so that the psychological needs of the negotiators for both parties are satisfied. But it would be wrong to deny its value as a means of showing 'good faith' through the making of 'concessions' and achieving what Cross has described as 'organised co-operation'.[4] This will be discussed in more detail later – see Chapter 27, pp. 183.

Notes

1. Statement from the Chartered Institute of Purchasing and Supply which appeared in *Purchasing and Supply Management*, September 1986. This is very similar to the definition given by the Government's Central Unit on Purchasing (CUP) in its Guidance Note No. 19, *PTN Update*, July 1989.
2. See note 8 to the Introduction, p. 8.
3. The use of PTN was recommended in the report entitled 'Government Purchasing', CUP Guidance Note No. 1, issued May 1986, which gave guidance on the use of PTN.
4. J. G. Cross, *The Economics of Bargaining Behavior* (New York: Basic Books, 1969), p. 177.

4 SECURING A BETTER BARGAIN

4.1 Introduction

Aside from strict tendering, there are many situations in which a firm will simply request another to submit a quotation or to make a proposal, for particular goods or services on a one-off basis. The degree of formality with which the request is made will vary, from the issue of a form with the Purchaser's conditions attached to it, to a simple letter which is not accompanied by any conditions.

In this type of situation when there is no history of repeated dealings and no intent to set up a long-term relationship, the field is wide open for both parties. Each has the choice as to whether to behave in the negotiating mode or not. By behaving in the negotiating mode is meant asking for more than one expects to get in the expectation that one will at least secure more than the point at which one prefers the bargain to no-bargain. The alternative is to frame one's proposal whether as buyer or seller in terms which you consider would be acceptable without negotiation to the other side and beyond which you would be unwilling to concede.

4.2 The argument for negotiation

The difficulty which was referred to earlier when discussing post tender negotiation (see page 15) is that the terms which would immediately be acceptable to the other side are bound to be terms which are less favourable to yourself than you would wish to secure. One has only to look at the differences between a buyer's conditions of purchase and a seller's conditions of sale to see what the effect would be if either were to agree to contract on the terms of the other. The same applies to price and all other issues.

Neither buyer nor seller can be certain as to how the other will behave. The buyer in preparing his enquiry does not know the terms and guarantees which any of the suppliers will accept. What he can be sure about is that if he does not ask he will not get. His enquiry is a declaration of his opening position and should therefore include all his needs and wants.[1] In subsequent negotiations he may be persuaded to concede some of his wants but he will not secure more.

Likewise, the seller in formulating his quotation does not know the price and terms on which the buyer would be willing to place the order. What he does know is that he has little chance, once he has submitted the quotation, of improving on it in any subsequent negotiations, unless the terms of his quotation allows him a measure of flexibility.[2] In a state of uncertainty the seller has every incentive therefore to protect himself by building the necessary safeguards into the price and terms of his offer.

Since the buyer must expect that this is what the supplier has done, this in turn means that the buyer would be foolish not to negotiate to remove at least some of the 'fat' built into the supplier's offer.

Assuming that the seller has behaved in the way expected, then an immediate acceptance by the buyer of the seller's offer would mean that both parties would have lost. The buyer's loss will be both a material and a psychological one. The material one will be the difference between the price and terms which he accepted and those to which the supplier would have retreated under pressure after taking into account the costs and time of negotiation. The psychological loss will be his inability to demonstrate either to himself or to others his prowess as a negotiator.

The supplier will also have lost in both the material and psychological senses because he will never know what the buyer would have accepted if his original proposal had been more to the seller's advantage. The ready acceptance by the buyer of the seller's offer is an indication that the seller did not achieve the best bargain that was available to him.

Neither of them would then find it easy to live with their own thoughts or to explain to their peer group[3] why they had failed to negotiate. This issue is referred to again later on p. 80.

4.3 *The argument against negotiation*

Against the above propositions it can be argued that if the buyer only sought to contract on terms which were favourable enough to the seller that he was willing to accept them without amendment, and the seller initially put forward an offer attractive enough to the buyer that he was willing to accept it without reduction, then both sides would have achieved a deal without the cost and time involved in negotiation. This is true but it will only happen if the parties have somehow communicated to each other their intention to collaborate and not compete. In game theory terms, that outcome will only be reached by 'unarticulated collusion' between the parties (see Appendix 1, p. 280).

Moreover those terms which were so easily accepted by the seller may leave the buyer exposed to risks and additional expense and the seller's low price will not have secured him the profit margin that he would really have liked. Further, neither party will have been satisfied psychologically. Both will have been left feeling that they could have achieved more had they been more competitive in their approach.

4.4 *Conclusion*

With low-value and low-risk contracts, where the costs incurred and time spent in negotiation are out of proportion to the benefits to be secured, then rationally at least the collaborative approach, if both parties can trust each other, is advantageous to both. In all other cases, both parties will have a strong incentive both rationally and psychologically to negotiate and secure the best deal that they can.

Notes

1. Needs are those items which are referred to later as 'Must Haves' (see Chapter 13, p. 68). If they are not secured, then the negotiator would have to break off the negotiations. Wants which are referred to later as 'Desirables' are the items which it is the objective of the negotiator to secure but he recognizes that he may have to exchange securing one or more of them for at least an equivalent concession from the other side.
2. Quotations which are submitted in response to a formal invitation to tender which includes the purchaser's terms of contract often do not reject these outright but indicate that the bidder would wish to discuss them. If, for example, the purchaser has asked for a price to be held fixed for a long period, the bidder may refer to the difficulty of doing this under current trading conditions and ask for the price to be adjustable on a basis to be agreed after the first twelve months.
3. By peer group is meant the negotiator's colleagues whose opinions are influential amongst the social group at work of which the negotiator is a member.

5 ADJUSTMENT OF LONG-TERM CONTRACTS

5.1 Introduction

We live in a world of continuous and often rapid change and yet the running of business requires us to use contracts as a method of trying to plan for the future. But planning for the future does not mean that the parties use the contract to allocate, almost irrevocably, risks which are unknown at the time of contracting. To the extent that contracting in the commercial world is often concerned with continuing relationships which are expected to last over a significant period of time, the parties to a modern contract will usually seek to provide means by which the contract can be adjusted to meet whatever changed circumstances arise.[1]

Unfortunately English law does not make this easy for the parties to achieve and does not provide them with the kind of support which is needed.

5.2 Flexibility

In any long-term contract, there is a need for flexibility. Although a particular risk may be foreseeable in general, this does not mean that it is foreseeable either in the specific terms or the extent which eventually materializes. A simple example is that of escalation. A rigid formula may define in detail, for example, the proportion of the contract price which is to be adjusted according to some defined index for changes in the cost of a particular material. That works well provided that the changes in the price of the material are not so dramatic that they completely alter the proportion of the contract price represented by that material. It also does not cater for technological change which increases or decreases very significantly the proportion of that material used in the finished product.

However, under English law, there is no available way under in which the courts can act in a commercial context to adjust the terms of a contract which because of some unforeseen event has become unduly onerous to perform.[2] The doctrine of frustration is concerned only with the impossibility and not the difficulty or excessive costs of performance. Further, if the contract is held to be frustrated, the result is its automatic termination at the time of the frustrating event.

5.3 Hardship clauses

In many long-term contracts, usually international but sometimes domestic, a so-called 'hardship' clause is often included to deal with the problem. The clause provides that in cases where an event has caused 'substantial economic hardship' or 'substantial and economic disadvantage to one of the parties', then the party affected may call for renegotiation. An example would be:

> If during the course of the contract either party considers that it has suffered undue prejudice or obvious hardship, that party shall have the right to require the other party to participate in a joint examination of the position with a view to determining whether revision or modification of the provisions hereof is required and if so what revision or modification would be appropriate and equitable in the circumstances.

The problem which English law has with such clauses is that they are simply agreements to agree and as such are not legally enforceable.[3] To overcome the problem there must be a provision that in the event of disagreement then the matter is to be referred to a third person who is required to act as an expert and not as an arbitrator in making a decision which is then binding on the parties.[4] An example of such a clause would be:

> If the parties have not reached a mutually acceptable solution within 60 days after the issue by either party of the notice requesting discussions, the matter shall be referred for a decision to three independent experts. Each party shall have the right to nominate one expert and the third shall be nominated by mutual agreement by the parties or in default of agreement shall be nominated by ——. Such persons shall act as experts and not as arbitrators and shall reach their decision in accordance with the principles of equity and good faith. Their decision shall be final and binding on the parties and any revisions to the prices or to other conditions of the contract shall take effect from the date when the notice of reference was first given.

In practice such a clause should be supplemented by procedural details and time limits, as well as a confirmation of immunity of the experts from actions in negligence.

5.4 Good faith

Furthermore, English law has no general doctrine that the parties are required to negotiate in 'good faith' or of the unconscionability of bargains. As was said in *Walford* v. *Miles* 'because the duty to carry out negotiations in good faith is inherently repugnant to the adversarial position of the parties in negotiations . . . each party to the negotiations is entitled to pursue his or her own interests so long as they avoid misrepresentations.'

It is clear that this statement represents the position in negotiations pre-contract. But does the same apply once the contract has been entered into, so that there is no general restraint on the ability of one party to exploit his dominant bargaining position in exercising his contractual rights? There seems to be a distinction here between the general power to negotiate and the exercise of a specific power. In the former situation there is probably no difference; the party is entitled to pursue his own interests. However, in the latter situation it seems that there may be a requirement only to exercise the power, say, to grant an extension of time or to terminate an agreement, in good faith.

In one case where the employer had the right to decide on extensions of time, and there was no appeal to arbitration, it was conceded by the employer that such power had to be exercised 'honestly, fairly and reasonably' even though there was no express term to that effect in the contract.[5]

It seems probable from the judgment in the Court of Appeal that had no concession been made in that case then the court would have implied a term to that effect. Indeed, exceptionally, a court has imposed a restraint in particular cases, through the use of the fiction of an implied term, but this does not appear to be based on any general principle of law.[6] Furthermore, as an implied term, if there were express provisions in the contract that one party was to have the right to act without having to consider whether or not his actions are reasonable, then the courts would appear bound to give effect to the express term although they might well seek to interpret it restrictively.

This is of particular significance in so-called 'strategic partnering arrangements' under which a buyer and seller agree to cooperate together over a period of time but their agreement does not constitute in law a partnership. However, a court may well interpret the meaning of a binding obligation to work together in good faith by analogy with principles derived from partnership law. If so then this would impose a restraint on either party by limiting their right under that partnering agreement, and any resulting supply contract, to take particular actions which are solely to their own advantage only when this is justifiable because of a need to protect their substantial and legitimate interests. In all other circumstances they would be required to act to the mutual benefit of themselves and their 'partners' even if this does not lead to the optimal outcome for themselves. It is not clear that a non-binding partnering arrangement would lead to the same result.

With that possible exception, the adjustment of long-term contracts is a matter of negotiation between the parties with little in the way of legal protection for the weaker party.

Notes

1. P. S. Atiyah, *The Rise and Fall of the Freedom of Contract* (Oxford: Clarendon Press, 1979), p. 713.
2. The best that English law has been able to achieve is that if the contract is of indefinite duration, then either party is allowed to give the other a reasonable period of notice to terminate so allowing the parties the opportunity to negotiate. The court has no power to modify the terms of the original contract – see D. Harris and D. Tallon, *Contract Law Today*

(Oxford: Clarendon Press, 1989), and cases cited there. See in particular *Staffordshire Area Health Authority* v. *South Staffordshire Waterworks,* where on a fixed price contract the cost of supplying water had risen over 18 times the contract price in the period between 1919 and 1975. It was held that the Water Company had the right to give seven months' notice to terminate, although there was no express termination clause in the contract which was of indefinite duration.

3. *Walford* v. *Miles* (1992) 2 AC 352.
4. M. Fontaine, *Droit des contrats internationaux* (Paris: FEDUCI, 1988), p. 284.
5. *Balfour Beatty Civil Engineering* v. *Docklands Light Railway* 1996 78 BLR 42.
6. *Timeload Ltd* v. *British Telecom* unreported (1993), but discussed in *Construction Law*, April 1997, p. 82.

6 RESOLVING CONTRACT DISPUTES

6.1 Introduction

Negotiation, either directly between the parties or in a structured form using one of the methods of Alternative Dispute Resolution (ADR),[1] is the preferred way in which to resolve many contract disputes. It is cheaper, simpler and quicker than going to law or arbitration and makes far fewer demands upon the time of the managers and professionals involved.

But negotiation in whichever form is only appropriate and likely to be successful if:

- Both parties want it to succeed.
- The parties have an interest in their continuing business relationship. This may be just in connection with the particular contract or project on which there remains work to be completed, or maintenance obligations to perform, or it may be for other work in the future.
- The issue which divides the parties can be expressed in terms of time or money or both and can therefore be divided. If, however, the issue is one of legal principle, to which there is only a 'yes-no' answer, then unless the one party is prepared to set this aside, no amount of negotiation will succeed.

An example would be an exclusion of liability clause which is raised as a preliminary point in a defence to a claim for the right to reject and/or claim damages for allegedly defective goods. Unless the seller is prepared to waive the clause, the buyer has no option but to refer the matter of its validity to law.

6.2 Disputes in the construction industry

Contract disputes are destructive in terms of what they cost, the time they take to resolve, the resources which they tie up and the deterioration they cause to the relationships between the parties. If they can be avoided in the first place by the preparation of sensible contracts and the adoption of non-adversarial behaviour then so much the better. If a dispute does arise, then its early settlement by negotiation is the sensible way to proceed. Unfortunately in the construction industry, which has a disproportionate share of contract disputes, it has been fashionable for these only to be settled after the contract has been completed. The evil consequences of this, to which reference was made in the Introduction, are that:

- The negotiations for settlement only take place long after the events to which they relate and the people involved have often been transferred to other projects. In consequence, memories will have faded and those concerned may have little interest in what happened in the past.
- In the same way as people's memories may have faded, records may have become lost or mislaid.
- If the dispute concerns a claim by the main contractor against the employer the contractor will already have been kept waiting some time for his money and he in turn will have kept his sub-contractors waiting. The hardest hit will be the suppliers/sub-contractors with the least cash resources.
- Failure to have settled the dispute will affect attitudes towards the project and to those believed to be responsible for what caused the events leading up to the dispute and in all probability will result in a lack of progress.

The conditions of contract traditionally used in the industry do nothing to help this situation. Only the New Engineering Contract (the NEC) provides positively for what it terms 'compensation events' to be determined by the Project Manager within a short time of their happening subject to the right of either party to refer the matter to Adjudication.

Contract disputes do have a particular characteristic in that the parties will already have been in an established relationship for some time and the subject matter of the dispute is normally allegations by one party of default by the other or of a failure to apply the contract correctly. These allegations will reflect back on the individuals concerned and cause them in turn to react emotionally and form a one-sided view.

Because of this, contract dispute situations are bedevilled by the blindness, stubborness and unwarranted beliefs of those involved in the righteousness of their own cause. Minor issues can become magnified out of all proportion.

It is against this background that the use of ADR, in particular mediation as a structured form of negotiation, can be useful in defusing the emotion and bringing the negotiators for both sides to an understanding of each other's position from which a settlement can then emerge.

Buying and selling are essential parts of human economic activity and as has been shown earlier, negotiation is both materially and psychologically an important ingredient of such activities. Contract disputes are not essential and serve no useful purpose. But, due to their destructive potential, which can easily cause the ruin of a substantial company, the need for negotiation is all the greater.

Note

1. Under the new civil procedure rules introduced following the Woolf Report, it was reported in November 1999 that there had been a massive increase in the number of commercial mediations. The Centre for Dispute Resolution stated that they were then currently running more than fifty commercial mediations a month. The use of ADR in its various

forms is described in the Central Unit on Procurement's Guidance Note No. 50 published by HM Treasury and in *Croner's Special Bulletin,* issue 34 of January 1996, published by Croner Publications Ltd. The most important advantages claimed for ADR are that:

- The parties are guided to reach agreement by a mediator or conciliator. No decision is imposed.
- The proceedings are short – usually not more than two days.
- The costs are much lower.
- The settlement can involve non-legal issues such as future business.

PART 2

PLANNING FOR NEGOTIATIONS

7 INTRODUCTION TO PART TWO

The process of negotiation is one of progressive commitment. Depending upon the strategy adopted, a party will increase his commitment as the negotiation proceeds in one of the following two ways:

1   Continuing to repeat his previous proposal, each repetition making it that much more diffi-cult for the negotiator to concede without losing his reputation for firmness.
2   Moving towards the other party so that, with each move made, the area for further move-ment between his present position and his walk-away point is automatically reduced. If the move is absolute and not conditional, only exceptionally will a negotiator be able to increase his area of movement by returning to, or withdrawing from, a position previously conceded while at the same time retaining his integrity.

Planning for negotiation is necessary therefore in order to ensure that:

1   The initial offer and the timing and extent of subsequent changes are in accordance with the degree to which the management of the company are willing to be commited.
2   At all stages the moves have been fully prepared for in advance, the facts established and the strategy selected.

In this activity, planning and action are partners not opposites; they are successive stages of a single process, the third stage of which, monitoring and review, completes the total cycle. This illustrated in the activity cycle, Figure 7.1.

During a single negotiation this cycle will be repeated many times. The review and planning stages may be the subject of a formal review meeting held away from the negotiating arena, or a quick ten-minute adjournment part way through a negotiating session. Whatever their form the purpose of such meetings must be to satisfy the two requirements stated above. If these are not met then the negotiators should not continue or they will be drawn inevitably into the position of making unscheduled concessions or establishing unwanted precedents, from nei-ther of which will it be possible for them later to withdraw. When afterwards called on to justify their actions the negotiators may well recall the lines of W. H. Auden:

> Look in your heat for there lies the answer
> Though the heart like a clever conjuror or dancer
> Deceives you oft into many a curious sleight
> And motives like stowaways are found too late.[1]

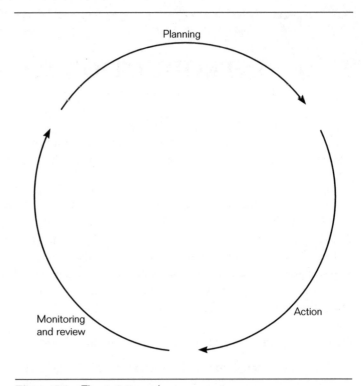

Figure 7.1 The activity cycle

Planning should cover the following areas:

- The scope of the negotiations
- Data acquisition – the environment and the other party's decision-making processes
- Data acquisition – objectives of the other party, their level of commitment to them and the characteristics and personalities of their negotiators
- Means of acquiring data
- Choice of negotiating style
- The negotiating team
- The objective and choice of strategy
- Organization and administration
- The negotiating plan.

Not all these areas may need to be covered in the same detail; much of the data may already be known to us and some may be inappropriate for the particular negotiation because, say, the negotiation is wholly domestic. Further, while time spent in planning is always important, it also costs effort and money and needs therefore to be related to the benefits which the negotiation is expected to achieve.

In order for us to be able to undertake the necessary planning, we have to acquire information relating to the legal and commercial environment within which the negotiations will be conducted, the objectives of the other party and his commitment to them, and the strength of his negotiating position in relation to our own. As the negotiations proceed we will be able to check and either confirm or amend our original assessments of all these. This is the dynamic side of planning which has to be sufficiently flexible to deal with the unexpected.

However, there is in this a danger against which we need to guard. Much of the information which we gain will be obtained either directly or indirectly from the other side or from others whose primary concern lies in furthering their interests rather than our own. All such information is therefore biased. To the extent that we cue in blindly to that information we will be led to adjust our own independently conceived ideas and objectives downward so that they conform to what we now believe to be feasible. The classic commercial example of this is the Dutch auction in which two or more competitors are each led by the buyer to believe that their prices are higher than those of their competitor(s). If each is deceived and responds to the deception, the result is a free-fall downward spiral in price. If, in private life, we have little real idea of what is a realistic price for the item we are buying or selling, and we believe that the other side is an expert in the matter, say a builder or an antiques dealer, we are easily led to cue into the price which he first suggests and to start any haggling from that level. So far as it is practical therefore, data gained from those whose interests are not the same as our own need verifying from an independent source.

Note

1. W. H. Auden, *The Dog Beneath the Skin* (London: Faber & Faber, 1938).

8 IDENTIFYING THE SCOPE OF THE NEGOTIATIONS

The identification of the scope of the negotiations covers the following issues:

- The purpose of the negotiations
- The points which the negotiations are expected to cover

8.1 The purpose of the negotiations

The questions to be answered (even if sometimes the answers are obvious) are 'Why are we negotiating?' and 'What do we hope to get out of the negotiations?' The answers will vary widely but a basic distinction can be made between sets of circumstances:

1. Each of the parties wants the deal to go ahead for reasons of their own which are not the actual subject of the negotiations, and
2. At least one and sometimes both parties are concerned solely with the terms and price which are the subject of the negotiations. One or both are largely indifferent as to whether these particular negotiations result in a deal or not since in the event of their not getting what they want they have what appears to them to be a viable alternative.

8.2 Both parties want the deal to go ahead for their own reasons

Some suggestions as to the type of answer to be made under these circumstances are:

- We have selected John Smith & Co Ltd as the preferred bidder for the X Project but their tender price is still a little too high and certain of their qualifications to our conditions of contract are not acceptable. However in order to maintain the project programme we need to get an acceptable revised tender within two weeks.
- As a result of a delay caused by the purchaser to our contract programme we have incurred additional costs for which we have submitted a claim for £30,000 which the purchaser is refusing to pay. Our claim is well founded but we do not want to go to adjudication,[1] even although we are confident we would be successful, because it would be harmful to our relations with the purchaser from whom presently we have real hopes of receiving further business. However, we do need some cash quickly. As the purchaser we realize that we did

delay the contractor for which we must pay him some money now, since otherwise he could get into financial difficulties which would have a serious impact on the project. At the same time we don't want him to think that either we are an easy touch or completely unreasonable. There's a long way to go on the contract and we are likely to use him again.

● We know that the purchaser is generally in favour of our tender but we cannot accept certain of their requirements, the most onerous of which is that we have unlimited liability for consequential damages. At the same time we need this order both to fill a hole in our order book and also because it will establish us in the marketplace, so we have to find a way to compromise.

● We like their idea of a long-term partnering arrangement covering our supply to them of a range of parts for their new ABC models; this would retain our position as a preferred supplier but we have to be careful about confidentiality and industrial property rights. Their present proposals could cause us a problem. There is a lot at stake here and we need a solution.

In each of these examples, there is a conflict which needs to be resolved so that some further benefits can be obtained. This is a characteristic of negotiations in this category which it is important to recognize at the outset. The negotiation is not simply about money or the terms of contract. Its primary purpose is either to:

● Place or secure the contract within a defined time-scale, or
● Avoid damaging future relationships, or
● Not create harmful precedents, or
● Obtain the partnering agreement to maintain a preferred supplier position.

Under these circumstances, failure to agree may not be an option either party wishes seriously to consider. If this is known to the other party it impacts strongly on the level of power which that party possesses. The amount of power which a negotiator has is closely related to the other party's perception of the importance to the negotiator of the outcome and of the alternatives which realistically the negotiator has available to him were the negotiations to break down.[2]

In the first example the key factor is whether or not the bidder is aware of the purchaser's need to get an acceptable revised tender within two weeks in order to maintain the project programme and that there is no realistic alternative to his bid. If he is aware of this, and of the adverse consequences to the purchaser if the programme is not maintained, then in the short term it is the bidder who possesses the power but he needs to exercise caution over the way in which he uses it. To antagonize the purchaser will do nothing to ensure the co-operation between the parties necessary to ensure the smooth running of the contract.

8.3 At least one party is indifferent to the success of the negotiations

Some examples of this situation would be:

● We know that the contractor has submitted a claim for £100,000 but this is obviously grossly inflated. He has finished the contract at last and he can wait for his money. We were not too pleased with his performance and we doubt if we will be using him again. We can afford to wait and let him take us at least to the door of the adjudication/arbitration tribunal. Time and costs are on our side not his.

● We have received three good offers, all from firms whom we have used before and been happy with their performance. There are some variations in their delivery promises which need to be sorted out and on terms of payment but after that it's a matter of who is prepared to give us the best price reduction. We are really not bothered which of them wins the order.

● We have got the best product of its type in the marketplace at the moment and we are running at near capacity with a full order book. If they want to order from us they will have to accept our terms and prices unless they can offer us something very special.

In none of these instances is there any purpose beyond securing the best terms. It is evident where the negotiating power lies and why. The party without the power has nowhere else to go. It is only if the contractor can hang on until he gets to the door of the adjudication or arbitration tribunal that he will get a sensible offer, always assuming that his claim possesses some validity.

The purchaser with the three firms he judges to be equally competent competing for his business is clearly in a strong position to bargain for a significant reduction off the quoted prices; on the facts given, it is irrelevant to him which of the three wins the order. He needs only to be careful that after his negotiations the supplier can still afford to be in business and operate efficiently.

The supplier taking advantage of his market position also has the power at the moment to dictate the terms on which he will do business. But he should remember what happened to IBM, who at one time used just this approach and whose arrogance caused such ill-will among the buyers whom they treated in this manner.

The rather loose way in which in each of the above examples of the purpose has been expressed is good enough for a first approximation. It will be refined and developed later in more detail when deciding on the negotiating strategy.

8.4 Points which the negotiations are expected to cover

The lists will again vary with the subject matter of the negotiation and the extent to which the parties have negotiated before and already reached agreement on particular issues. The golden rule when starting from scratch is to include everything, even if it is a point which for you is of little significance. Initially you often have little idea of how much it may be of value to the other party. By making it a negotiating issue you are at least creating the possibility of building up a concession which you can make later in exchange for one of greater value to you from the other party.

As an example there is set out below a typical agenda which might be put forward by the buyer on the negotiation of the commercial terms of a major electrical/mechanical or process plan contract following the submission of the contractor's tender.

1   The programme: when will the plant be ready for commercial operation?
2   The payment terms
3   Format of the performance bond and the parent company guarantee
4   The level and maximum of the liquidated damages for delay
5   Right of the contractor to an extension of time
6   Performance guarantees
7   Definition of the tests on completion and test methodology
8   Definition and effect of take-over
9   Performance tests: when are these to be carried out and what are the test methods?
10 The level and upper limit of the liquidated damages for failure to pass the performance tests; the purchaser's right to reject
11 The contractor's overall limit of liability and consequential damages including the purchaser's loss of profit
12 Definition and effect of *force majeure*
13 The defects period, its length and the contractor's obligations; effect of the Final Certificate
14 Industrial property rights, especially on process plants
15 Spares
16 Training
17 Definition of the purchaser's obligations
18 Requirement, if any, for collateral warranties from specialist sub-contractors
19 Means of dispute resolution
20 The contract price.

It might be objected that many of these issues will have been covered in the general conditions of Contract. That is true but it is equally true that the purchaser will often have introduced special conditions modifying the general conditions in his favour. The contractor will also have made reservations on many of these issues when submitting his tender since they are the ones which experience has shown are the most contentious. In any event, it is wise to ensure that there are no misunderstandings which could cause difficulties during the progress of the contract.

The order of the agenda is important and is discussed in more detail later – see Chapter 25, p. 164 – but it will be noted that the contract price has been left to the last. There are two reasons for this. Price is an emotive issue, discussion of which is likely to be prolonged and heated, and thus not a good way to get the negotiations started. Even more importantly, all the other issues relate to risk and until these have either been agreed, even conditionally, or at least explored, and the respective positions of the parties clarified, any discussion on price would therefore be not merely non-productive, but counter-productive.

Notes

1. Adjudication was introduced by Part 2 of the Housing Grants, Construction and Regeneration Act 1996. It is compulsory in all construction contracts as defined by the Act

for either party to have the right at any time to refer a dispute between them to adjudication. If the contract does not provide adjudication provisions conforming with the Act then the statutory scheme for adjudication will apply. The emphasis is on speed. The adjudicator must make his decision within 28 days of the dispute being referred to him. His decision is binding on the parties unless and until the dispute is finally resolved by agreement, arbitration, if the contract so provides, or by the court.

2. Note that it is the other side's perception which is significant. You have the power which the other side believes that you possess. So long as only you know your weaknesses you can afford largely to disregard them. It's when you know that he knows them as well that you may have a problem. You need therefore a contingency plan against his discovering them while trying never to disclose them however indirectly. As a purchaser, your time-scale, your budget, your desperate need for those supplies of which you believe he is the sole source, are all state secrets only to be disclosed in an emergency.

Kennedy on Negotiation at p. 82 and following refers to the work of Bacharach and Lawler on the concepts of dependence and commitment as being the basis of negotiating power and defines commitment as being 'the degree of importance to you of the outcome of the bargaining' (G. Kennedy, *Kennedy on Negotiation* (Aldershot: Gower, 1998)). It is agreed that the importance to you of the outcome, if known to the other side, gives them greater bargaining power. However, the term 'commitment' is used throughout this volume in a slightly different sense, more in accordance with its dictionary meaning, to refer to an obligation imposed on the negotiator which restricts his freedom of action. In this sense a commitment may actually increase the negotiator's power since it provides him with means to support his arguments and strong reasons why he should achieve that to which he is committed. Unlimited freedom to agree to demands from the other side is a weakness. For examples of commitment, see Chapter 10, p. 49.

9
DATA ACQUISITION – THE NEGOTIATING ENVIRONMENT AND THE OTHER PARTY'S DECISION-MAKING PROCESSES

9.1 The environment

The environment includes the legal, economic, cultural and political environment within which the negotiations will take place and the contract will be executed. The importance, and the extent to which each of these represents an unknown to the negotiator is a function of:

- Whether the negotiation and place of performance of the contract is purely domestic or one in which one party is located overseas from the other and the contract is to be performed overseas. The environmental factors will be of particular significance where the negotiator is the seller, the purchaser is resident in another country and the works, the subject matter of the contract, are located in that country or the goods are being delivered there.
- Whether or not the parties have dealt with each other previously in recent times and if so what was the outcome.
- Whether or not the parties intend to go on doing business with each other or intend to enter, or have already entered into some form of long-term relationship.

9.2 The negotiating environment – overseas bidding

If the negotiator has done business recently with the particular territory then answers to most of the points listed below ought already to be known. However it is worth checking them to see that the previous information still applies. Some regimes change course rapidly. Always remember that what applies within one state in a country may not apply in another. Equally, if the previous business was done with another entity then the character of the new one may differ sharply from the old especially if the new one is in the private as opposed to the public sector.

IDENTIFYING ALL FACTORS WHICH MAY BE RELEVANT

The following lists identify those environmental factors which may be relevant.

The political system
1 The extent of state control of business enterprises.
2 If state control exists how is it organized:

    (*a*) Centrally or regionally?

    (*b*) What are the limits of delegated authority from the centre?

    (*c*) With which state authority/enterprise must the negotiations take place – i.e. are there more than one, and if so what are their interrelationships?

3 What is the extent of political interest in the particular project:

    (*a*) Who is interested?

    (*b*) What are the respective powers of those who are interested?

4 What is the stability of the present regime? It is likely to change in the lifetime of the project?

    (*a*) When are elections scheduled to take place and is the project in question an election issue?

5 What are the political relations between the governments of the seller and purchaser?

    (*a*) How susceptible are these to the acts of the others (e.g. human rights activism)?

    (*b*) Are they likely to change if there is a change in the political persuasion of the government of either country?

6 Is it likely that:

    (*a*) One's room is bugged or telephone tapped, or conversation recorded?

    (*b*) Attempts will be made to compromise one sexually?

Religion

1 What is the predominant religion of the country of the purchaser?

2 Does that religion influence significantly the conduct of:

    (*a*) Political affairs?

    (*b*) The legal system?

    (*c*) Nature, or country of origin of products which may be purchased?

    (*d*) Social relations and individual behaviour?

    (*e*) Entry of personnel having particular nationalities or other religious beliefs/political affiliations?

    (*f*) Incidence of holidays and working hours, e.g. Ramadan?

Legal system

1 What is the legal system? Is it codified or derived from the English common law?

2 Is it mandatory to accept that the contract must be governed by the purchaser's legal system?

3 What is the level of enforcement of laws and regulations in practice?

4 To what extent are the courts and the judiciary independent of the executive?

    (*a*) What level of influence in practice could the purchaser or a major sub-contractor exercise over the judiciary?

5 What is the time-scale for court proceedings?

6 What means exist for the enforcement of court judgements?

7 Is there any procedure, and if so what, for the enforcement of foreign judgements/arbitral awards?

8 Is the purchaser's legal system such as to:

(*a*) Inhibit his negotiations in making agreements, granting concessions etc.?

(*b*) Restrict the authority of those able to conclude, award or amend contracts to specified officers of the purchaser's corporation?

9 Is there a reliable local firm of lawyers independent of the purchaser?

10 Is it necessary legally to establish a local company to carry out local work? If so, what are the rules in particular on the proportions of overseas to local shareholding, fees for management service and remittance of profits?

11 What are the relevant laws on employment, and social security? How are those applied to foreigners? Is there a required ratio of local foreign staff? Must an engineer be employed who is a member of the local engineering institute? These may differ if you establish a locally registered company as opposed to operating, if this is permitted, as a foreign company.

The business system

1 How is business conducted? Is it primarily between the principals of firms (as is largely true of the Arab world) or are all levels involved (as is the case in Japan)? Is there any real delegation of authority?

2 Is everything expected to be put in writing or are verbal agreements treated as binding? What significance is given to contracts?

3 Do professional advisers, e.g. lawyers, play a major role in negotiations and the decision-making process as in the USA, or are they regarded as subordinates whose primary function is to 'get the words right'?

4 Are formal meetings conducted only between the leaders of both teams with the other team members only speaking if they are specifically asked to do so?

5 Is industrial espionage practised? How careful must one be with locking away papers or even not bringing them at all?

6 Is bribery necessary to secure and/or carry out business? If so, how is it operated and what are the usual terms?

7 Can contracts be negotiated with one firm or must they by law, or as a matter of practice, be put out to competitive bid? If the latter, what are usually the key criteria for securing the award? Is it just a matter of price?

8 Do negotiations proceed in two stages, first the technical and then the commercial (as in Eastern Europe and China)? Are negotiations conducted by levels each of which will expect to obtain some concession?

9 In what language is business conducted? Can documents be in two languages, one of which is English and both be of equal validity?

10 Will negotiations be with an export/import agency, or direct with the operating company? Even if direct there may be a purchasing department involved who can be expected to have different motives to the actual users.

The social system

1 What is the level of formality expected in terms of dress, use of first names, use of titles, etc.?

2 Is business conducted only in the office or also after-hours, e.g. over a drink or dinner or on a golf-course?

3 Do social meetings involve wives and visits home or is all entertaining done in restaurants, clubs, etc.?

4 What is expected in the way of gifts?

5 Do people willingly accept criticism in front of others or only in private? How important are questions of honour or loss of face?

6 Are there particular issues, e.g. matters of religion or politics or sex, which are not openly discussed here?

7 Do women participate in business and if so is it on terms of equality with men?

The financial and fiscal system

1 What is ECGD's financial rating of the territory concerned? What country limit has ECGD established?

2 What is the country's debt service ratio? Has the country applied to the IMF for assistance and if so what was the result?

3 How large are the country's foreign exchange reserves? On what commodities does it primarily depend for foreign earnings?

4 Is the territory's currency freely exchangeable? If not what are the restrictions?

5 What is the country's record on honouring payment obligations including likely delays?

6 Can one obtain Letters of Credit confirmed in London?

7 What procedures must be gone through with the Central Bank or Ministry of Finance for obtaining payments in foreign currencies?

8 What are the applicable tax laws, in particular on what does the liability for tax depend? Can tax be limited to work performed in the country concerned? Are there any double taxation conventions in force and if so with which countries?

9 Is the remittance of the final payment subject to the issue of a tax clearance certificate? If so how is this obtained and how long does it take?

10 Can profits earned by a local company be remitted overseas? If so what are the rules and procedures?

11 What are the regulations on the payment of customs duties or can the contract be duty exempt?

12 Are there any other fees such as stamp duties, taxes or invoices which the contractor will have to pay?

Infrastructure and logistical system

1 What is the availability in the territory concerned of:
   (*a*) Necessary labour both skilled and unskilled?
   (*b*) Professional staff?
   (*c*) Materials for construction?
   (*d*) Constructional plant?
   (*e*) Maintenance facilities?
   (*f*) Competent and financially sound sub-contractors?

2 What restrictions are there on:
  (*a*) Importation of staff labour?
  (*b*) Importation of materials which are made locally?
  (*c*) Importation of plant?
3 Will the contract be negotiated and administered in the local language? If so, what is the availability of reliable and secure translators?
4 What are the local logistical problems relating to:
  (*a*) Port unloading facilities and waiting time?
  (*b*) Road and rail access to site relative to the foreseen size and weight of loads to be transported?
  (*c*) Internal air transport if this must be by the national airline?
  (*d*) Customs clearance, particularly at peak holiday periods?
5 What problems are foreseen relating to weather such as:
  (*a*) Rainy seasons?
  (*b*) Winter, snow and frost?
  (*c*) High summer temperature?
  (*d*) Dust?
  (*e*) Earthquakes?
  (*f*) High humidity?

Each of these may affect the programme or the design and therefore the cost of the works.

9.3 The negotiating environment – buying from overseas

Although a UK purchaser, when negotiating with a contractor from overseas, has the advantage of doing so within his own environment, he needs to be conscious that such environment will be different to that which applies in the contractor's own country. For instance, the meanings which the contractor will attach to particular words and phrases may be based on translations into English which give a misleading impression. As an example the French legal term *vices cachés* would normally be translated into English as latent defects. But while French law has a distinct set of rules governing *vices cachés* there are no such rules on latent defects in English law; indeed a well-known standard English textbook on the law of the sale of goods does not include the term 'latent defects' in the index. A knowledge of the contractor's home environment will be important in providing a dictionary of what the overseas contractor would normally understand by particular words, expressions or behaviour.

The overseas firm will also be accustomed to a set of norms which will differ from those in the UK in particular relating to:

● The employment of labour – note that the foreign contractor domiciled in another member state of the EU must adhere to the UK's minimum wage legislation but does not have to pay contributions to social funds in the UK where it is already paying similar contributions in its own country.[1]

- Health and safety legislation, regulations and codes of practice: their interpretation and application.
- Methods of doing business.

It would be foolish of the UK buyer to seek to take advantage at the negotiating stage of the foreign firm's ignorance only to end up with a losing contractor or a contract dispute, neither of which, will contribute to the contract's success. Far better to see that the foreign firm is properly advised and educated in these matters, which may even mean requiring that they enter into a joint venture with an experienced UK company.

9.4 The negotiating environment – buying or selling within the UK

Both parties either know or can easily find out the legal environment, a key factor of which is the impartiality of the courts and their freedom from political or financial influence. This is not to say that before the courts or an arbitrator both sides are equal in practice. Some firms can afford more expensive lawyers than others and can take the risk of paying the costs of losing. Some just do not have the financial resources to take that risk or wait until judgement.

But at least in the construction industry the new quick procedure for adjudication (see note 1, on p. 35) is providing a welcome measure of relief for the smaller sub-contractor.

Given the general economic and political stability within the UK and an effective legal system, the environmental factors which may be of importance to the negotiations are limited to:

- 'Green' issues which may lead to protests affecting the time and costs of the project, e.g. road protestors.
- The character of the organization with whom Party is dealing and its reputation for the way in which commercially it behaves. Is it for instance what Kennedy refers to as a 'red' bargainer interested in only its own short-term advantage?[2] Does it operate in a spirit of adversarialism, as many construction firms do, with claims specialists ready at hand to take advantage of every opportunity which the contract gives to them? Alternatively, does the organisation genuinely believe in and practise the development of long-term relationships of mutual benefit to both parties?
- As a client, does the organization really practise the policy of buying not on the lowest price but on selecting the most economically advantageous offer?
- Has the firm as a client adopted and, does it actually when buying adhere to, an established and published Code of Ethics?
- Again as a client, is the organization constrained by having to comply with certain rules, e.g. those of the European Community Procurement Directives and if so which apply?
- Does the firm as a client operate within the culture of a particular industry which will impact on the contractor's methods of operation?

9.5 The negotiating environment – contract dispute

Although probably neither side wants to take the dispute to law or arbitration, whether or not that is a feasible and practical alternative is one of the three major issues which establish the negotiating environment.

FEASIBILITY AND PRACTICALITY OF GOING TO LAW OR ARBITRATION

This depends upon:

- Whether or not a contract exists and if so what its terms are. The parties may believe that a contract exists and have acted according to their beliefs. If so then an English court will endeavour to find a contract even if perhaps it means stretching the rules.[3] However it may well be that although the parties have agreed on the essential elements of a contract they are not in agreement as to whose general terms of business form part of the contract. This happens not infrequently in commercial practice since once having agreed on the goods, the price and the delivery period, businesspeople tend to ignore the general conditions of contract until something goes wrong. They then wish to rely on their own terms of either sale or purchase only to find it is uncertain as to whose terms apply.[4]
- The extent of the assets which the other party possesses to satisfy any judgement made against him. No matter how good our case, if he does not have the money to pay we are wasting our time and money in even thinking about litigation/arbitration.
- In which territory does the other party have its assets and is the legal system prevailing in that territory such that a judgement can in practice be enforced against those assets? There are still many countries where the obtaining and enforcement of a judgement against the state or a state-owned enterprise would be impractical. This is something which we should have discovered before entering into the contract, although it is always possible that the regime may have changed during the contract.
- What are the means of dispute resolution provided for in the contract?
- By what law is the contract governed and which country has jurisdiction? These are two different questions. Hopefully for us the contract is subject to English law but if jurisdiction (the place and tribunal before which any action must be brought) is overseas this may make any legal/arbitration proceedings difficult, expensive and time-consuming.
- Are we in a position to spend the necessary resources in terms of money, time and management effort in undertaking legal/arbitration proceedings and can we afford to wait the time it will take to obtain judgement?

Litigation/arbitration necessarily involves a risk. Assume that both parties are resident in England with a contract under English law, we have a claim of £100,000 and we know they are good for the money. Our lawyers have advised we have a 60 per cent chance of success. However, they estimate our costs at around £60,000 of which if we win we will recover about £50,000. It will take two years to obtain a judgement. If we lose we shall have to pay their costs in addition to our own – say they are about the same. Using the expected value techniques described in Appendix 1, we can calculate the EV of the outcome:

EV = (Total of our claim and our recoverable costs multiplied by the probability of success) minus (the total of our costs and their costs multiplied by the probability of failure) minus our unrecoverable costs, or

$$(£150,000 \times .6) - (£100,000 \times .4) - £10,000 = £40,000$$

That does not take into account the two-year delay, the hassle and the disruptive effect on management time.

On this analysis we have every justification rationally for trying to negotiate a settlement which at any level above say 40 per cent of our claim would be preferable to a fight. If we look at it from their point of view and assume that their lawyers have given them similar advice to our own, then their assessment should be a loss of £90,000. In negotiations a settlement within the range £60,000–70,000 could be expected.

At this stage, cool heads are required to avoid our being drawn into a legal battle because of emotional arguments such as ' we have a legitimate right to the money', 'we ought to stand and fight' and 'we shouldn't let them get away with it'.

Obviously if the contract is with a foreign company and has to be litigated and any judgement enforced outside the UK then, dependent on the country concerned, the risks may be that much higher and the probability of success lower. Ultimately arbitration/litigation may just not be a practical possibility and this must be recognized in the preparation of the negotiating plan. There must be no wild talk of 'suing them if they won't agree' or 'enforcing the contract'.

EXERCISE OF FINANCIAL POWER

More potent than legal power, because the effect is both direct and immediate, is the ability of either side to act in one of the following two ways:

1 Withhold payment from the other for goods already delivered or services performed
2 Make deductions from monies or security belonging to the other which the one side holds in his possession.

The data which we need to know must therefore include:

1 Amounts unpaid and owing to the seller
2 Retention monies held by the purchaser
3 Performance bonds, bank guarantees or parent company guarantees held by the purchaser.

The first two are straightforward issues of fact; the third may involve problems of law. Performance bonds fall into two categories:

1 A cash bond or bond on first demand which, as its name implies, the purchaser can take to the bank at which it is payable and demand the value of the bond *without the need for giving any proof of the supplier's default.*

2 A conditional bond usually issued by an insurance company which the purchaser cannot cash without fulfilling the condition, which is to prove that the contractor is in default and that the purchaser has suffered a loss at least equal to the value of the amount which he is claiming from the bond.

A parent company guarantee is different as this is a guarantee from the parent company of the supplier to perform the work which the supplier has failed to perform or to pay monies due to the purchaser which the supplier has failed to pay. It is, however, important to establish whether or not the guarantee allows the parent to defend any claim against him by setting up against the claim any defence open to the supplier, e.g. a counter-claim which the supplier has against the purchaser.

The above is a very brief summary of the general position under English law. Expert advice should be taken based on wording of the security in question and the applicable law.

COMMERCIAL POWER

In practice the threat, open or implied, of the application of commercial sanction is the most widely used means of coercing settlement of a dispute and data is need on the means which both parties have of bringing commercial pressure to bear on the other.

- *By the purchaser against the supplier:*
  1 Removing a supplier from an approved list
  2 Downgrading the supplier's vendor rating
  3 Withholding the placing of an order about to be awarded to the supplier.
- *By the supplier against the purchaser:*
  1 threat by the supplier to cease reciprocal trading with the purchaser
  2 threat by the supplier in a monopolistic position or where demand substantially exceeds industrial capacity either to withhold supplies or at least to give a lower priority to future orders from the purchaser.

Apart from the possibility of the exercise of legal, financial or commercial power, there is the commercial position to be considered as to whether we expect to do business with the other side again, even set up a long-term relationship with them, or whether it is a one-off deal which we do not expect to be repeated.

If it is a one-off situation, then it is suggested that we should be guided solely by what rationally is in our short-term best interests. If, having evaluated the costs and benefits to ourselves and those for the other side, we come to the conclusion that our interests would best be served either by proceeding to exercise the power which we possess or allowing them to take action against ourselves, then so be it. But it should be a coldly calculated and not an emotional decision.

If we expect to do business again and even more so if we contemplate a long-term relationship, then we should only consider negotiations, either directly or, if these fail, through some structured form of alternative dispute resolution (ADR).[5] Specifically we should only take action based on the power which we possess and which would necessarily prejudice any long-term relationship if and when it becomes clear that any such long-term relationship is no longer feasible.

9.6 The other party's decision-making processes

Prior to entering into negotiations, our object should be to learn all that we can concerning the other side's formal organizational structure and decision-making processes and also how power is informally distributed. The kind of information for which we are looking is:

- If the entity with which we are dealing is a subsidiary or division of a larger organization how is power distributed between that entity and the organization's centre?
- What particular issues, or contracts/claims above a certain value must be referred to the centre before they can be approved?
- Where does the balance of power lie as between line management and functional departments?
- What is the degree of authority delegated to whoever is designated as project manager? This is a much misused title. Often the person concerned has little real authority and is more of a coordinator.
- Who, if anyone, has the real authority to commit the company? Do not be misled because someone has the right to sign an order. He or she may only be entitled to do so when specifically authorized by a Board or a committee or general manager.
- What influence on the decision making is possessed by advisers or consultants ?
- To what extent is the entity politically attuned so that its decision making will take factors into account such as 'green issues' or local unemployment?

The above is based very much on a Western model of management and decision making which is hierarchically ordered and individualistic. It would be quite different if the entity followed the traditional Japanese way of consensus management with decision making spread throughout all those managers who would be involved in or influenced by the negotiations.

Notes

1 This was decided by the European Court of Justice on 23 November 1999 joined cases C-369/96 and C-376/96.
2. G. Kennedy, *Kennedy on Negotiation* (Aldershot: Gower Press, 1998) p. 217.
3. In *Percy Trentham* v. *Archival Luxfor Limited,* it was said by Lord Justice Steyn that 'The fact that the transaction was performed by both sides will often make it difficult to submit that the contract is void for uncertainty. It also makes it easier to imply a term resolving any uncertainty or, alternatively, it may make it possible to treat a matter not finalised as inessential', [1993] 1 Lloyd's Rep. 25 at 27.

4. This is what happened in the recent case of *Hertford Foods Ltd* v. *Lidl UK* in the High Court, 5 November 1999. The only terms which the parties discussed and agreed over the telephone were the quantity and description of the goods, the price, packing delivery period and terms of credit. However when a dispute arose between the parties regarding failure in deliveries, and the right of the buyer to recover the additional costs incurred as a result of such failure, both maintained that the contract was governed by their own standard conditions of contract. Reported and discussed in *The Buyer*, January 2000.
5. See note 1 to Chapter 6 on p. 35.

10 DATA ACQUISITION – OBJECTIVES OF THE OTHER SIDE, THEIR LEVEL OF COMMITMENT AND PERSONALITIES/ CHARACTERISTICS OF THEIR NEGOTIATORS

Although in formulating our objectives we want to avoid the danger of cueing, referred to in the Introduction to this Part, we cannot avoid taking into account in setting our objectives, those of the other side and their level of commitment to them. It will be remembered that the definition of negotiation included 'at least satisfying the minimum needs (of both parties)'. Demanding unconditional surrender, which ignores the needs of the other side is not negotiation.

10.1 Their objectives

When it is a matter of price, it is reasonable to assume that their objectives are the opposite of ours. But this is not necessarily so across the range of issues with which we are concerned. In trying to put yourself so far as you can in their shoes and consider the problem from their perspective, it may well prove to be that some of their objectives are the same as ours and they may have some which we have not even considered, for example, the buyer's need to have the contract placed by a certain date because of its effect on the overall project programme. Of course, as the supplier, the sooner the contract is placed from our point of view the better but the date is not of the same critical importance to ourselves as it is to the buyer. It may also be significant to the buyer that the price does not exceed a certain level, since beyond that point he may have to refer the purchase to a higher authority for approval which he may be reluctant to do. It may be possible for us to meet his wishes by removing something from the scope of work, e.g. spares which can be ordered separately at a later date. Knowledge of this type gives us leverage.

10.2 Their commitment

It was stressed earlier that the moment either the buyer issues his enquiry, the supplier submits his quotation, or a party to a contract submits a quantified claim, then they are making a commitment, since each of these documents will normally set an upper limit on their demands. Before setting those limits we need to make some assessment of the reaction which we expect from the other side, their probable counter-demands and the strength of their commitment to achieving them. On investigating their level of commitment we may find at the extreme that the issue is non-negotiable and our only alternative to accepting their demand is to withdraw from the business. In those circumstances the early discovery of the non-negotiable item can save us a great deal of time and money which would otherwise have been wasted.

The other important discovery which we ought to be able to make is the sort of time-scale which the negotiations will take, from which we can roughly assess the time-costs of the negotiations and their effect on the value of any bargain we achieve – see further Chapter 16, p. 105. In arriving at their level of commitment we must make sure that our assessment is made looking through their eyes. It may be that the issue is one of no real concern to ourselves but we can see that it is of importance to them. In that event we have something useful with which to trade and, when it comes to defining our objectives, makes it in effect a major rather than a minor issue.

A commitment by either side may arise for one of six reasons:

1 A diktat from an external authority, e.g. a legal rule which requires that all contracts for public works must be placed subject to the law of the country in question. The public body placing the contract must comply with the rule. The overseas contractor has no alternative but to accept it or look elsewhere for business. The issue is non-negotiable.
2 An internal diktat from the Board of parent company, e.g. that for reasons of group policy, no subsidiary must accept joint and several liability in a joint venture.[1] Since joint and several liability of all the joint venturers is something upon which the client will insist, and the issue is non-negotiable, the other partners must either exclude that firm or make them a sub-contractor.
3 An ideological belief by the contractor's management, often supported by their industry trade association, that certain terms are so unfair that they should never be accepted, e.g. the requirement in the UK to provide on-demand performance bonds.[2] Rational arguments by the buyer are unlikely to persuade the firm to change its stance and if the term is judged by the buyer to be an essential one the negotiations will almost certainly fail.
4 Maintaining adherence to what has become an industry norm for the type of contact in question, e.g. in electrical, mechanical and process plant contracts which limit the liability of the contractor after the plant is taken over to the making good of defects and excluding any right for the purchaser to claim damages for loss of profit or of use. This commitment is weaker and it may be possible to negotiate, say, liquidated damages for any time when the plant is out of action during the warranty period because of a defect.
5 Guidelines prepared by the firm's management as to what they expect their negotiators to achieve either in terms of overhead and profit margins, delivery periods or certain contractual provisions included/excluded. Here the commitment is much weaker. Guidelines of that type usually represent a wish-list of what management would like to see achieved but don't represent a set of walk-away points if the deal is sufficiently attractive as a whole.

6 Desire by the negotiator to achieve success and earn the esteem of others and of himself by demonstrating his ability to achieve his negotiating objectives. Pre-negotiation planning by a group which is significant to the negotiator will increase this commitment.[3] It is, however, open to be changed by tactics designed either to lower the negotiator's aspiration level or his estimate of success – see Chapter 31, pp. 229.

10.3 Personalities and characteristics expected of their negotiators

The personal interrelationships between our negotiators and those for the other side will be an important factor in the success or otherwise of the negotiations. For good interpersonal relationships, it is not required that the negotiators for the two sides should be friends, even in a business sense, but that they should each have respect for the legitimacy of interest and integrity and of the other.

Legitimacy of interest means that I recognize that what the other is demanding is, in the circumstances of the case and of his position, what it is understandable for him to demand. It is not arbitrary or made with the intention of humiliating me. I still may not agree with it but at least I can respect the point from where he is coming.

Integrity does not require that the negotiator will always tell the truth or tell all of the truth. However, the deception is expected to be one which is determined by the structure of the bargaining situation, and the extent of and motive behind the deception are expected to be consistent with the legitimacy of the negotiator's position.

A deception can be said to be determined by the bargaining situation when it is required to counter the position or tactics adopted by, or expected to be adopted by, the other side. For example, in price negotiations the buyer would be foolish to reveal the actual level of his purchasing budget at a time when he suspected the supplier's price still included a margin for negotiation; he would use a figure which was substantially lower. His motive would be consistent with the legitimacy of his position and would be recognized as such by the supplier.

A distinction is drawn between acts of deception which flow naturally from the structure of the bargaining situation and those which are free acts, in the sense that they are not predetermined by that structure. A promise made to undertake some future act which was never intended to be implemented, but was made solely for the purpose of obtaining some benefit from the other side, would be a *free act*. An example would be a promise by the buyer to award the supplier future business if the supplier will give the buyer a discount on the present order, when the buyer knows, but the supplier does not, that there is no prospect of future business.

As a generalization it is maintained that each party to a negotiation will expect that the other may exercise deception when giving information and will accordingly apply their own judgement to such information when evaluating its significance. Moreover, to the extent that a negotiator adopts a position or tactics the obvious counter to which is deception, he is assumed to accept the use of deception as legitimate within that framework, falsehood ceases to be a falsehood when it is understood on all sides that the truth is not expected to be spoken.[4]

Expressions of intention to act in a particular manner which are designed to influence the other party's actions will be expected to be made in good faith at the time, although they may be subjected to reconsideration in the light of subsequent events. The distinction is important; a negotiator's effectiveness depends largely on his reputation of integrity. It is suggested that this will not be impaired by factual distortions within the framework determined by the negotiating structure, which will be anticipated by the other side, but may be destroyed by the expression of false intentions. This appears to be due in part to moral upbringing, and in part to the advantages derived from being classified as people whose word can be trusted.

ATTITUDES TOWARDS THE NEGOTIATOR FOR OPPONENT

The attitudes which negotiators have towards those for the other side will be derived from:

1 Any previous direct experience of negotiating with the other negotiators
2 Information obtained from others who have negotiated with the other side
3 Prejudices which they have developed towards the character and class of person whom they believe the other's negotiators to be.

Prior experience

Distinction must be made between prior experience of the actual individuals who will be involved on behalf of the other side and prior experience of negotiating with others in the other's firm or in the industry to which it belongs.

When the prior experience relates directly to the persons concerned then it may be of positive value in enabling us to prepare for the encounter ahead. Even then great care is required. At previous meetings the negotiator for the other side may have been playing a part, acting the part of the 'hard guy' to allow his colleague to be conciliatory. (See the discussion of the negotiating tactic of 'partners as opposites', p. 245.) On another occasion he may appear in his natural role of a reasonable fair-minded individual.

If, however, the experience is a generalization, e.g. 'buyers in the other side's industry demand discounts', based on what happened at the last two negotiations, this provides no certain guide for action. Because the last two buyers encountered in that industry wanted a discount, it cannot be stated that *all* buyers in the other side's industry want a discount. Unless this can be stated, it cannot be inferred that the other's buyer will want a discount. To make such an inference would be committing what the logicians call 'the fallacy of composition'; asserting that what is true of a part is also true of the whole. (It would not of course be unreasonable to assume there was a good chance that he would ask for a discount and therefore to allow for this in the pricing.)

Prejudices

The less intimately people are known the more they tend to be categorized by reference to such factors as their job, their income, the house/district in which they live, the school to which they went and the one to which their children go, the clubs and societies to which they belong, etc. From these 'labels' we tend to draw a composite picture and assume that those whom we identified as fellow members of a particular socio-economic group will share with us common values and beliefs. If we find that the other negotiator does not belong to a particular group, but nevertheless belongs to one for which we have high regard and to which certain virtues are ascribed, then we will similarly assume that all the members of that group possess those same virtues. Conversely if the group is one for which we have little regard, or with which we may actually consider ourselves to be in conflict, then we will assign to its members all the failings we associate with that group.

In practice, generalizations of this type are made continually; placing people into categories and drawing conclusions from this as to their character, for example, 'Managers are sound chaps. John is a manager, therefore John is a sound chap.' The inference is logically sound but the truth of the inference depends wholly on the first generalization which can only be based on very limited knowledge and be entirely subjective. We may believe it, but we would find it difficult objectively to justify our belief, and a union negotiator who had never met John and was told only that he was a manager might have a very different picture of him.[5]

Therefore, in preparing for a meeting with the negotiators for the other side, whom we have not previously met, our negotiators should listen to the views of others and consider such of their own past experience which is relevant but, equally, they should keep an open mind. In particular they should not draw firm conclusions as to the likely behaviour of the other side's negotiators because they happen to belong to a certain 'class', although, naturally, the more statistically significant their experience of a common behaviour pattern of people in that class the more they should, in a game-theory sense, 'maximize their security', by preparing for that common pattern to be repeated.[6]

INTERPERSONAL ATTITUDES

Rubin and Brown[7] have provided a useful concept which they refer to as a negotiator's IO (Interpersonal Orientation). A negotiator with a high IO is responsive to his interpersonal relationship with his opposite number. He is sensitive and reactive to how the other behaves. A person with a low IO is non-responsive to such relationships and is concerned only with his own interests and achieving his own objective without regard for the other. A further distinction is drawn in this analysis between high IO negotiators who are competitively orientated, i.e. are out to take advantage of the other and are suspicious of any apparent generosity on his part, and those who are cooperatively orientated, i.e. are prepared to trust the other and to behave themselves in a trustworthy manner, e.g. reciprocate concessions.

The following table sets out the result of the possible pairings of the three types.

Ourselves	The other side	Results
1 High IO competitive	High IO competitive	We will respect him as being someone similar to ourselves. Bargaining will be tough but professional and the outcome will be largely a function of the relative power positions of the two sides. Social relationships will develop

Ourselves	*The other side*	*Results*
		between the two but be confined to business i.e. they will lapse if the business relationship itself terminates.
2 High IO competitive	High IO cooperative	We will respond to his cooperative acts by exploiting every possible advantage which we possess. He can be expected initially to react with hurt surprise: 'I would never have believed anyone could behave like that.' Later his re-action will take one of two forms. First he may turn vicious and respond aggressively even if it means losing the bargain. Secondly he may avoid any outward show of resentment and take the best bargain he can get this time. Either way he will determine if possible never to have any more dealings with us. If he is compelled to have further dealings then he will change to being strongly competitive from the outset. Our gain will at best therefore be one good bargain.
3 High IO competitive	Low IO	He will act solely in his own interests regardless of our behaviour. Since he is not interested in us as a person, he will tend to react to our com-petitiveness as if it were solely the result of the structure of the bargaining situation. The negotiations will be difficult because whilst he would accept an outcome which satisfied his own interests, we would only accept it if it gave us a bigger share of the cake. So the classic 50/50 split could be acceptable to him, if it met his objective, but we would reject it.
4 High IO collaborative	High IO competitive	This is the reverse of 2 above.
5 High IO collaborative	High IO collaborative	The bargaining period will be short, with both sides concentrating on essentials and not inter-ested in scoring points. The outcome will be one which is recognized by both sides as fair but will not be optimal for either. Since the two sides will have enjoyed dealing with each other, repeat business can be expected.

Ourselves	The other side	Results
6 High IO collaborative	Low IO	Having no interest in our attempts at collaboration he will pressurize us to the point at which he has secured his own objective, assuming this is feasible given the relative power structure of the two sides. As in 2 above we may become so frustrated at his misunderstanding of our moves that we explode emotionally and the negotiations either terminate or continue with our being embittered and suspicious.
7 Low IO	High IO competitive	This is the reverse of 3 above.
8 Low IO	High IO collaborative	This is the reverse of 6 above.
9 Low IO	Low IO	Both of us are now interested solely in achieving our own ends. We will behave rationally ourselves and expect the other to do likewise. The negotiations will therefore be coldly impersonal. Each will recognize the validity of an argument from the other side only if it is supported by power or if it is in their overall interests to do so, e.g. by creating a trade-off situation which gives them what they want. Negotiations will be prolonged as both sides test the other to the limit. Also because of their low IO the two sides will lack any mechanism for informal or 'off-the-record' discussions over dinner or the golf course and they will be unable to trust each other as persons.

It is not suggested that in real life we often meet people who are at either end of the IO continuum or are either wholly competitively collaborative. However, it is important to discover at least the general direction which the tendencies of the negotiator for the other side take, and match our own team accordingly, avoiding cases 3 and 6. Even if we lack knowledge of the particular negotiator for them, we can often obtain a guide from the national characteristics of the country. As a generalization, if negotiators from that country can be expected to be concerned over 'losing face', would regard our negotiator as having insulted them were he to raise his voice in real or apparent anger or would be seriously disturbed if they felt that by our behaviour we were being insensitive, then we should not select a negotiator with a low IO – and that range of characteristics is to be found in many countries in Latin America, southern Europe and the Far East. The importance of this point is that persons who are low IOs do not change irrespective of the person with whom they are negotiating. They are insensitive to the other's behaviour and will go on behaving as if the world consisted only of persons like themselves. A naturally cooperative high IO will change his behaviour according to that of the person with whom he is dealing so that if that person is competitive he will change to being competitive and more strongly so than if it were his natural manner of behaviour.

PERSONALITY PROBLEMS

Reference will be made later (Chapter 12, p. 64) to what Kennedy has referred to as the 'Red Negotiator', that is someone wholly concerned with securing his own demands to the detriment of everything and everyone else. Such a person may be either a buyer or a client. Only exceptionally will the seller ever have enough negotiating power to employ him – although that was once the case with IBM.

As the supplier we don't need to fear him but we do need to be aware of his existence and of the ploys which he is likely to use in order that we can prepare accordingly. Some of these are described later in Chapter 11, p. 65 with suggestions as to how they can be countered.

NEGOTIATING WITH PEOPLE FROM DIFFERENT CULTURES

It is only to be expected that people from different cultures will behave in ways which are different to our own. They are unlikely to share our value system. Even when we recognize this, our immediate reactions are likely to cause us difficulties in one or more of the following ways:

● We tend to have stereotypes of people from other cultures often derived from what our family have told us, and from films, books, television programmes or chance encounters on holidays. Most of these stereotypes are hopelessly inaccurate as any sort of guide to the value system of the overseas negotiators.
● We divide people into 'in' and 'out' groups. The 'in' group, comprises in business our company colleagues and, to a lesser extent, people from other companies in our group and others of our own profession, even sometimes those working for 'the other side'. It is this group in whose company we are most relaxed and with whom we share most cultural characteristics in common. We empathize with their problems, help them out of difficulties and even make excuses for them when things go wrong. All others are in the 'out' group, upon whom we blame our misfortunes and with whom we only associate when we are compelled to do so. Most foreigners in business, outside perhaps a few from other group companies or firms with whom we have formed successful alliances, are in this category.
● We fall into the trap of ethnocentrism, the evaluation of other cultures by criteria specific to our own, and so make the assumption of our own cultural superiority. We deceive ourselves into thinking that our own prized cultural values are objective and from there it is only a small step to believing that other people ought to adopt them and indeed would do so if they recognized their value. But these values are not objective and there is no reason for oth-

ers to follow them. In northern Europe and North America we tend to value blunt, even rude, speech, involving the open criticism of others, as showing a person to be honest and straightforward. In the Middle East or South East Asia, such behaviour would be regarded as unacceptable and destructive of the harmonious relationships which it is important for the negotiators to establish before they can do business together. Can it possibly be said that one is right and other wrong? No, they are just different.

When we are dealing then with people from another country, especially if the work is to be performed within their country, we need to have a sensitivity to their culture and to their ways of doing business. Remember that they will probably expect that we will perform in accordance with their stereotype of us; often one which characterizes us as being rude, aggressive, impatient to get results, uninterested in local business etiquette and regarding as binding only what is written down in the contract. If, while remaining firm in the conduct of the actual negotiations, we can behave in ways that contradict this stereotype, not only are we more likely to get a favourable result but we will have laid the foundations for a successful ongoing business relationship.

Notes

1. Joint and several liability refers to each of the joint venturers being liable for the whole of the damages suffered by the purchaser regardless of the extent of his own liability for the loss. If the joint venture is, say, for the design and construction of a railway electrification scheme or a new tramway, it is the type of liability which those in the joint venture with the maximum of assets, e.g. manufacturing companies, usually try to avoid since the major risks are probably in the civil work and yet the civil contractor probably has the least assets with which to meet any claim.

2. On demand performance bonds are bonds which can be called by the purchaser at any time without the need to prove loss. They are favoured by purchasers but objected to by contractors because of the power which they place in the hands of the purchaser if he unscrupulous.

3. This has been shown in bargaining experiments and is intuitively correct because, as the negotiator, I now have a commitment to achieve not only to myself but to the rest of the group who participated in the planning. If I am not successful in fulfilling the plan they will probably be my sternest critics. For experimental results, see D. Druckmann, 'Prenegotiation experience and dyadic conflict resolution in a bargaining situation', *Journal of Experimental Social Psychology*, 4 (1968), pp. 367–83.

4. Henry Taylor, British statesman, is quoted as having said of international negotiations 'falsehood ceases to be falsehood when it is understood on all sides that the truth is not expected to be spoken', cited in P. R. McDonald, *Negotiation of Government Contracts* (Covine, CA: Procurement Associates Inc., 1970), pp. 1–8.

5. Haire conducted an experiment in which managers and union representatives were introduced, through photographs and written descriptions, to Mr B, an ordinary middle-aged,

reasonably well-dressed man with no distinguishing features. The view which each took of Mr B differed widely according to whether they were told he was a representative of management or of a union. M. Haire, 'Role perception in labour management relations: an experimental approach', in *Social Perception*, edited by H. Toch and H. C. Smith (London: Van Nostrand, 1968).

6. 'Class' is used here in the sense of belonging to a certain group who may be considered as negotiators to have certain defined characteristics, e.g. lawyers, accountants, buyers, salesmen, and to subgroups of these who belong to a particular country, industry or firm.

   Sherif in a provoking study has shown how intergroup relations can be seriously affected by sterotyped images: 'group prejudices and derogatory images of other people, though products of historical processes forming part of a people's cultural heritages may exert a fateful influence on the ongoing process between groups. *In the context of immediate encounters the past becomes a heavy hand*' M. Sherif, *Group, Conflict and Cooperation* (London: Routledge and Kegan Paul, 1966) (original emphasis).

7. J. L. Rubin and B. P. Brown, *The Social Psychology of Bargaining and Negotiation* (London: Academic Press, 1975), pp. 158 ff.

11 MEANS OF ACQUIRING DATA

As indicated in Chapters 9 and 10, the data which we need to acquire relates to:

- The negotiating environment
- The other side's organization and methods of negotiation and their objectives for this negotiation
- The personalities and characteristics of those who are likely to be negotiating for the other side.

11.1 The negotiating environment – buying and selling

Sources of information relating to the negotiating environment, if the negotiations are with an overseas buyer, are set out below. If the negotiations are with another UK firm then the environment ought to be sufficiently well known to us from our own internal sources.

OBTAINING DATA

The sources of generalized data sufficient to understand whether a problem exists or not include:

- *Within the UK*
  The Department of Trade
  Chamber of Commerce and Trade Associations
  Councils or Committees established for the particular territory or region, e.g. Committee for Middle East Trade
  Banks having a particular interest in the territory or region
  Friendly UK firms already trading with the country
  Newspaper and journal articles

- *Overseas*
  Any local company established by your own company or within the group of companies to which you belong
  The local British Embassy or High Commission
  Local banks
  Your own agent
  Other businesspeople operating in the territory
  Your own observation and experience
  Local newspaper and journal articles

In collecting and assessing data it is essential to bear in mind any bias which may exist in the person from whom the data is obtained and hence in the data itself, which will cause the data to appear either more or less favourable to your company. Bias may arise because:

1 The person providing the data may have an interest in your future actions. So anyone concerned to promote trade between your company and the country/purchaser in question will tend to minimize risks and present opportunities as favourably as he can.

2 The person wishes to please you, so he will tell you what he believes you would like to know. This is particularly true of the Far East.

3 The person does not really know the answer to your question but cannot bear to lose face by admitting this. Again particularly true of the Far East.

4 The person may genuinely believe he does know but his information is incorrect because he consistently fails to obtain data from reliable and objective sources. This will usually apply to data based on the cocktail-party gossip of those who rely on the Embassy circuit instead of going out to learn the hard facts.

5 The person who, while appearing to support your interests, is in reality concerned to support those of one of your competitors or even your customer since he believes showing favour to them will bring him the greater reward.

Essentially the gathering of data is an intelligence-type operation in which a number of separate facts are collected and fitted together to form a composite picture which is coherent and 'hangs together' in a way which is likely to resemble reality. But the emphasis here is on the facts being separate. All too often Fact A is regarded as being supported by Fact B when in reality they are both derived from a common source. The opinion of the commercial counsellor on a matter, and an article in the local financial journal on the same subject, are not supportive of each other unless both have obtained their data from unrelated sources. What is more likely in practice is that either (a) the counsellor read the journal or (b) the journalist obtained the copy from the counsellor or (c) they both met separately with a senior official of the central bank.

ACQUISITION OF DETAILED KNOWLEDGE OF RELEVANT ISSUES

Unless the company is already operating in the territory, there is only one way in which such knowledge can be obtained and that is by one or more visits to the territory concerned, made by suitably qualified personnel from the company's staff. The key factors which will make such visits successful are:

1 Time spent beforehand in preparation and obtaining as much generalized data on the territory and issues in question as possible.

2 Having a limited number of meetings set up in advance with those likely to be able to provide access to the data required.

3 Allowing enough time for meetings being cancelled and for other and further appointments/visits being made.

4 Getting out of the hotel and officials' offices and seeing something of the country first-hand.

5 Retaining an objective and enquiring mind and not allowing particular events or limitations to affect one's judgement.

6 Writing up reports as one goes along, recording the facts impartially and refraining from making judgements until one is able to do so in a balanced manner.

7 Not relying on second-hand data but insisting politely on being referred to primary sources.

11.2 The negotiating environment – contract dispute

Reference has already been made in Chapter 9 to the environment in terms of the feasibility and practicability of taking the dispute to law or arbitration and of enforcing any judgement or arbitral award which may be obtained. Although neither party may seriously want to consider this step, whether it is feasible or practicable or not will strongly influence their attitudes towards negotiation and towards taking arbitrary action.

As regards the other data which is necessary for the assessment of the probability of success either in negotiation or in legal, arbitral proceedings, this is essentially to be found in the contract itself and the records of the correspondence between the parties and notes of progress or other review meetings which have been held during the course of the contract. There are only two situations in which, legally, documents and evidence of discussions pre-contract may be relevant:

● The dispute relates to representations of fact which were made by one party to the other before the contract was entered into, or

● The contract was not reduced wholly to writing but consists partially of documents, correspondence and oral statements.[1]

Of course that assumes that there actually is a contract and it is not uncommon either commercially or, in the construction industry in disputes between main and sub-contractors, for the preliminary issue to be taken that no contract exists, but perhaps only a letter of intent.[2] The correspondence and documents which passed between the parties and records of work performed, will then need to be researched.

If the dispute relates to delay or disruption, then essential data will be the notices which the contractor gave to the employer at the time, together with the records of how the work was disrupted as compared with the planned level of activity. It has often been said that claims are won on records, records and more records. Where appropriate, written records can often usefully be supplemented by photographs which can provide telling evidence as to the then current state of construction and of plant standing idle.

11.3 The other side's organization, business methods and decision-making processes

If we have dealt with the other side previously, even if the negotiations were not successful then we ought to have records available as to the other side's organization and the way in which they behaved; if not records, then our staff who participated. Remember, however, that especially if we were unsuccessful as a bidder, that information from the people involved will be biased. Their descriptions of the other side's negotiators and their behaviour will seek to provide justification for our failure. It is, however, important to try and look beneath the bias to obtain some genuine assessment of the way in which the other side approached the negotiations. We should also try to establish how they viewed us at the end of the negotiations and, if we were successful, at the conclusion of the contract. Was their attitude positive towards us or were there criticisms of the way in which we behaved?

In any event, people's records and their memories will need updating. Any organizational change will almost certainly have been accompanied by cultural change. Any changes in senior personnel will almost certainly have led to changes in thinking; it is trite but true that new brooms do sweep clean and previous policies will have been discarded for no other reason than that they were those followed by the '*ancien regime*'.

11.4 Those who are likely to be negotiating for the other side

If we have dealt with the other side before, and there have been no significant changes in their personnel, then we will already be aware of their attitudes, beliefs and motivation, and of the tactics which they are likely to employ. If there have been changes, even more so if we have not negotiated previously with the other side, then we need actively to see to obtain this information in respect of those whom we believe we will be likely to be facing across the table. Information can be obtained directly by establishing informal contacts with the other side at differing levels within the organization This can often be done through the shared membership of clubs or societies. Information can be acquired indirectly in ascending order of particularity from:

● The reputation generally of firms within the industry
● The reputation of the other party as a firm in that industry
● The reputation of the negotiators for the other side.

Generalized information is often readily available to us from our competitors or associates. The difficulties are:

● Allowing for bias in the person providing the information,who may genuinely have had a bad experience but equally may be wanting to put the blame on others for his own folly or is happy for his own purposes to mislead you.
● Avoiding stereotyping, such as 'All firms in the UK construction industry are tough and unscrupulous. X is a civil engineering contractor. Therefore all his negotiators are tough and unscrupulous.' The logic is correct but is the first statement true? Civil engineering is certainly a tough industry and there are unscrupulous characters in it, but, while remaining on our guard, it would be a mistake to believe that all within the industry were tarred with the same brush.

● Separating out the grains of truth from the mountains of gossip and hearsay picked up, for instance, at conferences, often in the bar and sometimes in the toilets.

Given all these problems is the effort to obtain reliable information worthwhile? The answer is 'Yes'. While what is learnt is unlikely to be wholly accurate, it will usually be possible to sift out sufficient information to at least put us on our guard as to what may be the case. The old saying 'forewarned is forearmed' remains a useful guide to action.

Notes

1. It has been held recently that the strict rule, that under English law evidence cannot be given as to what the parties believed that the contract meant or their conduct, only applies when the whole of the contract has been reduced to writing. In other circumstance, when the contract was formed by documents, correspondence and oral discussions, such evidence is allowed in order to interpret objectively what were the obligations of the parties – *Carmichael* v. *National Power Plc, The Times*, 23 November 1999.
2. Work is often started by sub-contractors and others in reliance on the issue by the purchaser of a letter of intent or some other instruction to proceed. Unless the letter of intent or instruction to proceed sets out at least the major terms of the contract, in particular the contract price, then the court is likely to hold that there was no contract because the parties never came to an agreement on those terms. If, in reliance on the letter or instruction the contractor has gone ahead and done the contract work, then the contractor may be entitled to be paid a reasonable sum for such work under the doctrine of 'unjust enrichment'. However, as there was no contract the purchaser will have no contractual remedies against the contractor if the work is late – *British Steel Corporation* v. *Cleveland Bridge and Engineering Co Ltd* [1984] 1 All ER 504.

    Alternatively, if the letter or instruction authorized the carrying-out of certain specified preliminary work which the contractor has performed, then the court will probably find a collateral contract covering just that work.

12 NEGOTIATING STYLE

12.1 Introduction

Since the last edition of this book was published, there has been a virtual avalanche of texts recommending so-called 'win–win' negotiating, the concept that the outcome of the negotiations should be a win for both parties, as opposed to the older view that viewed negotiating as about winning for yourself without paying too much regard to how that left the other party. This seems to be part of a trend in which firms are encouraged to think of long-term relationships with their suppliers, even partnering with them, and adversarial-type behaviour is frowned upon and contracts should be 'fair'.

Clearly there are situations in which the establishment of long-term partnering-type agreements is appropriate and can be beneficial to all concerned. Within such agreements, there must be trust and commitment by all involved, since contracts are usually on an 'open book' basis, and adversarial behaviour would be out of place. Further the idea behind partnering is that those involved should be concentrating their efforts jointly towards the achievement of goals which will be of benefit to both. If, for example, the supplier working with the buyer's production engineers can find ways in which a product can be redesigned to reduce costs then both should share in the resultant gain. Similarly, if a contractor can demonstrate that a change in construction methodology would reduce a project's costs and time-scale then the benefit should be shared between contractor and client.

However, in all these situations, and the same applies in many industrial relations cases, one is not talking about how a given cake is to be shared but how to increase the size of the cake with the concept that it is to be shared already agreed. Most commercial negotiations outside of the partnering arena are much more closely aligned to the cake-sharing position in which more for you usually means less for me. Of course this does not necessarily mean that the value of the more for you is balanced by an equivalent reduction in the value of the less for me. It is usually possible to structure the bargain in such a way that you can have your 'more', which you value highly, at a cost to me which is significantly less. If this were not so then negotiations would become that much more difficult.

12.2 Single-factor negotiations

Assume that we are negotiating about the price to pay for an article which already exists and nothing else – no terms of payment, no guarantees and no warranty period. We would never know the real difference between us. You know my opening figure, say, 100 and I know your opening figure of say, 150. But I don't know the lowest figure which you would accept for the article and you don't know the highest which I would offer. Equally I don't know how anxious you are to sell and how much you really need the money. You don't know how keen I am to buy, what it would mean to me to possess the article, and how much money I could really afford to give for it. If I desperately wanted the article as an anniversary present for my wife and I was leaving town tomorrow I would obviously pay more than if I were on an extended stay and rather liked the article but had no particular requirement for it.

We would each try to find out the strength or weakness of the other's position whilst concealing our own. We might reach a bargain, but where would depend on the value you attached to selling and the value I attached to buying. It would be pure bazaar haggling.

12.3 Multi-faceted negotiations

Fortunately, in commercial practice single-factor negotiations of that type are rare. Even in contract dispute situations, where it may appear to be only a matter of money involved, there is the contractual basis for the claim to be established and there are often issues relating to bad workmanship, delays and extended warranties to be negotiated.

Negotiations for a contract are always multi-faceted, covering the price, delivery, specification and the key terms of contract. There is always the opportunity therefore for the packaging of offers in such a way that there is a benefit to both sides. 'If you agree to a reduction in the rate of liquidated damages for delay then we could consider bringing forward the date for delivery' would be a typical example.

But it is often argued that the buyer could gain more for himself without having to give anything away in return if he were to adopt a negotiating style in which he aggressively sought to further only his own interests – what Kennedy has referred to as 'red' behaviour.[1] There are two problems in the commercial world with the red approach. First it 'takes two to tango'. The red buyer is relying on the seller to give way to his demands. 'If you cannot do better on price than that you are wasting my time' is the typical red buyer's opening line. If the seller is also a red negotiator, he may well decide that he is wasting his own time and depart. The buyer must then look elsewhere for someone to bully without having learnt what else the seller might have been able to offer.

The second problem for the company employing the red negotiator is that his having secured all those concessions at the contract negotiation stage is likely only to mean grief and pain for his company when it comes to contract implementation; the more complex the contract the further the opportunities which will arise for the seller to recover through extras and claims.

Kennedy contrasts this red behaviour with 'blue' behaviour, where the negotiator is so concerned with the creation of harmonious relationships with the buyer that he will give almost anything away in order to secure this and to reach agreement. Such negotiators may well exist in the domestic world when we are dealing with friends and neighbours but hardly in the real world of commerce. If they do, then it cannot be for very long since their company would soon be out of business.

12.4 Trading

There is nothing wrong with the objectives of both reaching agreement and establishing a harmonious relationship with the other side, but the way to achieve these is not through a process of continually making concessions. This will only encourage the other side to ask for more. Genuine agreement and good relations arise from the respect which two professionals have for each other when they have learnt how to trade together to their mutual advantage. But the harmonious relationship is a by-product from the way in which the negotiations have been conducted, not an objective of the negotiations. Further, the perception of the harmonious relationship is not that it is a good in itself but that it will benefit the negotiator's company when it comes to difficulties which may arise during contract implementation or in the negotiation of follow-on business. Personal friendships which we form in the course of domestic social relations are valued for themselves, but friendly relationships in business are there to serve a purpose: a long-term gain for one's company. They are a means to an end and not an end in itself. Few business 'friendships' survive the departure of the negotiator from office.

Trading is the negotiating style of give and take except that in formulating our proposal we should start with what we want to take and then indicate what we would be prepared to offer in return. It's in the general form of 'If you will . . . then we would be prepared to . . .' – a specific example would be 'If you will agree to our proposal on excluding liability for damages for loss of profit then we would be prepared to consider an extended defects liability period'. What we want is stated clearly without equivocation. What we are prepared to give is left a little fuzzy until we get their reaction. While we have indicated flexibility, we have not made an unconditional concession.

A trader would have no difficulty with a blue negotiator, but how about when faced with a red one? Assume that the red bargainer is the buyer and that as the seller we have sent him our written quotation. He starts by pulling this to pieces: our price is absurd, our delivery period is ridiculous and the only terms he ever does business on are his own. What should be our reaction? Do we want to do business with him at all? If we have done our planning in advance we already know the type of person he is and the fact that we have bothered to send him a quotation and visit his office indicates that we do want to do so. That he has agreed to see us is an indicator that he is also interested in us. Our response is quietly to counter his allegations one by one and lead him into starting a dialogue. Whatever we do we must not allow ourselves to be intimidated by his outburst or allow it to influence our own behaviour. We are traders and as soon as we can we move towards exploring his possible flexibility, for example, 'Our price is based on your requirement for special packaging. If you were prepared to use our standard packaging which we would be happy to demonstrate to you then we could look at the price again' and so on through his list of comments.

It may not work. He may not be willing to trade. If so it will soon become obvious and we can take our leave.

The suggested style of negotiation is therefore trading and this applies whatever the negotiating situation or the style adopted by the person(s) acting for the other side. What we are willing to trade and what we want for it can be loosely formulated as part of our negotiating plan and developed further when we listen to their reactions to our initial proposals. Obviously if there is something which we want to secure but expect to have to trade for and they offer it for nothing then politely we accept. Equally we need to be aware of and have set down in our plan any issues which are strictly non-negotiable, e.g. because of company policy – (see p. 69).

Our style therefore does not alter, whether we are negotiating a partnering deal or a strictly arm's-length transaction. All that alters is the substance of what is being proposed for inclusion in the agreement. Suppose that on a partnering arrangement we as the manufacturer are asked to accept open book costing as part of the deal on continuous improvement and cost reduction. Our initial response might be 'If you are willing to agree strict confidentiality, a reasonable sharing of your savings on improvements which we originate and that we are not going to penalized for our efforts, then yes we would be willing to consider open book.' That leaves plenty of detail over which to negotiate while indicating broad, conditional, acceptance of the principle. Trading as a negotiating style still remains and we should never apologize for it.

Trading demands integrity from both sides. Deliberate falsification and any tactical ploys which depend upon it are out of the question. Of course the trader is expected to bluff, to leave himself room to negotiate when first declaring his prices, but not deliberately to lie or cheat – this applies as much to buyers as it does to sellers.

Note

1. G. Kennedy, *Kennedy on Negotiating* (Aldershot: Gower, 1998).

13 SETTING THE CORPORATE OBJECTIVES

Negotiations for a contract or for the resolution of a dispute are carried out within the context of the total business operations of the parties concerned. Negotiation should not be considered or be allowed to become an isolated act. It must be integrated within the totality of the firm's business and subordinated to the firm's overall business strategy. In this chapter we are concerned only with corporate objectives so that the negotiator is expected to behave normatively and solely in the company's interests. In the next chapter we will look at the negotiator's personalistic objectives and how these should be take into account.

13.1 Interests

Success in negotiating is to be measured therefore in terms of the contribution which such negotiations make to the attainment of the corporate strategic goals.

This can be seen most easily in the case of a firm bidding for a project or the procurement of goods, services or construction work. These activities only have significance in the extent to which they contribute to the company's profitability. The same applies, however, to the settlement of disputes which, until they are resolved, cost money and tie up both funds and management resources.

The objectives set on both sides for the negotiators need to take account of their overall impact on the firm's business. It's no use 'winning' the negotiations and losing a good client or customer or the reputation of the firm in the marketplace.

The objectives are also an expression of the party's interests which he wants to be satisfied by the negotiation. A primary interest for the contractor is earning a profit and for the purchaser that of securing the equipment or works that he needs for his operations at the most economically advantageous price.[1] It is not just the initial price which decides whether or not the contract will earn a profit or be economically advantageous. There is associated with the initial price all those other factors directly affecting price, such as terms of payment, together with everything which relates to quality and contractual risk. The difference here is between those factors which will occur in any event, e.g. that 90 per cent of the contract price for each stage of work will be paid on completion of that stage, and the risk that completion may be late or there will be defects. The latter will only affect profitability or value if they do occur. They can to some extent be discounted therefore, the more so if an action plan to reduce risk can be implemented in time.

13.2 Risk avoidance

Another primary interest for both sides therefore is that of protection against risk. A purchaser wants protection, for example, that if he pays out money for a product which is defective he can at least get it put right with preferably some recovery for the additional losses he has suffered. A contractor wants to be protected against the risk that if the contract goes wrong that it will not be the ruin of his business. Remember that there is no relationship in law between the damages which the contractor can be called upon to pay if he is seriously in default and the contract price. Further, that although the law on remoteness of damage may protect the party in default from true consequential damages, a foreseeable loss of profits is treated as direct damages, which, subject to the terms of the contract, will be recoverable.[2] In a recent case, the damages which the contractor could have been called upon to pay, had he not been protected by the terms of the contract, were over £1 million while the value of the machine, the subject of the contract, was under £300,000; at most, the profit margin of the contractor would have been around 15 per cent, i.e. £45,000. The terms of contract made the difference between a profit of, say, £45,000 and a loss of perhaps £950,000. Looked at of course from the client's side he had paid out £300,000 and because of the defects in the machine he was looking at a £1 million reduction in his profits. The judge referred in his judgement to the contract terms as making 'good business sense'. They certainly made good sense to the seller.[3]

Protection interests cover therefore a wide range of objectives, such as making good of defects, completion on time, satisfying performance guarantees, recovery of damages and rights of termination.

In particular contracts, there may be other interests, for example, gaining entry to a market, establishing long-term supply arrangements or, in a contract dispute, settling it in a way which will not prejudice future business relationships. Each of these will lead to the setting of different objectives.

13.3 Categories of objectives

Not all objectives possess the same value. They can conveniently be divided into three categories:

● The 'must have items' – If the negotiation is only about price, then this is our genuine maximum or minimum level we would accept, dependent upon whether we are buying or selling. It is likely that it will also include issues of risk such as the level of damages to which we would be exposed. If we cannot achieve the 'must have' items, then we walk away no matter how attractive the deal may be in other respects. It is assumed that in settling our 'walk-away' points we have considered the alternatives which are open to us in order to satisfy our interests. As a contractor we need to consider the disadvantages to our business of not securing this particular order. Do we have other alternative opportunities open to us within the same time-frame which would provide the same benefits and avoid the unacceptable risks? The value to us or the utility of the bid at any particular combination of price and contractual risk will differ according to our answer to that question (see further, p. 106 and for a discussion on utility see Appendix 1).

If we are the purchaser, then we may have no alternative but to procure the goods or services concerned although there may be the option of redefining the specification and/or our terms of contract so that they do not conflict with a 'must-have' of the firms with whom we are negotiating.

- The 'desirables' – These are items we would very much like to have or a price level with which we would be well satisfied. We recognize that if there are multiple items to be negotiated we are unlikely to achieve all of them and that we will have to develop trade-offs.
- The 'nice to have' items. It would be of benefit if we could achieve at least some of these but they are not essential. We would be content to use them as bargaining counters to obtain one or more of the desirables.

13.4 The 'must haves'

The first category, 'the must haves', cause the most difficulty because in effect these are non-negotiable. If we want to reach agreement then we should try and keep these to a minimum and ensure that they are clearly defined. Since they normally arise because of some instruction to the negotiating team, we must be sure that the instruction is fully understood and if necessary seek clarification from higher management. As a contractor it is one thing to be told that there must be an overall limit of liability and quite another to be told that such liability must be limited to 10 per cent of the contract price. Assuming that the principle of some limit can be agreed, the former at least allows us some flexibility on the amount. The latter allows for no flexibility on either the principle or the quantum. The same applies to damages for delay or for low performance and for the rates and maximum at which these are to be set.

The earlier that the 'must haves' of the other side can be identified the better. If as a contractor we can discover them before bidding, then if they are diametrically opposed to our own 'must have' objectives we should avoid the expense of preparing the bid. If for example we know that the deal is project financed, and so can anticipate the mandatory requirements of the lenders, we are in a position to decide before committing to substantial expenditure, whether or not these are acceptable to us. To adopt in those circumstances a policy of 'wait and see' or 'let's cross that bridge when we come to it' is a waste of time, money and resources.

13.5 The 'desirables'

These are usually linked together so that what we want to achieve is an overall package which imposes on us, whether as contractor or client, no more than an acceptable level of risk commensurate with the profitability of the contract. As both client and contractor, it is likely that in most instances we will have established norms of risk for the type of contract in question which are based on the standards generally in use in the industry concerned. If that is so then the area for negotiation is reasonably limited.

The problems start when the contract form proposed is either non-standard or a standard which has been heavily modified, since the approach of those drafting such forms or modifications is usually to throw as much of the risk as possible on the other side without regard to commercial reality. This happens regardless of whether it is the client or contractor who proposes the form. The negotiations are then likely to be prolonged, and to cover all the significant areas of risk listed below, the time implications of which are considered later (see Chapter 16, pp. 106–107).

MAJOR AREAS OF RISK

The following list identifies the major areas of risk that will need to be negotiated:

- Method of pricing related to information available
- Responsibility for ground conditions
- Design responsibility. If placed on the contractor, is it strict or due skill and care, and right of client to be involved in design process?
- Site or premises availability
- Right of the client to order variations and consequences of variations
- Time for completion and definition of completion
- Payment procedures, time for payment and, if contract is overseas, currency of payment
- Price escalation
- Performance guarantees and test procedures and methods
- Circumstances allowing extensions of time
- Liquidated damages for delay or low performance and the maximum of each
- Performance bonds, the amounts of these and whether or not on first demand
- Parent company guarantee
- Definition of *force majeure*
- Period of defects liability, extent of defects liability and residual liability at the end of the period for latent defects
- Responsibility for damage to the works and for injury or damage to others and insurance
- Liability of contractor for nominated sub-contractors, if any
- Overall limitation of liability, if any
- Termination for default and extent of liability on termination
- Method(s) of dispute resolution, and law, language and jurisdiction if the contract is overseas
- In a long-term contract, changes in economic conditions.

13.6 The 'nice to have' items

These are issues which do not have a major impact on risk but on which either client or contractor would like to see the proposed contract modified in their favour. They might include such issues as the periods for the giving of notices, use by the client of the contractor's drawings, form of the contract programme, and other matters primarily of an administrative nature such as arrangements for inspection. Dependent on the degree of importance which either party attaches to any of these, it may be possible to trade a concession on, say, two or three such issues in return for a concession on one of the major risk items. None of them should be given away without the party conceding/obtaining something in return.

13.7 Their objectives and ours

In our planning we are as concerned with what we perceive to be the interests and objectives of the other side as we are with our own. It is not necessarily the case that our objectives and theirs will be completely opposed to each other although our interests may be different. For example, they may see liquidated damages for delay as a convenient way to recover damages if we are late. We may see such damages as being a limit on our delay liability, which could be helpful to us provided that the rate and the maximum are set at levels which we can accept and perhaps have made some allowance for within our price.

Within our list of 'desirables', we need to set priorities for each item and the range of positions which we will take on each one. Continuing with the example of liquidated damages for delay, our initial position as a contractor could be 0.5 per cent per month to a maximum of 5 per cent, and our final position 1 per cent to a maximum of 10 per cent *depending upon our overall assessment of risk*. This proviso is vitally important. Although we prioritize and set a range for each 'desirable', the value to us of each is not self-contained but is dependent upon the totality of risk relative to price which we are accepting. If we say the maximum risk potential we are prepared to accept is 15 per cent then we could only go to the maximum of 10 per cent on delay provided that we had already agreed restrictions to 5 per cent on the remainder of the contract. This point will be explored further later in Chapter 27, p. 198.

13.8 Our negotiating interests

It is suggested that as part of the negotiating plan we should prepare in tabular form a summary of our negotiating interests and objectives and their anticipated response – this is illustrated in Figure 13.1, though, for simplicity the list of 'desirables' has been restricted to just six items.

This list is necessarily simplified and the entry is the basis upon which our bid was submitted against our standard conditions. In practice we would have identified more of our key clauses in the list of 'desirables' prior to the negotiations. Those under the heading of 'Nice to have' could not be ones we would foresee as leading to a 'walk-away' situation. At the moment we do not have their response to our tender. Once we have it or otherwise learn of their reaction we would add to the table their response.

Notes

1. This is the wording used in the EU Procurement Directives as the alternative to lowest price and allows the purchaser to take into account all such matters as technical quality, delivery,

---

Interests

As proposed in the Marketing Plan for 1999, we need to secure the contract for the Orpheus system which represents 25 per cent of our planned order intake for 2000.

Objectives

Must haves
1 Gross Margin: not less than 15%
2 Total liquidated damages: limit 15%
3 No liability for unliquidated damages for loss of profits.

Desirables	*Entry*	*Walk-away points*
Defects period	12 months	Above 18 months
Damages for delay	0.5 % per month	1% per month
Maximum damages	5%	10%
Completion	24 months	22 months
Low performance damages	None	Above 5% maximum assuming 10% for delay
Design liability	Due skill and care	Open-ended fit for purpose

Nice to have		
All our standard clauses		Not applicable

Figure 13.1 Sample summary of negotiating interests and objectives, and anticipated responses

running costs performance, after-sales service, etc. Another form of wording expressing the same idea would be 'the best value for money'.

2. Recent decisions of the courts, in particular *British Sugar plc* v. *NEI Power Projects Ltd* (unreported) 1996 have established that a normal loss of profits falls within the first rule of *Hadley* v. *Baxendale* as arising naturally according to the usual course of things from the breach of contract itself. Such damages are therefore direct damages and are not therefore covered by the word 'consequential'. According to the Court of Appeal, what the term 'consequential' actually means is not clear and its meaning could vary according to circumstances. What the courts have concentrated on what it does *not* mean in clauses excluding liability.

3. See *British Fermentation Products Ltd* v. *Compair Reavell Ltd* 8 June 1999, where the judge held that the exclusion of liability clause was reasonable under the Unfair Contract Terms Act 1977. Case reported in *The Buyer*, September 1999.

14 PERSONAL OBJECTIVES OF THE NEGOTIATORS

The previous chapter considered the setting of corporate objectives. The assumption was implicit that the negotiators involved were acting purely rationally in the best interests of their organization. However, negotiation is a matter of human behaviour and humans do not behave as models of rationality. Whether it is in the setting of objectives or the carrying through of the negotiations themselves, negotiators will act not only to meet corporate objectives but also in order to fulfil their own personal agenda. To the extent that the negotiators can influence the setting of the corporate objectives, they will bend these so that they conform to their personal ones.

14.1 Personal bias

In discussing the gathering of data, the difficulty was stressed of ensuring that such data was objective. When the data must be gathered from the behaviour of those representing either competitors or the firm with whom the negotiations are taking place, then bias in the reporting or assessment of such data is almost inevitable. Such bias will be linked directly to the personal subjective aspirations of the person doing the reporting or making the assessment. However objectively rational the result may appear, underlying that apparent rationality will be what the negotiator is seeking for himself.

14.2 Personal objectives

The needs of a negotiator, expressed in psychological terms, do not differ in principle from those which are possessed by other humans. This proposition may appear so obvious that it is not worthwhile stating. A common error, however, is to assume that those selected to undertake important commercial, industrial or political tasks are in some way different from normal people and then to be constantly surprised and somehow disappointed when it is found out that they are not. It is just because of this that explanations for the events of history are to be found more often in the personality characteristics of the principals concerned than in the grand strategy which is afterwards supposed to have directed their decisions.

14.3 Motivational drive

Following the classification suggested by Maslow the following are identified as the needs which supply the negotiator's personalistic motivational drive.[1]

1 Security
2 Self-esteem achieved through the satisfaction of others
3 Self-esteem by satisfying the negotiator's evaluation of himself
4 Self-actualization by the fulfilment of the negotiator's professional potential.

This list of needs is in descending order of dominance so that generally the rule holds good that until the more basic need has been satisfied to a point which the individual finds acceptable then the next need will not operate, or only weakly, as a determinant of behaviour. A negotiator in a position where he considers that his security is threatened is unlikely to be worried about earning esteem. It follows that in developing negotiating tactics based upon our views as to the other side's needs, regard should primarily be had to the one which we consider to be most basic.

14.4 Security

In general psychological terms the need for security expresses itself in the individual's preference for being within a stable ordered society surrounded by familiar things. The strength of this need is easily demonstrated by putting an individual in conditions which expose him to the unknown, e.g. taking a town dweller and making him cross an area of countryside which is strange to him on a dark night. He is at once disoriented and his immediate reaction is to seek a means of escaping back to that which provides him with the comfort of familiarity. Until that need has been satisfied it will dominate his entire thinking.

One particular instance of the operation of the security need is found in the behaviour of purchasers both in the domestic and the industrial field when deciding on the firm from whom to purchase or repurchase.

The domestic buyer tends to rely heavily on buying goods of a well-known brand or from a source on which, based on advertising or from past experience he believes he can rely, even if the price is higher than that offered elsewhere. The more substantial the potential risk associated with the purchase, due to the nature or value of the goods concerned, the stronger this tendency will become.

Equally the industrial buyer will tend to place repeat orders with the same supplier so avoiding the risks associated with the introduction of a new source and will tend actively to seek to implement a change only if the existing supplier becomes unsatisfactory. Again this tendency will be stronger the more technical the nature of the goods, so the buyer must press his case more strongly with his colleagues in the technical department in order to obtain their consent to any such change, and also the tendency will be stronger the more insecure or relatively junior in status the buyer feels his own personal position to be in the company hierarchy. True initiation of change, i.e. without the necessity for such being forced upon him, is only likely to come from the buyer whose need for security has already been satisfied, and who is reasonably assured of the esteem of his colleagues and seniors.

The consequences of this for the industrial marketeer, wishing to introduce his firm as a new supplier, are that the he must first discover whether the buyer feels secure or not, and, if not, plan his campaign initially on the basis of working to satisfy that need. He must minimize the apparent risk by offers of free trials or supply on a sale and return basis, arrange (through the buyer) technical demonstrations for the engineers, suggest to the buyer ways in which he would gain personally in prestige, etc. The existing supplier on the other hand must be continually alert to the possibility of losing the business and seek to counter this by showing the buyer how exposed he would be if he did make any change; the risks he would be running with a new product which was not proven for his particular purposes, or by buying from a firm not acquainted with the problems of the buyer's particular industry.

The negotiator's need for security is shown also in the demand for adhering to past precedents; the request by the other side that we should accept the contract on the same terms as those which they have agreed previously with other firms. This demand, which is frequently made, originates from a need to achieve security – this is indicated by the way in which the strength of the demand varies with the experience and confidence possessed by the negotiators. The greater their familiarity with understanding of the matters under negotiation, the range of possible bargains and the effect which each would have, the more willing they will be to move away from a strict adherence to the terms of past contracts. Conversely the greater their uncertainty as to the effect of any change to what had previously been agreed, the more difficult it will be to persuade them to make amendments.

This difficulty is reinforced if the review of the proposed contract by their management is to be conducted, not in terms of its intrinsic merit, but by reference to whether it conforms or not to the agreements signed on previous occasions. Then, not only must their negotiator possess the confidence to agree the new conditions himself, he must also be both able and willing to argue the case for their acceptance to his superiors. Obviously he is not likely to do this unless his need for security has been satisfied and the once unfamiliar arrangements have become well understood.

Under these circumstances, satisfying the need of their negotiator for security should be regarded by us as a major negotiating objective but one only likely to be achieved through a process of patient education, and the attainment by the negotiators for the two sides of a state of mutual respect and confidence.

Such education must, however, not be seen as patronizing nor must confidence be eroded by behaviour which is less than honest. This applies particularly to situations in which we represent a Western contractor or supplier and we are negotiating with a purchaser in a developing country. To the insecurity felt by their negotiators will be added the ingredients of national pride coupled with a sense of technical inferiority. The resultant mixture is explosive indeed and bitter resentment, if not complete disaster, will follow any use of hard-sell or bulldozing tactics which indicate contempt for, or display impatience with, the attitudes and arguments adopted by their negotiators.

14.5 Self-esteem achieved through satisfying others

Of all the drives which motivate the negotiator, this is perhaps the one most commonly encountered, and when present will most strongly influence the negotiator's behaviour. The negotiator is aware of the reasons for its existence, and these may vary from fear that incurring the displeasure of his seniors or colleagues may cause him to be punished or despised, to the hope that achieving results more favourable than could be expected will lead to him being rewarded or praised.

In a Western-style culture, this motivational drive appears to be largely derived from childhood training in which the child as an individual is encouraged to gain the respect of his parents, teachers and fellow pupils through the achievement of success. Equally, anti-social behaviour is punished through public humiliation (wearing the dunce's cap was an ancient example of this). Many children have suffered anguish from being made to look foolish before the rest of a class by continued public questioning, on a subject to which clearly they did not know the answer, coupled with sarcastic comments as to their stupidity or laziness.

In other cultures, development of the child takes place almost wholly within a group – family, school, youth association and state – so that respect for, and loyalty to, a group becomes the dominant factor of the young person's motivational behaviour. An individual brought up under such a system will go to almost any length to avoid acting in a manner which the group would consider unworthy.

Therefore, this drive is expected to be present in both forms of culture but to be stronger in those which place particular emphasis on the group.

When acting under this form of motivational drive, once the negotiator has secured concessions, which in his view are sufficient to satisfy that drive, his need to negotiate will cease and he will be content with whatever bargain has been reached at that point, regardless of its objective value. The only valuation which will be significant to the negotiator is his subjective estimate of the bargain he believes would cause him to gain the respect of the group with which he is concerned. Having secured that bargain he will not look further and this blinkered approach will extend to the suppression of knowledge not otherwise shared by the group, which would indicate that a more favourable bargain might be obtained but only through the application of greater effort and perhaps at the risk of disturbing his personal relationships with the negotiators for the other side.[2]

By providing the necessary concessions in the form of preplanned giveaways, so allowing their negotiator to at least appear to have performed his function, we can secure both our own negotiating objective and the goodwill of their negotiator. The converse is equally true. If we refuse to make concessions and so prevent the fulfilment of their motivational drive, then their negotiator will become frustrated. He may then seek release from the tensions so created either through an immediate emotional outburst or by a later act of spiteful revenge such as issuing an unfavourable report, making semi-false accusations, etc.[3]

Alternatively, since goal orientation tends to be retained, even against extremes of frustration, so that the individual seeks a way round the obstacle rather than abandon course, the negotiator may continue to try to satisfy his motivation even if this means adopting a pretence and deluding those whose favour he wishes to win. This is made easier for him to the extent that those concerned have not themselves participated directly in the negotiations, and it is open therefore to the negotiator to influence strongly the standards by which his conduct is judged. He can report in exaggerated terms on the strength of our resistance and on the difficulties which he had in securing even minor concessions.

Many instances of behaviour of this type have been noted in labour negotiations when the union negotiators have reported back to their membership or delegate conference.[4] Such behaviour in my impression is no less common in commercial negotiations, and in a later discussion consideration will be given to tactics which are designed to give their negotiator the opportunity of behaving in just this way.

A negotiator may continue to act as if motivated by the need to achieve self-esteem through satisfying others long after he has earned that esteem and the original causes of the motivation have ceased to apply, for example, the buyer who always demands a discount, the inspector who must always find something to reject, the cost investigator who must always find some item to disallow. Psychologists refer to the concept of the retention of such habits, after the motives which led to their existence are no longer operative, as *functional autonomy*.

Whilst the original motive may not apply, this does not mean that the behaviour is without any extraneous motivation. The negotiator may feel that he cannot act otherwise than in accordance with his previous pattern without running the risk of being accused of favouring a particular contractor/supplier and even perhaps of being suspected of taking a bribe. In such cases of functional autonomy in respect of the original motivation the negotiation takes on the character of an artificial exercise in role-playing, the conventions of which are well understood by both sides.

This is not to suggest that such negotiations are without value. They defuse the relations between the parties, prevent the risk of genuine emotion and permit the development between the negotiators of what Cross has referred to as 'organized cooperation'.[5] They also enable the negotiators for both sides to predict the outcome with greater certainty and to plan ahead accordingly.

In these respects such negotiations may positively facilitate the achievement of the matter of common interest to both parties to which reference was made at the beginning of this book; the less the time spent in haggling the sooner the project can get under way. At the same time removing all genuine tension and 'edge' from the negotiating process will result eventually in our negotiator being content with the achievement of a target which, although satisfactory, is significantly less than the optimum which could be obtained. The quiet life of the agreed bargain is preferred to the discomfort of hard bargaining. The distinction, and the effect on the personalities involved, is similar to that which applies between a price cartel and a state of genuine competition.[6]

It has been suggested in this chapter that in seeking to achieve self-esteem through satisfying others, one of the effects may be to cause the negotiator's personal level of aspiration to be lower than the objective his company would set if they possessed adequate data. Further, to the extent that the company can obtain such data only from the negotiator this will lead to his suppression of that data.

If, however, the group which is significant to the negotiator engages in extensive pre-negotiation planning, which includes the formulation of specific negotiating objectives, this will tend to have the opposite effect. In order to obtain the group's esteem the negotiator must achieve at least the objective so defined, to which he will therefore feel a greater commitment.

14.6 Self-esteem by satisfying the negotiator's self-evaluation

Apart from achieving recognition by others an individual within a Western-style culture will also seek the attainment of some goal for his own satisfaction. The goals he chooses will vary as he proceeds through life but the conditions under which he makes that choice will be determined by the decision he has already made as to the direction his path should take. Once, for example, a person has decided upon a certain course of action relative to his career he must afterwards accept the consequences of that decision or change the basic decision itself. The student who elects to go to university must accept the need to take examinations; the executive who takes the post of sales manager must accept that he will be involved in commercial negotiations. If either objects then their only alternative is to leave and pursue some other occupation. They are committed to following through any choice decision which they might make.

The significance of this commitment is that the individual's choice preference for any goal objective is made under real rather than imagined conditions and can be expected to take into account the consequential effects flowing from that choice. The student might prefer to study art rather than mathematics, both of which he is equally good at, but in a commitment situation would choose mathematics because it offered the prospects of a more secure career.

Psychologically these two situations, that of the student taking his examinations and the executive conducting a negotiation, have two factors in common. Both are ego-related, i.e. success is more closely related to the effort and skill of the person concerned than to chance factors. Both are achievement oriented, i.e. there is considerable pressure on the individual to succeed as opposed to a related situation in which, for example, he was playing a game for its own sake rather than to win.

Under business conditions which are both ego- and achievement-oriented, and in which the person will be committed to the choice he makes, the following propositions are made as to the level of goal objective which the individual will select:

1 The worth which the individual places upon any level will be a function of its achievement value to him and the subjective probability which he places upon succeeding at that level. Generally this function would appear to be a product of the two factors and the individual will select the level which maximizes that function.

2 The achievement value will have a relationship to the difficulties which the individual considers are involved. In general, the greater the difficulty, the higher the individual will value the achievement.

3 The individual's estimate of his subjective probability of succeeding at any level will be biased in the direction in which his motivation is stronger. If he is strongly motivated towards achievement he will overestimate his chances of success; if he is strongly motivated

towards avoiding failure he will underestimate his chances and overestimate the risks involved.

4 Success at any given level will result in the individual reassessing both the achievement value and the probability of success at that level and at those which are more difficult to achieve. Over a short range of values, this will cause the individual progressively to select those levels which objectively are more difficult to achieve. With each success achieved, however, the consequence to the individual of failure in terms of public humiliation are also increased. In the end he will be driven to aim for the extreme, which is beyond that which anyone could possibly expect, simply in order to fail with minimum loss of face and so return again to his natural level.

This is akin to the phenomenon of the football team who start the season with a winning run. Everyone now expects them to go on winning and although after their first defeat the team feels an immediate depression their secondary reaction is one of relief. The tension associated with the impossibility of always winning has been lifted.

5 If the individual fails then his immediate reaction will be one of the following:

(a) If he is motivated positively towards achievement then he will repeat the effort. The apparent increase in difficulty has added to the value of the goal objective which will tend to balance the reduction in his estimate of success probability, so that the product of the two will remain roughly the same.

(b) If he is activated towards avoidance of failure his reaction will be either to reduce his level drastically so as to eliminate the risk completely, or alternatively, raise the level to a point at which failure is very probable but no blame could be attached to him on that account.

The above represents a necessarily brief summary of what is generally referred to as *level of aspiration theory*. The parallel is clear between this theory and that of the maximization of subjective expected utility discussed in Appendix 2. The level of the goal objective is obviously closely related to that of the utility which a particular result possesses at any given time.

There is a significant difference between this personalistic approach to goal setting and a range of utility values based on corporate objectives. Simon has arrived at the same distinction for a decision. If the decision is oriented to the individual's goals it is *personally rational* and if oriented to the organization's goals it is *organizationally rational*.[7] When we assess the utility to us under risk of any bid, the only truly subjective factor which we consider is our attitude towards risk taking. All other factors are objective: the profit which would be realized if the bid were successful, the need to obtain the order, the contractual risks involved (see pp. 70 and 297). The function so derived represents as far as possible the corporate utility of the bid.

The level of goal objective under discussion is, however, entirely personalistic with its emphasis on achievement. The utility to a company manager of a particular bid, when he is acting under corporate motivation, is not affected by the ease or difficulty of securing the order. It is irrelevant since the resultant contract, if the bid is successful, will return the same profits, employ the same people and involve the same risks. To the sales manager, however, the challenge of the competition and the sense of exultation felt when he wins, enter very strongly into his personalistic worth assessment, so that to him the difficult order will possess a higher level of achievement value than the easy one. Two conclusions follow from this: first, the sales manager is likely to apply greater effort to securing the difficult order, and secondly, he is likely to overestimate his chances of success.

When acting under personalistic motivation therefore there is a tendency to aim for the highest level which it is believed can be achieved and conversely it is also believed that the level aimed at can be achieved. Beliefs are reinforced or otherwise by past record of success or failure; success encourages sights to be raised still higher; failure, particularly if it is repeated, will tend to cause selection of some lower goal.

An individual may keep some goals to himself but those which relate to his business or social life are likely to become the common property of the group with which he is involved. A husband's ambition to obtain promotion will become known to, if not shared by, his wife; a manager's ambition to become a director of his company will be known to his immediate colleagues. Although the hurt to the individual if these aims are not realized will be substantial, it will be greatly increased if he is aware that his failure is apparent to the group, and the closer his ties to the group the deeper that hurt will be.

Because this group awareness of his failure is something that the individual will wish to avoid he can be expected to both:

1 Take action to prevent it happening.
2 React strongly against any person whose activities could be the cause of such failure.

PREVENTIVE ACTION

The individual will deliberately select a target in negotiation which is lower than he expects to achieve. He will overstress the difficulties and problems to be encountered: the skill of the other side and the strength of their negotiating position.

Provided that such behaviour is only a contrived outward show, designed to protect the negotiator from loss of self-esteem within the group under circumstances which the negotiator never seriously envisages happening (i.e. he does not allow it to affect his real goal or the effort which he makes to achieve it), then no harm should result. It is a pretence for which he may gain credit as being a person not inclined to exaggerate his own prowess.

If, however, the negotiator comes to believe in such a target as representing his own genuine level of aspiration then this must have the effect of reducing the effort which he puts into the negotiation, and so ultimately the absolute value of the results which he attains. He will become an expert in achieving mediocrity.

In Japan where the primary motivation is that of the shame of failure, the effect of any failure can either be to provide an incentive to even greater efforts, or to cause a loss of confidence accompanied by anger and aggression. In order to defuse this potentially dangerous situation, the Japanese will act to minimize direct competition, and therefore the number of occasions on which they run the risk of feeling the need to act so as 'to clear one's name'. The proverbial politeness of the Japanese is one example of this, as also are their consensus methods of decision making which involve people at a number of different hierarchical levels and departments within the organization so that the decision emerges from the process of consultation and is not handed down from the top. In that way there is neither loser nor winner.

RETALIATORY ACTION

A negotiator expects to win and lose points; he does not expect to be humiliated in circumstances in which his humiliation is in front of, or must become known to, members of the social group whose opinions and respect he values, which would include other members of the negotiating team. If such humiliation occurs his first reaction is likely to be to regard his opponent's conduct as trickery and unfair, and to maintain that he as an honest man has been taken advantage of. If, due to lack of experience or sophistication, he already feels insecure in dealing with his opponent then this reaction will be even stronger.

It has been suggested that up to a certain point a negotiator will ignore such humiliation and even treat it with contempt but that after that point has been reached he will retaliate in such a way as to demonstrate the ability to handle himself.[8] The suggestion is persuasive and my experience of many negotiations throughout the world shows that people when bargaining do indeed behave in this way. The first reaction is either to ignore the insult and treat it with contempt or to deny the accusation indignantly. The second reaction is that of retaliation; the negotiator for the other side must pay for his behaviour and, which is even more important, must be seen to pay by the members of the social group (members of the negotiating team, other office colleagues), whose valuation of him as a negotiator we find significant. Moreover, at this stage, our negotiator's behaviour would not be expected to be a model of rationality. He will still retaliate even if such retaliatory action causes him to suffer an economic loss greater than the gain he would achieve if he did not take such action.

The experimental work in this field has concentrated inevitably on the short-term relationships between our negotiators, those for the other side, and our negotiators' social group, and may be summarized briefly as follows:

1 Having suffered humiliation, subjects will retaliate even at some cost to themselves.
2 Their retaliatory action is much stronger if the humiliation becomes known to a social group which is of significance to them, and because of the humiliation they have suffered that group regards the subjects as being 'weak'. They will be willing in that event to suffer much greater losses themselves in order to carry out the retaliation.
3 Subjects will tend to exercise restraint and not take retaliatory action if the reaction of the social group is unfavourable towards the person initiating the humiliation and sympathetic towards the subjects.

Of more interest, but more difficult from the viewpoint of experimental work, is the situation in which such relationships are long term thus creating opportunities for future adjustment.

With a long-term relationship it seems likely that minor acts of humiliation will be forgotten, if not forgiven, provided that the subject is not continually reminded of them. For most people, the expression 'life's too short' probably sums up their general attitude.

However, if the humiliation has been serious, if the subject has been driven through what we term his *resentment level,* then the motivational drive for retribution will continue. Resentment level is defined as the level of humiliation beyond which a subject feels a permanent sense of antagonism towards the person who inflicted the humiliation. The hurt he has suffered is something which he can neither forgive nor forget. Once an emotional state of this nature has been created, further negotiation between the persons concerned will be difficult, if not impossible. Further, it is likely that the person humiliated will be supported publicly by his colleagues against the person responsible for the humiliation, even though, internally, they may criticize his weakness.

Public humiliation by our negotiators of those for the other side is therefore a dangerous act which is likely to cause us to suffer the greater loss, even if the original act which caused the humiliation was inadvertent.

Given therefore that we possess the power to humiliate the other side, it is suggested that we should act in one of the following ways:

1 Deliberately disarm himself so that the power no longer exists. If, for example, the other negotiator has made a mistake, we can ignore it and act publicly as if it has never happened. If through ignorance, he has already committed himself by agreeing, say, to the wording of a contract clause, we may have to extract him from the commitment by, in this instance, pretending that he has made a mistake himself, and withdrawing the clause in question.
2 Indicate privately to him that he does indeed possess such power whilst at the same time offering him a way out which leaves the balance of advantage just in our favour, provides him with some benefit, and certainly does not expose him to humiliation.

For this to succeed, we must make sufficiently credible to him not only the threat, say to expose a mistake, but our determination to carry through the threat should he not respond. It is not necessary that he should believe that we actually would execute the threat, but only that there is a sufficient risk of our doing so, to make acceptance of our proposal the more attractive alternative.

In practice, in order to avoid embarrassment, we would minimize his open communication both of the threat and his willingness to carry it out, leaving him to understand the implications behind our words which might be: 'I appreciate this is a problem for you. However, things cannot be left to stand as they are, but at the same time we do not want to make them any more difficult as that is not going to do either of us any good. How about if we...'. Notice how we clearly implied we *could* make matters more difficult but would prefer not to, and emphasized collaboration to solve a joint problem. This is aimed deliberately at reducing the conflict and defusing emotion.

14.7 Self-actualization through professional fulfilment

If a person wishes to develop his potential to the fullest then this type of motivation is generally referred to as *self-actualization.* It is being used here in the rather narrower sense of a person whose motivation in the field of negotiation is the achievement of the highest possible level of professional attainment. Neither the 'roundness' of that person's personality nor the development of harmony between the parts of his personality are being considered here.

It might be thought that if the negotiator's motivation were so based on the need for self-expression at the highest level of professional attainment then no psychological problems of adjustment would arise. Because of his professionalism the negotiator's personal objectives would be consistent with those derived solely from a study of economic factors and the use of objective decision-making techniques. There would be total identification between his own goals and those of the organization.

Even if it is assumed that self-actualization provided the negotiator with his sole motivational drive, and this is an assumption which in practice would be made reluctantly (as human beings are much too complex for such simplifications), that motive in itself is liable to incline the negotiator away from a purely economic and objective approach.

As stated earlier, negotiation, like any other business technique, is never an end in itself but only a means to an end. Further, the success of any negotiation must be judged in relation to the contribution which it makes to the welfare of the business as a whole. It may for instance be preferable in the total interests of a group of companies as a whole for a negotiator, or a claim for breach of contract against a client, to 'fail', if the final result is the award of a new contract at an enhanced profit margin to another member of the group.

Such a result would be unlikely to bring the negotiator charged with the handling of the claim any personal satisfaction and, indeed, he can be expected to react strongly against any suggestion that group interests make it necessary for him to 'lose'. He would regard this as a denial of his professional skills. On a similar basis a member of our negotiating team, whether lawyer, engineer or accountant, will find it hard to accept an opinion from his opposite number on their team with which professionally he disagrees, even if he is told that it is in the interests of our overall negotiating plan that he should accept it.

Whilst beneficial, therefore, in that the individual will not degrade corporate negotiating objectives for personalistic motives in the sense discussed, self-actualization can still be a hazard in preventing the development of the total negotiating plan which, in the case of long-term relationships, is always looking to the future.

14.8 Conflict and adjustment in the negotiator's motivation

At the beginning of this chapter, reference was made to the conflict inherent in any negotiation between the need to reach agreement and the desire to do soon the most favourable terms achievable. In Section 16.3, this will be amplified by showing the relationship between the time spent in negotiation and the terms obtained; that the more favourable bargain takes longer to achieve.

These parameters of the negotiating situation necessarily create a conflict in the mind of the negotiator. He is motivated to achieve two positive goals which are mutually opposed: the optimum terms and the certainty of agreement today. As a result he is placed in the conflict situation which is generally referred to as *approach–approach,* in which there is a choice between two positive incentives; holding out for optimum terms carries the risk of losing the bargain altogether; reaching agreement today involves the risk of doing soon terms which are unfavourable.

Therefore the negotiator has also a dual conflict of *approach–avoidance;* the choice between two aspects of a goal, the one positive and the other negative. This situation can be represented diagrammatically as shown in Figure 14.1.

Figure 14.1   Approach–avoidance situation for the negotiator

The strength of the negotiator's tendency to approach or avoid is clearly related to the strength of the motivational drive concerned, although both tend to be stronger the nearer they are to the goal objective. Although it is not so obvious, experimental results have established that the strength to avoid increases more rapidly than that of approach as the subject nears the goal objective.

This is confirmed in relation to negotiation by the following observations derived from my own experience:

1   In the early stages of negotiation a sales negotiator will be willing to argue strongly for the best terms. The positive aspects of achieving favourable terms are immediately attractive; he knows there is no question of an immediate agreement and also that the risk of losing the bargain altogether at that stage is equally remote.
2   As the number of items left for discussion diminishes, he will become unwilling to argue strongly in favour of any point to which the buyer appears to be seriously opposed. The fear of losing the bargain altogether will become the dominant motivational drive.

Ambivalence of this type is typical of situations in which the decision to resist, or to take a strong line, is first expressed at a time remote from the point at which we will be faced with the consequences of following through that decision. At a distance the real advantages to be gained are the attraction whilst the disadvantages are seen as hypothetical. 'Let's cross that bridge when we come to it' is the favourite expression of those who think this way.

Later, as the time for final action or decision approaches, the consequences, once so lightly discarded, loom large, and we are compelled to change course even at the risk of suffering some humiliation.

The negotiator's internal conflict is not, however, lessened by final agreement being reached. The brief moment of exhilaration is quickly followed by the longer period of doubt and self-criticism, even of remorse.

As a defence against such anxieties, and in order to retain self-esteem, the answers are rationalized. The other side is credited with greater strength or skill; the need for preserving goodwill is given as a reason for not having pressed home the advantage possessed. The process as a whole is illustrated in Figure 14.1.

Such rationalizations are helpful in moderation because they enable an adjustment to take place and a return to other business without an obsession with failure. They only become harmful if they are used as reasons for lowering the level of aspiration.

It is necessary, however, to be aware of this conflict of motivation problem when developing a negotiating plan. By setting limits on the negotiator's authority the motivation to obtain favourable terms is reinforced and the tendency to snatch at early agreement is lessened.

14.9 Implications of personal objectives in negotiation planning

There are three implications in the planning for negotiations of the existence of personalistic motivations among the negotiators:

1 The first is the bias to be expected from our own negotiators in their assessments and recommendations. At any level above that which satisfies their need for security and earning esteem they are likely to be strongly risk aversive. Their attitude will be rationalized by some such saying as 'That would be a good bargain – let's not be greedy and waste time and money by pressing for more.'
2 The second is that we should set firm corporate objectives which it is the negotiator's objective to achieve, so that we reinforce his own motivation for success and define success in a way which is clear and easily identifiable in an objective manner.
3 The third is that we should anticipate the existence of personalistic motivation in the negotiators for the other side and allow for it in our planning. We need to provide them with the opportunity to obtain enough to satisfy their security level and earn sufficient esteem to justify their actions to their peers and superiors. Further we must make them work hard enough to earn their 'gains' so that there is no suspicion of complicity on our part. They must be required to bargain hard to secure any planned 'give-aways' or dig deep to discover any 'mistakes' which will need therefore to be well hidden.

Notes

1. A. H. Maslow, 'A theory of human motivation', *Psychological Review*, vol. 50 (no. 1, 1943), pp. 370–96.
2. This can be regarded as equivalent to H. A. Simon's 'satisficing' hypothesis in which the negotiator divides the utilities of all perceived outcomes into satisfactory and unsatisfactory, and then acts so as to achieve that outcome which meets the criterion of satisfactory for the minimum expenditure of effort. The term 'effort' here includes search resources so that once a course of action is found which is regarded as satisfactory no further search will be made. For example, see W. H. Starbuck, 'Level of aspiration', *Psychological Review*, vol. 70 (no.1, 1963), pp. 51–54.

3. Union leaders who are elected by their members for the precise purpose of bargaining are always placed in an extremely difficult position when the offer made to them initially is, in fact, management's final offer. The practice by management of acting in this way (often referred to as Boulwarism, after the man who developed it at General Electric in the USA) always gives rise to emotional resentment in union leaders who are thereby deprived of the opportunity of demonstrating to their members that they have acted effectively on their behalf. This applies irrespective of the size of the offer. This was clearly the case in the miners' dispute in UK in the winter of 1973/4. The package offered by the National Coal Board (NCB) had extracted all that could be offered within the limits of the Government's phase 3 policy, to the point at which it was described by the union's leader as: 'Having done more than scrape the barrel; it has scraped some of the paint off the outside too.' Unfortunately the very extent of the initial offer had left the NCB nothing to bargain with and the subsequent reaction of the union's leaders was predictable to an offer which, as one of them stated, 'was an offence to everyone's negotiating instincts; there was scarcely any room for manoeuvre'.

4. See the examples quoted in R. E. Walton and R. E. McKersie, *A Behavioral Theory of Labor Negotiations* (New York: McGraw-Hill, 1965), pp. 327–29.

5. J. G. Cross, *The Economics of Bargaining* (New York: Basic Books, 1969), p.177.

6. It has been proposed by R. M. Cyert and J. G. March, *A Behavioral Theory of the Firm* (New Jersey: Prentice-Hall, 1964), pp.119–20, that a major objective of businesspeople is to control their environment and eliminate uncertainty. One way of doing this is for contracts to be negotiated which impose no strain on either party. The delivery period contains slack so the penalty clause can be accepted; the price contains a substantial margin for profit so that costs are not under severe pressure; the equipment is proven so performance guarantees present no problems.

   Pressure by the purchaser to tighten on these factors must initially create stress as the contractor's organization adapts in order to respond. New methods and procedures will be adopted to speed manufacture; cost savings will be introduced to safeguard profit; new developments will be perfected to improve performance standards. The same must apply to the commercial negotiators. Because of the pressures imposed on them by their superiors the standards by which the group judge the negotiators' achievements must rise, which in turn must compel the negotiators to demand more of themselves. They will look for new safeguards in the wording of clauses, tighten up on ambiguities and avoid leaving loopholes. But this will only happen if the bargaining is 'for real' and that in turn will only happen if the other side has elected to adopt an aggressive policy of maximization.

7. H. A. Simon, *Administrative Behaviour* (London: Macmillan), pp.75–76.

8. See M. Deutsch and R. M. Krauss, 'The effects of threat on interpersonal bargaining', *Journal of Abnormal and Social Psychology*, vol. 61 (1960), pp. 223–30, and 'Studies of interpersonal bargaining', *Journal of Conflict Resolution*, vol. 6 (1962), pp.52–76; I. Goffman, 'On face work', *Psychiatry*, vol. 18(1955), pp.213–31.

15 CHOICE OF STRATEGY

15.1 The first offer – bidding and procurement

In relation to the level and terms on which any offer is submitted or accepted, there are only two basic negotiating strategies which can be employed. These may be conveniently described as:

1 'Quick kill' (sometimes referred to as 'final offer first')
2 'Hold back'.

Quick kill is the strategy of selecting an offer which it is anticipated the recipient will accept without further negotiation, or of responding to an offer by accepting it at the level and in the terms in which it was made.

Hold back is the strategy of selecting an offer which is sufficiently attractive to the recipient not to be rejected out of hand, but at the same time contains a margin for negotiation which is considered adequate:

1 To enable the party submitting the offer to meet the recipient's demands.
2 To ensure that at the end of the negotiations the party submitting the offer obtains a bargain which at the least satisfies his minimum negotiating objective.

Alternatively, to the recipient it is the strategy of bargaining with the party, or parties submitting offers until terms are secured which meet at least the recipient's minimum negotiating objective, and which he considers are the most advantageous he can obtain taking into account the time factor for negotiation.

It is important to note that the concern here is only with strategies which are aimed directly at securing a bargain, so enabling the venture which is the subject of the bargain to proceed. Obviously if a party were indifferent to the result he could make any proposal he chose, regardless of whether it would be acceptable to the recipient or not, i.e. he could submit a tender at a price level which, if accepted, would meet his own negotiating objective, without considering the bids likely to be made by his competitors or the price level at which the purchaser was likely to place the order.

In practice, the strategy of final offer first is used, regardless of whether it will be acceptable to the contractor or not, in contract dispute situations where the purchaser is sufficiently certain of the strength of his position not to care about the contractor's reactions. If the contractor does not accept the offer then the purchaser knows that the contractor does not have the ability to take him to law and it is made clear to him that he will not receive any more orders. Such behaviour may be arbitrary and contrary to the modern ideals of maintaining good business relationships but it happens.

Leaving aside arbitrary behaviour what strategy should we use as the best means of securing our objectives? The answer depends on the domination/subordination relationship which exists between the two parties.

15.2 Relationship between ourselves and the other side

The correct strategy for us to select is determined by our state of domination/subordination or uncertainty relative to the other side in accordance with Figure 15.1.

Our state relative to the other side	Correct strategy to select
(a) Domination	Quick kill
(b) Subordination	Quick kill or hold back depending on strategy assumed to have been selected by the other side
(c) Uncertainty	Hold back

Figure 15.1 Strategy selection

OUR DOMINATION AS A SUPPLIER

1 If we know we are a single-source supply for the purchaser then we will be in a dominant position provided that:
   (a) The worth of our offer to the purchaser is marginally greater than the minimum which the purchaser would accept.
   (b) The worth of such an offer to ourselves would at least meet our minimum negotiating objective.
2 If in a competitive situation the worth of our offer to the purchaser taken as a whole is marginally greater than the worth of any competitive offer, and we know this, then we will be in a dominant position within the limitations that:
   (a) The worth of the offer to the purchaser is just greater than that of any competitors and at the same time meets the purchaser's minimum acceptable level.
   (b) The worth of such an offer to ourselves would at least meet our minimum negotiating objective.

If we are the supplier, the significance of the domination relationship is that, within its limits as described above, we are free to set our offer at a level which maximizes its value to ourselves and having done so are in a position to resist departing from that level. Our strategy is therefore quick kill.

The second case of domination may not be immediately recognized as such and an example may help to clarify the concept.

It is assumed that the purchaser will value the factors comprised in the subject offer, and in the most favourable competing offer, by comparing their utility values and selecting the offer which has the highest utility in the manner described in Appendix 1. Three such factors are identified: price, delivery and technical merit. Using the same notation as in Appendix 1, the components in each tender will be regarded as ordered pairs, where x_1 represents price, x_2 represents delivery and x_3 technical merit. The first component x_1 is a member of set K_1 in which $x_1 > y_1 > z_1$ and similarly for sets K_2 and K_3.

The comparison between our offer and the competitive order is given in Figure 15.2.

Factor	Maximum utility value	Our offer	Competitive offer
Price	3	y_1 (1.5)	x_1 (3)
Delivery	2	y_2 (1)	x_2 (2)
Technical merit	5	x_3 (5)	y_3 (2)
	10	7.5	7

Domination exists since $U(x_3 - y_3) > U(x_1 - y_1) + (x_2 - y_2)$

$(5–2)>(3–1.5)+(3–2)$

Figure 15.2   Comparison between offers of the parties

Because of our technical superiority we are able to increase the price and extend our delivery to the point at which the bid is just preferable to the competitive offer. Knowing this, we could resist any request by the purchaser to reduce our price based on comparisons between our price and that of the competitive offer.

DOMINATION BY OURSELVES AS A PURCHASER

We will be dominant if we know for certain that we will receive at least two genuinely competing offers from bidders who satisfy the following conditions:

1 The bidders know that each of them will meet the purchaser's minimum requirements for acceptance of a tender in respect of all relevant factors, e.g. price, delivery, etc. Obviously if a bidder knew that one competitor did not meet, say, a particular mandatory specification, then he need no longer consider the price level which that firm would submit, and the bidder would move into a position of at least partial domination under the previous analysis of ourselves as a supplier.
2 Neither bidder possesses any non-price advantage which would enable him significantly to raise his price level above that which would satisfy that bidder's minimum negotiating objective. Again possession of any such advantage would move the bidder into a position of some domination as illustrated in the example given in Figure 15.2.

3 The bidders are confident that we will award the contract to the most economic offer submitted, without post-tender negotiation directed towards securing discounts or other reductions. If the bidders do not have this confidence then the case is treated as one of uncertainty, unless the opposite applies and they know we will expect to bargain. In that event we are in a quasi-dominant position, in that we can compel the bidders in their own interests to adopt a hold-back strategy. We are not strictly dominant, however, since all bidders can now be expected to have included a negotiating margin.

Again our strategy is that of quick kill, and this should enable us to buy at the most economic level related to the conditions under which, and the firms from whom, we have invited tenders.

SUBORDINATION BY OURSELVES AS A PURCHASER

If we are as a purchaser subordinate to the other side as a supplier, i.e. the converse of the situation illustrated in Figure 15.2, then it is presumed at the start that our strategy should be hold back. The other's bid is most likely to be at a level well above the minimum which would be preferred by him to no bargain. Through negotiation we would hope to reduce that level. However, this presumption would be reversed by the existence of any factor which would lead us to believe that we would lose rather than gain from any such negotiation. Such factors could be:

1 A feeling of mutual confidence between ourselves and the other side developed through a long-term and continuing business relationship. We are satisfied that the other side will not have sought to take unfair advantage and we do not wish to encourage the other side into adopting a hold-back strategy in the future and adding negotiating margins.
2 Delay which would be caused by the negotiation in award of the contract and as a result of this probably also in the final completion of the project (see p. 32).
3 Our recognition of the basic weakness of our negotiating position and our unwillingness to lose face by starting a negotiation which would most likely prove to be abortive. This would again apply most strongly to the situation in which there was a long-term relationship between the parties.

It would be expected in practice, therefore, that we would only adopt a hold-back strategy if:

1 Our buying in that particular market was random and so no long-term relationship was to be considered.
2 We were in a position to develop a genuine 'threat' strategy, for example, by threatening not to place the contract at all or to adopt a different solution which would reopen the whole tendering on a basis less favourable to the other side, e.g. reducing the technical standards or eliminating particular specification requirements which had given the other his advantage.

SUBORDINATION BY OURSELVES AS A SUPPLIER

When we are in a strictly competitive position bidding to an authority known not to indulge in post-tender negotiations then we have no alternative. We *must* basically adopt a quick-kill strategy; we have only one chance open to us. However, depending on circumstances and the degree of strictness of the authority concerned in applying their rules, we may employ a partial hold-back strategy by making non-specific reservations on the terms and conditions of contract or the specification in such a way that customer must call him in for discussions before being able to complete his tender appraisal or place a contract. We would then adopt a negotiating strategy related to the knowledge we had been able to glean of our competitive position. If within certain limits this was favourable then our position within those limits would be one of quasi-domination, and so we could afford to take a hard line up to the point at which the domination equation was no longer true. If our position was unfavourable we could relax the reservations or discard them altogether, in the hope that this would compensate for the factors in which our offer was otherwise inferior.

However, when we know that whatever offer we submit the purchaser will expect to bargain, then equally we *must* select a hold-back strategy and submit our first offer at a level which includes a defined negotiating margin. It is a common delusion of firms dealing with a known bargainer for the first time to believe that if they submit a truly competitive or 'fair' offer then the recipient will recognize the fact and be prepared to accept it without bargaining. Such firms fail to realize that to a bargainer the willingness of the other side to negotiate and to have concessions extracted from him forms a significant part of the emotional worth of the offer. Depending on the motivation of the bargainer, a refusal to negotiate will create suspicion, anger or even contempt and may lead to a rejection of an offer even in circumstances when objectively it would be in the purchaser's interests to accept.

UNCERTAINTY

So far in discussing domination and subordination it has been assumed that both parties know with reasonable certainty the facts of the negotiating situation. In practice the reverse will often be the case: the supplier will be uncertain as to the degree of domination (if any) which he enjoys or the price level above which the purchaser will not place the order. The purchaser will not know the realities of the competitive situation nor the minimum price level or other terms which the supplier would be willing to accept.

Because of these uncertainties neither party may feel inclined to risk all on a single throw. The purchaser may find the lowest price too high for his budget; the supplier may find that he could have obtained more for his goods and services. Both have some incentive to employ a hold-back strategy but are reluctant to lose the possible advantages of quick kill. Neither can be certain of each other's intentions. Suppose one of them, perhaps through a misjudgement does decide to use quick kill, what would be the position of the other? In a state of uncertainty what should be the strategy of each party?

| Strategy/choice | | Description | Conditional |
Ourselves	Buyer		utility value
HB	QK	Contribution value of an award which would result from the buyer's acceptance of an offer which contained a margin for negotiation over the level of the supplier's minimum negotiating objective.	6
HB	HB	Contribution which the supplier considers would result from a successful negotiation with the buyer, following submission by the supplier of a bid which contained a margin for negotiation. The supplier has allowed for a proportion (but not all) of the negotiating margin to be conceded.	5
QK	QK	Contribution value of an award to the supplier at the level which just meets his minimum negotiating objective.	4
HB/QK		Loss which would result to the supplier from failure to secure an award.	−1

Figure 15.3   Strategy values – the supplier bidding in a state of uncertainty

Strategy choice for the supplier

The situation will be looked at first from the viewpoint of the supplier. Using the method outlined in Appendix 1, it will be assumed that the supplier is able to establish a scale of the utility values of the possible outcomes of submitting the bid, dependent on the strategy choices of the buyer and himself. These are set out in order of preference in Figure 15.3. The values shown in the figure are themselves quite arbitary and selected only for the purpose of providing a numerical example. The format of the table and the order of preference, however, are of general application.

It will be noted that no reference has been made to the fourth possible strategy combination of the supplier selecting quick kill and the buyer seeking to negotiate. It is considered that having selected a bid which just satisfies his minimum negotiating objective, the supplier would prefer to lose the award rather than secure it at a level below that objective.

In order to arrive at the expected utility values for each outcome the supplier must now estimate his subjective probabilities of achieving success and these are as shown in Figure 15.4.

Strategy/choice		Probability		Notes
Supplier	Buyer	Success	Failure	
QK	QK	0.7	0.3	Supplier's estimate of his chances on a straight competitive bid.
QK	HB	0.1	0.9	The low chance of success reflects the supplier's refusal to reduce below his minimum negotiating objective.
HB	QK	0.3	0.7	Reduced chance of success on a straight competitive bid due to addition of negotiating margin.
HB	HB	0.6	0.4	The slightly lower chance of success than for QK/QK reflects the risk of a competitor cutting his price.

Figure 15.4   The supplier's success probability for possible strategies

Using the technique described in Appendix 1, the expected value can now be computed for each outcome, as shown in Figure 15.5.

Finally in order to select which strategy he should adopt the supplier must choose the decision rule which he wishes to use. In Appendix 1, two such rules are identified:

1 The maximin criterion which would lead the supplier to select the strategy row which is the maximum of the row minima.
2 The Bayes procedure of assigning subjective probabilities to the buyer's strategy choice and choosing that strategy for the supplier which is optimal against that assumed probability distribution.

	Buyer's strategies	
	QK	HB
	QK $(0.7\times4)+(0.3\times-1)=2.5$	$(0.1\times4)+(0.9\times-1)=-0.5$
The supplier's strategies		
	HB $(0.3\times6)+(0.7\times-1)=1.1$	$(0.6\times5)+(0.4\times-1)=2.6$

Figure 15.5   Expected value of the supplier's strategies

So far in the discussions all situations have been treated as situations of risk and, therefore, it has been considered realistic to assume that the supplier is able to make some meaningful assessment of the probability that the buyer will prefer one strategy to another. Since this situation has been identified as one of uncertainty it is important to include now the case in which the supplier has no 'feel' for the situation and cannot, therefore, make any such assessment.

This does not mean that the Bayes procedure must be abandoned. Under such circumstances the supplier would be justified in adopting the Laplace criterion which states that if absolutely no information is available about the relative probabilities of the buyer's strategies then each should be judged equiprobable. This principle (also known as that of insufficient reason) is older than any other but has often been criticized on the grounds that it is not always easy to identify which events should be considered equally probable and that by changing the number of events the probabilities are automatically changed. However, its use can be justified in a simple case where the alternatives can be strictly limited to two or three.

Also it is recognized that it is usual to apply the Laplace criterion only to games against nature and not to games against an opponent in which the supplier is expected to act on the basis of his knowledge of the buyer's pay-off function and the assumption that the buyer's strategy will be optimal. But because this situation is one of uncertainty the supplier will have no knowledge of that function, and that being so the game becomes analogous to one against nature.

If the assumption of equal probability is applied to the buyer's strategy choice then the utility value to the supplier of his two strategies becomes:

$$\text{Quick kill} \quad (0.5 \times 2.5) + (0.5 \times -0.5) = 1$$
$$\text{Hold back} \quad (0.5 \times 1.1) + (0.5 \times 2.6) = 1.85$$

The supplier's strategy choice would therefore be hold back. It is also interesting to note from Figure 15.5 that the same result would be reached if the supplier adopted the maximin criterion.

Although this result has been obtained with particular figures it is maintained that in a state of uncertainty, in which the supplier cannot make a rational subjective probability assessment of the buyer's strategy choice, the result is quite general and the supplier's strategy choice should always be hold back. The reasons for reaching this conclusion are set out in Appendix 1.

Strategy choice for the purchaser

It is assumed that the purchaser is free to select whichever negotiating strategy he prefers, i.e. he is not restricted by public tendering rules which forbid him from negotiating with the lowest, or indeed any other bidder, after receipt of the tenders.

The case in which the buyer will receive at least three competitive tenders may be considered as typical. This means that there are four possible ways, from a bidding strategy viewpoint, in which the bidders could act:

1 All bidders select quick kill
2 The majority of bidders select quick kill
3 All bidders select hold back
4 The majority of bidders select hold back.

The buyer is unable to assess the subjective probabilities of each course of action occurring but using the method outlined in Appendix 1, he is able to estimate his preference for the outcome associated with each possibility. The results of this are shown in Figure 15.6.

| | | The buyer's strategies | |
		QK	HB
	All QK	8	9
	Majority QK	7	8.5
Bidder's strategies			
	All HB	1	5
	Majority HB	4.5	6

Figure 15.6   Purchaser's strategy choice

Notes on Figure 15.6

The buyer adopts a quick-kill strategy:

1 If all the bidders adopt QK then the result will be favourable to the buyer since all bidders will by definition of the QK strategy have put forward a price which just satisfies their minimum negotiating objective.
2 If only a majority select QK there is some reduction in the buyer's expected utility since there is now a chance that the bidder who was previously lowest will have added a negotiating margin which would put his bid above that of the next lowest bidder. The buyer would therefore be obliged, having decided to adopt a QK strategy himself, to accept the tender from the bidder who was previously next to lowest.
3 If all bidders adopt HB and therefore add a negotiating margin the result is extremely unfavourable to the buyer. Such a margin would be likely to be around 10 per cent and this is the extra which the buyer would have to pay. The matrix assumes that the outcome is still just above the buyer's minimum acceptable level; if it was not then the buyer would have to re-tender.
4 If one bidder adopts QK then there is a marked improvement since there is a chance that this will be either the original lowest or next to lowest bidder.

The buyer adopts hold-back strategy:

5 If the bidders have all adopted a QK strategy it is assumed that either the lowest or the next to lowest will, under pressure, be willing to grant a small discount.[1]
6 In the straight bargaining situation where all bidders have adopted hold back, the outcome is based on the buyers being able to secure a concession of approximately half the negotiating margin.
7 If one bidder has adopted QK then the buyer's expectations improve slightly on the chance that this could be either the original lowest or the next to lowest bidder, so that his bargaining would start from a lower base. It is still assumed that the buyer will seek to bargain on the grounds that his decision is based on personal motivational drives as much as rational thinking.

The above reasoning is quite general and does not depend on the particular values selected. (The complete working out on which the matrix in Figure 15.6 is based is given in Appendix 1.) Therefore in any case of uncertainty the purchaser would select hold back as his negotiating strategy since this is clearly dominant over quick kill *particularly if the supplier were himself to select hold back* which is the supplier's preferred strategy in a situation of uncertainty.

GENERAL CONCLUSIONS

Bringing the respective utility values for the supplier and the purchaser together in one game-theory type matrix produces the pay-off position illustrated in Figure 15.7. It must be stressed that no comparison can be made between the utility values of the events for the two parties since the utility scales are personal to each and have no relationship with one another.

		Purchaser's strategies	
		b_1 QK	b_2 HB
	a_1 QK	(2.5) (7.5)	(–0.5) (8.75)
Supplier's strategies			
	a_2 HB	(1.1) (2.75)	(2.6) (5.5)

Figure 15.7   Matrix of supplier's and purchaser's strategy choice expected values

The supplier will not select a_1 for fear that the purchaser will choose b_2. The purchaser will equally not select b_1 for fear that the supplier will select a_2. Therefore the strategy choice a_2b_2 represents the 'solution' in the game-theory sense, i.e. both parties will adopt hold-back strategies.

The outcome a_1b_1 will *not* be reached by both parties acting independently of one another. There must be cooperation between them to the extent that both have complete confidence in the strategy which will be selected by the other, i.e. the situation is no longer one of uncertainty.

Purchasing conclusions

From the purchasing viewpoint four important conclusions can be drawn from this analysis:

1 If the buyer is continually in the market he should seek to gain the confidence of genuinely competing suppliers and *always* adopt quick kill. He will thereby maximize the gain to himself.

2 If the buyer is only occasionally in the market so that suppliers have no opportunity to obtain such confidence, the buyer should adopt hold back since this will maximize the gain to himself *irrespective of the strategy selected by the suppliers*.

3 The buyer who is continually in the market will lose rather than gain by mixing his strategies. Assuming he goes out of tender five times with the strategies set out in column 2 of

Figure 15.8, then the strategies likely to be adopted by the suppliers (assuming they start with confidence) are set out in column 3 and the pay-off to the buyer is given in column 4. All suppliers are regarded as knowledgeable and will therefore use the same strategy. It will be seen that the total pay-off to the buyer is 28 compared with 40 for adopting quick kill every time.

The crucial tender is number four. It is believed that having been caught once the suppliers would select hold back. Having then been proved to be correct, in that the buyer tried it again, they would adopt hold back next time and from then onwards.

4 Provided there is genuine competition the buyer who is regularly in the market and who adopts hold back as a strategy will lose, as compared with quick kill, once confidence has been established in the suppliers so that they too adopt quick kill as a strategy.

The values shown in the matrix are the end worth of the strategy to the purchaser in present value terms. They do not take into account the time and trouble in which he would be involved by continual negotiation.

Tender number	Buyer's strategy	Supplier's strategy	Pay-off to the buyer
1	QK	QK	8
2	HB	QK	9
3	QK	HB	1
4	HB	HB	5
5	HB	HB	5
			28

Figure 15.8 Pay-off to purchaser of varying his strategy choice over a series of tenders

5 The above has assumed there is genuine competition. Suppose, however, the purchaser suspects that the suppliers have formed a cartel and that there are no suppliers of the particular goods or services which he requires outside of the cartel. What then should be his strategy if he is going to be in the market on a regular basis?

He can assume that the bidder who has been allocated the contract within the cartel, and who has no reason therefore to fear competition, will have selected a price level which is above that at which he would have bid competitively. Competition will therefore serve no purpose. The purchaser's only hope is to persuade at least one of the firms to defect from the cartel. Assume that there are five firms, which we call A to E, and the purchaser knows that he will be placing four contracts of roughly equal value for the same goods or services over the year. It is suggested that he should act as follows:

Tender 1 Go out to tender and use a hold-back strategy with the lowest bidder, say A, to negotiate the best available terms.

Tender 2 Go out to tender, assume the best offer this time is from B. Negotiate with B and then offer the contract to firm C provided that they match the lower of the prices negotiated with A on the first tender or B. If C declines repeat the process with the other firms.

Tender 3 Don't go out to tender but negotiate with both A and the firm who obtained order 2 to secure the best deal.

Tender 4 Go out to tender, assume the best offer is received from D. Offer the contract to firm E provided that they at least match the lower of the offers negotiated on tenders 1–3 and that received from D. If E declines, which is unlikely if so far they have received no business, then repeat the process with the other firms.

It may not work, it depends on the firmness of the cartel and there are of course other variants which could be tried. The essential aim, however, is to stop the cartel members from being able to forecast that you will simply select the firm whom they have nominated to secure the business. Cartels thrive on predictability. If you can keep them guessing at what you are likely to do then the members will probably start to become disillusioned and at least one will defect. Of course if you are a public authority bound by the EC Public Procurement Directives you may not have the necessary commercial licence to behave like this as there are no provisions in the Directives allowing you to select and negotiate because you are dealing with a cartel.

15.3 Contract dispute

The distinguishing feature of contract dispute negotiations is that the two sides are already in a contractual relationship. Each has therefore at any time five alternative options open to it:

1 Accept the contract situation as it is and the actions, proposals or interpretations of the other.
2 Maintain the contract in being and accept its validity, but object to and seek to negotiate further within the contractual framework, the actions, proposals or interpretations of the other.
3 Terminate the contract.
4 Act outside the contract provisions recognizing that this could lead to an action for breach of contract by the other. That is the assumption is made that either party may decide to act knowingly in breach of contract if it perceives such a course to be to its advantage.

In deciding as between alternatives 1 and 2, the supplier, as the recipient of proposals from customer, must always weigh up the benefit to be gained from showing resistence and establishing a reputation for firmness, as compared to the ill-feeling he may engender in customer's staff which may have unfortunate repercussions at a later date. Even if the supplier is right on a minor issue, it may not pay him in the long run to prove this to customer, particularly if such action would bring public discredit on a member of customer's staff. It is easy to be right and dead.

The supplier, as the initiator of proposals which he considers are based entirely on a proper interpretation of the contract and factual matters capable of proof which he has provided, may reasonably expect the purchaser to accept. However, at this point emotion may take over from reason and this is a reaction which the supplier should anticipate.

By preventing the purchaser from developing any counter-proposals the supplier has deprived the purchaser's negotiators of the opportunity to be seen to be carrying out their function. They may therefore react violently and substitute abuse for rational argument or become bitter and wait their chance to even the score. An example from the field of labour relations, in which abuse was used in reply to the company's policy of proposing a package which they intended should be accepted by the unions without substantial modification, is given by the following exchange between the chief negotiators for General Electric of America and the IUE, quoted by Walton and McKersie.

> Moore (GE's chief negotiator): 'Your items are inflexible.' Carey (for the IUE): 'Yes, they are inflexible. We have an inflexible position on them. You can mess with the small items but not with the principles. All of our items in this proposal are important. Mr Moore we are going to get all of them even if we have to walk over your face. Understand that? Even if we have to walk over your face, Mr Moore.[2]

The supplier should anticipate the possibility of this reaction in putting forward his case and be at pains to show that he has taken note of the purchaser's views in developing his own position. In this way he will enable the negotiators for the purchaser, when reporting to their own management, to achieve credit for having been responsible for moderating the supplier's claims, or improving his offer, from that which he first intended to submit. If this is not sufficient then the supplier must consider modifying his strategy and adopting a limited form of hold back which will be adequate to satisfy the personal motivation of the purchaser's negotiators. Again it is stressed that situations of contract dispute are the most difficult to treat normatively. The degree of personal and emotional involvement is too great.

INTANGIBLE SITUATION

Here the supplier's case is based to a significant extent on matters which are resistant to absolute proof and depend on factors of subjective judgement. In arriving at the supplier's strategy a distinction is made between intangible issues which are related to circumstances genuinely outside the control of either side and intangibles which arise from the purchaser's default including that of an agent from whom he is responsible, e.g. a consulting engineer. A further distinction is necessary between the acceptance of a claim in principle and agreement to its quantification. We arrive therefore at four possible combinations and these are listed below together with the supplier's suggested strategy.

Case No.	Circumstance	Issue	Strategy
1	Happening outside control of either side	Agreement to claim in principle	QK
2	Happening outside control of either side	Quantification of claim	HB
3	Happening due to the purchaser's default	Agreement to claim in principle	QK
4	Happening due to the purchaser's default	Quantification of claim	HB

Although in Case 2 the strategy proposed is hold back it is considered that the negotiating margin to be added by the supplier should be minimal in the absence of any prior knowledge as to the purchaser's bargaining behaviour which would lead the supplier to make a different assessment, e.g. the purchaser is known always to cut any claim in half. The reason is that the purchaser will also under such circumstances have suffered a loss himself through no fault of his own and he is likely therefore to regard any demand by the supplier, which he considers to be excessive, as unjust and an attack upon his status. His response will accordingly be both emotional and antagonistic. If, however, the supplier goes out of his way to express understanding of the purchaser's position and presents his claim as modestly and deferentially as possible he is much more likely to be treated sympathetically. At the same time the supplier must not appear to be so weak that the purchaser treats him with contempt. 'Fair but firm' should be taken by the supplier as his guideline.

The problem arises in an even more acute form with Cases 3 and 4. Here what is significant is not the purchaser's loss as such, but the certain loss of esteem and possibly even the disciplinary action which would be suffered by the members of the the purchaser's staff involved, if the supplier's claim were to be accepted. Additionally, it must be expected that those same members of the purchaser's staff will be amongst those detailed to investigate and advise on the validity of the supplier's claim. An example of such a situation would be a contractor's claim for additional costs of site working due to loss of productivity caused by the employer's frequent design changes, the Engineer under the contract responsible for adjudicating on the claim, being the employer's Chief Engineer in charge of his design department.

As regards acceptance of the claim in principle it is contended that the strategy here should be quick kill on the basis that the supplier should submit his claim strictly in accordance with the facts and the contract documents without exaggeration so that should the claim be rejected he has an irrefutable claim to present either to the purchaser's directors or whichever tribunal has jurisdiction under the terms of the contract. On the quantum of the claim, the supplier must expect that the purchaser will bargain, since it is the only means by which he has objectively minimized what he pays, and subjectively, from the viewpoint of the negotiator, the only way in which they can secure their objective of protecting themselves against loss of esteem if not actual security. The supplier must be willing to explore with them ways in which the claim can be structured, by for example introducing a scapegoat such as the R & D Department on whom the necessity for the design changes can be blamed, so protecting them whilst allowing the supplier to achieve his objective. The supplier's negotiating margin should represent his belief as to the concessions which the purchaser's negotiators will need to be able to demonstrate to their own management they have secured so that they are protected and management's approval to the settlement will be forthcoming.

In all claim negotiations it will be to the supplier's advantage if he can support his statements with factual evidence so removing them from the arena of 'pure' bargaining and providing the purchaser's negotiators with justification for their acceptance. No problems are foreseen with this where the factual evidence relates to events outside the control of either side, e.g. unusually severe weather conditions. There can, however, be a problem when the facts are concerned directly with the conduct of one or more of the purchaser's staff. Any public reference to this by the supplier can only lead to the negotiators for the purchaser closing ranks, much as any criticism by an outsider of any member of a family will be bitterly contested by the other members, however much they might agree with the criticism in private amongst themselves. If possible the facts should be stated without reference being made to the individual concerned either by name or title. If this is not possible then the reference should be made in such a way as to imply that anyone might have done the same and that no personal criticism of the individual is intended. Obviously, there are difficulties with this type of approach if the basis of the supplier's claim is negligence and he wishes to preserve his legal rights. In the event that the supplier has decided – along the lines indicated earlier (see pp. 43 and 44) that he both possesses legal power and is willing to use it – then his approach will necessarily be that much harder.

Because of this the supplier must expect the purchaser to bargain; it is the only means which he has for ensuring that he pays the minimum which the supplier will accept. It follows that the supplier's strategy must be hold back and also, by way of corollary, the better the factual evidence he can present to support particular items in his claim, the more he will remove such items from the pure bargaining arena and so give the purchaser's negotiators justification for their acceptance. An example of this would be a claim for extension of time and extra costs due to exceptionally inclement weather, supported by local Meteorological Office figures showing rainfall 50 per cent above average for the period in question.

CONSULTANTS

The supplier's strategy may also be affected by whether the purchaser's negotiators are members of the purchaser's own staff or are a professional firm of consulting engineers or quantity surveyors engaged by the purchaser to undertake the task of contract administration. If the latter, relevant points to be considered are:

1 If the purchaser's team are professionals of the same discipline as those of the supplier then this may make it easier for the supplier to present his case factually and gain the purchaser's consent. It can also lead to the establishment of informal alliances between members of the supplier's team and those of the purchaser even to the point at which formal meetings are held only to record agreements reached the evening before during a social drinks session.

2   The supplier must recognize the purchaser's need to justify himself to his client and the fees he is charging. This applies particularly overseas where the concept of the consultant acting in an independent role between contractor and employer is virtually unknown and the consultant is regarded quite simply as the agent of the client employed to protect his interests.

ACTION OUTSIDE THE CONTRACT

Not in every situation will either party follow the contractual route in the resolution of their differences, nor will they be willing to allow that the existence of rights under the contract, uncontestable on any proper interpretation, shall be decisive of the matter. Examples of the type of situation in which this can happen are alleged excessive profits being made by a firm working on a government fixed-price contract, contracts made under one government which its successor alleges were obtained by corruption, and projects for which a government agency finds it cannot pay or no longer wants to, because of changed economic or political conditions.

Under any of these circumstances not only is the employer's action likely to be arbitrary as regards the main contractor's contractual rights, but the main contractor himself is likely to follow a similar course with his sub-contractors. Equally a main contractor working overseas faced with a payment default which he believes will not be remedied, may decide that immediate stoppage of work and withdrawal of his staff will minimize his losses as compared with the cost of carrying on working and shipping equipment, whilst he follows the often tortuous route of giving the proper notices required under the contract and waits for the employer's response.

There is a strong temptation for the side against whom arbitrary action has been taken to act emotionally in the presentation of claims and issue threats which cannot in reality be sustained. It is, however, a temptation which should be resisted. What it is feasible for the contractor to do and to demand will depend on his rational assessment of the strength of his bargaining position considering all the factors referred to earlier on pp. 43–45. It is indeed on these factors that the decision in favour of arbitrary action itself should be taken in the first instance. The success of arbitrary action in either an offensive or defensive situation depends on the possession of real power and the willingness to use it. Power here is the ability to hurt in the sense of depriving the other side of what they most want and which they cannot, at least easily, obtain in any other way. Willingness to use it means being tough and not departing from the selected course even when subject to abuse or threats. It usually means the end of any possibility of future business relationships but then this is a factor taken into account before the action is started. It falls clearly under the heading of a quick-kill strategy.

SENSITIVE ISSUES

Apart from the two cases stated above the supplier must also consider separately his strategy on any issue on which he is vulnerable and to which he knows that the purchaser is sensitive. The supplier's strategy on such an issue should be quick kill in order to avoid further bargaining. Specifically his offer should be made at a level which he believes will be recognized by the purchaser as acceptable. If in doubt the supplier should offer more rather than less. Since the issue is sensitive, and emotions may well run high, the purchaser is likely to regard any offer which does not satisfy him as insulting and either terminate the bargaining or insist on the acceptance by the supplier of a much higher offer. Whichever way the purchaser reacts, the supplier stands to lose and will suffer the additional disadvantage of having antagonized the purchaser and so created further problems for the future.

An example, based on my own experience, will illustrate the type of situation under discussion.

The supplier had failed to comply with a contractual obligation which would not affect the performance or operation of the equipment concerned. The purchaser, however, regarded the contractual non-compliance as insulting. To remedy the problem by modifying the equipment would cost the supplier 25 per cent of the contract value. The supplier ascertained that the purchaser would be willing to consider the offer of a discount in settlement of the issue. The problem then arose as to how much discount should be offered.

The supplier considered that 5 per cent would be the lowest offer acceptable to the purchaser, and the highest likely to be asked for would be 10 per cent. The danger of an offer at 5 per cent was that the purchaser would not consider it sufficient to eradicate the insult in view of his known feelings on the subject and the consequences of being made to perform the contract were disastrous. The supplier drew the matrix in Figure 15.9 as an aid to making his decision.

| | | Purchaser's strategies | | |
		Quick kill	Hold back	Strategy EV to supplier
	Quick kill	7.5×0.8	10×0.2	= 8%
Supplier's strategies				
	Hold back	5.0×0.1	10×0.9	= 9.5%

Figure 15.9   Expected value to the supplier of varying strategies in a situation of contract dispute

The supplier's assessment was that an offer at 7.5 per cent had an 80 per cent chance of being accepted. It was high enough to reflect the supplier's contrition and could not possibly be regarded as insulting. An offer at 5 per cent was not considered likely to be accepted and any bargaining would be likely to finish at around 10 per cent since the purchaser would act in one of two ways:

1 Offer 10 per cent on a take-it or leave-it basis.
2 Start the bargaining at 15 per cent which would mean a final deal at around 10 per cent.

Although the matrix shows a very low probability of the 5 per cent offer being accepted, the two strategies do not have an equal value until the probability rises to 40 per cent.

In fact the offer was made at 7.5 per cent and accepted. I will never know whether I could have got away with any less.

Notes

1. It is recognized that this could be considered as contradicting the statement made on p. 93, that having submitted a quick-kill bid, the supplier will not be willing to grant a discount. However, the values shown in the matrix represent the purchaser's assessment of how he believes that the bidders will behave and, in practice, it is thought that a purchaser would consider that he would be able to secure a small discount from at least one of the bidders.
2. R. E. Walton and R. E. McKersie, *A Behavioral Theory of Labor Negotiations* (New York: McGraw-Hill, 1965), pp.362–63.

16 SHORT-TERM CONTRACTS – LEVEL OF THE FIRST OFFER

16.1 Bidding

For the purpose of this chapter, a short-term contract is one in which the objectives of the parties do not involve the establishment of long-term business relationships. The possibility is not ruled out that the parties may go on to continue to do further business together, but the possibility of establishing such relationships does not form part of their current objectives. Because of this the way in which they will set the levels of their first offers will be related solely towards the worth to them of the contract under negotiation.

The importance of the level at which the first offer is made (using the term 'level' to refer just not to price but to all other conditions of the offer) is that it establishes one of the following:

1 The level at which the bargain will be made
2 The level below which the bargain will be made
3 That no bargain can be made.

The possibility is excluded that the bargain will be made at a higher level than that of the original offer, that is, one more favourable to the person making the offer.[1] Of course there are occasions when a contract is settled at a price higher than that originally bid, but invariably it will be found that this is due to a change in the technical content, delivery period or some other factor affecting price. Because from the viewpoint of the person making it the level of the original offer can effectively only move downwards, the choice of that level is of crucial importance to his success in the negotiations. A wrong decision at this point will be virtually impossible to correct.

16.2 The golden rule

The golden rule is that the level of the first offer should be such that it will maximize the subjective expected value to the supplier of the outcome at the conclusion of the negotiations. Subjective expected value is discussed in Appendix 1, p. 265. If the offer is a bid being put forward in competition, then one of either two circumstances will apply:

- The bidder knows that the purchaser will not negotiate, e.g. it is to a government department or local authority bound by the Public Procurement Regulations,[2] or
- The bid is being made to a purchaser known to negotiate after receipt of the bids, or the bidder is uncertain whether he will negotiate or not.

16.3 Outcome of negotiations

In the first circumstance it has already been established that the bidder's strategy is quick kill and the outcome will be either a straightforward acceptance or rejection of the bid. The value of the outcome is therefore the value of the bid. The suggested methodology for establishing the level at which the bid should be made is given in Appendix 2.

In the second situation there will be negotiations over a period of time and the outcome of those negotiations is a function of:

- The supplier's original bid
- The purchaser's initial response to that bid
- The supplier's concession factor
- The purchaser's concession factor
- The time taken by the negotiations.

The supplier's original bid over the period of the negotiations will be reduced by the concessions which the supplier is obliged to make in order to obtain the maximum concessions which he can from the purchaser. The face value of the outcome is then the supplier's original bid less the concessions which he has been obliged to make. However, the true value of the outcome to the bidder is its face value less the negotiating costs incurred over the period of the negotiations and discounted back to the date of submission of the bid. The bidder's influence on the time taken by the negotiations arises from two factors:

- The higher his initial offer, provided it is not so high as to be summarily rejected or recognized as 'pure' padding, the longer the negotiations will take, and
- The rate at which the bidder plans to concede in order to obtain the maximum concessions out of the purchaser and the minimum bargain which the bidder is willing to accept. The more favourable the bargain which the bidder wants then again the longer the period of the negotiations.

There is therefore an interrelationship between the five factors identified above as determinative of the outcome. The manner in which they interact is described and illustrated in detail and a mathematical model of their interaction developed in Appendix 3. The key points which emerge from this are:

- That there is no advantage to the supplier in artificially inflating his bid above the level which maximizes the subjective expected value of the outcome
- The influence of time costs and the discount factor in reducing the final value of the outcome to the supplier
- How the supplier himself influences the time taken to reach the final bargain by the level at which he sets his initial demand and the minimum bargain which he is prepared to accept: the influence on the final value of the outcome of the supplier's assessment of the purchaser's concession factor will be heavily reliant upon the reputation for firmness of the negotiator for the purchaser.

A simplified example is set out below in order to illustrate numerically the method proposed for the selection by the bidder of his optimal demand. Although the example refers only to price there would in practice be other factors to be taken into account, such as delivery period and contractual risks.

16.4 A numerical example

In selecting his initial demand the bidder is concerned to balance the gains to be derived from increasing his demand with the time costs and discounting effect necessarily associated with the bargaining period, within the limitations of:

1 The concessions he can expect from customer
2 The concessions he would have to make himself
3 The period of bargaining which would be required.

Assume that the bidder believes that customer's initial offer will be £140,000 and that the maximum which customer would ever be willing to pay is £180,000. The bidder's costs of carrying out the negotiation are £1,500 per month and the discount rate, which takes into account escalation in costs and the reduction in profitability due to the later receipt of the profit contribution, is 6 per cent per annum.

The bidder wishes to establish the level at which to submit his initial offer so as to maximize the outcome. For the present it will be assumed that he attaches no special significance to securing the order earlier rather than later, other than the effect of the discount factor.

For each demand which the bidder considers feasible, he estimates:

1 The maximum concession which he believes customer would make relative to customer's initial offer of £140,000 and the minimum concession which the bidder would have to make in order to obtain that maximum concession from customer.
2 The minimum time which he would expect to elapse before agreement was reached. In this example no constraint is placed on the time available for negotiation, i.e. it is regarded purely as a function of the bargaining process.

He then prepares a table in the form shown in Figure 16.1. It will readily be seen that his optimal demand is £180,000 with an anticipated negotiating period of four months. This can also be represented in graphical form, Figure 16.2, in which the total gain derived from any demand and the time costs involved have been plotted against time. The net gain is the difference between these two and is at a maximum at the point at which the marginal net gain from increasing the demand would be zero. It will be appreciated that this is the point at which using the differential calculus the first order derivative of the net gain curve is equal to zero.

Therefore it is proposed that the bidder should demand £180,000, with the expectation that the bargain will be made at £165,000, provided that this bargain would satisfy at least his minimum negotiating objective and that he is willing to allocate four months' effort to the negotiation.

Bidder's initial demand £'000s	Bidder's expectations of time which would elapse before agreement month	Concession allowed by the bidder up to time of agreement £'000s	Contract value at time of agreement £'000s	Discount factor 0.005 per	Discounted value of agreement £'000s	Cost per month £'000s	Cost to time of agreement £'000s	Value of outcomes at present value less time costs £'000s
200	12	20	180	0.06	169	1.5	18.0	151
190	7	20	170	0.035	164	1.5	10.5	153.5
180	4	15	165	0.02	162	1.5	6.0	156
170	2	15	155	0.01	153.5	1.5	3.0	150.5
160	1	10	150	0.005	149.25	1.5	1.5	147.75
150	0.5	5	145	0.0025	144.5	1.5	0.75	143.75
140	nil	nil	nil	nil	140	–	nil	140

Figure 16.1   Value to the bidder of possible outcomes to an initial offer, discounted to present value and taking time costs into account

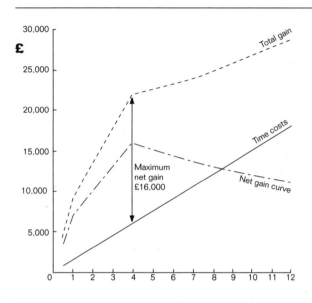

Figure 16.2   Net and total gain curves

If the assumption that the bargaining period is a function only of the bargaining process is amended by imposing an external restriction on the time available for negotiation, then the bidder must limit his demand to that which will result in the most favourable outcome within that period. Thus from Figure 16.1, if only one month is available within which to settle the bargain, then in that example he should not demand more than £160,000.

16.5 Procurement

The Issue of the selection by the purchaser of an initial offer only arises when the purchaser has elected to use a hold-back strategy. A hold-back situation is classified as the case when the purchaser seeks to bargain directly on price and also the other case in which he seeks to do so indirectly through bargaining on those terms of contract which significantly affect risk, e.g. penalties, warranty liability and terms of payment.

In arriving at his decision as to the level at which to make his offer, the purchaser faces the same basic problems as those which confronted the supplier: the more favourable the terms demanded, the longer it is likely that the negotiations will take and the higher will be the time costs. From the purchaser's viewpoint the time costs will essentially be:

1 The loss of revenue or additional expenditure in which the purchaser will be involved due to the delay in starting work and therefore in completion. Postponement of the opening of a new productive facility will mean a loss in earnings, at the same time involving the purchaser in paying interest charges on capital already expended. Delay in completion on non-revenue earning capacity, e.g. new office premises, will prolong the period before the benefits to be derived from such capacity can be realized.

2 If the tender is not on a fixed-price basis, the escalation costs resulting from the work being completed later and therefore, in a time of inflation, during a higher cost period. Even if the particular contract being negotiated is on a fixed price some extra cost may arise if the delay causes postponement of related works to a later period. For example, if the purchaser spends six months negotiating a fixed-price contract, the tender being valid for six months, he will not incur any additional costs under the contract. But if after the award of that contract the purchaser plans to place separate contracts for, say, foundations and off-site facilities, the six-month delay will certainly cause these contracts to cost more.

3 Actual costs of the negotiation itself in terms of the allocation of staff involved in both the buying or contracts departments and staff in other departments called upon to provide support.

Unless the particular contract involved is subject to price escalation, then, provided that the negotiations are concluded within the validity period of the tender, the time costs with which the purchaser is concerned are wholly independent of the value of the contract. The extra costs or loss of revenue are a function only of time and the cost/revenue factor concerned and, in general, can be treated as linear with time. It follows that in many instances a potential concession is simply not worth the effort and time costs which would be required to secure it; a conclusion which if appreciated by the supplier must encourage him to remain intransigent.

16.6 The overall bargain

In developing his reply to an initial offer presented by the supplier the purchaser should be concerned with the worth to him of the overall bargain and not with whether any one particular element appears to be out of line. Treating costs, overheads and profit as separate negotiable entities seems wrong in principle and can lead only to distortion. It is interesting to note that support for this view is to be found in the American Policy Instructions to contracting officers on price negotiations:

> Profit or fee is only one element of price and normally represents a smaller proportion of the total price than do such other estimated elements as labour and material. While the public interest requires that excessive profits be avoided, the contracting officer should not become so preoccupied with particular elements of a contractor's estimate of costs and profit that the most important consideration, the total price itself, is distorted or diminished in its significance. Government procurement is concerned primarily with the reasonableness of the price which the Government ultimately pays and only secondarily with the eventual cost and profit to the contractor.

Further, there is the danger to the purchaser that unless he can bring equal pressure to bear on all elements at the same time, which is unlikely, what he gains in one direction he will lose in another. The supplier may, for example, seek to compensate for a reduction in the rate of profit or overheads allowed by increasing material estimates through, say, adjustment of scrap allowances, or increasing labour estimates by, say, reducing the effect of learning.

16.7 Negotiation with a single supplier

The purchaser would be expected to respond to an initial offer made by the supplier rather than make the first move himself. He will, therefore, have the advantage of knowing the maximum which he might have to pay and is in a better position to assess the concessions which he could anticipate the supplier making.

As before, the example will be simplified by limiting it to price alone. Following the example set out in Figure 6.14 it will be assumed that the supplier has proposed his apparent optimal demand of £180,000. In order to develop his response the purchaser needs to establish:

1   The time costs; these will be assessed at £2,000 per month representing the loss of profit which would be incurred by a delay in completion.
2   The maximum level at which he would prefer a bargain to no bargain. It is decided that this is £165,000.
3   The related outcomes and negotiating periods which he would anticipate over a range of possible replies within the limitation that no outcome is acceptable over £165,000. These together with the related time costs are set out in Figure 16.3.

Purchaser's response	Expected negotiating time	Expected bargain	Time costs	Expected outcome
(£'000s)	(months)	(£'000s)	(£'000s)	(£'000s)
140	8	150	16	166
145	4	155	8	163
150	2	160	4	164
155	1	165	2	167

Figure 16.3   Expected outcome to the purchaser arising from his initial response to the supplier's offer

It will be seen that the purchaser's optimal outcome is given by a response of £145,000, which should lead to a bargain well within his upper limit of £165,000. If, therefore, the purchaser's estimate of the supplier's concession factor is wrong, and purchaser has to concede more than he anticipated, he can still do so and remain within an acceptable limit as far as the actual bargain is concerned. In that event, in order to minimize the effect on the final outcome, the purchaser will be compelled to either:

1 Make the larger concession at a more rapid rate so reducing the time-cost effect, but weakening his reputation as a firm negotiator.
2 Concede slowly, so retaining his reputation for firmness, but incurring the higher time costs.

Rather than risk having to take either of these courses the purchaser may prefer to select the safer response of £150,000. His choice will depend ultimately on his confidence in the estimate he has made of the supplier's concession factor.

Notes

1. Theoretically, if the purchaser were to concede more than the supplier had originally anticipated on the terms of the contract, then it would be possible that the supplier could obtain a better bargain than his original bid. The bidder would simply going on asking for more. I have however personally never known this to happen. When the bidder's strategy is hold back, it is of course possible that the outcome is better for the bidder than he expected if the purchaser concedes more than the bidder had originally allowed for when planning his own initial demand.
2. Although not expressly stated in the Directives, the Commission have issued a policy statement that 'in open and restricted procedures all negotiations with tenderers on fundamental aspects of contracts variations of which are likely to distort competition in particular on prices shall be ruled out; although there may be discussions for the purpose of clarification' (1994 O. J. L.111/114, quoted in S. Arrowsmith, *The Law of Public and Utilities Procurement* (London: Sweet and Maxwell, 1996)). It is believed that in practice this is not strictly observed and that the term 'clarification' is interpreted widely. Given that there will often be qualifications made by the bidders to the purchaser's terms of contract it can hardly be otherwise.

17 LONG-TERM CONTRACTS – THE INITIAL APPROACH

17.1 Introduction

Long-term contracts, even those on a partnering basis, do not form a separate category of contracts in English law. It is therefore necessary for the parties to set down in the contract the rights and obligations which each is to possess and the way in which they intend to collaborate for their mutual benefit. An important point to be established at the outset is that the agreement does not refer to the parties as being 'partners' and expressly states that it does not create the relationship of partners between them. If they were legally to be partners then each would be liable for the acts and defaults of the other within the scope of the partnership and, unless the partnership agreement provided otherwise, they would share their profits or losses derived from the partnership equally.

17.2 Collaboration

The point which distinguishes long-term/partnering contracts from others is not the period of time over which the agreement is intended to last, but that the agreement foresees the creation of a relationship between the parties which transcends the merely contractual obligations involved in the exchange of goods or services for a monetary consideration. It is the intention of the parties that they will collaborate together in good faith for their mutual benefit. With a short-term or one-off contract of course there is a degree of cooperation between the parties, otherwise the contract would be unworkable, but the purchaser's cooperation with the supplier is so that the supplier can complete the contract work for the benefit of the purchaser. There is no intention that the cooperation should be directly for the benefit of the supplier and it is the same the other way round. It follows from this that any such cooperation can be expected to be limited to those matters which indirectly benefit the cooperating party, so that if as a purchaser I can see no benefit to myself in cooperating, I will be unlikely to do so, especially if it is going to cost me money.

It is often suggested in relation to partnering that there should be a partnering agreement which is stated not to be legally binding but which expresses in broad terms the intentions of the parties; then each order to supply would be covered by normal conditions of purchase, perhaps leaving out those conditions which are judged to be too adversarial. The problem with this suggestion is that in any dispute the terms of the non-binding partnering agreement may not be of any assistance[1] and those of the particular purchase order might very well not cover the dispute in question. As an example, consider the question of intellectual property rights in a development which the parties had jointly funded. To whom do these belong and can either party use the results for the purpose of supply to others? Unless the answers have been clearly stated in a legally binding partnering agreement, the result will almost certainly be a dispute which might well finish up in court. The same would apply to investment in new tooling. Can this be used by the supplier, who made the investment as part of his contribution to the partnering arrangement, to enable him to trade more profitably with third parties?

It is also important not to be misled by provisions in an agreement, even if that agreement is expressed to be legally binding, which are dependent for their effectiveness on the parties reaching agreement. As an example consider the following clause in a long-term/partnering agreement dealing with hardship, which was referred to earlier on p. 20.

> If during the course of the contract either party considers that it has suffered undue prejudice or obvious hardship the party prejudiced shall have the right to request the other to enter into joint discussions in order to determine whether revision or modification of the provisions hereof is required and if so what revision or modification would be appropriate or equitable in the circumstances.

Sounds impressive but in English law this clause is unenforceable because it constitutes merely an agreement to agree. Nor does English law recognize a duty to negotiate in good faith because, as was said by a member of the House of Lords in the case of *Walford* v. *Miles* 'the duty to carry out negotiations in good faith is inherently repugnant to the adversarial position of the parties involved in the negotiations each of whom is entitled to pursue his or her interest so long as they avoid making misrepresentations.'[2] It might equally have been said that the obligation is too vague to be enforceable.

The only way to make an obligation such as the one illustrated above legally enforceable is to provide that in the event of disagreement there is a nominated third party, usually an independent expert, who is empowered to make a decision binding upon the parties.

17.3 Proposals for partnering

The objectives of a supplier putting forward proposals in response to an invitation to enter into a long-term/partnering agreement are very different therefore from those when he was submitting a bid for a short-term contract. Obviously price remains important but the non-price criteria by which the purchaser will assess the bid are likely to be even more important. They would include satisfying the purchaser on:

● The willingness to partner and a commitment to partner from top management which would include a partnering charter[3]
● Their commitment to continuous improvement of the product or services, the subject of the partnering agreement, and proposals for the monitoring of performance in the achievement of those improvements

- How they would involve their principal sub-contractors and suppliers down the supply chain into the partnering arrangement
- How they would establish good communications between the partnering firms at all levels and ensure the involvement of all staff in both organizations
- The definition of the key players who would manage the relationships between the firms
- Objectives of both parties to be reviewed, probably annually, for achieving a reduction in the total acquisition costs to the purchaser of the goods/services, the subject of the agreement
- Proposals for any capital investment, including the criteria for such investment and how the return from such investment will be handled
- Their proposals for 'open book' costing which would include a formula for materials, labour, general overheads and profit plus any other foreseen items, e.g. return on capital investment . These would again need to be reviewed, say, annually having regard to technology changes and the progress made in cost reduction
- Proposals for the training of the staff of both parties
- Confidentiality provisions
- Proposals for the sharing of rights in intellectual property resulting from the work done under the agreement
- Liabilities of the parties for default, e.g. of the supplier for late delivery or defective work and the purchaser for default in payment.
- A hardship clause which provides for expert determination if the parties cannot find a solution upon which they agree
- Provisions for termination if the parties find that the agreement does not work
- Means for the handling of disputes.

17.4 Partnering negotiations

The purchaser should have set the 'partnering' criteria by which he will assess the bids in his enquiry document – it is of course mandatory for him to do so if he is inviting tenders under the restricted or negotiated procedures of the European Procurement Directives. (It is doubted whether partnering is possible under the current rules relating to restricted procedure if the literal interpretation of the prohibition on post-tendering negotiation is followed.) Whether the purchaser has done so or not, the bidder should show an awareness of all the implications of partnering and of his commitment from the directors downwards actively to implement these in both letter and spirit.

Although the supplier and purchaser are entering into a partnering agreement it would be wrong to see either side as a 'soft touch'. Indeed, the agreement is far more likely to be successful if each of the above points and any others considered to be important are the subject of hard but straightforward bargaining. The interests of each in some of the above points will not be the same and compromises will have to be made. What is essential is that both sides want to partner, and recognize at the outset that they share the same objective of achieving a mutually satisfying partnering agreement.

17.5 Long-term agreements – not partnering

Of course, not all long-term agreements involve partnering. A purchaser may decide to have a number of long-term agreements with a reduced list of its principal suppliers; this would raise a number of issues, some of which will be similar to those in a partnering arrangement but with the difference that the parties remain at arm's length with each concerned only with their own interests. Each would be free to pursue their own advantage, without regard to the disadvantage which that would impose on the other, even when by modifying their actions they would impose less harm on the other although they would achieve less for themselves.

A simple example would be a right to terminate otherwise than for default. In a partnering arrangement the exercise of this right would be preceded by discussions aimed at reducing to a minimum the effects of such termination on the supplier and with a lengthy period of notice. In a long-term agreement without partnering, the purchaser would be entitled to proceed strictly according to the contractual provisions of the agreement relating to notice and any compensation payable to the supplier, regardless of the effect of the termination on the supplier and with no obligation to reduce its adverse impact.[4]

In putting forward proposals for a long-term agreement without partnering, the supplier must be even more concerned with the protection of his own interests. If, say, the purchaser expects the supplier to invest capital in new equipment, then the supplier's proposal must contain provisions as to how this investment is to be recouped either through guaranteed sales or compensation.

It would be unwise for the supplier to rely upon his usual terms of sale since they would probably be inadequate to cover all the points which are necessary for his protection. Certain clauses will take on an added importance. The major points which should be considered are:

- Price – depending upon the nature of the contract work and the proportion which it represents of the supplier's business, there can be cost advantages or disadvantages from a long-term contract. If the supplier must set up new facilities specifically for this contract, then the cost of this must be allowed for separately and amortized over the anticipated contract period or quantity of work. It must be capable of being proved if the contract is terminated early. If no special facilities are required and the contract represents a significant part of the supplier's business, then this will guarantee a recovery of a substantial portion of the supplier's fixed overheads which will be of benefit to him when bidding for other work. In putting forward his price the supplier must be aware therefore of its implications for the whole of his business over the period for which the long-term contract is to run. The supplier must ensure that he is covered against future increases in costs by a suitable escalation clause or formula.

    Similarly, if any goods are to be imported then the supplier must ensure he is covered against currency fluctuations or changes in import duties.
- Contract work – as always, it is important to define what must be done and to what quality, but the consequences of any error are magnified because of the number of times the work has to be done over the period of the contract.
- Although this is not a partnering-type agreement, the purchaser may be looking for con-

tinuous improvement and to share in cost benefits. Unless the contract is to be on an 'open book' basis, this may be difficult to achieve. If it is to be 'open book' then the costing method to be used and the verification of costs must be set out in detail by the time the contract is agreed.

- Termination – the purchaser is likely to want termination for convenience. If so, then the supplier must ensure that he is protected against the interruption to his business, unrecovered overheads, etc. and that there is a significant period of notice.
- Intellectual property rights which may arise out of work undertaken under the terms of the contract, e.g. the development of new tooling, must be covered. If it is work jointly undertaken or for which the purchaser contributes to the costs then provisions for the sharing of the rights must be included.
- Confidentiality – both sides are likely to learn much about each other's business which is confidential but may not be protected by intellectual property rights. A broadly drawn confidentiality clause should be included.
- Other standard-type clauses such as terms of payment take on added significance because of their impact on the business as a whole.
- A legally binding 'hardship' clause should be included to cover against major economic changes.
- A dispute resolution clause, providing for alternative dispute resolution (ADR) in the first instance with final recourse to arbitration, is required.

Obtaining, say, a three-year contract for the provision of all the canteen facilities at a manufacturer's sites may appear attractive but only if it is profitable and on the right terms. Further, the supplier must ensure he makes provision for what is to happen at the end of the three years if the contract is not renewed.

In general it is suggested on a long-term contract that the supplier should put forward his price utilizing the same methodology as was proposed earlier (see pp. 106–108 for a competitive hold-back situation, i.e. at a level to maximize the subjective expected worth to the supplier of the outcome at the conclusion of the negotiations). These could be expected to take some time and the time costs and associated discount factor will probably be significant. The supplier's problem arises if the intended contract, especially one on a partnering basis, is to be 'open book' with some formula for sharing cost benefits from improvements. This will mean the supplier disclosing his total price make-up including profits and overheads. It is important that the make-up is presented in such a way that when it comes to sharing cost benefits the supplier is not penalized by a lower overhead and profit recovery.

Notes

1. The non-binding partnering agreement would by definition not be the term of the contract. Since it would only be a statement of the intentions of the parties as at the date of contract as to how they intended to behave, it would not be a representation of fact and could not therefore be the basis of a claim in misrepresentation. Further assuming that the actual terms of

contract were expressed in a written contract document, in which case the parties cannot give oral evidence of their intentions, it is equally thought that there may be difficulties in producing a statement of intentions as evidence as to how the contract should be interpreted. However, if in the Partnering document the parties have agreed not to enforce strictly their contractual rights under the construction contract, as to say the giving of notices, and have followed this out in practice, then so long as the Partnering document is in force, a court or arbitrator would be likely to take this into account in deciding on their respective rights, applying for this purpose the doctrine of promissory estoppel – see *Birse Construction Ltd* v. *St David* TCC 12 February 1999.

2. *Walford* v. *Miles* [1992] 2 ACX 352.
3. It is recommended in the European Construction Institute publication, *Partnering in the Public Sector,* that a workshop should be held at the beginning of the contract, the results of which should be incorporated in a partnering Charter. Items to be covered in the Charter should include:

● A statement of behaviour which should be followed and what should be avoided, e.g.
  – Co-operation and trust on all matters
  – Fair allocation of risk to those best able to manage it
  – Continuous search for improvements
● Expression of intent to communicate freely – giving early warning of problems and not allocating blame
● Acknowledgement by the client that contractors and suppliers should make a fair return on their efforts
● Recognizing that problems will occur which will need to be dealt with expeditiously in a cooperative manner and action taken to avoid their recurring
● Rapid action needed to resolve disputes as they occur
● Strong expression of ownership of the partnering process and commitment to perform
● Commitment to attend to all matters which will either lead to success or impede it. List to be attached to the Charter.

The Charter is to be signed by all concerned and displayed prominently in the project offices and at progress meetings.

4. The problems which can arise from long-term relationships which have not been properly set out in contractually binding agreements is well illustrated by the dispute at the time of writing between Marks and Spencer and their supplier William Baird. Although they had been a supplier to Marks for very many years, it is understood from press reports there was no express long-term contract or partnering agreement between Marks and Bairds, only a series of individual orders. Therefore Bairds had been forced to rely on the argument that because of the course of dealing over all these years with Marks, there was an implied contract which did not allow Marks unilaterally to cancel all existing orders without a three-year period of notice, which is reported to be likely to cause 4,500 redundancies amongst Baird's workers.

18 CONTRACT DISPUTE – THE FIRST OFFER

18.1 *When an offer is to be made*

In Chapter 6 when discussing whether negotiations in a contract dispute situation would be successful or not it was pointed out that, if the issue were a legal point of principle, then the only way in which that issue could be resolved would be by a reference to a judicial tribunal. If therefore the issue is one of contract interpretation, say, whether or not one of the parties possesses a specific right under the contract to additional payments or to recover damages, then negotiations can only proceed if it is agreed to set that issue aside and proceed on the basis of equity or fairness to both sides. You cannot negotiate on the existence or otherwise of a right but only the amount of money which, in the events which have happened, it would be fair and reasonable for one party to pay to the other. By setting the issue on one side one has dispensed with the legal rules relating to additional payments or damages.

Offers are only expected to be made therefore if either the existence of the right is not disputed, and the negotiations relate solely to the amount to be paid, or it has been agreed that the issue will be set aside and negotiations will proceed on the fair and equitable basis.

In deciding upon the level of our first offer two situations need to be distinguished:

- The submission by ourselves of a claim under the contract
- Responding to a complaint by the purchaser of our contractual default.

18.2 *Submission of a claim*

The first difficulty with contractual claims is that invariably they are based upon some default by the purchaser or consultants acting on his behalf in their performance of the contract. It follows that they are likely to cause a highly emotionally charged situation. People do not normally react rationally to public criticism of their behaviour however justified such criticism may be, especially when it is criticism of them as professionals.

It is important therefore that in preparing and presenting the claim we do so in a calm and unemotional manner, do not resort to hyperbole or over-statements and avoid so far as possible criticism of individuals. As regards their cause, claims should be stated in a cold, flat, rational and unemotional way and linked as closely as possible to matters of contractual default capable of objective proof.

The major difficulty is often the relating of cause and effect. It may be easy to identify that we were delayed, say, in the making available to us of key data necessary for the development of our design, but quite another to demonstrate the effect which that delay had initially upon our design office work and subsequently in either manufacture or site construction. Moreover, while it was appropriate to establish the causes rationally and without over-statement it is another matter when it comes to the effect whether this is expressed in terms of time, money or both. If it can be shown that data contractually due to be provided at week 10 was not actually provided until week 20, then clearly there can be no doubt as to contractual default which establishes cause.

However, proving the effect linked to that cause may be much more difficult and it is made more so in practice since if there is a delay in providing data it is unlikely that there is only a single delay. It is much more probable that there will have been a whole series of delays and that not all of them will have been due to the purchaser's default. It follows that in presenting our claim as to the effects of delay we must recognize that the purchaser will seek through bargaining to reduce the value of the claim. He knows we will have anticipated this and will therefore have inflated the claim's value. On the effects and therefore the value of the claim neither side can trust the figures of the other.

The value of the claim as presented is then the amount which the contractor wants to secure plus the concessions which he considers he will have to make to the purchaser in order to obtain that amount and taking into account the time-costs involved.

The amount the contractor wants to secure is not necessarily related strictly to his extra costs. Contractors often view claims not just as a means of recovering their additional costs, but as a way of bringing back the margin on the contract to the level at which they would have liked to have tendered but were unable to do so because of competition. A construction contractor, say, would have liked to have tendered with a gross margin of 10 per cent; in fact his tender price was at break-even in order to secure the work. His objective now through claims and variations is to recover that 'lost' 10 per cent irrespective of whether or not he incurred any additional costs as a result of the purchaser's default. Of course any additional costs actually incurred will be added to the 'lost' 10 per cent. The claims culture in the construction industry is due to many factors: each job on a different site is to some extent a prototype, clients spend too little time and effort in deciding what they really want before they invite tenders, tender periods are too short, contract conditions too harsh and so on, but a major factor is the under-pricing of work by contractors believing, only too often correctly, that it is the lowest price that wins the day. Then the battle starts.

Reference was made earlier to setting legal issues aside and proceeding to negotiate on a fair and equitable basis. It can be objected that seeking to include in the claim the recovery of margin 'lost' at tendering stage is neither fair nor equitable. This is agreed. If the firm has elected to tender at a given level then that is their risk and the employer should only agree to negotiate on that basis.

It can also be argued that if the firm chose to ignore when tendering a particular term of the contract of which the interpretation is clear, then equally it would be wrong to allow them later to submit a claim in contradiction of that clause. The issue here, however, is not so clear-cut. If the events which form the basis of the claim were completely unexpected, e.g. the contract was on a fixed price but there were substantial and unforeseeable increases in the contractor's costs, the employer may agree to consider such a claim on an *ex gratia* basis but should only do so if the contractor successfully completes the work on time and to specification. Even then the amount which the employer pays should be a matter for his discretion, based on his assessment of the facts, including the contractor's performance, and not a matter for negotiation.

18.3 Responding to a complaint by the purchaser

In a situation of contract dispute the supplier's initial offer should be such as to:

1 Point the way towards a settlement which would just satisfy what the supplier believes would be the purchaser's minimum negotiating objective, given that both sides were agreed on the facts of the dispute.
2 Ensure that in any settlement the supplier achieves at least his own minimum negotiating objective.

The distinguishing feature of contract-dispute negotiations as opposed to those relating to bidding and procurement is that the two parties are already jointly involved in a venture from which both stand to lose or gain. As a result the degree of emotional involvement of the negotiators is much higher and the worth to either side of a particular outcome must be conceived as much in psychological as monetary terms. Further the socio-legal system under which the relevant part of the contract is being executed must be taken into account.

Under these conditions it is likely that there will be a substantial difference in the worth of the subject matter of the dispute to the two sides. Thus failure to comply with some minor requirement of the specification may have little significance to the contractor who is confident that it will make no difference at all to the operating standards and performance of the equipment. To the purchaser's engineers, however, such failure may appear both as an insult and as something which, if they do not insist on it being corrected, could be the cause of their being severely censured if the facts came to the notice of their superiors.

18.4 Valuation of the purchaser's negotiating objective

The supplier's negotiators should try therefore to see how the issue in question looks through the eyes of their opposite numbers, and in so doing take into account variations in national temperament, social structure and cultural background.

Ideally the facts of the matter in dispute should have been agreed before any offer is made at all. It is dangerous to start establishing positions unless there is common ground between the two sides on at least the factual issues. If, however, such agreement has not been reached, and the supplier is forced into the position of having to make an offer, then he has the difficult task of assessing what he believes would be the minimum negotiating objective of the purchaser if the facts were agreed. For example, if the supplier believes that the purchaser is only taking a hard line because the purchaser believes wrongly that the factors are in his favour, then the supplier may assess that once the purchaser knows the truth, the objective of his negotiators will be simply to get themselves off the hook with the minimum loss of face. Under these circumstances the supplier's initial offer must be aimed at allowing the purchaser's negotiators a graceful way out, preferably without exposing them to censure from their own management.

Suppose that the dispute concerns the purchaser's claim for delay damages and the supplier's contention that he is entitled to an extension of time. In reality the supplier's case for an extension of time is based four-fifths on the purchaser's own contractual default and one-fifth on *force majeure*. However the purchaser's management are unaware of the extent of their own default and quite genuinely believe that the supplier is to blame. It is suggested that in his initial approach the supplier should stress the *force majeure* and play down the purchaser's contractual default thus giving the purchaser's negotiators a way out from exposure to their own management. The supplier would of course, behind the scenes, ensure that the significance of this move was not lost on the purchaser's negotiators and that they were aware of the consequences which would follow from its rejection.

One particular circumstance because of its importance to the supplier as a contractor, and its unfortunate frequency of occurrence, needs particular mention and that is customer default in payment. In this event the supplier has the initial decision as to whether to turn the issue into an openly recognized one of dispute or to simply record the default and continue with the contract work.

The primary factors in reaching that decision are:

1 Whether the supplier believes that customer will ultimately correct the default provided that it is not publicized, but that if it is, it will cause adverse and possibly irrational action by the customer, e.g. unfair calling of a performance bond.

2 The magnitude of the default relative to the supplier's ability to continue to provide financial support.

3 The attitude of the supplier's bank and credit insurers, if any, who must be advised of the default.

4 As an alternative to 1, whether or not the supplier believes that, by administering a sharp shock, the customer can be made to realize that he must conform to the contract terms otherwise the supplier will take action not only as provided for under the contract, e.g. suspension or termination, but will so advise his government which, if customer is a public agency, could cause political problems. Implicit in this is the supplier's belief that customer *can* pay and that the sharp shock, e.g. notice of intent to suspend, will be treated by customer as credible. It further follows from this that the supplier must never threaten and then not act if the default is not remedied, as this would totally undermine his credibility. If the supplier believes customer cannot pay then he must consider the alternative of arbitrary action provided this would not invalidate any insurance cover he has against non-payments i.e. if he has such cover he must first consult his insurers.

5 Whether or not the contract is within a legal system which provides the supplier with a full and fair opportunity to recover the debt, protects the supplier against arbitrary action by customer, and customer has assets within the jurisdiction. If the answer to these questions is 'no', so that for all practical purposes the debt is irrecoverable by action, then the supplier can look only to his insurers and take such arbitrary action as that to which they agree to minimize the loss.

Again it is stressed that in deciding on the use of tactics of this nature the supplier must take fully into account the factors personal to the customer and his negotiators; in particular that of sensitivity to criticism and the emotional reaction which such criticism would be likely to generate.

Depending on the nature of the dispute, the purchaser's negotiating objective will fall into one of the following categories.

NON-TERMINATION OF CONTRACT

Security

Because of some failure fully to meet specification, the purchaser requires guarantees or assurances on the performance or reliability of what has been supplied. His objective will be expressed in terms of:

1 Items covered by the guarantee
2 Extent of the guarantee
3 Time for which the guarantee is effective
4 Consequences if the guarantee is not met
5 Extent to which the guarantee is in full satisfaction of the supplier's liabilities.

Discount

Because of failure to complete the work on time or failure to meet specification, the purchaser requires a reduction in the contract price, either directly by way of discount or indirectly by way of damages. His objective will be expressed in terms of:

1 Amount of the discount
2 Extent to which payment is in full satisfaction of the supplier's liabilities.

Rectification

Because the work does not comply with the specification, the customer requires it to be modified or additional facilities provided. His objective will be expressed in terms of:

1 Extent of the work to be carried out
2 Time within which the work must be carried out
3 Extent to which the rectification is in full satisfaction of the supplier's liabilities.

It will be understood that the three categories are not mutually exclusive. Thus the customer may consider that the default by the supplier is sufficiently serious for him to require both security and discount.

TERMINATION OF CONTRACT

The customer's objective will be expressed in terms of:

1 To the extent that work is not complete to costs of repurchase from another supplier

2 Minimizing his liability towards the supplier in respect of money which he already owes to the supplier or which the supplier is entitled to in respect of work in progress, etc.

3 Recovery of damages covering delay in completion of the contract and consequential loss of revenue or additional expenditure incurred by the customer arising out of the cancellation.

The customer's objective is therefore unlikely to be singular. There will be a number of objectives, each of which in some measure will be related one to another, so that a concession by the supplier on one will be prejudicial to his negotiating position on another. Not all of the customer's negotiating objectives will be of equal importance to him. He may, for instance, value the giving by the supplier of a guarantee more highly than the recovery of a discount if his primary concern is that of ensuring system reliability.

It is the supplier's task to seek out the customer's value structure and to discover in which way he can satisfy the customer's minimum negotiating objective in a manner which is least prejudicial to himself.

18.5 The supplier's negotiating objective

It follows from the discussion of the customer's negotiating objective that in any contract dispute one or more factors will stand out as being of major importance quite independent of actual cash payments. The supplier's offer should be structured in such a way as to ensure that as a minimum his objective in relation to these factor(s) is achieved. In considering how the supplier actually does this, two cases may be distinguished:

1 The supplier believes his principal objective to be directly opposite to that of the customer.

2 The supplier believes that his principal objective is either of secondary importance to the customer or its existence may even not have been appreciated by the customer.

SUPPLIER'S AND CUSTOMER'S OBJECTIVES DIRECT OPPOSITES

Leaving aside actual monetary payments, this is the less common case and will only occur when there is one central issue to the dispute, the loss or gain of which virtually ends the matter. An example would be an admission by the supplier that the customer was entitled to terminate the contract for the supplier's default when the supplier was liable under the terms of the contract for substantial and easily proven consequential damages.

Even if the customer does not initially raise the issue directly, the supplier must bring it out into the open. In so doing the supplier would make it clear that any settlement to be acceptable must satisfy him on this point; a line to which he would consistently stick.

THE SUPPLIER'S OBJECTIVE OF SECONDARY IMPORTANCE TO OR NOT APPRECIATED BY THE CUSTOMER

It has been indicated already that there may be a difference in the worth of the dispute to the two sides. Equally each may have a totally different principal objective. As an example consider a dispute regarding the quality of work carried out by the supplier. The customer's principal objective may be simply to obtain rectification of the work plus an extended guarantee period which would provide him with security. The supplier may be quite willing to meet him on these issues but will want to ensure, as his main objective, that he is not penalised for delay or does not lose his performance bond. Neither of these is of primary interest to the customer and even may not have occurred to him.

The supplier should conceal his anxiety and deliberately avoid raising the matters which concern him until at least the final meeting. Even then he should treat them as of minor importance and, if possible, as mere formalities.

It is not suggested that when dealing with a sophisticated negotiator this strategy will deceive the customer. By not raising the issues initially the supplier will not have brought them openly within the scope of the negotiation. He will therefore have allowed the negotiator for the customer the opportunity to ignore them. This is an illustration of the process of tacit communication and coordination. The supplier has tacitly agreed to meet the customer by not raising the consequential issues: the customer has tacitly agreed that in return for the supplier's concession on the customer's negotiating objective he will give the supplier the assurance he wants in terms of the final bargain.

The difficulty in practice is how can the supplier be sure, without open communication, that he has correctly understood the customer's intentions? If the supplier assumes, as he should, that the customer is at least as much aware as the supplier of the importance to him of the concealed issue, then the customer's behaviour may be explained in one of the following ways:

1 The customer is deliberately not raising the issue until a late stage in the negotiations so that he can use it then as a lever to exert maximum pressure on the supplier.
2 The customer is willing not to raise the issue at all as a major negotiating point.

Since the supplier cannot openly ask the customer which tactic he is employing, and even if he did could not necessarily believe the customer's answer, how can he satisfy himself as to which explanation is correct? The same dilemma may face the customer. If he has decided on tactic 2, how can he do so in a way which the supplier will find credible while at the same time not totally committing himself in case, if the negotiations are not going successfully, he wishes to change his mind?

Recognizing the dilemma the supplier can arrange to give the customer the opportunity to raise the issue and at the same time collaborate with the customer in defining their agreement on all other points. In so doing, he creates the situation in which if the customer were to raise the concealed issue as a major negotiating issue at a late stage, the supplier could legitimately withdraw from the agreements already reached and accuse the customer of bad faith. The supplier therefore uses the development of a bargaining situation first as a means of testing the customer's intentions and secondly as a method of ensuring that it is no longer in the customer's interests to change his mind.

18.6 Determination of the level of the initial offer

The basic approach to the establishment of the initial demand in a contract-dispute situation is similar to that adopted for bidding and procurement. The supplier assesses what he believes the outcome will be, based on his judgement of the customer's range of negotiating objectives and his concession factor, and selects the demand which he believes will lead to the optimal outcome. It has been seen that these objectives are not as clear-cut as in bidding/procurement and that the value which one side puts on a particular issue may differ widely from the value which it possesses for the other.

Time costs will only be significant where the dispute concerns a major financial claim or the payment of other money is dependent on the issue being settled, e.g. release of retention money dependent on the settlement of a dispute relating to spares.

More so, however, than in bid/procurement negotiations, the supplier must consider the effect which any concession will have on the future and that it is the ultimate not the immediate cost associated with any action which is significant. The correct, small, concession made at the right time can be very useful in avoiding future difficulties. The wrong, small, concession made at the wrong time can be very costly to the supplier in the encouragement which it gives to the customer to ask for more, and the precedent it gives him on which to base future demands.

Because there will normally be a number of issues involved, the importance of which will vary, it is essential that in formulating his initial demand and his belief as to the customer's concession factor the supplier assesses the worth to him of each issue in terms of money (or utility values if the amounts involved are of sufficient significance). The importance of each issue can then be compared and the demand structured so as to achieve the optimal outcome.

Such comparison will also indicate any anxiety issues which the form of the supplier's initial demand should be designed to protect. Emphasizing the point made earlier (p. 106), the supplier's initial demand is a function of a total negotiating plan which foresees a particular outcome based on the supplier's judgement of the customer's concession factor, and the concessions which the supplier considers will be necessary for him to make.

This process of formulating the initial demand is illustrated with the following simple example.

The supplier is five months late in completing a contract for the customer. Responsibility for the delay is disputed since neither side is wholly to blame. The defects liability period runs for twelve months from the original date for completion, extended by any period for which the supplier is in default. During the period of delay, spares to the value of £500 have been used on maintaining the plant which the customer considers should be paid for by the supplier, as free replacement of defects, and the supplier asserts should be paid for by the customer since their use only became necessary through maloperation of the plant by the customer's staff. Liquidated damages for delay are at the rate of £1,000 per month and the supplier assesses the cost of extending the defects liability period at £200 per month.

The supplier prepares the following analysis of the position:

1 Negotiating area. Liquidated damages: £1,000 per month to a maximum of £5,000. Defects liability period: £200 per month to a maximum of £1,000. Spares: £500.

2 Negotiating objective. The supplier's preferred objective £3,000; minimum acceptable £4,500. The customer's expected minimum objective £2,500; expected preferred objective £5,000.

3 The anxiety factor. This is clearly the damages. If the preferred negotiating objective is to be achieved then the damages payment must not exceed £2,000 on the basis that at least £1,000 will have to be conceded on the other two points. If the minimum negotiating objectives is to be achieved then assuming the other two points have to be conceded completely the damages payments must not exceed £3,000.

Additionally a concession on the period of delay will automatically involve a similar concession on defects liability. However, the converse is not necessarily true. A concession on a longer defects period could be traded for lesser damages.

In deciding on his initial offer the supplier has the choice of either:

1 Offering the limit to which he is prepared to go on damages, making it clear that this issue is not a matter for further negotiation, whilst at the same time indicating a greater flexibility on defects liability

2 Saying nothing, or reserving his position on damages and making an offer only on spares and defects liability

3 Making some offer on each issue but indicating on which he would prefer the initial negotiations to be concentrated.

Unless the negotiating position on damages is considered to be very strong, so that the offer could be kept down to say £2,000 as a maximum, the preference would be for alternative 3. Damages is a major issue for both sides and as such must form an important part of the negotiations. On the other hand, unless his position is very strong, the supplier would not wish to commit himself to too firm a position too early. The negotiating plan would therefore be:

1 An initial offer of
   (a) The minimum damages thought to be acceptable and not regarded as insulting, say, £1,000.
   (b) Acceptance of defects liability for half the disputed period which would cost £500.
   (c) Half the value of the disputed spares which would cost £250.

2 To concentrate the subsequent negotiations first on the damages issue, conceding slowly and reluctantly to £2,000. At that point make no further concessions on damages but offer the balance of the defects period for a final settlement. This would leave half the value of the spares as a final 'sweetener'. The cost therefore of the final bargain on this basis would be £3,500.

19 THE NEGOTIATING TEAM

19.1 Character and composition of the team

The performance of our team depends as much, if not more, on the way in which its members function together as it does on the technical expertise which each individual member possesses.

In considering the character and composition of the negotiating team it is necessary to look beyond technical skills to the personality and temperament of the proposed members and the way in which these are likely to interact between themselves and with the anticipated members of the other side's team. The character and composition of the negotiating team must therefore be such that:

1 The members have the technical expertise to deal effectively with the whole of the area which it is foreseen that the negotiations will cover
2 The members are compatible in temperament with one another and with those whom it is believed will represent the other side.

SIZE OF THE NEGOTIATING TEAM

The area covered by any contract negotiation may be divided broadly into four sectors:

1 Commercial: price, delivery, commercial policy on risk taking
2 Technical: specification, programme, methods of work
3 Legal: contract documents, terms and conditions of contract, insurance, legal interpretation
4 Financial: terms of payment, credit insurance, bonds and financial guarantees.

If the scale and importance of the negotiation justifies it then the negotiating team for each side would comprise a negotiator qualified in, and responsible for, each of those areas. These four persons would then constitute the permanent team for the negotiation, and would be supplemented by other specialists on particular issues as they arose, e.g. production methods, inspection, installation. For negotiations of lesser significance one negotiator would double for another and cover two areas, after having been fully briefed on the subject with which he was less familiar. Thus the legal negotiator might cover the financial area, and the commercial negotiator, if he had an engineering background, might assume responsibility for the technical area. Alternatively the commercial negotiator might cover both his own and the legal plus financial areas, with an engineer to support him on the technical side.

On lesser negotiations therefore the team of four could be reduced to two; it should not be reduced to one, no matter how well-qualified the negotiator concerned. It is demanding too much to expect the same person on his own to:

1 Present his own case and study his opposite number's visual reactions
2 Listen to and makes notes on his opposite number's reply
3 Plan and present his response to his opposite number's reply
4 Consider the possible outcomes on each point, and their effect on the bargain as a whole and develop a trade-off strategy
5 Identify and conclude the final bargain
6 Record the final bargain.

Additionally the presence of a colleague will give the negotiator the advantage of:

1 Being able to employ team tactics
2 Not having to develop all the arguments on his own. It is more effective for arguments on different points to be developed with differing styles
3 Having someone to support him in the case of sickness or overtiredness. This is particularly valuable when negotiating away from home base
4 Having someone with whom to share his problems. This is again especially valuable when operating abroad with poor communications back home and faced, inevitably, with the doubts and uncertainties present in that type of situation.

It is preferable that a negotiator has the support of an assistant or trainee to make notes, do calculations and remind him of any points which he has missed, and thus not leave him to handle the whole bargaining process by himself. If a company maintains that they cannot afford to send two people then really they should not be in the business to which the negotiation relates.

Equally, however, the negotiating team should not be too large. At any time it should not exceed five, although they will not necessarily be the same five over the whole period. If a basic team of three is assumed, one commercial, one legal and one technical, then this might need to be augmented on a major negotiation at different stages by specialists from the engineering, production or finance functions. Beyond five it becomes extremely difficult for the team to be kept under control and for its activities to be directed towards a single outcome. Separate and uncoordinated discussions are likely to start between the functional specialists on both sides, and arguments are likely to develop between the members of the team themselves during the negotiating session. The retention of a united front and the direction of all argument towards a single goal are essential preconditions for an effective team operation and with more than five permanently in a team these are most unlikely to be achieved.

In certain industries with which I have been associated, it has been the practice to involve in the negotiations both local and higher levels of management, plus representatives from all staff functions. An assembly of as many as 25 people cannot be referred to as a negotiating *team* because it is certainly *not* a team. Arguments between assembly members are numerous and based on the lines of traditional disagreement between staff functions or the entrenched views of their representatives. The practice may be effective as a means of communication, so that everyone concerned is informed about the proposals under consideration, but it is highly ineffective for the purpose of negotiation and from that viewpoint has nothing to commend it.

It will be noted that the preceding paragraphs have referred to the negotiators and also to functional specialists. A clear distinction is drawn between those whose function on the negotiating team is to negotiate and those who are there to provide specialist advice or information. A quality assurance manager may for example be asked to join the team when matters affecting his function are being discussed but is not his task actually to carry out the bargaining with the other side. That would be the task of the commercial negotiator who would look to the quality assurance manager to provide him with the necessary specialist support.

A further distinction is drawn between the risk-taking function of the commercial negotiator and the functions of the other specialists who do form part of the negotiating team. These other specialists have a dual task to perform. They negotiate with their opposite number on the wording or interpretation of the documents with which they are specifically concerned. However, when the issue raised is one which involves commercial risk then their function is to act as an adviser to the commercial negotiator and to apply his policy decision. Take the simple example of a warranty clause. The commercial negotiator will ask his lawyer to interpret for him the risk which acceptance of the other side's proposals would create, and then take the decision on the policy line which he wishes to adopt. As necessary he argues this policy line with his opposite number but leaves it to the lawyer to express that policy in the form of an amended clause and argue the drafting of this with the lawyer from the other side.

These distinctions are important since much of the criticism which is made of functional specialists as negotiating team members arises from a lack of clear understanding of the role which they are there to perform. The major problems arise when such specialists stray away from their proper role and start to take the risk decisions which are the prerogative of the commercial negotiator. It is not lawyers who lose suppliers contracts because of their legalistic attitude but commercial negotiators who do not keep lawyers in their proper place and attending to their proper function.

SELECTION OF THE NEGOTIATING TEAM

As part of their normal business function, purchasing and sales departments can be expected to provide people to take part in negotiations. Negotiation is a major part of the activity of both departments. Although the academic training of the junior may be deficient in the theory of negotiation, he is likely to be introduced to the subject in a practical way from quite early on in his career, and his further advancement may well be dependent upon the degree of success he achieves.

It is not so, however, with other departments. Negotiation does not form part of the professional training of an engineer, lawyer or accountant nor is it an activity in which the individual will necessarily be engaged for any significant portion of his time or one which will influence his future chances of promotion. One cannot therefore expect to be able to take any engineer, lawyer or accountant away from his office desk and send him straight out on a major contract negotiation. Accordingly, if a company is likely to require the services of these professional people as members of negotiating teams, they should arrange for them to receive the necessary training.

In addition to his professional abilities the person should be selected on the basis of his suit-ability *as a negotiator* for the negotiation in question. If it is a major negotiation then he would be expected to have significant negotiating experience, and be judged to be compatible with the other members of the team and with what is known of the attitudes of the other side's team. If the negotiation is of lesser significance then it might be judged a suitable opportunity for someone of less proven ability to gain experience. The important factor is that the selection is made positively from the viewpoint of the best interests of the company in regard to that nego-tiation and for the future. It may for instance be decided that one negotiator specializes either in a particular product or with a particular customer, so that a sense of continuity is achieved. Alternatively if the company identifies its market as a particular overseas country with its own peculiar environment then one or more negotiators should be trained as specialists in all aspects of that environment and encouraged to obtain at least a colloquial knowledge of the local language.

When referring to someone's ability as a negotiator the following qualities seem to be the most important:

1 Sound technical knowledge of his own discipline and of the techniques of negotiation, in particular, the art of asking questions
2 Understanding of the product or service involved in its relationship to his discipline/function. Thus the lawyer engaged on contract negotiation should have sufficient knowledge of the subject matter of the contract to appreciate the practical significance of the clauses which he is negotiating
3 Facility of expression
4 Ability to listen to what the other side are saying and analyse their arguments objectively
5 Willingness to look at issues from the viewpoint of the other side
6 Ability to stay in command of himself even when exposed to severe pressure
7 Mental/physical stamina and a sense of determination
8 A sense of humour
9 Readiness to retain a sense of proportion and stay with the main issues and not be diverted onto side lines
10 Possession of a 'feel' for the relationship of the negotiating points with another and being willing to trade one for another
11 Ability to get on with people of differing nationalities, religions and social classes and to avoid nationalistic, racial or social prejudice.

To what extent can these qualities be taught and to what extent are they determined either genetically or by the social conditioning to which the individual has been subjected from birth?

Clearly 1 and 2 must be taught; the remainder are a function of the individual's personality and the environmental influences to which he has been subjected. In practice it is my view that by the time people start to carry out commercial negotiations their personality and attitudes have been so far developed that they are unlikely to undergo significant change. Therefore, whilst a person can refine himself and gain experience of the way in which others behave, so that he develops a sense of either anticipation or understanding of their actions, he will still retain the essential personality and attitudes with which he emerged as an adult.

Imaginative training may develop any particular characteristic, such as ability to understand the other's viewpoint, to the extent that it is latent within the individual. It is argued that such training is unlikely to create the ability where previously it was non-existent.

THE ROLE OF THE AGENT

The role of the agent will vary widely between two extremes. At the one end of the spectrum is the agent who is solely a 'contact man' with those who are supporting the supplier in their efforts to secure the business. At the other is the agent who permanently represents the supplier in the territory or with a particular customer, has some knowledge of the supplier's products/services and is able and willing to provide the supplier with a range of services such as translation, office and communication facilities, and assistance with local legal and taxation advice, and joins the negotiating team at least for certain meetings.

The agent whose function is limited to being a 'contact man' will not be a member of the negotiating team as such, although he will be involved in any discussions between the team leader and those who are assisting the supplier and stand to benefit, should the supplier be successful. Because of the delicate nature of his role it would not be appropriate for him to become involved in the formal working sessions. His task lies outside these in the informal discussions which may be necessary so that the supplier can attain his objective. He is also there to brief the team leader on how to handle particular situations or personalities.

The agent whose role is wider can be co-opted as a member of the negotiating team although this will generally be one of his younger staff rather than the principal himself. If the language e.g. Chinese, is totally unknown to any of the supplier's team then he may act as the interpreter. Certainly he should be there to check on any interpretation being done by customer's interpreter. The difficulty in practice is that the agent only stands to gain if the supplier is successful in obtaining the contract and he has therefore a vested interest in the supplier making the concessions necessary for this purpose. He will be resistant to the supplier taking a tough line which could cause the business to go to a competitor and will often seem to the supplier to be more on customer's side than his own. There are other difficulties as well. The agent, especially in the Far East, will almost never tell you directly any bad news. He wants you to be happy and therefore will tell you what he believes you want to hear. Somehow he will have an explanation for each reverse and 'a cousin' who can put matters right. It is up to the team leader to see through this and get to the truth, otherwise time and money will continue to be spent on what is a lost cause. Also can you be sure that he is working for you alone and is not also involved with one of your competitors? Or again the ubiquitous 'cousin' who is the source of information in the customer's office may be receiving as much information about your proposals as he is providing about customer's plans.

These problems must be anticipated and guarded against both in as careful selection as possible in the first instance and with continued attention subsequently to testing him as you go along. This will either prove him to be the right man whom you can reasonably trust or provoke him into taking an unexpected holiday. One such person, known to the author personally, who was a very non-devout Muslim, suddenly decided when the going got rough to disappear on the Haj!

But despite all the above the agent in many territories is essential to success. It is rare for the team leader or other members of the negotiating team to be sufficiently familiar with their opposite numbers or others who are part of the decision-making process, that they can ever become part of the local 'old-boy' network. They will never be able to obtain access to genuine 'inside' data or exercise informal influence on the decisions to be reached. Only the agent has the possibility of belonging to the 'right' local family or tribe or of having been in the same year at college with one or more of the decision makers, and can take advantage of the reciprocation of favour for which such links provide the framework. Only he may be able to get you that vital appointment ahead of the crowd or ensure that it is your proposal which the real decision maker has in front of him at the appropriate moment.

19.2 *Appointment and duties of the team leader*

APPOINTMENT

In discussing this topic at seminars on negotiation it has been suggested to me that the question of *choosing* a team leader does not really arise; he chooses himself because of the position which he holds in the company or organization concerned. Reference has been made specifically to the sales manager and chief buyer as two obvious examples.

There are many occasions when these two managers will act as leaders of their respective teams, but there are also numerous other occasions when an alternative candidate will be proposed. Some examples drawn from my own experience are set out below and the reader is left to make his own choice.

Subject matter of negotiation	Candidates for team leader
Purchase of raw materials for production process	Raw materials buyer Plant manager Production manager
Purchase of major item of capital plant	Purchasing/contracts manager Chief engineer Divisional manager or other line executive
Major sales contract	Marketing/sales director or manager Senior line executive from managing director downwards Project manager designate for the contract
Contract dispute	Project manager Contract administration manager Sales manager or other executive who originally negotiated the contract

When deciding whether or not to appoint an executive as a negotiating team leader, two criteria by which he should be assessed are suggested, as follows:

1 His ability to lead a negotiating team as opposed to any purely technical skills which he may possess
2 His degree of personal responsibility for the profit or loss which may follow from any decision taken during the negotiations.

Specifically a person should not be selected for any of the following reasons:

1 He can be spared, having nothing else to do at that time.
2 He is *the* technical expert on the product.
3 He happens to be the senior manager concerned with the outcome of the negotiation.
4 He once knew personally the territory concerned or members of the other team for the other side.

Although it has been indicated that the team leader does not have to be a technical expert on the product upon which the negotiation is centred, it is not suggested that either buying or selling is a mystique on its own which can be conducted without any product knowledge at all. The leader for a sales team who cannot answer any of the buyer's questions directly, but must refer him to one or other of his colleagues, is unlikely to earn the buyer's respect. Equally the buyer without product knowledge can too easily be fooled in a situation in which an informal alliance develops between his own and the supplier's technical experts. Such alliances are not uncommon in industries in which the engineers, although commercially on opposing sides, were trained together, are members of the same professional institute and have collaborated together technically in finding solutions to common problems.

The negotiating team leader should possess therefore sufficient knowledge of all the problems involved in the negotiation, commercial, technical and contractual, to enable him to make an intelligent contribution to each item discussed and to direct and coordinate the activities of the functional specialists.

DUTIES

The specific duties of the team leader are to:

1 Select the remainder of the negotiating team
2 Prepare the negotiating plan
3 Conduct the negotiations and in particular take all decisions on:
    (a) Timing and level of concessions
    (b) Selection of items to be traded off against each other
    (c) Calling of team review meetings
    (d) Requests for an adjournment
4 Make the bargain with the other side
5 Ensure that the bargain is properly recorded
6 Issue the negotiating report.

Additionally, as a leader, he has the more general functions of leadership to perform: of generating enthusiasm in his team, maintaining their morale under all conditions and by his own example obtaining from each the maximum contribution which he is capable of providing.

The team leader is there to lead and, within the scope of his authority, to make decisions. Certain of those decisions will involve the question as to whether a particular risk should or should not be taken, and the team leader can expect to receive advice on the issue concerned from the appropriate specialist on the team. Ultimately the decision is for the team leader to take and he must be permitted to go against the specialist advice if he considers this necessary.

It is in this respect that the departmental organization of a company can be prejudicial to the proper conduct of negotiations. The specialist will come from one of the functional departments, e.g. engineering, law, finance. Whilst his technical advice must be considered by the team leader (or the specialist dismissed from the team as being someone in whom the leader has no confidence), this does not mean that the leader must act upon that advice. The engineer may, for example, advise that the company's product does not conform with a particular requirement of the buyer's specification. But the decision whether to ask for an amendment prior to contract and risk losing the business, or to take the risk and seek to negotiate a concession during the course of the contract, should that become necessary, is for the team leader to take. If he is in any doubt he refers back to his own line manager.

19.3 Visits by senior personnel

A problem which often arises on major contract negotiations abroad is whether or not at some stage to involve a person senior in the company hierarchy to the team leader, such as a group board director. In negotiating contracts with overseas ministries, government corporations and similar bodies, it may be necessary to do this in order to gain access at the highest political level. It also may be appropriate if the assistance is being sought of a minister from the UK government to visit the territory concerned to support the supplier's efforts. The following are the suggested guidelines for such visits which can be helpful but which can equally be disastrous:

1 The advisability and timing of the visit should be left to the negotiating team leader.
2 The visit must be handled in such a way to reinforce and not derogate from the authority of the team leader. There should be no suggestion of opening up a new line of communication with the visiting director so that he can be used to overrule the team leader's decisions. This applies both to the client and to the agent.
3 The visiting director must allow himself time to be briefed and for the possible postponement of appointments. His schedule must be kept flexible and not overloaded with a rapid succession of meetings. If necessary he must be prepared to stay an extra few days to secure that vital appointment remembering, that the people he wants to see will have many other important matters to deal with.
4 The local British embassy must be informed in advance of the proposed visit and intended meetings with ministers and their support enlisted.

5 The visiting director must take the trouble even if it is only on the outward journey to inform himself of the basic political, economic, religious and social facts relating to the overseas territory.

6 Never must the visiting director appear as patronizing to the local minister or senior government officials whom he meets. He may be at or near the head of a major UK company but there are many other companies in the world. There is only one President or Prime Minister of that territory. His approach should be courteous and respectful but firm on the points he wishes to establish.

19.4 The negotiating team overseas

There are some rules which apply specifically to the behaviour of the negotiating team when they are in an overseas territory, especially one which differs significantly from Europe or North America. The following table lists these:

Do	Do Not
1 Be sensitive to the local social, business and religious customs	1 Go native
2 Be aware of the local political scene and how it may affect both your project happening and your chances of success	2 Involve yourself in any form of political activity or express publicly your opinion on political affairs
3 Behave courteously and be respectful to ministers and officials	3 Be subservient or allow yourself to be intimidated or overawed by their status or by the shock tactics they may use to impress upon you their superiority or power
4 Prepare yourself in advance for all meetings and stay calm	4 Be surprised at the unexpected or allow yourself to get flustered
5 Take every opportunity to get out and about and talk to people	5 Succumb to local temptations!
6 Have as team members those whose personality and technical abilities are likely to fit in with those with whom negotiations will be conducted	6 Allow your expert, however brilliant, to patronize the client or try to teach him his business
7 Be flexible and willing to adjust to their conceptions provided you can still obtain your objectives even if the means are different	7 Be rigid and insist that yours is the only way
8 Be careful on security of your papers and discreet in referring to people, particularly your contacts, by name	8 Be eager to show off your limited knowledge

9 Listen to your agent's advice with an open mind

10 Be patient

9 Try and teach him his business or impose your preconceived ideas

10 Leave the territory unguarded at critical stages even if you miss a board meeting or your holiday

20 COMMUNICATION AND SECURITY

20.1 Communication

The communication which is referred to here is that between a negotiating team operating away from home base and their home management. The need to communicate arises from the requirements of the negotiating team and the home office:

1 The negotiating team require:
    (a) Factual information
    (b) Specialist advice
    (c) Management decisions
2 The home office requires reports on how the negotiations are proceeding.

Preferably such communications should be minimized, for the following reasons:

1 Communication links are not necessarily secure (see p. 142).
2 Even with modern methods of communication, the need to communicate inevitably imposes a delay in the negotiating team being able to make a decision. This puts the negotiator at a definite disadvantage against a competitor who is able to make decisions on the spot, and creates a bad impression on the buyer.
3 It is difficult for a negotiating team to be able to convey an adequate impression of the problem with which they are faced and of the atmosphere within which the negotiations are being conducted. When therefore they receive the advice and/or decision from home base it is frequently inappropriate in the particular circumstances.
4 Frequent reference back to home base weakens both the negotiating team's own morale and their standing in the eyes of the overseas buyer.

In preparing his negotiating plan, positive action should be taken therefore by the negotiating team leader to reduce the need to communicate with home office to an absolute minimum. In so far as information and advice are concerned, the following suggestions are made as to how this can be achieved:

1 The necessary back-up data is assembled to enable answers to be given to each question which it is foreseen that the buyer may raise. For this purpose all prior correspondence, notes of meetings, etc., should be reviewed and note taken of issues which have arisen on similar negotiations in the past. Consideration should certainly be given to having the capability of the negotiator being able to communicate via his laptop to files which are held on his computer at head office. This will be valuable in saving time and make it unnecessary for the negotiator to carry paper files around with him.

2 Points on which it is known that any competitor may be regarded as superior to the supplier are similarly reviewed and information put together to rebut such criticisms.
3 Supporting information and precedents which may be helpful in negotiation are collected. Some examples would be:
   (a) Precedents of clauses from other contracts
   (b) Copies of official records showing changes in wages and material costs since the last order/tender with this particular purchaser
   (c) Specimen test specifications of the type which will be provided to the purchaser on inspection and acceptance.
4 Sufficient data is assembled to enable price changes resulting from simple amendments to the specification to be calculated on the spot. This would include unit rates and prices for such work as cabling, trenching and plant installation. In particular the detail of the steps by which the costs have been developed into a selling price must be available in a form convenient for easy reference. A suggested format is given in Figure 20.1.
5 If the contract is to be subject to other than English law, advice is obtained in advance from a local lawyer so that the effect of any major differences can be assessed. Similarly the taxation position is investigated to ascertain whether. or not the supplier will be subject to sales tax, tax on profits earned in the foreign territory, etc.

The requirement for reference to home management for decisions can be reduced if not eliminated by the way in which the negotiating brief is prepared (see Chapter 21). There are, however, two major exceptions to the general rule of minimal communication.

1 The opening phase of the negotiation shows that no bargain is foreseeable within the terms of the negotiating brief. This is discussed in detail in Section 26.3.
2 The negotiations are prolonged and interim action is required to be taken at home. In that event the safest course is to send back the member of the negotiating team within whose field the action required falls. If the technical discussions have resolved the issues on the equipment to be supplied and delivery is tight, then the technical negotiator might return home early to enable editing, and even advance ordering, to proceed whilst contractual discussions continue.

   It is recognized that this course of action may be expensive and at times inconvenient, but it is the only sure way in which the correct information is likely to be transmitted. In addition, secondary questions, which the receipt of such information generates back home, can be answered first hand and with the minimum of delay.

REPORTS FOR HOME OFFICE

Inevitably management at home are concerned to know of the progress their negotiators are making. Managers who are accustomed to daily contact with their staff, by telephone if not face to face, do not take kindly to a situation in which they feel out of touch. They hate the uncertainty of not knowing.

Reporting is not necessarily an easy matter. It has all the disadvantages enumerated earlier as applying generally to communications and the special problem of being concise without

Plant and materials

Unit cost ex-works	Quantity	Total ex-works cost	Freight and insurance	Duty	Commercial overheads	Profit	Agent's commission	FCBD premium	Interest and bank charge	Selling price

Installation

Basic man-hour rate	Premium rate	Living allowance	Total man-hours	Total cost	Commercial overheads	Profit	Agent's commission	ECBD premium	Interest and bank charge	Selling price

Plant hire

Basic hire rate	Fuel	Total weeks	Total basic cost	Freight and insurance	Total cost	Commercial overheads	Profit	Agent's commission	Interest and bank charge	Selling price

Figure 20.1 Composition of selling price

being misleading. If delivery is a key issue and the team leader reports back that he has settled for a period which hardly satisfies the supplier's minimum negotiating objective, the manager is at once concerned. He wonders why the negotiators have not done better. At best he will react to the situation by requesting clarification and suspending judgement until it is received. At worst the manager will jump to the conclusion that the negotiator has let him down and will initiate panic action accordingly, possibly to the extent of flying off immediately to the scene of the negotiations.

In fact the negotiating team may well have achieved an acceptable result, for example, by tying the delivery promise to the performance by the purchaser of certain obligations, such as the supply of full technical data to enable the supplier to proceed within stated time-scales, which the negotiator knows in practice the purchaser cannot achieve. The shorter delivery promise may be a device to enable the purchaser to place the order within authority he has already received from his board and without having to go back for revised authority which would lose the buyer face and perhaps lead to the negotiations being reopened with a competitor.

The old saying 'no news is good news' applies also to negotiations. If these are proceeding within the negotiating brief then there seems little point in the negotiator saying so. However, security was earlier identified as a motivational drive, and if the home manager's need for security can be satisfied by a simple communication saying 'Discussion proceeding. All well' then no harm is done. But for the reasons already given, any detailed reporting by telex, or e-mail, or telephone on specific issues is strongly opposed; it leaves far too much room for misunderstanding. The manager ought to be able to work on the basis that the team leader will only come back to him in specific terms if he finds that he cannot satisfy the terms of the negotiating brief.

Throughout this chapter reference has been made to the negotiator communicating with his manager, and this has intended to imply a single line of communication between the negotiating team leader and the manager having the profit-and-loss responsibility for the contract. Parallel lines of communication between other team members and their respective functional departmental heads should not be permitted. If, say, the lawyer on the team wishes to communicate with the company's legal adviser then he should do so through the team leader and the message should similarly be relayed at the other end from the manager to the legal adviser.

This may sound a laborious and even time-wasting procedure but it is essential if the team leader is to retain control of the negotiations. To start with, he must approve of the need to communicate and check the security aspects. Secondly, any request for advice is bound to contain a mixture of pure professionalism and commercial risk taking. For example, the drafting of a clause on exclusion of liability for consequential damages must be related to the degree of risk that such damages could be recovered and the company's attitude towards the taking of that risk. This is not a matter which the lawyers can settle on their own,. and any communication to home office for advice needs to describe both the practicalities and commercial implications of the risk issue as well as the legal position on recovery of damages.

Finally the team leader should never be put in the position in which a team member has communicated with his functional chief at home and obtained support for his views which he then uses as a weapon in argument against the team leader who may well, in the company's hierarchy, be junior to the functional head.

The rule as to a single line of communication between the team leader and his line manager at home is one therefore that should never be broken.

20.2 Security

The problem with security is that no one takes it seriously until he has personally been involved in an incident in which he has been the victim – if security is going to be taken seriously this demands constant care and attention especially at moments of relaxation.

A person's approach to security will differ according to whether he believes that deliberate attempts will be made by others to obtain confidential information from him or that people may simply take advantage of an act of carelessness. The first instance is generally rare, confined to certain territories and reasonably well publicized. The negotiator knows in advance to expect bugged hotel rooms and searches of his luggage, and to avoid contact with local nationals whose objective may be to obtain evidence of compromising behaviour.

Much more difficult is the territory which is seemingly innocent and in which therefore the negotiator is liable to be that much more careless. This includes the UK. If asked the question directly, 'Would you expect the buyer to take advantage of a lapse in your security?', the negotiator may well reply 'I suppose he might.' This would still not prevent him from going to lunch and leaving papers in the buyer's office in an unlocked briefcase!

Security in those circumstances is very much a matter of habit and it is suggested that the negotiator should adopt the following habits:

1 Do not talk business in a place where conversation can easily be overheard and there is no idea of who is listening. This applies especially to aircraft, trains, hotel lounges and chauffeur-driven cars. Do not assume that others can understand only their own language.
2 Do not put temptation in the buyer's way. Specifically do not:
    (a) Leave papers on the table in his office or conference room when at lunch. If they are left in a personal office or conference room make sure the buyer cannot re-enter first.
    (b) Ask him to make copies of any document or arrange for him to do any typing, unless it is in order for him to take an extra copy for his own use.
    (c) Have the negotiating brief with the figures clearly displayed open on top of papers. He may be very good at reading upside down.
3 Do not trust hotel porters with cables or hotel/public telex operators. This may run the risk of the message being sold to the competitor or the foreign buyer. In some countries this is a recognized trade.
4 Do not assume that people employed by a personal agent or local company are necessarily to be trusted. Their nationalistic ties with the foreign buyer may be stronger than their commercial loyalty or they may simply be underpaid.
5 Do not leave business papers lying about in public or hotel rooms, and do keep those of a strictly confidential nature securely locked away.

Sometimes the negotiator may be offered information of a confidential nature regarding either the competitor or the buyer. How should he react?

It is suggested that the first reaction should be one of suspicion. Is the information a 'plant' intended to mislead the negotiator? Remember it may be so, even though the actual informant believes it to be genuine; he may have been deceived as well.

Only if there is complete satisfaction that the information is genuine would it be prudent to use it and even then with the greatest of care. If it really is genuine then this is a source of further information which will have to be concealed. Neither competitor nor the buyer must ever be allowed to suspect the transference of information. Alternatively, if it is after all a 'plant', the person concerned must not be allowed to think he has succeeded; preferably he should remain in a state of uncertainty.

An example would be a case in which the supplier had received information as to the buyer's budget. In negotiating the price the supplier would act initially as if he believed the budget to be higher than the information indicated. If the information is indeed correct then the supplier can allow himself gradually to be persuaded by the buyer that he cannot afford to pay more than the lower figure. If the information is false then the supplier's figure will be nearer the truth and he will have minimized any reduction in the upper level of the bargaining zone (see p. 317). The supplier will also have taught the buyer that he is not easily fooled.

CODES AND E-MAIL ENCRYPTION

Communications between the negotiating team operating abroad and their home office may be subject to surveillance by the authorities of the country in which the team is operating, as well as possible exposure to the team's competitors. Items which are politically sensitive or commercially revealing should be coded, therefore, in a way which will at least make it difficult for either the authorities or competitors to interpret and would not expose the team or their agent to political action. Such issues would include:

1 Names of any persons who are politically or commercially sensitive. This would include the supplier's agent, government ministers, the supplier's competitors and top personnel within customer's organization.
2 Price level and discounts.
3 Acceptability or otherwise of particular propositions.

If any form of coding is to be used then it should be easy for the recipient to interpret, not be capable of being misunderstood and still make sense as a message. The last point is important since otherwise it may not be accepted for transmission and could certainly arouse strong suspicions.

The need for coding must therefore be identified at the planning stage of the negotiations and the system to be used agreed between the team leader and his home manager. Code names may be given to persons whose identity is sensitive and a numbers translation agreed.

An example of the use of a simple code might be:

Coded message: 'Uncle still not well. Paul believes another visit to hospital may be necessary. Will make arrangements to-morrow. Do not worry as condition still amenable to treat-ment.'

Translation: Customer still not satisfied. Agent's contact man thinks further discount necessary and will make offer tomorrow. Proposals still within negotiating brief.'

If the facilities can be made available, consider instead of using a code to use e-mail with encryption. Both a public and private key are used for this purpose. The sender uses the recipient's public key when he encrypts the message and the receiver uses his private key to decrypt it. Most Internet service providers give users access to some form of encryption. Again, if this method is to be used it must be planned in advance.

21 THE NEGOTIATING BRIEF

21.1 Formulation of the brief

A distinction is drawn between the negotiating brief which consists of the instructions given to the team leader by management and the negotiating plan which is developed by the negotiating team and represents the manner in which they propose to implement those instructions.

The negotiating brief is prepared in writing and signed by the manager having profit and loss responsibility for the outcome of the negotiations in question. It may vary in form from a short informal memorandum to a more lengthy formal paper. In general the simpler and shorter the brief the smaller the risk of misunderstanding and the greater the chance that the instructions will be followed.

Although the preparation of the brief is the responsibility of management, its terms must be acceptable to the team leader as representing a feasible target at which to aim and allowing him sufficient latitude within which to negotiate. He and possibly other team members should participate in the formulation of the brief.

The brief should:

1 Define the negotiating objective in terms of the major issues to be discussed
2 State the minimum acceptable level for each of the major items
3 Establish the time period within which the negotiations should be concluded
4 Identify the team leader and other members of the negotiating team
5 Set up the lines of communication and the reporting system.

The format of the brief will be common to each of our negotiating situations, selling, procurement and contract dispute, although the details to be included will obviously vary. The example and notes which follow deal with a brief for a sales negotiating team about to go abroad to negotiate an export contract for which their company has earlier submitted a tender. It is believed that the buyer has called the seller and one other firm for contract negotiations. The seller also believes that there is very little between his offer and that of his competitor as regards price.

21.2 The negotiating objective

The negotiating objective will usually be expressed in terms of the expected return on sales, taking into account the risks involved in performing the contract and the contract terms. At the time of tender, allowance will have been made in the price for terms which are more unfavourable to the seller than those the risks of which are allowed for in his standard commercial overheads. It would be an objective of the negotiations to persuade the buyer to amend these terms to ones which are more favourable to the seller in exchange for a reduction in the risk allowance made in the contract price.

As an example the original tender was submitted at a price of £348,000 which included a margin on sales of 42.5 per cent arrived at as follows:

Commercial overheads	15%
Profit	12.5%
Negotiating margin	15%, made of:
Terms of payment	5%
Delay damages	2%
Additional warranty period	1%
Margin for price reduction	5%
Time costs allowance	2%

It will be remembered that in arriving at the level of his first offer in a hold-back situation, the seller would have submitted a bid which was optimal in relation to his estimate of the concessions he was likely to have to give the buyer in order to obtain the maximum likely concessions from the buyer and the time it would take to secure the contract. The seller has assumed that he will need to make a concession of 5 per cent of the contract price in order to secure a price which contains his above-stated overhead and profit margins and that the time costs will amount to 2 per cent of the contract price.

The negotiating margin for the terms of contract was arrived at by examining each of the purchaser's conditions which adversely affect the seller as follows.

TERMS OF PAYMENT

The buyer's terms are 80 per cent on interim payments, 10 per cent on takeover and 10 per cent at the end of the defects liability period.

The seller would normally expect 90 per cent on interim payments, 5 per cent on takeover and 5 per cent at the end of the defects liability period. He estimates the difference between the two will cost him 5 per cent.

DELAY DAMAGES

The buyer has asked for 1 per cent of the contract price per week to a maximum of 15 per cent.

The seller's normal terms are 0.5 per cent per week to a maximum of 5 per cent. The seller estimates that the real possibility of delay is four weeks and the difference could cost him 2 per cent of the contract price. He has considered carefully the completion period proposed by the buyer in his enquiry and is satisfied that he can meet it unless something goes horribly wrong. The provisions in the buyer's contract terms as to extensions of time are reasonable enough to protect him against events genuinely outside his control but he takes the risk of his subcontractors.

DEFECTS LIABILITY PERIOD

The buyer has asked for a 24-month defects period while the seller's normal terms of business are for twelve months. He estimates the additional risk is equivalent to 1 per cent of the contract price.

The negotiating objective would then be stated as:

- Improve the terms of payment to at least 85 per cent on interim payments and only 5 per cent to be held during the defects period
- Reduce the delay penalty to at the most 0.75 per cent per week
- Reduce the defects period to, at the most, 18 months. This would help also with the earlier release of the retention money.

For each of these objectives secured the seller would be willing to grant the buyer a proportionate reduction in the contract price within the allowance included in the tender if this was demanded by the buyer.

21.3 Minimum acceptable terms

The negotiating brief for these might read:

- *Price level:* Maximum reduction in profit after concession of the negotiating margin on price and provided that the negotiations are concluded within one month after the expiry of the validity period of the tender is 2.5 per cent.
- *Terms of Payment, delay damages and defects liability period:* The buyer's terms can only be accepted provided that the allowances made in the tender are retained in full.

21.4 Period for negotiations

The validity period of the tender is 90 days as requested by the buyer. The 2 per cent allowed in the tender for time costs, including the discount factor, is based on the negotiations lasting for four months from the submission of the bid, i.e. the bidder would be prepared to extend validity at no additional cost to the buyer for one month. After that the bidder would have to requote. It is now six weeks from the submission of the bid and assuming negotiations start two weeks from now this would allow a maximum of two months for the negotiations to be concluded.

21.5 The negotiating team

The brief should state the names and job titles of the team members and indicate any duties they will be required to perform outside of their own function. In the example the brief might read:

Team Leader   Mr Jones, Export Sales Manager
Team members   Mr Brown, Assistant Manager Systems
                 Engineering
                 Mr Smith, Assistant Legal Adviser

Mr Brown will cover all production aspects in addition to engineering and is responsible for obtaining instructions from the production manager for this purpose. Mr Smith will look after the financial requirements and is responsible for obtaining instructions from the export finance manager.

21.6 Communications and reporting

The brief might read:

Mr Jones will report to me on this negotiation and I will be responsible for advising functional and departmental heads of any issues affecting them. In my absence Mr Williams will assume this responsibility.
Signed .... General Manager, Engineering Contracts Division

The above is necessarily simplified and in practice there would be likely to be other terms of the contract which would require negotiation but the same principles would apply. What the supplier has to watch is that there will be a relationship between several terms so that what is agreed on one will affect the other. For example, whatever is stated in the contract regarding the definition of completion and the tests on completion will affect the risk of paying the delay damages. The risks on defects liability will be affected by what is stated in the defects liability clause. No unconditional agreement therefore should be reached on any of these issues until all the ramifications have been explored so that, ideally, there should be a single bargain covering all of them.

22 THE NEGOTIATING PLAN

The functions of the negotiating plan are to:

1 Define the initial strategy ⌣
2 Develop the supporting arguments✓
3 Identify the data required to support such arguments ⌄
4 Allocate responsibility for the collection of such data⌄
5 Decide on the location for the negotiations ✓
6 Ensure that the appropriate administrative arrangements have been made.

22.1 Definition of initial strategy

THE SUPPLIER HAS SUBMITTED AN OFFER

In relation to each issue which has been identified as forming part of the negotiating area, the supplier is likely to have at least some knowledge of the purchaser's views. Obviously he knows that his own initial offer is not wholly acceptable. There are then broadly three possibilities:

1 The purchaser has replied with proposals of his own. Alternatively, if the supplier has taken objection to a term of the purchaser's call for bids, the purchaser has stated that he insists on that term. In either event the negotiating area is defined.
2 From discussions or preliminary informal encounters with the purchaser, the supplier has been advised on the items which the purchaser disputes and why, but not the precise terms which the purchaser is going to demand.
3 The supplier merely knows his own offer is in some respects unacceptable to the purchaser.

In regard to 1, the supplier's initial strategy is to defend the position he has taken in his offer. Specifically he does not make any concessions (p. 166).

With situations 2 and 3, whilst similarly defending his own position, the supplier must explore the purchaser's views and seek to identify the width of the gap between the two sides and the intensity with which the purchaser objects to the supplier's proposals.

In all three instances the supplier must seek to reassess his preliminary estimate of the purchaser's concession factor. In the negotiating brief example on p. 146 the supplier would seek to establish whether or not his estimate of 5 per cent for the price concession factor and four months for the negotiating period was correct or not.

THE SUPPLIER HAS RECEIVED AN OFFER

If the supplier has received an offer his initial strategy will depend upon whether or not he has already made any reply which defines the terms the supplier would be willing to accept.

1 The supplier has replied stating his own terms. The negotiating area is defined and the supplier's initial strategy is to explore the purchaser's position without making concessions.
2 The supplier has not replied with a statement of his own terms. His initial strategy is to persuade the purchaser to reveal the strength of his own commitment to the terms of his offer, whilst making the minimum disclosure of his own position.

22.2 Supporting arguments

The actual argument which the supplier will use to support his strategy on any issue will be particular to that issue and to the negotiation in question. An example may clarify the way in which it is suggested that the supplier should approach the problem.

Let us take the two issues on the terms of contract, relating to the level of delay damages and the length of the defects liability period referred to in the preceding chapter on the negotiating brief. The plant which is the subject of the contract is basically a standard item for supplier and he has supplied it previously to other purchasers. He has not identified any unusual risks either in design or manufacture.

The supplier must be careful in how he develops his arguments for reducing the level of damages and the length of the defects period, otherwise he will lay himself open to the argument from the buyer that he has no confidence either in his ability to complete on time or in the quality of his product.

It is assumed that from the enquiry documents the supplier will have an understanding of the purpose for which the plant or system is required by the buyer and therefore will be able to estimate approximately the likely loss that the buyer would incur by late completion. It seems unlikely that the rate of 1 per cent per week proposed by the buyer represents a genuine estimate of his probable loss since £3,480 per week would equate to an annual loss of profit of about £180,000, which is almost 50 per cent of the value of the contract. It would rather appear therefore that the rate of damages has been chosen as a stick with which to encourage the supplier to complete on time – not in practice all that unusual, although not legally correct.[1] The seller's plan would be to question the buyer as to why he wants damages of that level. If the supplier can establish that what he suspects is the case, namely that the purpose of the level of damages is to provide the seller with confidence in the seller's likelihood of completing on time, through the use of a stick, then the seller can look at other ways of providing the seller with security. For example he could produce evidence in a document signed by the company secretary, of the number of times the seller has been contractually late in completing similar contracts in the last ten years, which hopefully will demonstrate the supplier's good record of completing on time. He could then argue that with that record a stick of 1 per cent per week is unnecessary and that the supplier's proposal of half that amount is adequate.

On the extended period of defects liability, the argument would be that it is the first twelve months after the plant goes into operation which are critical. After that there are always going to be arguments if anything goes wrong as to whether it was due to a defect or not and the extra period is again really unnecessary for the buyer's protection.

What the seller will be looking to do is finally to offer the buyer a packaged deal under which if the buyer accepts the seller's proposal on penalty then the seller would be prepared to offer him an extended defects period of 18 months. Although this is unlikely to be immediately successful it ought to point the way to a compromise solution.

The essential point is that whatever the issue the arguments are directed towards the seller's belief as to the buyer's views and problems, in this example of being provided with security, and not related to the seller's problems which are of no concern to the buyer. It is not a valid argument to say as a supplier that the price cannot be reduced because of the level of costs. The costs are the supplier's problem, not the buyer's. It is, however, a valid argument that if the buyer is wanting the supplier to accept a particular risk then the buyer must expect to pay for it and that it may be more economic for the buyer to agree on sharing the risk.

22.3 Supporting data

From the nature of the arguments to be presented will come the definition of the supporting data required. In the above example it would be the statement certified by the company secretary. Also, if it can be produced, similar evidence on the incidence of defects in the second twelve months after completion of similar plants compared to the first twelve months. It may be that the supplier can obtain evidence of this from other purchasers of similar plant.

If the issue is related to the period for completion, then a programme in network or barchart form would be needed.

The plan needs to allocate responsibility for the collection of such data and its presentation in the required format.

22.4 The location of the negotiations

For both sides there is usually a strong preference for 'playing at home'. The environment will be familiar, it is easier to bring in additional support, the 'home side' are in charge of the administrative arrangements including those for hospitality, there is the psychological advantage that 'they have come to you', and the saving in costs for hotels and air fares.

However, there are some advantages in 'playing away'. The negotiators can devote their whole time to the negotiation without being distracted, it avoids the risk that the negotiator for the other side can argue that he does not have authority since there is the option if he tries that of insisting on going to the top, the team leader does not have his own management on his back and is able to exercise a greater degree of freedom within the overall scope of his negotiating brief.

22.5 Administrative arrangements

If we are 'playing at home' then it is up to us to ensure that the arrangements for the meetings have been made in a way which is conducive to agreement being reached. Specific points to be considered are:

1 The choice of the meeting room. It should be large enough to accommodate comfortably all taking part, well ventilated and should not have a telephone.
2 There should be at least one side room which can be used for an adjournment meeting, and which should have a telephone.
3 A secretary should be available in a nearby office for taking messages, arranging for photo-copying and typing up draft proposals.
4 If appropriate, visual aid facilities should be available and although most negotiators will have a pocket calculator with them, a larger machine with a print-out facility is often useful.
5 Refreshments should be ordered in such a way that they create natural breaks. Ideally they should be served in an ante-room to give a chance for informal discussions.
6 The table and seating plan should be worked out in advance. The author's own preference is to avoid having a 'head of the table' and to have the two sides opposite each other with the respective team leaders in the middle.

If we are 'playing away' then unless we are fortunate enough to have a subsidiary company operating in the territory or we can arrange facilities through our local agent, we must be pre-pared to operate on our own and to provide our own back-up. We should therefore give attention to the following:

1 Typing facilities. It is a great advantage if one member of the team can type reasonably well so that drafts and telexes, etc., can be produced quickly. A typed telex is much more accept-able to a telex operator and therefore much more likely to be sent that day than one in an unfamiliar form of handwriting.
2 Headed notepaper and visiting cards. The latter may have to be specially produced to give the senior members of the team titles which will impress the other side as to their status. In many countries a manager is a nothing compared to a director.
3 Staying at a hotel which has the best available business facilities. The team leader should if possible have a suite so that one room can be used for private discussions.
4 A file of newspaper and magazine cuttings appropriate to the project in which we are inter-ested, which is updated daily. A typical file might contain data on:
   (a) Economic situation in the country
   (b) Recent finance deals concluded or financial offers made on other projects
   (c) Inflation
   (d) Rates of pay for grades of local staff and labour
   (e) Union activities
   (f) Reports on the industry in which the supplier is operating
   (g) Local contractors of possible interest to the supplier
   (h) Changes in laws, insurance regulations, workers benefits, etc.

5 Other portable office equipment such as typewriter or laptop computer, calculator with print-out facility, stapling machine, punch, file covers, typing ruled and graph paper, ruler, scissors, eraser and visiting card file. The author's own practice is to have one brief-case which contains permanently all of these items, other than the typewriter (but including a laptop) and to add to it with experience, so that one can operate to the greatest degree practicable independently of local facilities which may be unavailable, expensive or, in the case of typing, constitute a security risk.

Note

1. If the rate of damages is substantially in excess of anything which the purchaser would suffer, then the damages would be considered a penalty, which in English law is unenforceable.

23 CONDUCTING THE REHEARSAL

As the final stage of their preparations for the negotiation both sides need to test out their plans in a rehearsal for the live performance. If the time can be allocated and the importance of the negotiations justify it, the rehearsal should be made a formal negotiating session with a team representing the other side, drawn from the appropriate departments within the firm's organization. It is surprising how often a session of this nature can develop more 'needle' than the real event.

23.1 Value of the rehearsal

The value of a mock negotiation of this nature is that not only will it expose any weaknesses in the negotiating plan, it will also constitute a training exercise for the negotiating team. The whole performance can be recorded on videotape and later played back to expose deficiencies in technique of which the participants were totally unaware, for example, irritating mannerisms, poor control of facial expression, muddled presentation of arguments, excessive use of English colloquialisms in talking to foreigners.

This is the ideal and it is appreciated that time and expense may not permit it to be achieved, although I hold strongly the view that it is only by training of this nature that a company's success ratio in negotiation can be improved significantly. Considering its importance to a company's profitability, it is remarkable that the need for training in negotiation continues largely to go unrecognized, except for the type of training which consists of learning from mistakes made in practice, the cost of which must exceed that of any training programme.

However, if a full session cannot be arranged the team leader should insist as a minimum on a colleague playing the part of a 'devil's advocate' and using the arguments which he thinks the other side will adopt in order to attack the firm's case. This may cause the team leader to recognize the need to change the presentation or strengthen certain arguments and identify the requirement for additional supporting data. Scrutiny by the 'devil's advocate' of such data which the team leader is intending to show the other side will often reveal inadequacies or the inclusion of statements which the firm would find embarrassing.

*P*ART *3*

STRUCTURE AND SEQUENCE OF THE NEGOTIATIONS

24 INTRODUCTION TO PART THREE

All recognized works on negotiation emphasize planning as the first phase of the negotiations. We have now concluded that phase and are entering what many people would consider the negotiations 'proper', that is, when the two parties either meet or correspond with each other. It is interesting to note that most books on the subject seem to exclude the possibility of the negotiators sending or receiving written proposals in advance of, or sometimes in substitution for, verbal ones as if negotiation was only about face-to-face meetings.[1] Of course in most negotiations face-to-face discussions will be held at some time but often only after the ground has been prepared by written communications. Negotiations for a sales contract will only be held after the supplier has submitted his quotation, usually in writing; negotiations on a claim will only follow its written submission. The formulation of the written approach is as much a part of negotiations as the face-to-face dialogue.

All books seem to agree that there are stages in the negotiation process following the planning although not on precisely how many or the names by which they should be known. What does seem to be missing from most of the lists is the vital stage of 'the opening' which, as referred to above, may well be in writing. It is only then that the side to whom the opening is presented, either in writing or verbally, is first placed in the position of being able to assess what the opener wants, and to some extent from the language used, how strongly the opener is attached to achieving those wants. Then, at least in commercial negotiations, there is usually a pause while both sides review what they have learnt and decide on their next step – this is the review stage.

What follows next is a period of debate and search for mutually acceptable trade-offs at the conclusion of which either the shape of the final bargain starts to become clear or it is apparent that the parties are never going to reach agreement. I have called this stage the 'follow-up' since it follows up on the review after the opening. One experienced writer on negotiating refers to it as 'debate'[2] and it is true that most of this stage is spent on debate interspersed with further reviews as the negotiators check the position they have reached against their planned targets.

Assuming that the two sides still consider an agreement is feasible, this leads to the stage I refer to as 'identifying the bargain'. As a result of their debates so far, both parties can identify the conditional offers which are on the table and what they would have to do in return to turn those offers into firm agreements. 'If you will reduce the maximum of the delay penalty then we could consider accepting your proposals on the extensions of time clause': this sort of conditional offer raises the immediate question as to how much the reduction would have to be, but it does open the way for agreement to be reached. If the answer to that question is a figure to which the supplier either could agree or is near enough that he can see that agreement ought to be possible, and if there is no other factor still outstanding which would affect his overall risk assessment, then the supplier can feel that he is getting near to a bargain. The last point is vitally important on complex contract negotiations. It is tempting but highly inadvisable to conclude an agreement on one major area of risk while agreement on other such areas remains outstanding. They need to be coupled together so that the response could be 'Yes, that seems reasonable enough but before we go any further on that one we must deal with your proposals on liquidated damages for low performance which as they stand are unacceptable.' Again such a response is inviting the question 'In what way do you consider them not acceptable?', which would hopefully lead to a constructive dialogue on that issue also.

Note that throughout I have referred to *conditional* proposals or offers and during the follow-up stage that is the form which they should take. Whenever during this stage the term 'concession' is used in the text, it is meant in this conditional sense. The general form of the concession is 'If you could agree to X (i.e. the term which is important to me to secure), then I don't think we would have a problem with Y (i.e. the term which you want and which I am prepared, as part of an overall bargain, to trade for X) provided we can reach agreement on the other outstanding issues.'

It is recognized that bargaining in this way on the terms of an entire lengthy contract with a number of contentious issues is both tedious and involves the negotiator in keeping track of all the points, which is one of the reasons why it was suggested one member of the negotiating team should have the specific task of keeping the records of the discussions. Also periodically the team leader should call a recess so that the team can review where they have got to on each item and ensure that nothing gets overlooked. Remember also that in some circumstances it is not a question of exchanging an X for a Y but of collecting together a number of issues of lesser value to you but of higher value to him and exchanging all of them for the one that you really do want to secure. This is another reason for not giving anything away which could be of value to him; instead the approach is if he wants it then he has got to pay for it.

Finally we enter into the last stage of concluding and recording the bargain. Concluding the bargain means turning those conditional offers or concessions which both sides made earlier into definitive agreements which spell out not only the principles but also the detail. Additionally, it means going over what has been agreed while at the same time not allowing people to have third thoughts and say something like 'Just a moment, surely we didn't intend to include *any* industrial disputes as a reason for an extension of time', when it is quite clear that that was exactly what was intended by both sides. Maybe the purchaser should not have intended it but that is what he did and it was on that basis that the liquidated damages were agreed. Open that up again and you open up the whole bargain. Finally, if all the time and effort put into the negotiations is not to be wasted, then it is essential that the final agreement is recorded in writing and signed by both parties before they disperse. If that means working late or staying another night then so be it.

The stages in the negotiations following up from the preparation and planning are therefore:

1 The opening
2 The review
3 The follow-up
4 Identifying the bargain
5 Concluding and recording the bargain.

Notes

1. G. Kennedy, *Kennedy On Negotiation* (Aldershot: Gower, 1998) does not mention it. C. Karass, in *The Negotiating Game* (New York: Thomas Y. Crowell, 1970), refers on p. 84 to a choice of media 'always being available in negotiation', which clearly is not so in many commercial situations.
2. G. Kennedy, *Kennedy On Negotiation* p. 101.

25 THE OPENING

It is assumed that the preparation and planning for the negotiation has been carried out in the manner described in Part Two and that the time has now arrived for the initial presentation of our case in accordance with the terms of the negotiating plan. We may be in the situation that we are required to either take the initiative and submit a proposal ourselves or to respond to one already provided by the other side. In either event there are three possible ways in which we may proceed (although it may be found in practice that one or more of these are eliminated by the rules under which the negotiation is being conducted):

1 Submit a written proposal/answer without supplementing this by verbal discussion.
2 Submit a written proposal/answer to be supplemented by face-to-face discussions.
3 Present verbal proposals at a meeting.

25.1 Written proposal/answer without discussion

It is suggested that a written proposal/answer which is not to be supplemented by discussion should be submitted only when:

1 We have no other choice under the rules of the negotiation, e.g. tendering to a strict public authority which does not permit discussions with tenderers during the adjudication period.
2 We intend the written proposal/answer to be our initial move and also our last. An offer of discussions, whether expressed or implied from the wording of the proposal/answer, will be taken by the other side as a clear indication that the terms offered do not represent our final position. If they do, or we wish to give the impression that they do, the document should be complete in itself and drafted in such a way that:
    (a) If it is a proposal, it can be replied to on a simple yes/no basis without the need for clarification.
    (b) If it is an answer, it can be accepted without qualification in the terms in which it has been presented.

Whilst a written proposal has the obvious advantages of being complete, and permitting the expression of complex ideas in a detailed form which the recipient can read and reread until these have been fully assimilated, it has certain serious disadvantages:

1 It is a permanent record of our adoption of a certain line of action. As such it will give rise to a feeling of commitment and make it more difficult for us at a later stage to make concessions.[1] This difficulty will be reinforced if we have circulated the document widely within our own organization.[2]

2 Any written presentation is necessarily 'cold' and although English is a wonderfully flexible language it is often difficult to choose words which convey precisely the meaning intended and avoid misunderstandings or the giving of offence. This becomes even more difficult when the document must be translated and the finer shades of meaning will inevitably become lost in the process.

3 People tend to use more formal expressions and therefore state their positions with greater apparent firmness in written as opposed to verbal proposals.[3] Again, if the proposal is to be circulated within our own organization, we may feel it necessary to defend or explain our position at length which in turn will increase the degree of commitment we feel to that position.

As an example of the difference between written and verbal expressions of the same idea compare the two statements:

'We regret that we are unable to see our way clear to ...'

'I'm sorry, but I don't really see how we are going to ...'

Putting aside for the moment considerations of the need to maintain good interpersonal relationships between negotiators as a basis for a long-term continuing business relationship between the parties, it can be argued that the extent to which the use of formal communications is a disadvantage will vary inversely with the strength of our case. The stronger our case the more we stand to gain from a formality in communications between the two sides.[4]

The more formal the communication medium the more the negotiations will be centred upon objective interparty issues and the less time will be spent by the negotiators on self-presentation. Conversely the less formal the communication system, the more the negotiators are dealing face to face and the less easy it is for the stronger side to remain totally adamant and refuse any concessions. Interpersonal feelings between negotiators will tend to create what has been termed the *norm of reciprocity,* so that to some degree concessions will be made on emotional grounds which it would be difficult to justify on a strictly objective appraisal.[5] It is much easier to say no by letter, or even over the telephone, than it is to a person's face, particularly if that person is someone with whom one has already developed some form of interpersonal relationship.

However, reintroduction of the factor of a continuing business relationship between the two parties reduces significantly the value to us of this approach. The deliberate minimization of the element of interpersonal contact will prevent us from reaching informal agreements or understandings with the other side, will deprive us of access to information which the other side is only willing to release informally, and result in the contracts concluded being interpreted and applied strictly according to their legal terms.

Each of these factors may prove detrimental to our long-term interests. For instance, we can never be sure when the time will come that the only real safeguard which we have against the imposition of severe claims/penalties will be the goodwill existing between ourselves and the other negotiator, goodwill which has arisen out of the multitude of interpersonal relationships developed at all levels between our own and his staff.[6]

Given therefore the expectation of a continuing business relationship between the two sides it is suggested that we should:

1 As a norm seek to develop close interpersonal relationships with their negotiators.
2 When the issue is significant, and we possess the stronger case, increase to some degree the formality of the negotiation, perhaps by introducing a negotiator who is less well known to the other side and who is sufficiently senior to merit their respect.
3 Conversely, if we have the weaker case then we should maximize the informality of the negotiations, e.g. seek face-to-face discussions between negotiators whose interpersonal relationships are the best developed.

25.2 Written proposal/answer supplemented by verbal discussion

The advantages we would gain from the submission of written proposals in advance of a meeting with the other side are as follows:

1 They will provide an agenda for and give coherence to the discussion.
2 They will enable the other negotiator to consider the points raised, prepare for them and seek prior clarification of any items on which he is in doubt.
3 If the proposals embody any complex drafting, they allow this to be studied and, as necessary, permit advice to be taken from specialists who would not normally attend the discussions.
4 They provide a definite expression of the commitments into which we are willing to enter.

By defining the issues in advance, and giving time for preparation by the other party of his negotiating plan, our submission of prior written proposals means there may be a greater chance of decisions being reached in the meeting, and within a shorter time than would otherwise be the case.

This will only be so if the gap between our proposals and theirs is narrow and there is a substantial overlap between their respective minimum objectives. If the gap is wide, and little or no overlap exists between the respective minimum negotiating objectives, then the submission of written proposals in advance, to which we now feel a degree of commitment, will have the reverse effect, making agreement more difficult to reach and certainly prolonging the negotiations.

A common situation is that the bidder, having submitted his bid, is called by the purchaser for discussions – in reality, negotiations. It is to the purchaser's advantage if prior to the meeting he submits to the supplier an agenda for such negotiations. By so doing, he can dictate both the scope of the negotiations and also the order in which the various issues are to be discussed. The first issue he must decide on is whether the technical and commercial issues are to be dealt with together at the one meeting or whether they are to be the subject of separate meetings and if so which is to be taken first.

If the contract is for construct only to the purchaser's design, it is far less likely that there will be major technical issues to be discussed than if the supplier is to be responsible for design and there are performance requirements to be achieved. It is suggested that on a construct-only-type contract, the two sets of discussions could either be taken together at one meeting or the technical points could be discussed separately, but it is not significant whether such discussions precede or follow the commercial ones. If, however, the supplier is responsible for design and for meeting performance requirements, then it is fundamental to the award of the contract that the purchaser is satisfied with the designs, equipment specifications and guarantees on performance and reliability put forward by the supplier in his bid. If there are questions on what the supplier has put forward then these need to be settled before meaningful commercial negotiations can take place.

A possible disadvantage of the presentation of written proposals in advance, in addition to those referred to earlier, is that giving the other side advance notice enables them to prepare their plans with that much more knowledge of the line which we intend to follow. If their negotiators are inexperienced or naive, then giving them no advance warning may tempt them to deal with the issue unprepared, rather than admit their own inadequacy, and as a consequence lead them to concede more than they would have done had they been forewarned.

However, any advantage we may gain in this way will only be temporary if their negotiators, either on further reconsideration by themselves, or after censure by their own management, decide that they have been 'tricked'. This can only result in their passing through the resentment level (discussed on p. 82) and feeling a sense of continuing personal antagonism against our negotiators whom they consider to be responsible.

25.3 Verbal proposals only

The advantages of relying wholly on a verbal presentation at a meeting without the submission of any prior written statement are as follows:

1 Total flexibility – The negotiator can change his mind right up to the moment when he deals with the actual point concerned and even then he can strengthen or weaken his treatment of the issue dependent on his judgement of how the negotiations are going.
2 Exploration before commitment – The negotiator can test the reaction of his opposite number to a certain line before irrevocably committing himself to it.
3 Use of emotion – The negotiator can use emotion in order to emphasize a particular point or to disarm criticism and avoid giving offence.
4 The association by the other side of the integrity of the proposals with the personal integrity of the negotiator – A person's belief in the validity of a statement is strongly influenced by his belief in the veracity of the person making the statement.

Bacon expressed much the same thoughts when he suggested that to 'deal in person is good when a man's face breedeth regard; or in tender cases where a man's eye upon the countenance of him with whom he speaketh may give him direction how far to go: and generally where a man will reserve to himself liberty either to disavow or to expound'.[7]

In any event, even if the supplier has submitted no written proposals, he should at the least ensure that there is an agenda agreed with the purchaser in advance for the meeting. As suggested earlier, it is always an advantage to be the one who prepares the agenda as he decides on the items to be discussed and the order in which they are taken. It is the purchaser who should do this, but if he has not done so it is always open to the supplier to put forward his own agenda.

The order of the agenda will obviously vary from one negotiating situation to another but there are broadly three ways in which it can be prepared:

- The easy items on which there is likely to be little disagreement can be taken first. This can have the advantage of relaxing the negotiators and getting the negotiations off to a good start. If it's the first time that the parties have met, it provides a useful opportunity for them to get to know each other. The disadvantage is that if the negotiators start in the morning it means that the difficult and contentious items will be taken late in the day when the negotiators are likely to be tired.
- The most contentious item can be taken first, often, on a sales negotiation, the price, on the basis that once it's over the other items can be got through relatively quickly so the negotiations end on a 'high'. If the negotiations are starting in the morning the advantage is that the negotiators are fresh for handling the most difficult issues. Against this, if the negotiators are meeting for the first time, it means that they will be going in to talk about those items 'cold'.
- The order can be mixed so that one or more items on which we expect him to give us concessions can be followed by ones on which we expect to have to make concessions to him. If this approach is followed then it is again suggested that the more difficult issues are left to later.

Probably the most important factors in deciding which order to choose are the extent to which the negotiators already know and are comfortable with each other and the time which the negotiations are expected to last. If only one day has been allocated then you do not want to start discussing, say, the price late in the afternoon or early evening. It should be taken much earlier, say, no later than immediately after the lunch break. If two days have been set aside for the negotiations, then start with the contentious items first thing on the second day.

The disadvantages which are inherent in the concept of flexibility are:

1 Use by the negotiator of his opposite number's actions, remarks or even facial expressions, as a cue to the level which the negotiator selects for any demand and the firmness with which he pursues it. Lacking any definitive commitment in the form of a written proposal known to his opposite number, the negotiator must rely primarily on personalistic motivation – his own level of aspiration – for providing him with support. To that extent he is much more vulnerable to determined resistance by his opposite number which, as discussed earlier, may cause a progressive reduction in the negotiator's level of aspiration.

2 It is easy for the negotiator to lose the thread of his argument and to be diverted on to side issues.

3 It is difficult to present complex points involving figures or detailed drafting without at least some written back-up.

4 Misunderstandings may arise and apparent agreement be reached without genuine under-

standing. This is particularly likely to happen if the parties do not speak the same native language.

5 Not having had advance warning the other side may listen politely and then withdraw until they have had the opportunity to consider the points made and prepare their answer.

25.4 Conclusions

Drawing the various advantages and disadvantages of the three possible methods of presentation together the following guide lines are suggested:

1 A written statement should only be submitted, whether as a prelude to discussions or not, if:
   (a) It is required as a tender or for the submission of a claim.
   (b) It is known that it will not give offence. If there is any doubt on this point then the draft, or relevant parts of it, should be cleared informally with the chief negotiator for the other side before formal submission.
   (c) The negotiator is either totally committed to the points made in the proposal, so that he is prepared to lose the bargain rather than withdraw, or the points represent those on which he is willing to trade if this is necessary to secure the bargain.
2 If no prior written proposal is made then a statement summarizing the main items of our presentation and giving details of figures and particular points of drafting should be available both for use by the negotiator and as a handout (possibly in a censored edition) for the other side. To the extent that this brief has been prepared as part of the preparation of the negotiating plan, and endorsed by our management, it will provide the negotiator with a significant commitment and a strong reinforcement of his level of aspiration.
3 Any written proposal, whether given in advance or not, (other than a tender to a strict public authority) should refer only to those points which the negotiator wishes to disclose at that time in the negotiation, since agreement on point A may be difficult or impossible to obtain if the other negotiator realizes in advance the line the negotiator intends to take on associated point B, especially if B raises emotional issues.

   Where a draft contract is being tabled for negotiation this may be difficult to avoid but certain clauses can still be left blank to be supplied later, the drafting of these only being finalized when their attitude to the remainder of the draft as presented has been discovered.

25.5 Exposing the negotiating area

Our objective at the opening stage of the negotiations may be described as exploration without commitment. We want to ensure that the whole of the area to be covered by the negotiation is exposed, together with their views on each point. But at the same time we does not want to be drawn into making too firm a commitment of our own position on any individual issue; specifically we will wish to avoid at this stage any partial agreement or concessions.

Figure 25.1 on page 166 is a suggested guide to the way in which the negotiator should behave in the opening phase.

When a written statement has been submitted by the other side:

Do	Do not
1 Challenge each point, asking why he made it.	1 Speculate on his reasons or put words into his mouth.
2 Appear ignorant, even if this is not true, and let him justify his case.	2 Try to be clever and show depth of knowledge by answering questions put to him.
3 Note his answers and reserve the position.	3 Agree immediately even if agreement will be reached in the end.
4 Make certain each point has been fully understood even if this means going over the ground twice. This applies particularly if native languages are not the same.	4 Snatch at what appears to be a favourable bargain or interpretation of his views.
5 Test out the strength of his views of each point so that later on the probability of his sticking to his position under pressure can be assessed.	5 Be drawn into lengthy arguments on any individual point from which it may be difficult to withdraw.
6 Be aware of the interrelationship between different contract points and the possible counter-arguments which will be developed if success is achieved on any particular one.	6 Be conscious only of the particular point under discussion and of the immediate benefits to be derived from succeeding on that point alone.
7 Appear calm and quiet.	7 Betray feelings by showing anger, surprise or delight at his remarks.
8 Correct him if he is proceeding on a false belief as to a factual position for which you are responsible.	8 Improve his judgement unless it is advantageous to us to do so.

When we have submitted a written proposal:

Do	Do not
1 Limit answers to his questions to the minimum and seek to persuade him into talking again as soon as possible.	1 Elaborate at length on motives.

Figure 25.1 Guide to negotiator's behaviour in the opening phase (continued)

2 Test out the strength of his objections by seeing if he will withdraw them without requiring any corresponding concessions.

2 Concede anything or be drawn into trade-off negotiations before all points have been discussed.

3 Behave generally as described in points 6, 7 and 8 above.

When no written statement has been submitted by either side:

Do	Do not
1 Identify all the points to be discussed.	1 Let the discussions ramble on without any defined order.
2 Cover each point in sufficient depth for both sides to be aware of each other's position.	2 Concentrate the discussion on one point to the exclusion of all others.
3 Keep the discussions exploratory.	3 Be drawn into definite commitments either in the form of making a firm concession or taking up a position from which it may be difficult later to withdraw.
4 Behave generally as described in points 6, 7 and 8 above.	

Figure 25.1 Guide to negotiator's behaviour in the opening phase (concluded)

Notes

1. See P. C. Vitz and W. R. Kite, 'Factors affecting conflict and negotiation within an alliance', *Journal of Experimental Social Psychology*, vol. 6 (1970), pp. 233–47, in which the authors describe experiments in bargaining conducted by telephone and by written communication.
2. Of course, this may be done deliberately as a negotiating tactic (see p. 248).
3. This was certainly the case in the experiments referred to by P.C. Vitz and W. R. Kite in note 1. In my own negotiating experience, there is a continual need to review and rephrase the drafts of written proposals to try to overcome this tendency to harshness of expression and the inclusion of gratuitous phrases of exaggeration. A quote from one of the written messages in Vitz and Kite's experiment serves as an example: 'I cannot agree that *under any circumstances* our contributions are to be based upon resources.' The italicized words add nothing to the argument, are unlikely to be true, and are almost certain to annoy the other side. All they achieve is to make it more difficult for the person initiating the message to negotiate away from that position in the future.

4. E. Morely and G.M. Stephenson, 'Interpersonal and interparty exchange: a laboratory simulation of an industrial negotiation at the plant level', *British Journal of Psychology,* vol. 60 (no.4, 1969), pp. 543–45, and 'Formality in negotiations: a validation study', *British Journal of Psychology,* vol. 61 (No. 3, 1970), pp. 383–84.

5. This norm states that (1) people should help those who have helped them and (2) people should not injure those who have helped them. A. W. Gouldner, 'The norm of reciprocity', *American Sociological Review* (April 1960). Opportunities will arise during the development of interpersonal relations between negotiators for one to be of assistance to the other even in such simple matters as arranging transport or accommodation, providing secretarial facilities, etc. Such assistance at once places the recipient under some obligation to reciprocate.

6. A. W. Gouldner in his article 'The norm of reciprocity', *American Sociological Review,* vol. 25 (1960), p. 161, suggests that one important function which the norm performs is that of establishing stability given significant power differences between two persons and groups. The invoking of this norm by a contractor, in the relationship between himself and a purchasing authority is a clear example of this. Even if the supplier's first-order defence of non-contractual liability fails, he can still rely on the second-order defence: 'You should not impose the penalty because of the assistance which I provided to you in connection with . . .'.

The supplier may also suggest that he will withdraw in the future from his previous willingness to provide benefits if the purchaser does not recognize the moral obligations arising from those provided in the past. Assistance and benefits in this connotation do not refer to gifts or bribes but to services which a contractor regularly undertaking work for a purchaser performs without specific charge, e.g. technical consultancy on maintenance problems or the development of new specifications, sponsoring attendance at technical conferences. See also S. Macauley, 'Non-contractual relations in business', *American Sociological Review,* vol. 28(1963), pp. 55–66 for further examples.

It could also be implied (Gouldner does not mention this) that the norm of reciprocity would only be invoked provided that the person doing so considered that he himself was without significant normal guilt. Thus the contractor would not utilize his second line of defence, if the delay giving rise to the penalty claim was clearly due to his own negligence, but only if the default was in the nature of a legal technicality. On this hypothesis the reciprocation extends also to the social character of the acts involved.

Macauley makes somewhat the same point when he refers to a supplier having a commitment to conform to his customer's expectations which is largely independent of legal sanctions. The supplier is expected to produce a good product and stand behind it.

7. Sir Francis Bacon, 'Of negotiating', in *Essays of Sir Francis Bacon* (London: Grant Richards, 1902), p. 134.

26 REVIEW OF THE OPENING

Assuming that we are presenting the initial proposal then at the end of the opening phase we should be in a position to:

1 Know those parts of our offer which the other side is likely to accept.
2 Know those parts which he is unlikely to accept.
3 Deduce, from the line he took in his criticism of our offer and our own response, the strength of his opposition on any issue.
4 Predict the general form of the optimum bargain to us on each issue or groups of related issues which he is likely to accept.

Before proceeding further with the negotiations, therefore, we should first review the results achieved from the opening phase and decide into which of the following three categories the negotiations can be placed:

1 A bargain acceptable to both sides is immediately identifiable.
2 A bargain acceptable to both sides is foreseeable but will require further negotiations to achieve.
3 No bargain is foreseen which would both be acceptable to him and meet our minimum negotiating objective.

26.1 Bargain immediately identifiable

This is the simplest case and the one in which we may be tempted to merge the opening phase into the later commitment stages of the negotiation without allowing the opportunity for intermediate bargaining. Sensing the narrowness of the gap between the two side's positions we may jump at once to the point of making proposals for a final settlement.

Whilst recognizing the temptation, it is one which for the following reasons we should resist:

1 By making an immediate proposal, which must represent some concession from our initial offer, we may encourage the other side to believe that by prolonging the negotiations he can achieve further concessions from us.
2 By appearing over-eager, we may lead him to believe that we have some personal reasons for wanting early agreement. Again this would suggest to him that he could achieve more by holding out longer.
3 Unless we retract, any further negotiations will start from the level of his settlement proposals which can only be to our disadvantage. However, the withdrawal of any offer must

create emotional antagonism towards us and lead him to demand more than he would have done otherwise, as a penalty on us for our behaviour. Either way we will stand to lose.

Accordingly even if the bargain is immediately identifiable we should still allow time for the working-out of the negotiating process. This proposition may be illustrated with a simple example.

Suppose that we have made an initial offer of 100 to which he has responded with a counter-offer of 90. If asked separately their belief as to the settlement figure it is highly probable that both would reply 95. If we make an immediate offer of 95 it is likely that he, for the reasons given above, will respond with an offer to split the difference at 97.5.

On the other hand, if our first negotiating proposal is 92.5 to which he responds with 97.5, thus establishing a pattern of mutual concessions, we can then propose a further mutual concession of 2.5 so arriving at a final bargain of 95.

Following our review of the opening, it is proposed that we should decide on some intermediate step which will:

1 Act as a signpost to him of the form of the final bargain
2 Provide the opportunity for him to make a responsive concession[1]
3 Allow us to judge our next move according to whether he makes a responsive concession or not
4 Commits us to the minimum concession only which is necessary to obtain the desired concession from the other side.

26.2 Bargain foreseeable

REVIEW OF THE NEGOTIATING AREA

Provided that the opening sessions have fulfilled their primary objective of disclosing all the items to be covered by the negotiations, it should now be possible to identify the total negotiating area. This may be considered graphically as illustrated in Figure 26.1, which is based on the scenario given in the negotiating brief on p. 146. The dotted horizontal lines in the rectangle represent the offers made by the seller and the notes to the left of the rectangle represent comments on the offers made by the seller. The solid lines represent the seller's various walk-away points, depending on the concessions he has secured on the buyer's terms of contract.

It will be seen that the seller has three walk-away points, depending upon the contract terms negotiated with the buyer:

- £322,000 if the buyer's terms apply equal to a reduction in margin of 7.5 per cent
- £308,000 if there is a 50/50 split between the buyer's and seller's terms equal to a reduction in margin of 11.5 per cent
- £294,000 if the seller's terms apply equal to a reduction in margin of 15.5 per cent

From the opening the seller has concluded that the buyer is likely to:

Seller's walk-away points	'000	'000	Offers
	350	350	
	348 ------------- 348		Bid
	340	340	
	330	330	
If buyer's terms apply	322 ————— 322		
	320	320	
	315 ------------- 315		Seller's final offer with defects conceded but penalty secured and TOP much improved – see p. 216
	313 ═══════ 313		Seller's planned objective after review
	310	310	
If 50/50 split on terms	308 ————— 308		
	300	300	
If seller's terms apply	294 ————— 294		
	290	290	

Figure 26.1 Review of the bargaining process – the total bargaining area

- Show some flexibility on the terms of the delay penalty, although a reduction to the 0.5 per cent level will be difficult to achieve
- Show strong resistance to a reduction in the defects liability period to twelve months
- Although a concession on the terms of payment appears possible, the buyer will require a substantial reduction in the contract price in exchange for any such concession.

Before he can consider any significant reductions in price, the seller concludes that he should try to see if he can persuade the buyer to move on the issues of penalty and defects liability period. If he can achieve this, then he will know how much is available to bargain with on terms of payment and price. The seller is more concerned with securing a reduction on the delay penalty than with reducing the defects liability period. His negotiating margin on the delay penalty is twice that on the defects liability.

He has concluded that in order to obtain the contract, with improved terms of payment the buyer is going to want around a 10 per cent discount off the contract price. If he could, say, reduce the need for the delay penalty and terms of payment margins by some two-thirds then he could afford a total reduction of not more than 10 per cent and still achieve his negotiating objective. This is shown on the rectangle by the double solid line at £313,000. The seller decides that it would be dangerous even to discuss price, or indeed any concessions on price, until the issues of the delay penalty/defects liability period had been at least conditionally agreed. If that can be achieved then he could argue strongly for a concession on the terms of payment but without offering any price concession. He anticipates that at some stage the buyer is going either to propose the price concession he wants from the seller for a change in the terms of payment or require the seller to make a proposal. If he is going to secure his negotiating objective the seller knows that, as his absolute limit is a 10 per cent reduction, it would be dangerous for him to offer more than 2.5 per cent covering both penalty and terms of payment. He must then resist hard and get a counter-offer from the buyer.

At the conclusion of the review stage, the seller has a clear plan of his next moves:

- Concentrate the negotiations on the penalty/defects liability period and offer an increase in the latter, say, to 18 months against a reduction in the penalty to 0.5 per cent per week.
- Be prepared to indicate his willingness as part of an overall acceptable bargain to concede to 24 months with the penalty at 0.75 per cent to a maximum of 10 per cent. Although the maximum is judged to be largely irrelevant, it may affect the buyer's attitude when it comes to terms of payment since he may want to retain the maximum penalty until completion.
- Assuming that is conditionally agreed, then press for an increase in the terms of payment to those stated in the tender. If pressed, make an offer of a 2.5 per cent reduction in the contract price in exchange for this and the penalty. Make no further move until the buyer has put forward a counter-proposal. Review this proposal when received, knowing that his maximum concession in order to secure the negotiating objective is a total 10 per cent reduction in the contract price against terms of payment 85, 10, and 5 per cent.

There are two dangers against which the seller's negotiators must guard when deciding on action. First while being conscious of the walk-away points they must never confuse them with the negotiating objective. While certainly they represent the points at which the seller would just prefer to take the contract rather than abandon the negotiations, they are not objectives.

Second, they must not allow themselves to be lulled into a false sense of security because they have a reasonable negotiating margin with which to play. This must be conceded both slowly and grudgingly and only against concessions from the buyer. That a reduction of 10 per cent is available, if necessary, should not be allowed to influence their concession behaviour in favour of generosity. Instead they should be miserly.

THE BUYER'S APPROACH

The above illustration as to how the negotiations might proceed assumes that the buyer goes along with the supplier's approach. If he does, he is playing into the supplier's hands by allowing the supplier to decide on the format for the negotiations. Alternatively, the buyer could take the initiative and inform the seller at the outset that he was not prepared even to discuss the terms of contract until the supplier had made a substantial reduction in the tender price. If the supplier were not willing to do this then he might as well go home now.

In one respect this is a high-risk tactic for the buyer. Having made the threat, if the supplier declines to make a 'substantial' reduction then he will be left with only the other firm with whom to negotiate. At the same time, it is of course left to the buyer to interpret subjectively what he means by 'substantial' so that he has left himself some room to manoeuvre. The supplier's immediate response would be likely to be on the lines that before discussing discounts he would want to be able to assess risk, which he can only do after there has been a debate on the terms of contract. The buyer's response to this should be that the supplier knows the buyer's terms and he should proceed on the basis that these will the terms of the contract. This then leaves the buyer in the position of being able to ask for even further reductions if he eventually accepts any of the supplier's proposals for the modification of the terms.

If the supplier had carried out a rehearsal as recommended in Chapter 21, he should have been prepared for this reaction by the buyer. Although price is often the last item to be discussed, there is no rule which says so and it is often advantageous to do the unexpected. In our example, the seller has not had a rehearsal and is taken unawares. How should he respond? He has the following alternatives:

1 Decline to make any reduction.
2 Make an immediate reduction.
3 Say he is prepared to consider a reduction in the tender price but he can only assess how much after he has discussed the terms of contract.

The first course will almost certainly result in his being asked to leave. Having committed himself to requiring a substantial reduction before negotiations on the contract can start, the buyer cannot back down totally without completely losing his reputation for firmness.

Following alternative 2 will lead the supplier into disaster. He has at the most 9 per cent of the contract price available to offer as a reduction if the contract is to be on the buyer's terms and that would take him down to his walk-away point. Whatever he offers now, the buyer is going to want more and he can hardly offer less than 5 per cent. He runs the risk of even that being dismissed as derisory and told to do better if he wants the negotiations to start.

Alternative 3 must be the preferred course to take. The supplier has indicated a willingness to reduce the price but has not been specific and is clearly linking the reduction to progress in the negotiations. It ought to be sufficient for the buyer to feel that he has achieved enough to start talking. If it doesn't then the seller could answer along the following lines: 'If you are insistent that we refer to a figure now then it could only be say 1–2 per cent, which I am sure is not what you are looking for. We think that it would be better for both of us if we kept the negotiations on price until after we have sorted out the other issues. Then we could make you a sensible proposal.' If this is said firmly enough and the buyer is really interested in the seller's tender, then he must realize that further pressure is going to get him nowhere. To get himself off the hook the buyer could then respond 'OK we'll leave it there for the moment and come back to the price later but just so we understand each other, there has got to be a substantial reduction before we could think of awarding you this contract; if you cannot see your way clear to that then we are all wasting our time, understood?' The supplier's reply might then be 'Yes, your position is quite clear and I am sure we will be able to satisfy you once we have come to an understanding on the other points.'

But the lesson should be clear that it is no use believing that the other side will always agree to play the game your way. You must be prepared for them to make the rules and ready to respond accordingly. It would also in this instance be a definite sign of weakness if the seller was not able to respond immediately and had to ask for an adjournment. Again, this shows the value of a rehearsal.

What the seller would also have learnt if the exchange between them went as suggested above is that the buyer is probably after at least some 10 per cent by way of a reduction and he must be very careful to have enough in hand for the final negotiations. He would, however, also have understood that the buyer was seriously interested in his bid and that he was in with a good chance.

26.3 No bargain foreseeable

It happens not infrequently that as a result of the review of the opening it becomes clear that no bargain is foreseeable within the terms of the negotiator's current authority. If the negotiator finds himself in this position there are three possibilities open to him:

1 Break off negotiations and withdraw.
2 Continue and seek revised authority.
3 Influence the other side to seek revised authority.

BREAK OFF NEGOTIATIONS

No negotiator likes to break off discussions particularly if, as a supplier, he knows that there are competitors waiting in the wings only too eager to take his place. So this is a last resort which at this stage in the negotiations should be selected by the negotiator, whether as a supplier or a buyer, only if *all* the following conditions are satisfied:

1 The negotiator knows that he is in a strong position and that the other side must contact him again if the business is to proceed.
2 The negotiator believes that this is the only way in which to convince his opposite number to change his mind.
3 The issues involved are fundamental and if the other side will not give way then the negotiator genuinely would prefer no bargain.

Later, of course, we may have no option but to withdraw if we are satisfied that the other side will never concede on issues on which we would rather face the consequences of no bargain than accept. But this is a conclusion to which we should come slowly and with reluctance. Few statements made early in a negotiation should be taken at their face value.

The same principles should govern our conduct in a case of contract dispute. As indicated earlier (see 43) few firms like the idea of taking their disputes to law or arbitration. The difficulties and costs involved in obtaining and enforcing a favourable judgement are too formidable especially if the contract is for export. No matter how great the problems or the degree of patience required, the attempt to arrive at a negotiated settlement should be continued until all hope is lost.

CONTINUE AND SEEK REVISED AUTHORITY

This is the more normal course for the negotiator to follow. The negotiation is kept going on minor issues while the negotiator communicates with his management and seeks a revision to his authority which he believes will be sufficient to secure eventual agreement. In referring the issue back to management, the negotiator will be expected to make his own personal recommendations to management as to the action they should take, based on the range of bargains which he foresees as being possible to achieve, the time it would take to do so and the value to us of such bargains in comparison with that of no bargain. Because of his proximity to the negotiating table and to the other side, the negotiator must be careful, when expressing his views, to avoid becoming so emotionally involved with securing agreement, or identifying himself so closely with the other side's viewpoint, that he loses objectivity. It is only too easy for a negotiator widely separated from his home base in terms of time and distance to 'go native'.

The interesting point arises as to whether the negotiator should allow the other side to be aware that he is seeking revised authority or should endeavour to conceal this fact.

There is the obvious disadvantage that by disclosing his actions the negotiator admits that his company may not be totally committed to the position which he as the negotiator had adopted, and implies that their value system may be such that they would prefer making at least some concession to the other side's viewpoint rather than accept the outcome of no bargain.

Having made this admission once, the negotiator must expect that his opposite number will not in future, attach the same degree of belief in the negotiator's firmness of purpose, especially if management's answer is to relax the restrictions previously placed on the negotiator's powers. Naturally, this relaxation of restrictions becomes known to the other side, at least in principle if not in degree, through the manner in which the negotiator subsequently conducts his case. They will become more inclined to doubt the negotiator's word and to insist on his referring back any issues of significance. Clearly, if this process of reference back and amendment to the negotiator's power is repeated too many times, the negotiator's position will be destroyed.

To prevent this happening management must demonstrate their support for the negotiator and their general commitment to the terms which he is seeking to secure. They may do this by:

1 Sending written messages of support to the negotiator which he can either show openly to the other side or allow him to 'discover' them.
2 Selectively refusing to make any concessions. The negotiator deliberately refers back (and allows the other side to know he has done so) an issue on which it has already been predetermined that our management would not depart from the negotiator's stand.

3 Demonstrating that any concession had to be secured from the highest authority within the company and must be treated as a total exception. Again the negotiator should be provided with evidence that this is so in a form which he can produce for the other side.
4 Sending out a 'hard-line' support man from head office to take the pressure off the negotiator and to prove that the company solidly supports the negotiator in the job which he is doing.

A related point is the effect of the other side's knowledge that the negotiator is seeking revised authority based on his estimation of the negotiator as a person with whom to deal. Amongst sophisticated bargainers it is well accepted that an individual negotiator does not possess *carte blanche* to deal on any terms he chooses. There are always limits placed on his authority and provided that these appear reasonable to the other side he is not likely to think any the worse of the negotiator because he becomes aware of their existence. He will not consider that his pride or status have been offended because he has been called upon to bargain with a negotiator who is acting under instructions.

However, this is not always so with unsophisticated negotiators, especially those whose own authority is largely absolute, either because they are sole proprietors of their own business or princes of their territory. They may react emotionally to any admission by the negotiator that he must refer back on any issue for further instructions, and demand that if *he* does not possess the necessary authority then the company should send someone who does.

If this difficulty was foreseen in advance then it would be expected that the company would send someone who was sufficiently senior in the company, with sufficiently wide terms of reference and enough technical support, to be able to complete the negotiations without the need for reference back, even if ultimately this means no bargain. It is stressed that possessing wide terms of reference is not a matter of merely having the authority to make concessions; it is having the authority to make judgements as to whether the terms on which agreement is possible are to be preferred to no agreement at all.

If the problem was not foreseen in advance, and the negotiator does not in consequence possess the necessary authority, then three choices are open to him:

1 Admit his position and risk the strong possibility that he will be asked to withdraw.
2 Exceed his authority.
3 Seek to communicate with his management without this becoming known to the other side.

It is obviously impossible to lay down a single rule for deciding which of those three choices is the correct one in every case. However, the first preference would be for choice 3 but, if this was judged impractical, then choice 2 would be selected. The reason for avoiding any admission of lack of authority, and being compelled to withdraw, is that this would place any other negotiator who is brought in subsequently in a very difficult position. The very fact that another negotiator had been brought in would imply that the company was willing to make, at least in part, the concessions which the other side was demanding.

One advantage that the negotiator may be able to secure by allowing the other side to know that he is waiting for revised authority is that he can use the waiting time to identify and collect together all other significant issues which are in dispute and on which he requires concessions.

When he does receive the revised authority, the negotiator exchanges these concessions for the ones which the other side want and which are the subject of the revised authority. During the waiting time, the more the negotiator has been able to build up in the mind of the other side's negotiator the enormity of the concession for which he is asking, the higher the exchange price the negotiator will be able to secure. On one occasion in which I was involved in a situation of this type the chief negotiator for the other side replied to the terms of the exchange proposal with the question: 'Mr Marsh, you want the lot?' to which the reply was simply 'Yes'.

Obviously if the request for further authority is refused and the other side remains adamant, then the negotiator has no further options open to him; he must withdraw.

INFLUENCE THE OTHER SIDE TO SEEK REVISED AUTHORITY

As a course of action this is often used in conjunction with the two courses just discussed rather than on its own. Indeed the primary aim of breaking off the negotiations is to compel the other side to reconsider his demands.

Equally whilst the negotiator is seeking revised authority he should at the same time be working to persuade his opposite number at least to modify his demands to some degree. His primary methods of achieving this are:

1 Holding firm as long as he can to his own position.
2 Convincing the other side of the major injury which the company would suffer by agreeing to the other side's terms. As suggested previously it is in the negotiator's interest to exaggerate this injury in order to justify the demand for a larger concession from the other side in return.
3 Seeking to make the individual supporting members of the other side's negotiating team understand the company's real difficulties, and using these members as allies to work on the other side's management. The most effective allies for the negotiator in this respect are the professional advisers to the other side, such as lawyers and engineers, who can usually be relied on to take a more objective line.
4 Persuading the other side's negotiator that the benefits he would gain from achieving his demands would be appreciably less than he believes. Again reference behind the scenes to his professional advisers can be helpful in achieving this. Information can be 'leaked' to them which the negotiator indicates he would not reveal officially, and because the information is presented in this way it is more likely to be believed to be true.

Note

1. Concession is used here as previously in a conditional sense that is the concession is of the form 'if you will agree to . . . , then we would consider . . . '. Concessions in an absolute sense: 'As you have agreed to . . . , we will agree to . . .', should not occur until the bargaining has reached an advanced stage and the shape of the total bargain can be seen. This is often difficult when negotiating on the terms of a total contract – it may be necessary then to make it clear in the opening phase that nothing is to be regarded as agreed until everything has been

agreed. In that way, recriminations can be avoided if the negotiator starts to backtrack later, on something 'agreed' earlier, because of the way in which the negotiations have gone on another but related point.

27 THE FOLLOW-UP

It is in this stage of the negotiations that each side starts significantly to adjust its demand and attitudes to the observed behaviour of the other. The primary emphasis, therefore, is on adjustment and because each knows this, their initial behaviour is likely to contain a strong element of bluff although, as suggested earlier, bluffing too strongly can be self-defeating.

This is also the stage in which the unity of the negotiating team will receive its first severe test. One team member may regard the other side's violent criticism of his proposals as largely bluff, and so maintain strongly that we should stand our ground. Another may feel with equal conviction that from the other side's viewpoint the criticisms are justified, and that agreement will not be reached unless our original proposals are modified in a way which will substantially meet the criticisms. Therefore, temporary alliances may well be formed across the negotiating lines. Whilst this is inevitable behind the scenes, the team leader should never permit such alliances to appear openly at the negotiating table unless as part of a tactical ploy (see p. 129). However, it is necessary to recognize that interaction between the members of the negotiating team plays a major part in the adjustment process and that the degree to which we move towards the other side is to some degree a function of the personalities of the negotiators and the discipline established by the team leader.

The process by which the two sides adjust to one another within the framework of the variables which lead us initially to prefer one demand to another is now considered. The form of their concession factor and therefore the value of the outcome achievable, the time which will be taken to reach that outcome, the costs associated with that time, and the major strategic weapons at our disposal (commitment and threats) will all be discussed.

27.1 Reappraisal of their concession factor

It will be remembered (p. 105) that our initial demand was optimal in relation to:

1 Our expectation of their concession factor
2 Our expectation of our own concession factor necessary to secure that concession from the other side
3 The time at which we anticipated that a bargain would be reached related to our own and their initial demands and the respective concession factors
4 The costs associated with the time taken to secure agreement.

It is necessary to consider now the manner in which our demand may change, according to whether our expectations regarding their behaviour prove to be correct or not. There are three possibilities:

1 They act in accordance with our expectations.
2 They concede more and/or faster than we had expected.
3 They concede less and/or slower than we had expected.

THEY ACT IN ACCORDANCE WITH OUR EXPECTATIONS

In order for their initial behaviour to be in accordance with our expectations, we must have selected a negotiating strategy which will also lead at time T_{ij} to an outcome O_{ij} (using the same notation as that on p. 32). Accordingly, although we and they differ in their initial demands, they have both independently selected the same outcome. Assuming that they have behaved rationally in the choice of their concession factor, it must also follow that we have made a mistake. We have assessed a concession factor for them as a *maximum* whereas, in fact, it represents the *minimum* which they consider necessary to exact a maximum concession from ourselves.

By the same reasoning they are equally mistaken in their beliefs. The concession they have assessed as our *maximum* is that which we judged would be the *minimum* we would have to allow to them in order to obtain the *maximum* which we believed they would yield.

A simple numerical example to illustrate this behaviour is set out in Figure 27.1.

	1 Original demand	2 Assumed maximum concession factor	3 Expected outcome	4 True maximum concession factor	5 True level at which bargain preferred to no bargain
Us	100	−4	96	−6	94
Them	90	+6	96	+7	97

Figure 27.1 Comparison between true and assumed concession factors

The supplier makes an offer of 100 to which the buyer responds with an offer of 90. This defines the bargaining area. Column 3 shows that both sides expect that the bargain will be made at a price of 96, and both make the same assumptions regarding the other's maximum concession factor and their own minimum required to achieve this. In fact, both are wrong. Both could have adopted a harder initial line. The buyer could have tried to force the price down to 94 and the supplier to push it upwards to 97.

Generalizing, it may be stated that in any case in which at the commencement of the bargaining a negotiator's expectations as to the other's concession factor are immediately fulfilled, then the negotiator has underestimated the maximum concessions which the other would make. As a corollary to this, if either we or they are correct in our estimation of the other's true concession factor, our actual behaviour will differ from that which the other expects. In Figure 27.1, if they knew that under pressure we would concede to 94 then his initial approach would be considerably harder than we had expected, since they would only plan on making a concession of 4 whereas we had anticipated his making a concession of 6.

Coddington has proposed that in any satisfactory model of the bargaining process a bargainer does not revise his decision when his expectations are fulfilled.[1] However, it has just been demonstrated that, given a rational opponent, the fulfilment of our initial expectations must mean that we had underestimated their concession factor. Does this mean that in this particular case we should exhibit inconsistency and change our strategy even though our expectations have been fulfilled?

Provided he stays with his strategy, we can be confident that, as a result of the initial moves, our own strategy will lead to the outcome associated with our original demand. Although we now know that this outcome is less than optimal in terms of its value at the time of agreement, a more favourable outcome derived from our adoption of a hard-line strategy would take longer to achieve and therefore would be subject to a reduction in terms of its present value, due to the effect of the increased discount factor and time costs.

We also know that any change we make in our strategy is likely to cause the other side also to make a change. This could be more favourable to us, i.e. they could increase their concession factor or alternatively they could react unfavourably from our viewpoint by hardening their line of resistance. The latter is more probable. Rationally, they already have some guide to our true concession factor from our first moves; emotionally they are likely to react on the lines: 'All right, if you want to make things tougher, two can play at that game.

The result of the initial moves may be regarded as having created a temporary balance between the demands of the two sides. If the balance is confirmed by their next moves this will point the way to a specific outcome on which the two sides will focus their attention and coordinate their expectations. If the initial balance is disturbed by our change of strategy, neither side will be able to recognize immediately any such focal point, and time will be required for exploratory probing before balance can be restored at some new level.

Accordingly, in practice, unless the anticipated improvement in outcome is significant and the adverse effects of the delay in reaching agreement are small, there will be little incentive for us to change our strategy *provided that the other side do not change theirs*. If they were to change to a harder line and to concede less than we had expected in return for our own concessions, then we would be compelled either to change strategy ourselves, so prolonging the negotiations, or to make more concessions and so lower the value to us of the outcome. Either way we would lose. The same reasoning could be applied to the other side and at this point a similarity begins to appear in the situation facing the two sides and that of the two collaborators in the zero-sum game.

The decision problem facing us is now represented in game-theory form to see whether suspicions are confirmed. This is shown in Figure 27.2, the data for which is based on that previously used in Figure 16.2 for arriving at our original optimum demand. The assumption is made that if we switch to our hard-line strategy then we increase the value of the outcome to 170 but it takes longer to achieve: five months if they do not change their strategy and eight months if they do. Conversely if they change to a hard-line strategy, but we do not, it is assumed that we will reach a lower outcome than that originally predicted, but that it will only take three months to reach agreement. While the actual figures used in Figure 16.1 are arbitrary, the assumptions on which they are based as to the circumstances under which the value of the outcome to us will be increased or reduced, or the time for agreement extended or shortened, would seem to be of general validity.

This is in fact the situation considered in Appendix 1, p. 279. Our maximum strategy is clearly a_1, stay with our original choice, since, even if they do change to a hard line, we are still better off on present values than if he had selected a_2. However, as in the discussion in Appendix 1 and for the same reasons, we could still be tempted to change strategy if we believed that they would not, and some people might well decide to take this gamble.

The preference would be to stay with strategy a_1 and the argument to support this choice would be that the selection of the hard-line strategy would carry with it, in most bargaining situations, a higher than 50 per cent risk that they would follow suit and we would finish up, therefore, with outcome a_2b_2 which is the one we would most prefer to avoid. We would have to be convinced that both the risk of this happening was very small, and also that they would not become resentful and determined to exact retribution on a future occasion, before changing to the hard-line.

		Other side	
		Stays as predicted b_1	Changes to hard line b_2
Stays with original plan a_1		156	153.1
Us			
Changes to hard line a_2		158.25	151.2

Figure 27.2 Decision problem: stay with present strategy or change to hard line?

Assuming it is decided we stay with strategy a_1 then it is necessary to try to ensure that they also stay with their initial strategy, so that the outcome became a_1b_1, which might be termed the 'cooperative choice'. It is suggested that we should approach their negotiator informally along the following lines:

> We both want the best bargain we can get. The way for us both to achieve that is to continue the way we have started. If, however, you start to play it tough then I can do the same which will benefit neither of us. We both have to live so let's be sensible and not too greedy.

OUR DECISION RULES

From the above analysis it is suggested that we should adopt the following decision rules:

1 We should only change to a hard-line strategy if this is clearly optimal against any likely probability distribution of their strategy choice, and will not reflect adversely on us on a future occasion.
2 In any other case we should stay with our original strategy choice.
3 If we do decide to stay with our original strategy then we should 'signal' them to do likewise with the threat of switching to a hard line if they do not agree.

Whilst the analysis has been made by considering our decision-making process in relation to their reaction to our initial demand, the reasoning used is quite general and, therefore, the above decision rules can be applied at any stage in the negotiations. They are especially important to remember in the final stages of the negotiation when the temptation to defect, to ask for that little bit more, seems for some negotiators to be especially strong and can be the cause of serious delays and loss of the other side's goodwill.

Therefore the answer to the question of whether we should show inconsistency in our decision making or not, is that we should at each time make that choice which is optimal in relation to the knowledge which we possess at that time. To the extent that as the bargaining proceeds our knowledge increases, this may cause us to change our strategy, even if our expectations have been fulfilled, if we believe that to do so will be advantageous.

OPPONENT CONCEDES MORE AND/OR FASTER THAN WE HAD EXPECTED

As established in the previous section, their initial response to our demand, when judged from their viewpoint, represents their estimate of their minimum concession factor necessary to obtain a maximum concession from ourselves. If they now concede more or faster than we had expected, this must mean that their real concession factor is even greater.

We therefore are not wrong in our estimation of their concession factor by the visible gap between our expectations and their actions but by the far larger gap between his expectations and their true concession factor. Assume that in the example in Figure 27.1 we had expected them on the first bargaining concession to concede 2 and in fact they concede 3. We can now reason that if they are willing initially to concede 3 then this must mean that their maximum concession factor is probably of the order 8–9 and not the 6 which we had originally estimated.

We accordingly revise upwards our expectations as to their concession factor, in line with the maximum to which we now believe that they will concede and the time it would take for us to obtain such a concession. This in turn leads us to revise downwards our belief as to the minimum concessions which we need to make and so harden our bargaining line.

The process is an accelerating one in which each concession they make reinforces our belief as to the maximum to which they will concede, and so strengthens our determination to stand firm – this in turn persuades them that they have no alternative but to go on conceding. So it continues until they have conceded to the level of their point of final resistance, provided that this is less than our then current demand. If it is greater then they must at some time accept our current demand.

In a purely theoretical model, it would be possible to allow for us actually increasing our demand so that if we were prepared to allow the negotiations to go on for long enough, the end point of the bargaining sequence would always be their final resistance point. As stated earlier (see Chapter 16) it is considered that to increase a demand during the course of the negotiation would create such an emotional disturbance that it could not be to our advantage to do so. Accordingly this possibility is dismissed.

It may also be objected that although the other side originally conceded more than we had expected this does not mean that they must continue to do the conceding. Could they not at some stage stand firm themselves and compel us to concede? What if they made a mistake by conceding too much all at once and this has led us to assume a far larger maximum concession factor for them than is really true? In the extreme, what if they have already reached their point of final resistance?

The difficulty is that, by their initial action, they have persuaded us to a revised expectation of the final bargain to which we may already now be committed in the sense either that we have advised our management of the revised outcome, which we now anticipate being able to achieve, or at least our negotiator will feel a personal commitment to the other members of the team as a result of the planning meeting at which they revised our strategy. If they now try to change from conceding to standing firm they will simply not be able to convince us that, after having made those early concessions, greater than we had expected, they now mean their present intransigence. Our refusal to believe that their change of plan is genuine will be reinforced by the humiliation which our negotiator would suffer were it true. In terms of his personal reputation he cannot afford to allow it to be true, and the best means available for preventing it, is to stand firm and to demonstrate that he intends to continue to stand firm.

This is one example in contract negotiation of the moral of the old Aesop fable of the boy who cried wolf. A person cannot suddenly change his behavioural pattern and expect to be believed, not at least unless he can relate the change to some external event, the truth of which is easily demonstrable, e.g. as a buyer, being prepared to show a lower quotation, received late, to the supplier with whom negotiations are in progress. Merely to say the quotation has been received will be taken as bluff.

In the situation under discussion, we would assume that they are bluffing, in the absence of any overt act by them proving the contrary. We will make this assumption, either because we genuinely believe it to be true, or because we cannot afford to allow ourselves not to believe it. So long as we do this, and they prefer the outcome represented by our demand to no bargain, then they have ultimately no alternative but to give way.

This conclusion emphasizes the key importance of limiting the amount of initial concession. It must be no greater than the minimum which the negotiator believes is essential to initiate the bargaining process and exact the maximum concession from the other side. Any doubts as to the level of the concession should be resolved downwards. It also confirms the conclusion reached earlier (see pp. 106 and 126) that exaggerated demands do not operate in favour of the side who make them, since it is more difficult to minimize the initial concession when the demand has been artificially inflated.

Whilst the effect of the time cost have been allowed for in this representation of the bargaining process, in that our demand has been assumed to be optimal after taking these into account, no allowance has been made for the tactical effect of either side being under a time restraint, e.g. the existence of a defined date by which the buyer must place the order.

Clearly the pressure resulting from any such restraint will have an effect on both the tactics employed and the eventual outcome, and this is an issue which will be dealt with in Section 27.2.

THEY CONCEDE LESS AND/OR MORE SLOWLY THAN WE HAD EXPECTED

If we discover that they are taking a harder line than we had expected then there are two possible explanations for this:

1 We were correct in our original estimation of their genuine concession factor but they are bluffing.
2 We were wrong in our original estimation of their concession factor.

The consequences which flow from these two alternatives, in the manner anticipated and are set out in decision-tree format in Figure 27.3.

Our crucial decision is whether they are bluffing or not. The only real way for us to determine this directly is for us to adhere to our original plan, make the concessions we had intended to make, but beyond this to remain intransigent. The danger to us of adopting this strategy is that we become so committed to a firm line that, if we are wrong and they are not bluffing, our concessionary move when it does come involves much greater loss of face and reputation for firmness (see p. 324). As a result we may find it difficult to re-establish both our credibility and a firm line of resistance. Often we will feel compelled for just this reason to take a stand on some issue of doubtful validity on which otherwise we would have been prepared to concede.[2]

In order to minimize this risk and, whilst holding firm but with the minimum of defined commitment, we should seek to discover indirectly the extent, if any, of their bluff. We may do this by informal discussions with their negotiators, by cross-checking their assessment of the strength of their negotiating position from neutral sources and by looking for outward signs of the true attitude of their negotiators in terms of their personal behaviour. If the senior negotiator really has booked his flight home tomorrow, when home is 5,000 miles away from the scene of the negotiations, then this is some indication of how he feels.

Assuming that they are not bluffing and we behave rationally this will cause us as in branch 5 (Figure 27.3) to adjust our expectations downwards and lower our current demand. What will be the effect of this on the other side? This will depend on the relationship between the amount/rate at which we do concede related to their expectations. There are again three possibilities:

1 We concede at the amount/rate expected.	1 They adhere to their original strategy.
2 We concede less than they had expected.	2 If they believe we are not bluffing and behave rationally, then they adjust their expectations and lower their demand. This is what Cross has described as the general case of a convergent bargaining process.[3]

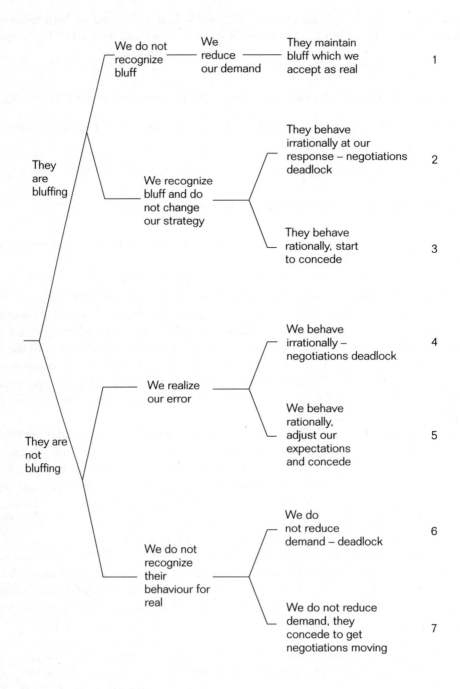

Figure 27.3 Decision tree – they concede less or more slowly than anticipated

3 We concede more than they had expected.

3 They amend their strategy by hardening their line and the negotiating process follows that described previously.

IRRATIONAL BEHAVIOUR

Even if our diagnosis is correct it does not necessarily follow that the negotiations will proceed smoothly. It has been indicated in branches 2 and 4 (Figure 27.3) that the negotiations may deadlock due to irrational behaviour. Being caught out or persuaded that he has made a mistake may create the reaction of: 'It was worth a try', accompanied by a philosophical shrug of the shoulders. Alternatively, the negotiator may react by showing stubbornness, a wilful refusal to face reality and by taking refuge in insults and rhetoric.

The patient coaxing of colleagues and the urge of economic necessity will both be needed in order to compel their negotiator into a more responsive attitude. Our own negotiators can assist by finding some small concession to smooth their way back to the bargaining table and by refraining from open signs of delight or triumph at their discomforture.

Finally being *right* in one's diagnosis and following this with the *right* response does not necessarily lead to the most favourable outcome. In branch 7, by failing to recognize that they are not bluffing and, therefore, failing to respond to their intransigence by making concessions, we compel them to reconsider their level of demand. If we had known why they were adhering to that level of demand, for example, that this was the minimum figure which they had been instructed by their management to achieve, then we by reason of our improved understanding would in all probability have moderated our own demand. Our negotiator's attitude would have been that there was nothing to be gained by pressing the point further as it was not going to be conceded, and that he was wise to accept the position and take what he could get.

It is in the hope of indicating this type of attitude that negotiators use commitment tactics by saying that, for example, they personally see the force of the argument but are bound by other decisions, other instructions or regulations.

Unfortunately negotiators over the years have debased the coinage of commitment tactics by bluffing; by pretending to commitments which either do not exist, or are far less restrictive than they have stated. Again the parallel may be drawn with Aesop's fable of the boy who cried wolf. If a negotiator wishes to be believed, when genuinely he is committed, he should not pretend to commitments when the falseness of his position can easily be exposed.

27.2 The influence of time

So far, discussions on the effect of time have considered only the time and costs incurred as a result of the duration of the negotiations and the discounting effect due to our later receipt of the benefits from the negotiations. It has been shown how the greater advantages which may be gained from prolonged bargaining must be balanced against these time costs and the discount factor so as to optimize the outcome. When doing this, no specific limit has been placed on the time available for the negotiations, and both this, and the time actually taken, have been assumed to be a function of the bargaining process itself.

Time limits, at least at some stage in the negotiations, are the rule rather than the exception in commercial practice and will affect the conduct of the bargaining in two ways:

1 Strategically by defining the negotiating period and compelling the negotiator at some predetermined point in time to change his strategy from that of hold back to quick kill.
2 Tactically by the pressure created on the negotiator himself through the need to make decisions against a defined deadline.

STRATEGIC EFFECT

In considering the strategic effect of time limits on a negotiation it is necessary to distinguish between:

1 The situation in which the time limit is established at the outset, is known to both sides, and constitutes therefore a negotiating time framework.
2 The situation in which no specific time limit exists initially, but one is subsequently created unilaterally by one side issuing a demand for the negotiations to be completed by a defined date, often accompanied by a statement as to the terms upon which he requires agreement to be reached.

NEGOTIATING TIME FRAMEWORK

The following axioms related to the behaviour of the two sides will apply to any negotiation which is conducted from the outset within a defined time framework:

1 The higher the initial concession rate of either side relative to time, the less favourable the bargain they will secure.
2 Both sides should therefore initially only make minor concessions or none at all.
3 At some period before the deadline both sides should make a series of moves designed to permit identification of a final bargain which is acceptable to both of them. These moves may be concessionary, or a repeat of earlier offers, depending on the bargaining strength of the two sides.
4 The side with the weaker bargaining strength is the one which is under greater pressure to reach agreement by the deadline, i.e. the one which has more to lose if the end result is no bargain.[4]

   If at the end of the final time phase of the negotiations we as the weaker side would prefer their initial offer to no bargain, then we must accept that offer. Specifically, at that time we will act so as to maximize our security and will not offer a compromise, which there must be some probability they might reject, so bringing the negotiations to an end without agreement having been reached.

   In order to reduce the risk of being faced with the choice between their initial terms and no bargain, in the penultimate phase of the negotiations we will make some concessionary move designed to secure reciprocal concessions from them.
5 The more even the bargaining strength of the two sides the later each can leave it before

making a concessionary move. Each will be aware that the other knows he would prefer a bargain to no bargain so both will expect that ultimately they will come to terms.

If the practice of making late mutual concessions happens several times, then this will become the norm of the two sides' negotiating behaviour and it would be unthinkable for either of them to depart from this, either by making concessions too early, or by failing to make the concessions needed for agreement to be reached, even if this happens only minutes before the deadline is due to expire.

6 The length of the period referred to in point 3 should be just sufficient to allow the two negotiators to reach agreement, taking into account any difficulties in communication.

If the period is too short, because neither side has made any move soon enough for the concession-making process to operate, then the side with the weaker bargaining strength having failed to set up a position of potential compromise will be exposed to the time-threat of accepting the other side's offer as it stands, or run the risk of no bargain.

If the period is too long, because one side has made a move too early, then this will be treated by the other as a sign of weakness and encourage him to remain intransigent, thus reducing the opportunity for reciprocal concession making and increasing the chances of no agreement being reached at all. The move will be misinterpreted because it was made at the wrong time.

27.3 Threat strategy

STRATEGIC EFFECT AND TIME THREATS

The imposition by either side of a time limit to the bargaining process necessarily carries with it a threat should the time limit be passed without agreement having been reached.

The function which this threat performs is related to the incentive to carry out the threat which the negotiator who is threatening would have, should his demands not be met.

If the demand represents the minimum negotiating objective of the negotiator who is threatening, so that he would prefer no bargain if it were not accepted, then the primary function of the threat is to convey that message to the other negotiator. The threat tells the other negotiator the scale by which the negotiator who is threatening values the terms of the proposed agreement.

One difficulty with the threat as a means of communication is that there is no commercial equivalent to 'cross my heart'. The person to whom the threat is made can only estimate whether the negotiator who is threatening really would prefer the implementation of the threat to no bargain, and he may get it wrong. This problem of the belief of the reality of the threat by the person threatened is crucial to the whole concept of threat strategy and will be discussed again.

If the threat does not succeed, suppose now that the alternative would represent a worse outcome to the negotiator who is threatening than accepting the bargain available without the use of the threat. The primary function of the threat then becomes to deter through 'its promise of mutual harm'.[5] The negotiator has no incentive to carry out the threat, whether his demands are met or not, although if they are not met he may be compelled to do so in order to maintain the other side's belief in his firmness of purpose.

The severity of the deterrent effect of any threat will depend upon:

1 The extent of the commitment which the issue of the threat places upon the person making it
2 The belief of the person to whom the threat is addressed that if he does not accede to the other's demands then the threat will be implemented
3 The injury which would be suffered by the person to whom the threat is made, if he accedes, in comparison with the loss he would suffer by resisting, were the threat to be carried out.

THE THREAT AS A COMMITMENT

The making of a threat in itself creates a commitment on the person who makes it to carry it out, should his demands not be met. The degree of that commitment which will be visible to the person to whom the threat is made, will be in proportion to:

1 The extent to which both the demand and the threat are specific – The more they are specific the less room there will be for adjustment, either in the demands or the threat itself, and so the greater the degree of commitment. Conversely the looser the phrasing the greater the opportunity of subsequent 'interpretation' and therefore the smaller the commitment. Compare these two statements:

> 'We must make the decision today. You have until 12 o'clock to accept the terms we have offered or we shall place the business elsewhere.'

> 'We cannot go on discussing any longer. You know the terms of our last offer. If we cannot reach agreement on these then we shall have to consider seriously placing the business with another firm.'

The first statement is explicit both in terms of the demand and of the time-scale in which it must be accepted. The commitment is total. If the supplier does not accept, there is no alternative left to the buyer. He must give the order to another company. To do otherwise would destroy the buyer's reputation for firmness and his credibility as a negotiator.

It follows from this that the buyer is unlikely to risk making a threat of the type in the first statement without the intention of carrying it out, and having the ability to do so in the form of an alternative source of supply. *These facts must be known to the supplier.* The second statement, however, is much less clear. No specific time limit is mentioned and the reference to 'reaching agreement on the terms of the buyer's last offer' indicate some flexibility in the buyer's position. The commitment is that much weaker.

2 The authority and reputation of the person making the threat – The more senior the negotiator, and the greater his reputation as being 'a man of his word', the stronger the degree of commitment.

3 The norms of social interaction prevailing in the business society within which the negotiation is being conducted – The commitment which a negotiator feels for a statement he has made depends, in part, on the expectancy which he believes others will have as to the likelihood of his telling the truth. If in a particular context it is recognized as legitimate to bluff, and no particular shame attaches to being caught out, then the commitment which a negotiator has to a verbal expression of intent will be small. If on the other hand the negotiator is operating within a business community in which his value as a negotiator is related strictly to the trust which others place in his word, and the penalty for being caught out is never to be believed again, the negotiator's commitment is absolute. He cannot afford to act otherwise than in accordance with his expressed intentions.

It is expected that in such a situation the negotiator would normally use statements in which the degree of commitment was only weakly defined and he had room left to manoeuvre. When, exceptionally, he made a definitive commitment then this would be regarded as a positive signal of his intentions to carry out the threat should the other side not accede.

THE BELIEF OF THE PERSON THREATENED

A threat which is designed as a deterrent will clearly be ineffective if the person to whom it is addressed does not believe it will ever be implemented. Our belief that they will implement a threat, should we not accede to their demands, will be related to:

1 The character of their negotiator and the consistency of his conduct on other occasions.

2 The loss of reputation for bargaining firmness which their negotiator would suffer were he not to carry out the threat, again taking into account the business environment within which the negotiation is being conducted.

3 Any overt act of commitment made by their negotiator from which he would find it difficult to withdraw, e.g. publicizing his intent to third parties.

4 The value to them of securing the concession to which the demand is related. Would they benefit to an extent which makes the threat sound sensible?

5 The economic loss which they would incur were they to carry out the threat. As a factor in their decision-making process this will clearly be in conflict with 2 and 3 but, whilst a generalization is difficult, it is believed that in any continuing relationship between the parties, the negotiator's reputation will be of greater importance than the economic loss. Expressed in another way, the negotiator is not likely in such a situation to put his reputation at risk unless he has already weighed the economic costs of threat implementation and decided they were worth risking.

THE LOSS WHICH WE WOULD INCUR

The general nature of a threat associated with a time limit is that if we do not accede then they will terminate the negotiation. Therefore, the comparison lies between the value to us of the bargain after making the required concession and the value of no bargain. As indicated in Section 13.1, a distinction must be drawn between a concession, such as discount, which is a certain reduction in value, and a concession, such as agreeing to an increased rate of penalty, which only creates the risk of loss.

OUR STRATEGY DECISION AFTER THEY HAVE MADE A TIME THREAT

Rationally, it is proposed that we should make our decision on whether or not to concede to their demand by comparing the two courses *accede* and *stand firm,* and selecting that which possesses for us the greater value.

If it is assumed that once we have given the concession, agreement is reached without further bargaining, then the value to us of acceding is simply that of the bargain after taking into account the effect of the concession. The value of stand firm, however, is not a certainty since it depends upon the other side's reaction to our decision. It can be expressed therefore only as an expected value according to the following equation:

$$(U_1 \times p_1) + (U_2 \times p_2); p_1 + p_2 = 1$$

in which:

U_1 = value of the bargain without the concession
U_2 = value of no bargain
p_1 = the probability of withdrawing their demand and agreeing to our terms
p_2 = the probability of them carrying out their threat and breaking off the negotiations.

The use of this decision rule clearly involves us in some risk, in the way described earlier in the discussion of the use of expected value techniques, whenever the value to us of the bargain, after accepting their demand, is higher than that of no bargain (see p. 111). Nevertheless, it is believed that it does represent in a quantified form the way in which most negotiators intuitively approach this problem in practice.

An alternative to the decision rule maximize security would mean that we would choose the strategy *accede* in any case in which the value of this course exceeded that of no bargain. In general, the adoption of this rule would be far too defeatist. It should only be considered in exceptional circumstances in which their commitment to the threat is regarded as very strong, and therefore the risk of its being invoked is high, and the importance of securing the bargain even after granting the concession is too substantial for risks to be taken.

REPEAT BARGAINING BETWEEN THE TWO SIDES

However, if we were consistently to adopt the decision rule of selecting the course which maximized expected value, and our dealings with the other side were on a continuing basis, then they would soon come to anticipate our decisions. By carefully selecting the threat, and ensuring that we were aware of their commitment to carrying it out, they would ensure that our decision was always to concede.

Our defence to any such tactics would be to pre-empt the other side by:

1 Defining in advance our own commitment to any issue on which we anticipated that they might develop a threat strategy.
2 Acting in a manner so as to avoid the gap on any major issue which they would be likely to use in conjunction with a threat being too wide too late in the negotiations. The narrower the gap towards the close of the bargaining period, the less they will be likely to stake their reputation or risk having to implement the threat, should we stand firm. By the same reasoning the lower is our credulity in the threat being fulfilled if we do stand firm.

Accordingly, if a time limit is foreseen in advance, at the penultimate stage in the bargaining we should ensure that on any issue which could be made the subject of a threat we have made an offer which we consider is sufficiently attractive to the other side to justify a compromise.
3 Randomizing our response to their threats by challenging them on certain occasions even though the rational decision would be to concede. The effect of this will be to confuse the other side in their attempts to build up a picture of our value structure and prevent them from making reliable estimates of the probability of which course we will select.

EMOTIONAL RESPONSE TO THE USE OF THREATS

The issue of a threat is an overt assumption on the part of the person making it that he has a power relationship with the person to whom the threat is addressed that allows him to make the demand which the threat carries and to expect the other person to obey. In considering the emotional reaction of the person threatened, two conditions are distinguished:

1 The existence of a power relationship which the person threatened finds acceptable in terms of his perception of the status differential between himself and the negotiator making the threat
2 The arbitrary assumption, by the negotiator who is threatening, of a power which the person threatened may be compelled to obey, but which he does not regard as legitimate and so does not respect or accept.

Under condition 1 the right to issue the threat is acknowledged and no sense of resentment will arise. Under 2, however, there will be a very strong feeling of resentment which is likely to give rise to an emotional outburst. A typical reaction would be: 'I will *not* give my agreement to those terms even if we do lose the order. It will serve him right too. He will have to pay more if he buys from anyone else.'

In this type of reaction the person threatened is concerned primarily with the results of his actions on the negotiator who is threatening and not with the effect on himself. He may be willing to accept significant punishment on his own behalf provided only that he can obtain the satisfaction of inflicting at least equal punishment on the negotiator who is threatening.

It has been suggested that the person threatened may regard the threat as legitimate if he regards the goal which the threat-issuing negotiator is seeking to obtain as legitimate.[6] This is especially so if, because of the identification of the means with the end, the person threatening is willing to regard the threat as depersonalized. If, as our negotiator, I can say that I understand and accept what the negotiator for the other side is trying to do and that I bear no personal grudge, then clearly I regard the threat he is making as legitimate, and will not feel emotionally disturbed because of it.

However, I may feel that he is going beyond his true function. If, according to my standards, he is trying to be greedy in order to satisfy his own personal motivation beyond a point which I can recognize as being reasonable, then I will react emotionally against any such threat.

The difficulty arises in practice because the standards of the two negotiators are seldom the same. Small differences may be tolerated but if the standards of the two negotiators are widely separate then emotions must be aroused, and the possibility of discovering an agreement which both sides genuinely accept that much reduced.

27.4 The tactical effect of time

By defining in advance the time limit within which our negotiator is required to make an irrevocable decision, the other side at once places the negotiator under pressure, the degree of which will be related to:

1 The importance of the decision
2 The time available
3 The extent of isolation of the negotiator.

IMPORTANCE OF THE DECISION

The more important the decision the greater the pressure which the imposition of a time limit creates. The negotiator, aware of the consequences of a wrong choice, will want the maximum opportunity to investigate, consider alternative courses of action and the wider issues involved, and to consult his superiors and colleagues.

Because of the time constraint he will be restricted to a greater or lesser degree in the extent to which he is able to follow through any or all of these opportunities. He will be compelled to act in some measure in a manner contrary to that in which he has been trained and even possibly to override the instructions he has received.

Inevitably, there will be conflict between the demands of the system, the ordered method of the company's negotiating control procedures, and the requirements of the negotiating situation itself. Under these circumstances the negotiator's behaviour would be expected to follow the sequence described below.

1 Initially the negotiator will react emotionally against the dissonance of the situation conflict into which he has been placed. He will describe it in exaggerated terms and put the blame on the negotiators for the other side or on his own head office, whom he will criticize severely.

   The psychological function of this outburst is to provide the negotiator with a defence mechanism. By defining the position as one of impossible difficulty, for which he is not responsible, he has lowered his own level of aspiration and provided justification for others to judge his actions according to that level. Despite the difficulties, if he is successful he will receive great credit; if he fails he will hope to escape censure.

2 The negotiator then seeks some course of action which minimizes the conflict between the system, or his instructions, and the demands of the negotiating situation. Within the time available, he tries to obtain revised instructions and to avoid commitments, which he knows would be totally unacceptable to his company, by redefining them in a way which appears to meet their demands but still provides us with essential protection.

Finally, he concedes to the limit he believes he could justify subsequently.

3 Having acted, he reduces the dissonance which still remains by altering his valuation of any possible course of action which he did not select, but which was attractive to him, so as to make it less attractive.

Suppose that he took the decision not to accept their demands on delay penalty, because these exceeded the company's norm for such clauses, but was nevertheless tempted to do so on the grounds that he personally did not believe the risk involved was substantial. He will now support this decision by changing his belief in the risk of paying penalty; from being a low risk it will now become significant.

TIME AVAILABLE

Clearly, in terms of making a final decision, the shorter the time allowed to the negotiator the greater the pressure to which he is subjected. From a personal viewpoint, he resists that pressure by adjusting his level of aspiration to that which he believes is the optimum he is likely to achieve within the time available.[7] Having made this adjustment he is no longer concerned with the amount of time involved, which then becomes a parameter of the decision-making process.

For example, if there is inadequate time to consult the company's head office lawyers on the drafting of the contract, the negotiator adjusts his level of aspiration for the preparation of the contract documents, downwards, from that of a legal expert to that which would be expected of a layman experienced in contract matters working on his own. Having made that adjustment, and in so doing provided himself with a defence against future criticism, the negotiator acts to achieve that level of competence without worrying about the improvement which could have been achieved had time been available for consultation.[8]

However, because the negotiator is successful in his defence to their time pressures in terms of enabling him to proceed with the bargaining without being subject to severe personal stress, this does not mean that there is no objective loss in efficiency. On the contrary, although the negotiator may rationalize away his inadequacies to himself, the inefficiency caused by such inadequacies still exists and will be reflected in the terms of the final bargain.

Time pressure often has an adverse effect by compelling hurried decisions, inadequate reviews, etc., all of which give rise to the risk of some vital point being overlooked. To a considerable extent, the negotiator can guard himself against this risk, if only he will take action to do so in advance, and before the time pressure becomes effective, for example, by:

1 Planning communication links with home base and ensuring that the right people will be available at the time when they will be needed.
2 Anticipating concessions for which the other side may ask and having approved answers available.

3 Ensuring that essential data for rapid reassessment of price or delivery periods are available.
4 Taking advice in advance on technical issues which may arise, whether these are of engineering, law or finance.

Extended negotiations

Time pressure can also be created in the opposite way by the other side deliberately extending the negotiations so that our negotiator is left uncertain about their real intentions. This tactic is most effectively used by a purchaser who is negotiating with two or more overseas suppliers.

The sales negotiator who wants to get down to business and conclude the bargaining is frustrated by the buyer's unwillingness to come to any firm decisions, by meetings being postponed, requests made for alternative or additional quotations, etc. He becomes fed up with life in the foreign hotel, despite its superficial glamour, suffers frequently in health from the effects of eating unusual food and the nervous strain of waiting and wondering, with the added worry of the effects of a prolonged absence from home on his domestic life.

These conditions, together with his natural desire to obtain the order, create an almost irresistible temptation to the negotiator to do anything, if only it will produce a definite answer. The purchaser obviously hopes that the 'anything' will take the form of significant concessions perhaps much greater than the negotiator is authorized to make, and often his hopes will be realized. The negotiator will make the concession for much the same reason as a political prisoner confesses; for the relief which he obtains from so doing. There may be problems in the future in justifying his actions but for the moment these are shut out by the release from tension which he now experiences.

Later when the negotiator does have to justify himself he would be expected to act again in the way suggested by the theory of cognitive dissonance and overestimate the disadvantages of the alternative courses of action which he rejected.

Is there any way in which the negotiator faced with this type of situation can be helped? From my own experience the answer is yes. There are steps which management can take and the most important are:

1 Sending a negotiating team which is tough, experienced and compatible.
2 Providing the negotiator with strong support from home base, e.g. quick and realistic answers to his queries.
3 Keeping in regular contact with the negotiator.
4 Giving management encouragement to the negotiator and giving credit to him for perserverence whilst sympathizing with his difficulties.
5 Helping out with domestic problems, for example, ensuring that a young wife with a baby is visited, that she is kept in touch and does not feel neglected.

If support of this type is given then it has been known for the position to be reversed; for the purchaser to have procrastinated too long so that eventually he comes under time pressures himself due to his need to get the order placed.

Natural breaks

Apart from any time limits imposed by the other side, time pressures are also created by natural breaks in the negotiations, especially if these are associated with social occasions.

When they have already made a concession during the morning bargaining session we will come under some pressure to reciprocate before the break for lunch, particularly if the two sides are lunching together. We will want the atmosphere to be relaxed rather than tense, for them to feel good towards us rather than the reverse. They can be expected to back up the pressure by making some remarks such as: 'Look, let us at least see if *something* can be settled before we break. I have given way on X, how about Y? Can you agree to that so we can achieve at least that much for a morning's work?' If we do not make the concession before lunch then we will be under even more severe psychological pressure to do so immediately after lunch. In such circumstances, continued refusal by the negotiator to make any sort of concessionary move must have the effect of alienating the other side and even members of our own negotiating team. They want the negotiator to respond to an atmosphere of goodwill by making the responsive concession.

Whilst pressures can be created by the existence of natural breaks they can also be induced by withholding a break, for example, the other side, who would normally have called the lunch recess, continue the arguments throughout the recess period. If we raise any objection we are at once put in the wrong by being told that if only we would be reasonable and agree then everyone could go to lunch.

DEGREE OF ISOLATION

Pressure on the negotiator becomes more intense the further he is isolated from his colleagues. This point has already been referred to in Section 19.1 when discussing the dangers of a one-man negotiating team.

Human beings are social animals who requires contact with other humans in order to operate effectively. The negotiator's needs are support, to review and reinforce his judgement, and balance, to correct any lack of proportion in his thinking.

If he is deprived of these needs by being isolated, and unable to communicate effectively with his home base, the negotiator soon becomes vulnerable. At the same time, if he is subjected to time pressures the situation can easily become one which it is beyond the capability of the negotiator to handle in a rational manner. He may then become either verbally aggressive, attacking the negotiator for the other side whom he treats as responsible for the situation, thus providing himself with a defence mechanism, or apathetic, refusing to participate further in a cooperative manner.

The measures to prevent this type of situation from arising are the same as those suggested previously dealing with extended time pressures.

27.5 Modification of the negotiating objective

Our original negotiating objective was formulated as the optimum outcome which we could foresee in relation to:

1 Their expected resistance to a range of possible demands
2 The time which would be expended to secure each outcome over the range of those foreseen as possible, and the related time costs and discount factors
3 The desirability to us of each outcome over the range of those foreseen as possible including
   the negative value of no bargain.

As a result of the initial contacts between the two sides it is probable that we will have been led
to modify factors 1 and 2. The way in which this modification may occur has already been discussed in Section 27.1.

The desirability to ourselves of each outcome should not have changed as a result of the
initial encounters between parties, unless, by their conduct, they have satisfied us that some
factor which influenced us in their original valuation was incorrectly assessed. Two examples
of the way in which this could occur would be:

1 They make it clear that our chances of securing worthwhile follow-on business are dependent on our willingness to establish local manufacturing facilities. We had not previously
   taken this point into account in assessing either our current costs or future returns.
2 They explain that our interpretation of their terms of contract is incorrect, and that the
   terms are much less onerous than we had believed, and we are willing to accept the explanation.

We are now in a position to draw together the three factors listed at the beginning of this
section, as modified by the experience which we have gained from the initial contacts, and to
reassess the potential outcomes over the spread of issues with which the negotiation is concerned, and the time which it would take to achieve each of these. This will enable us to determine the conditional value for each outcome and to estimate the probability of success.
Applying the techniques used previously we can arrive at an expected value for each outcome
and select the negotiating strategy which maximizes this expected value function.

Following on from the example of the supplier negotiating with the buyer as considered
previously in Chapters 16, 22 and 23, and assuming that the buyer has countered the seller
with the hard-line approach as set out on p. 173, the supplier now re-examines his position as
follows:

> I believe that the buyer is not bluffing and that he is looking
> for a reduction of about 10 per cent in the tender price. If I
> can achieve an exchange of the two-year defects period for a
> reduction in the penalty and a halfway position on the terms
> of payment then I would have 3.5 per cent in hand. If I then
> add to this my 5 per cent for the negotiating margin on price I
> have a total of 8.5 per cent available. This could be enough to
> get the contract and would allow me to just satisfy my negoti-
> ating objective. It would also leave me 2.5 per cent in hand
> before I reach my walk-away point. I think that should be my

preferred strategy but I will just check the expected value of that against the strategy of planning to concede down to my walk-away point. I need to know which to adopt since it will affect how much I offer initially against the improved payment terms and my further concession.

In order to do the expected value calculations, the supplier assigns a utility value to each of the outcome on a scale of 10 to –1, with the value of no-bargaining being assessed at –1. The supplier does not expect that the negotiations will last longer than the two months for which he has allowed. The supplier does not include any outcome more favourable to himself since he believes that would be impossible to achieve based on his view that the buyer is not bluffing. Nor does he consider any strategy of reducing his price below the total margin of 31.5 per cent since that approximates to his walk-away point as defined by the terms of his negotiating brief. It can be assumed that the supplier has a reasonable forward order book and, while interested in the business, is not desperate to secure the order.

Strategy number	Margin	Penalty cover	Defects cover	Terms of payment	Time costs	Conditional utility	Success probability
1	27.5%	1%	1%	2.5%	2%	6	40%
2	25%	1%	1%	2.5%	2%	3	60%

Utility of No-Bargain –1
Strategy 1 EV (Expected value) = 2.4– 0.6 = 1.8
Strategy 2 EV= 1.8 – 0.4 = 1.4

Figure 27.4   Expected value of alternative strategies

This confirms to the seller that he is right in going for the first strategy. However, it is critically dependent on his judgement that the negotiations based on that strategy are only going to take the two months.

27.6 Making the next move

In making our next move following from the opening, its review and our decision on the follow-up strategy choice, our primary concern is with the degree of commitment we attach to any issue. Commitment in this sense means that we adhere strongly to a defined viewpoint.

It has been established already that our firm commitment, which is demonstrated as such to the other side, is likely to cause them to reconsider their own estimates of success on the issue in question, and possibly to scale down their demands or their commitment to them accordingly. By demonstrating the strength of our commitment to any issue, we communicate to the other side the importance which that issue possesses for us. If we are successful in demonstrating a strong commitment, we will cause the other side either to concede outright or increase the value of the concession which they offer in exchange, unless they are prepared to accept the risk of no bargain.

However, extreme firmness of commitment will only be an embarrassment to us if we are compelled by pressures generated by the other side, or by external events, subsequently to withdraw. The loss of credibility which we will suffer will be even more serious than the immediate impact of the withdrawal on the outcome of the particular negotiation.

We are therefore in the dilemma that if we are not firm enough we will not convince the other side; if we are too firm, or firm on the wrong issue, we will lose credibility and will not be believed when later on we do genuinely intend to stand firm. The virtue of firmness lies only in its ability to be convincing to the other side.

In terms of the development of the negotiation the opportunities open to us, in order of their weakness of commitment, may be stated broadly as follows:

1 Exploratory talks – we give no indication of our commitment to any particular position but continue to explore the issues under negotiation as we did in the opening phase.
2 Negotiations on fringe areas only – we adopt a position of commitment only on minor issues; all major issues are put on one side for later discussion.
3 Negotiation on fringe issues; trade-off position developed on major issues – we negotiate and may reach agreement on minor issues; on major issues we define our position with varying degrees of commitment and seeks to develop an overall trade-off situation which will lead to a final bargain. This may be one single 'package' but is more likely to be several.
4 Repetition of initial offer on major issues; bargaining limited to fringe areas – we make it clear that in our view the negotiations are only about the fringe areas. Having defined our position on the major areas in our offer we are not prepared really to discuss these in any detail; we are willing only to restate our position from which we are not prepared to move.

Unless due to the commercial structure of the negotiation either party is in a position of significant bargaining superiority, the negotiations, when viewed from either side, would be expected to fall generally into category 3. Categories 1 and 2 are only a matter of 'putting off the evil day' and indicate a substantial weakness in our position. Category 4 can only properly be adopted by us if we are in a position of major strength. To select it we must be confident that the other side, faced with total intransigence on all major issues, will in the end concede.

The process of commitment will be progressive. On very minor points there may be almost immediate agreement unless any of these are retained as 'straw issues' (see p. 252) for use as bargaining counters at a later stage. On more significant points the parties will reiterate and expand on their previous proposals with varying degrees of commitment but without closing the door totally on the possibility of finding some way in which their respective viewpoints may be reconciled.

Some of the points already made in discussing the strategic aspects of the negotiation are relevant to the issue of how commitments can be made with varying degrees of firmness, and it may be useful to recapitulate these here:

1 A written commitment is firmer than one made verbally.
2 A commitment will be firmer:
   (a) The more formally it is made
   (b) The more senior the negotiator by whom it is made
   (c) The more final the terms in which it is made
   (d) The more specific the terms in which it is made.
3 A commitment can be increased by supportive action which is demonstrable as such to the other side.
4 Discussion of a proposal in advance within our own organization, and in particular its adoption as part of our negotiating plan, will increase our commitment to that proposal, and this commitment can be used by us to demonstrate to the other side the impossibility of our agreeing to anything else.
5 Commitment may be increased by reference to the authority or requirements of third parties.
6 Maximum commitment can often be demonstrated by a minimum response – a simple yes or no said with sufficient conviction is more effective than a long speech.

Once commitments have been convincingly demonstrated, individual trading off of points may then take place, on terms which will allow both sides to claim that they have secured their own underlying objectives, whilst giving recognition to the other's viewpoint.

Continuing our example, the seller proceeds with the negotiations on the rate and maximum of the penalty and the period for defects liability. The buyer has clearly committed himself to obtaining the two-year period. He refers to precedents already established from previous negotiations with other suppliers and to the difficulties he would have with his own management if the two-year period were not secured. The supplier senses that to agree anything less would cause the buyer's negotiators to lose esteem both in their eyes and with their peer group in their company. Without conceding the point the supplier concentrates on the penalty, maintaining that it is excessive in relation both to the value of the contract and to the buyer's foreseeable damages.

At length he proposes that if the buyer will reduce the penalty to 0.5 per cent per week with a maximum of 10 per cent then he thinks that he can meet the buyer on the two-year period for defects. The buyer's response is to indicate this could be acceptable but only as part of the final bargain and after the seller has made a significant reduction in the tender price. With that for the moment the seller must be content. At least it looks as if he will have available for the final bargaining the full 2 per cent margin included against the penalty risk.

There remain the major issues of the terms of payment and what proposal the seller is prepared to make on the tender price in return for an improvement in the payment terms. The buyer's negotiator now takes the initiative by telling the seller that they have spent quite enough time on the contract terms and he wants the seller's best offer tomorrow morning (Wednesday) as he is required to give his final recommendations to his board on the award of the contract by the end of the week.

This is the crunch point for the seller. He must now review the progress made and decide on the proposal to put to the buyer which will be sufficient not to cause an immediate emotional outburst of, in polite terms 'That's not nearly enough, you're just wasting time', but yet will both leave the seller with a little flexibility and protect his negotiating objective. The problem for the seller if he provokes the emotional response is that the buyer's negotiator, supposing him to have reacted like that, may then find it difficult to continue the negotiations on a constructive basis. How the seller and the buyer then proceed is discussed in Chapter 29, 'Concluding and recording the bargain'.

Notes

1. A. Coddington, *Theories of the Bargaining Process* (London: George Allen and Unwin, 1968), p. 93.
2. I have noted how some negotiators with whom I have dealt will immediately follow a concession with taking a hard line on some point of minor significance as if to say: 'Now do not misjudge me; just because I gave in a few moments ago does not mean I am a soft touch; I can be tough as well, when I want to be; so just remember that.'
3. J. G. Cross, *The Economics of Bargaining* (New York: Basic Books, 1969) p. 51.
4. T. C. Schelling, *The Strategy of Conflict* (London: Oxford University Press, 1963), p. 35.
5. See 'Threats in interpersonal negotiations', H. H. Kelley, *Journal of Conflict Resolution,* vol. 9 (no.7). The whole article is a thought-provoking analysis both of the use of threats and of the problems involved in the conduct of bargaining experiments, and the conclusions which may legitimately be drawn from them.
6. An example from my own experience concerned a negotiation in a foreign country in which the negotiating team, of which I was a member, was required to give immediate written answers to a series of propositions or withdraw from the negotiation. One of these propositions was for a three-month reduction in the delivery period! The answer given was to agree to the proposal but to provide that the delivery period started from the time when all technical information necessary to perform the contract was available, which in practice would have exceeded three months.
7. This follows the theory of *cognitive dissonance* developed by L. Festinger, described in *Scientific American* (October 1962).
8. The assumption is made that either the company's control procedures do not insist on the contract being reviewed by their lawyers or that if they do, the negotiator has decided to override them on the grounds that to insist on such review would cause the loss of the bargain. Again following the theory of cognitive dissonance it would be expected that the negotiator having made such decision would adjust his belief of the value of consultation with the lawyers, so that it became minimal. He would not allow himself to believe that a course of action which he had rejected possessed any significant value.

28 IDENTIFYING THE BARGAIN

28.1 Signalling to the other side

It was indicated earlier that one of the difficulties which face a negotiator is that of making his words credible. Since bluffing is universally recognized as an essential element in the real-life bargaining process, we expect the other side not to believe all that we tell them. Further, they will know that we do not expect them to believe everything and would regard them as a bargaining simpletons if they did. They are therefore constrained in two ways from believing what we tell them. First, in general, they have no absolutely reliable means of knowing whether we are telling the truth or not. Second, they are afraid of losing their own reputation as a negotiator with us if they permit themselves to be too easily deceived.

As the negotiations proceed, and each side makes concessions from the original starting position, the probability that they are telling more of the truth must increase. If either side actually does reach their minimum negotiating objective on any issue then they would actually be telling the truth if they stated they would prefer no bargain to making further concessions. But how is the other side to know this? How are they to distinguish our protestations, that we can concede no further, from those which we made earlier and from which we subsequently did concede?

The communication of credibility is a difficult task as many an unfortunate person has found when subjected to torture in order to compel him to disclose information of which he was ignorant. This is the serious disadvantage of any process of compulsion and perhaps of physical torture in particular; it may force someone to talk but cannot ensure that they will tell the truth.

How then do negotiators distinguish the truth from untruth? How do they know when they have secured the most favourable bargain which is open to them within the time-scale concerned?

One answer is that they do not make the distinction; they continue to be deceived all the way through the negotiation and the end bargain does not on any major issue represent the minimum negotiating objective of either side. This was the conclusion reached by Ann Douglas in the four cases which she studied in American union–management negotiations and is supported by my own experiences in the field of commerce.[1]

However, the end deception may be more apparent than real. The bargain which is negotiated constitutes, in Diesing's words, 'the terms by which the parties are to live together'.[2] He was referring to collective bargaining between unions and management, but in this respect the principles are identical with those which apply to long-term relationships between supplier and purchaser.

Since the bargain is of this nature, and because the implementation of the contract will afford the opportunity for either side to work for the adjustment of the terms, if they feel aggrieved, there is an incentive for both sides not to inquire too closely into whether the bargain really does represent the most favourable outcome they could achieve. The attitude of the negotiator might be described as that of the man who says:

> The bargain is good enough, even though I probably could achieve more. I know he is cheating a little, and if it makes him happy that's fine, but I've won the points I really wanted. It will probably help things along later; at least he will not be trying to score points.

Although this may represent the attitude of the negotiator at the time the bargain is made, it is not one which he will necessarily wish to disclose to his own management, or even later admit to himself. To his management he will rationalize the bargain as the best that was achievable; to himself he will adjust his beliefs so that they correspond to and support the action which he took. If this adjustment indicates that he may have been deceived the negotiator will look for a scapegoat which may be the other side or someone in his own organization.

The way in which the negotiator's attitude may change is illustrated by the three statements set out below which describe the way in which the same negotiator might represent the same bargain, first at the time at which it was made, then later to his own management and finally to himself:

1 At the time of making the bargain: 'I agree to a bargain of 100 although I suspect he would drop to 98, but a bargain at 100 satisfies my minimum negotiating objective, should keep him happy and ensure there are no problems in the future.'
2 To his own management: 'I settled for 100 which is well within the negotiating objective and shows a saving of £X on the earlier contract. I doubt if any further reduction was feasible and in any event could only have been secured at the expense of quality.'
3 Later to himself: 'I agreed to 100 because I thought it was the lowest to which he would go on the basis of his cost figures. He could have deceived me on that. If I find out he did he'll get no mercy next time.'

Another more positive answer to the question is that negotiators do keep certain words, phrases and manners of expression or behaviour intact in terms of honesty. They do so not because they feel constrained for any ethical reasons against telling untruths but for reasons of operational necessity.[3] As Diesing has expressed it: 'There must always be some way to communicate one's true position without deception and without misunderstanding.'[4]

However, as stated by Goffman, there must be strict limits placed on the use of such signals since otherwise the negotiator might be tempted to misuse them, and statements unaccompanied by such signs would carry little weight.[5] The limitation is created very largely by the norms and structure of the negotiation itself. In the early stages the other side's negotiator will bluff and exaggerate, and ours will expect this and act similarly. Later, as the bargaining moves to the stage of identifying particular concession-exchange situations, the negotiator will expect to receive signals from the other side which are genuine indicators of their position.

An example of a signal which is not totaly definitive but indicative of the availability of a bargain is: 'I'm afraid that we could not accept your proposals as they stand; however, you might like to see how they could be modified so as to meet the points we have raised.' This is a clear indication that the proposals *would be acceptable* if they were so modified. Another examples is: 'I have been thinking about the points which you raised on the defects liability clause. If you could agree to the wording we have suggested then I don't think we would have any difficulty on the issue of an overall limit of liability if this was at a significant level, say, the contract price.' The phrases 'I don't think we would have any difficulty' or 'I don't think there would be any problem with . . .' have become virtually standard ways of saying 'we would agree to' without being quite so specific. They are, however, clear indicators as to the bargain available.

Later on, when the negotiations have proceeded further the signals will be more specific and definitive of the details of the actual bargain, for example, 'We have discussed this long enough. We are not willing to depart from our standard clause on extensions of time. However, if you are prepared to accept that, then we will agree to your suggestion of reducing the liquidated damages to 0.5 per cent per week to a maximum of 10 per cent.'

When a negotiator recognizes that he has received such a signal he knows that a bargain is available to him on those terms, and that any other terms could only be secured, if at all, by the use of any power threat available to the negotiator. However, this would only be likely to result in driving the other side through their resentment level, so creating problems for the future.

The actual form of signal used will clearly vary from one negotiator to another but some which I have encountered in practice are as follows:

1 The negotiator states his position with the minimum of argument and includes some phrase indicative of commitment and the absence of bluff: 'That is my final position. It is now up to you.'
2 The proposal is complete and made in absolute terms; there are no loose ends.
3 The negotiator has left himself with no way out, other than to break off the negotiations, if his proposals are not accepted.
4 The negotiator's tone of voice is one of complete finality and his demeanour impassive. He looks straight at the other side and does not shuffle about, fidget, whisper to colleagues or engage in other forms of displacement-type activity which would be indicative of tension associated with lying.
5 The negotiator's answers to any questions from the other side are as brief as possible, often just a simple yes or no.

One method which the negotiator can use to be convincing to the other side on a particular issue is to transfer it from the area of intercompany relations to that of the interpersonal relationship between himself and his opposite number. By so doing he changes the norms of social morality from those which prevail between competing organizations to those which provide the basis for dealings between persons within the same social relationship group. In effect, the negotiator identifies himself and his opposite number as members of the club. During this period of identification the norms of morality which govern the negotiator's behaviour towards his opposite number, and according to which he expects his opposite number to behave, are those which apply between club members. Since it would be unthinkable for one club member to be dishonest to another, irrespective of how they treat outsiders, the negotiator by his actions has commited himself to telling the truth and equally has bound his opposite number to do the same.

This process will normally take place outside both the formal negotiating arena and the formal negotiating session, for example, at a coffee break or during pre-lunch drinks. The negotiator signals his intentions to his opposite number by treating him with a much higher degree of familiarity. He will use first names, perhaps take him by the arm, and will adopt a more intimate style of speech. If they have the same professional backgrounds or other common links the negotiator will refer to these.

28.2 Communication and coordination

In analysing the reasons which lead the negotiators finally to settle on one figure, or one set of words, in preference to any others, there is a distinction between:

1 Power point coordination
2 Focal point coordination.

POWER POINT COORDINATION

This refers to the situation in which the outcome is selected because it is preferred by both sides to no bargain and also represents the value which each believes the other only marginally prefers to no bargain, within the time period concerned. It is the outcome therefore which both sides believe is the minimum the other would accept within a specific time-scale.

The buyer agrees to a price of £100 because he was willing to pay up to £102 but believes the supplier will not sell today for less than £100. The seller agrees to £100 because he was in fact prepared to sell for not less than £98 but believes that the buyer today will not pay more than £100.

The beliefs of the two sides as to the other's minimum figure may or may not be true; in general, as in the example given above, it is maintained that they are not true. My experience over many years, first as a buyer and latterly as a seller, is that in almost every case the other side could have obtained more had they pressed their case further, although certainly the outcome would have taken longer to achieve. If that is our experience of the other side there is no reason to believe that their experience of us is any different.

The explanation for this failure to maximize advantage appears to lie in the reasons which have created the negotiator's belief. He can rarely have any independent knowledge as to whether the other side is willing to concede further or not. He must rely on the history of previous dealings with them, the way in which the negotiations have proceeded and his observations of what they say and do. His belief is accordingly entirely subjective and therefore subject to the family of motives which influence negotiating behaviour, some of which will favour proceeding further and others which will be in favour of settling now. The members of this family, which have been discussed already, are briefly identified in Figure 28.1.

Motives in favour of negotiating further	Motives in favour of settling now
1 Increasing the negotiator's self-esteem in which he is held by others of significance to him, by obtaining further gains.	1 The diminishing marginal utility of further gains and the adverse influence these may have on future relationships with the other side.
2 Satisfying the negotiator's need for self-actualization by achieving a better bargain.	2 The time it will take to secure further gains and the related time costs/discount factor.
3 Creating a more favourable precedent for the future.	3 The need for achieving certainty.
	4 The desire to end the conflict and establish or re-establish harmonious relationships with the other side.

Figure 28.1   Table of negotiating motives

The negotiator's belief as to whether the other side will concede further or not is a blend of prediction and motivation, in which the interpretation placed by the negotiator on his observations of their conduct is conditioned by the motives which influence the negotiator's own behaviour.

As the negotiations proceed and some concessions are made the degree of influence exerted by any particular motive will change. Initially the negotiator's need for achievement of esteem will pull him strongly towards holding out for better terms. However, once the negotiator's minimum negotiating objective has been secured, the influence of this particular motive will decline and that of another, say the fear of disturbing long-term relationships with the other side, will begin to influence the negotiator more strongly.

This change in motivation will in turn influence the way in which the negotiator interprets their behaviour. Initially he will disbelieve and therefore ignore their protests that they cannot accept some particular term but later he may be prepared to listen more closely and offer them a compromise – one that is designed not only to protect the negotiator but which will also, in the negotiator's judgement, satisfy their own motivation.

Provided that the negotiator's esteem motivation for continuing the negotiation is satisfied, to the point at which it ceases to be a matter of concern to him, no problem of dissonance will arise from his acting in a manner which will satisfy his other motivational drives. Suppose, however, that the esteem motive remains unsatisfied although the negotiator also recognizes that on balance other considerations, such as time costs, the need to obtain work for the company, preclude him from negotiating further. He will resolve the dissonance so created by 'interpreting' the resistance shown by the other side to mean that however long the negotiations had continued he could not have secured more from them. He will adjust his interpretation of their behaviour so that it eliminates any feelings of personal inadequacy which he might otherwise have possessed. Additionally he may look for a scapegoat, a previous precedent set by another negotiator, or a rash statement made in the tender for which he was not responsible.

Therefore, it is never recognized, in the objective sense, by the negotiator, that the other side will not concede further. He arrives at this belief in the compound way, from a mixture of observation and motivation. The influence of motivation has been discussed but how about the actual observation itself: what are the signs for the negotiator to read?

It is suggested that the following three signs are the most significant.

Continued repetition of a simple demand without change

By repetition the other side increase their commitment to the demand. This implies that they are willing to risk no bargain should we not agree and, therefore, securing the demand is a part of their minimum negotiating objective.

Establishment of a chain of logic which cannot be broken

If the other side can demonstrate that a chain of logic exists which supports a particular demand, this establishes a commitment to the achievement of that demand. They would suffer too serious a loss of esteem were they to abandon the demand after having made such a demonstration.

As an example of this type of commitment, in negotiating the terms of a supply contract I demonstrated that it was illogical to apply the same warranty terms to equipment, the failure of which would put the entire system out of operation, and to equipment which if it failed would only affect system operation to a minor degree. Having established this principle I was committed to the achievement of its acceptance by the purchaser.

Absence of any partial fall-back position

It is unlikely that the other negotiator will concede a demand if he has presented it in such a way that his only alternative to achieving success is capitulation. By denying himself the comfort of a fall-back position, which would allow him a partial gain at the expense of a partial concession, the negotiator puts himself into a situation in which he must either succeed or suffer serious humiliation. He is therefore strongly committed against making any concession.

Many examples could be drawn from other fields of human behaviour in which people have deliberately thrown away a safety mechanism in order to provide themselves with the strongest motivation for the achievement of their objective: the young swimmer who deliberately ventures out of his depth and throws away his plastic ring, the man with 'prospects' who takes on financial commitments slightly beyond his means and who must therefore ensure that the 'prospects' do materialize.[6]

FOCAL POINT COORDINATION

Focal point coordination refers to the situation in which each side recognizes that the *same* outcome would satisfy their minimum negotiating objectives and would provide a fair and reasonable settlement of the difference between them. If proposed to each of them by an independent mediator, each would separately agree that the point constituted a fair bargain.[7]

The conditions necessary for focal point coordination to occur are:

1 The two sides share a social and ideological background which is sufficiently common for them both to possess the same general views as to what is fair and reasonable.
2 The gap between the demands of the two sides is such that a solution which both recognize as fair and reasonable is identifiable as being preferred to any other mutual choice.

For example, if there is a prominent solution which balances almost equally the demands of the two sides, and both belong to a society which adheres to the equity of equal shares, then both are likely to identify a 50/50 split as being an acceptable outcome.

It is stressed that both conditions 1 and 2 must be satisfied if focal point coordination is to occur. For instance, if the buyer is concerned only with purchasing at the lowest price, and is uninterested in whether this policy in the long run provides sufficient rewards for suppliers to invest in efficiency, then focal point coordination will not arise, since the ideology of the two sides will be too sharply opposed. It is also worth noting in this context that different pairs of negotiators may differ in the focal point at which they coordinate or even whether or not they do coordinate.

The negotiator's attitude towards what he regards as a focal point on which to coordinate will depend upon:

1 His professional background – Coordination is easier if the two negotiators share the same background.
2 The extent to which his motivational drives for security and esteem have been satisfied – The less the negotiator feels the need to prove himself the more likely he is to be fair.
3 His emotional bias for or against the negotiator for the other side – Any prejudice against the other is bound to influence the negotiator to be less fair; conversely a favourable bias towards the other person will tend to influence the negotiator towards wishing to be fair and therefore he will more easily recognize a potential focal point.
4 His emotional bias for or against the principle which the other side is seeking to establish – Again any prejudice against the arguments being presented by the other side must prevent the negotiator from taking an objective approach.

Factors which will lead the two sides to recognize a particular outcome as a focal point will be:

1 A precedent set at a previous negotiation, the results or operation of which both sides have been satisfied.
2 The rounding down of a demand, usually so that the last two digits of a four-figure number, the last three digits of a five-figure number and the last four digits of a six-figure number are zeros. A supplier will often take advantage of this to arrange the price in such a way that the buyer reacts to the presentation accordingly. The fewer the number of zeros with which the price ends the more prominent the reduction to round numbers becomes as a focal point, e.g. £462,265 is a more powerful signal to coordinate at £460,000 than £462,200.
3 The gap between the demands of the two sides is not too large and can be divided in a manner which is intuitively appealing, e.g. 1:1 (50/50), 2:1 ($\frac{2}{3}$/$\frac{1}{3}$), 3:1 (75/25).
4 The existence of some formula, however crude, for apportioning the difference or relating payments, the facts for the calculation of the formula being easily ascertained and not in dis-

pute. The formula in this case takes on the nature of a scapegoat, as it does to some extent in factor 3. It becomes in itself the justification for the bargain and is at hand to take the blame should the bargain be criticized.

Sometimes the formula may not be so easy to agree. Consider the example of ten existing suppliers to a national retail chain being asked to agree to contribute a total of £50,000 towards the costs of a major in-store promotion planned by the retail chain of the suppliers' products. Which of the following formulae would you consider to be the 'fair' way in which the total of £50,000 should be divided between them assuming that all have agreed in principle to contribute:

1 Divide the total of £50,000 between the ten suppliers each paying the same amount?
2 Share the total of £50,000 between the suppliers in proportion to the turnover of each of the suppliers with the retail chain over the last twelve months?
3 Share the total of £50,000 between the suppliers in proportion to the total turnover of each of the suppliers over the last twelve months?

Formula 1 is simple and has the advantage that each supplier can then argue for the same treatment as each of the others in the promotion of his products. It suffers, however, from two disadvantages. It takes no account either of the relative size of the firms or of their current level of business with the retail chain from which they might be expected to benefit by the promotion. Formula 2 suffers from the first disadvantage but does get over the second one. Formula 3 gets over the first disadvantage but does not relate the cost to the potential benefit.

My own personal preference would be for formula 2, but I recognize there are arguments against it. It could for instance be argued that it is the firm who is presently doing the *least* amount of business with the retail chain which stands to gain the most and that therefore the sharing should be in reverse proportions to the current levels of business.

There is of course no right solution and certainly not one which would be likely to please everybody. That the costs should be shared somehow equally is unlikely to be disputed but what does equality mean? For the sharing to be genuinely equal there must either be equality in the initial position of the suppliers or the formula must take their initial inequality into account. It is this requirement which creates the problem; one well-known to those who promote schemes to create social justice.[8] In practice and in desperation, it is quite probable that formula 1, sharing the costs in the same amount each, would be the one which would be chosen. The others are just too difficult, which brings out the point that the simpler any formula can be made, even if it is only rough justice, the more probable is it that it will be chosen as the point upon which the parties will coordinate.

As suggested in the comment on factor 2, it is common negotiating strategy for one party to structure his demand or his response to the other's demand, in such a way as to create a situation which points towards a focal point. If the invitation is accepted, the bargaining is then concerned with the identification of the actual focal point upon which to coordinate and not with the principle of acceptance or non-acceptance of the negotiator's demand/response.

OUR STRATEGY CHOICE

The capability of the two sides to coordinate at all is primarily a function of the compatability of their needs. If these are compatible to a degree which makes coordination feasible, then the type of coordination and the point at which it occurs will be a reflection of the ideology and personality characteristics of the negotiators involved.

In deciding on his negotiating strategy, therefore, our negotiator is not a free agent. He is restricted in his choice by factors related to the others, at least some of which he cannot hope to change, e.g. their social and political ideology. If their belief system is such that they regard securing the most favourable price as more important than incurring delays to the project through protracted negotiations (which used to be the case with communist-state purchasing organizations), then the negotiator must expect him to be strongly motivated towards continuing the negotiations regardless of the consequences for the project. (I have been told by those with personal experience that this can apply in India to the purchasing of spares for a major plant construction.) Because of this need to secure concessions, he can also be expected to go on for a longer period of time refusing to believe the argument that no further concessions can be made. The conditioning effect of motivation on belief is not confined to one ideology alone.

Under these circumstances focal point coordination is clearly impossible and power point coordination something to which he will only move slowly and with reluctance.

Our negotiator makes his choice, therefore, taking into account his belief of the other side's attitudes. If these are in sympathy with coordination on a focal point, the negotiator's original demand and subsequent concessions are directed towards that focal point which represents the most favourable outcome he believes he can secure.

Alternatively, if the negotiator considers the other side will not be sympathetic towards a focal point, his strategy will be to convince them of his commitment to the achievement of some outcome which he believes is just acceptable to them, within a time-scale which makes that outcome optimal for him.

28.3 Policy issues

In their search for a solution upon which to coordinate, a factor which may inhibit the two sides is any issue of which the acceptance or non-acceptance would involve the negotiator in departing from a policy rule. If the rule is in the nature of a social custom then, under extremes of pressure, the negotiator may give way and correct the dissonance so caused by an adjustment of his belief as to the respective values of the custom and the bargain he has made. However, if the rule is a command which the negotiator (say, for the other side) is compelled to obey, no concession is possible and the negotiator's continued insistence on the point must cause the negotiations to deadlock.

The alternative is to search for a solution which does not directly involve any point of principle, but is concerned solely with practicalities. In a dispute between two nations over their rights in regard to a disputed piece of territory, to raise the issue of sovereignty directly must cause an emotional deadlock, as, for example, the dispute between the UK and Argentina over the sovereignty of the Falkland Islands. Provided that the negotiators concentrate on such practical matters as customs formalities, entry and exit documents, work permits, etc., a workable compromise may be achieved.

The same type of problem will arise in negotiations with government departments or quasi-governmental organizations. Sometimes the rules of these bodies have the force of law, for example, the Armed Services Procurement Regulations of the USA. In other instances, as with the standard contracting procedures of the British government departments and public utilities, they are a matter of departmental orders which, whilst lacking the force of law, are regarded as binding by the officials concerned and only subject to amendment with difficulty and at the highest level. To depart from them in a particular case would create a precedent which it would then be difficult, particularly for Ministry officials, to refuse to others.

The commitment of the government body to these rules clearly strengthens the bargaining position of the government negotiators. They cannot concede the issue and their lack of authority is demonstrable to the commercial negotiator who knows that if he raises the issue directly he cannot succeed.

By the establishment of such rules the issue is transferred outside the negotiating arena and converted into a parameter of the negotiating situation, inside which the commercial negotiator must seek the means to achieve his objective. If the negotiator is bound by a government accountancy formula for determining his overheads, he must look elsewhere for the recovery of these cost elements which the formula disallows. Instead of arguing the principle of whether a particular element of overheads should be allowed or not, the negotiator bargains on a percentage figure, as a figure, without reference to the elements of which it is constituted. This can be taken a stage further and the price, as a whole, negotiated without any settlement being reached on particular cost items, wage rates or profit margins, on which, if taken individually, the official negotiator may be unwilling to commit himself for fear of offending some rule or creating a precedent for the future.

Notes

1. A. Douglas, *Industrial Peacemaking* (Columbia: Columbia University Press, 1962), p. 199.
2. P. Diesing, 'Bargaining strategy and union–management relationships', *Journal of Conflict Resolution,* vol. 5 (no.4) footnote to p. 376.
3. Moral repugnance against lying arises only when to lie would be contrary to the social behavioural norm established by society for the particular circumstances in question. Society has not designated bargaining in general as an area in which there is a social norm against the making of self-disbelieved statements. On the contrary (see Section 10.3) it has been proposed that it is an accepted part of negotiating behaviour to make such statements, and no condemnation will be made of the person making them provided that they arise naturally out of the negotiations.

   It is only certain acts, e.g. shaking hands to seal an oral bargain, which society treats as a commitment from which it would be socially unacceptable for the negotiator to seek to withdraw.
4. P. Diesing, 'Bargaining strategy and union–management relationships', pp. 375–76. See also I. Goffman, *Strategic Interaction* (Oxford: Blackwell, 1970), p. 128.

5. I. Goffman, *Strategic Interaction*, p. 129.
6. For examples see T. C. Schelling, *The Strategy of Conflict* (London: Oxford University Press, 1963), p.19. Schelling also makes the point that the negotiator increases the effect of the commitment by making it clearly visible to the other side that he has no fall-back position.
7. For an example of a solution proposed by a mediator which provided a focal point on which the negotiators could coordinate see T. C. Schelling, *The Strategy of Conflict*, p. 63.
8. See A. McIntyre, *After Virtue* (London: Duckworth, 1981), Chapter 17.

29 CONCLUDING AND RECORDING THE BARGAIN

29.1 The final review

Immediately prior to the session at which the negotiator believes the final bargain will be reached, it is essential that he conducts a review for the purpose of:

1 Identifying *all* the points which are still outstanding
2 Deciding on the bargain on each point which he expects to achieve, and the limit on each point to which he is prepared to concede either singly or in combination with other issues
3 Determining any particular tactics to be used
4 Deciding on the arrangements for recording the bargain.

The duration and formality of this review will depend on the magnitude of the negotiations. It may be only a twenty-minute recess towards the end of a single day's bargaining; it may be a formal meeting, at which a director or general manager of the firm is present, before the negotiator and his colleagues depart for the final round of talks.

Irrespective of the form of the review, it is the time at which the final decisions must be made and the alternative of no bargain squarely faced. The approach to the review should therefore be in terms of the value of the agreement to us as a whole. Each outstanding point, on which the policy has been to resist the other side's demands, should be re-examined to see whether we really would prefer to walk away and lose the bargain rather than to concede. This is the time at which narrow departmental interests *must not* be allowed to prevail. This is not suggesting a policy of concession but one of realism in relation to our overall business objectives. Contractual risks may be unpalatable to the lawyer and every effort made to avoid the more serious ones, but, in the end, a contract should only be turned down if an evaluation of the risk shows that it is unacceptable relative to the contract as a whole and to the totality of our business circumstances.

Even if there has been an agreement on the trading of certain concessions it is expected, as advised earlier (see p. 171), that these 'agreements' are provisional until the whole of the bargain has been concluded. The stage has now been reached when these 'agreements' must be finalized and the bargain as a whole concluded unless either party decides that 'no-bargain' is preferable to what is on final offer and walks away from the table.

We need therefore to take all the provisional agreements as a package and make sure that we include everything on which there is any reservation on their part, anything where they have perhaps said 'Yes that seems OK, but we would just like time to think it over.' The time for thinking over is past now but you must make sure that you cover all these so that they cannot come back later and raise the issue again. This is where it's so important in negotiating a total contract that you have kept a running record as you have gone through the clauses on the provisional agreements reached and the points still finally to be agreed.

When it comes to what is often referred to as 'the close', my preference is for the summary method where you summarize all the 'provisional' agreements and trade-offs which have been made and any issues which have been left outstanding, and then make your final proposals as a complete package. Whether at that point you offer a 'sweetener' or not depends on your judgement as to its value in securing an agreement now. There is also the possibility with certain organizations that the final negotiations may be held by someone from their management who is of significantly higher seniority than the officials with whom you have been negotiating. If you suspect this may happen then you must allow for being in a position to give him a concession which is:

1 Large enough to just satisfy the higher dignitary in terms of his need to maintain his position, but
2 Not so large that he censures his officials for having failed to do their job and insists that they continue the negotiations further.

The concession is of course traded for an immediate agreement now and not made unilaterally.

When making your offer of the final bargain you make it clear that it is final and display total commitment towards it in the ways suggested earlier (see p. 201). The bargaining is over and it is up to the other side to accept or not. Any suggestions by them for further discussions should be courteously refused.

It is also only to be expected, however, that even if the other side have provisionally agreed to certain terms that they will try and extract at least one more concession. This has been named the 'quivering quill' ploy.[1] From the purchaser it runs along something like these lines: 'Just before we conclude everything could we please revisit the clause on the defects liability period. I was never quite sure we made it clear that your obligations at law continued after the expiry of the defects liability period.' Of course as the supplier we made it quite clear when the clause was discussed that our obligations in law did *not* extend beyond the end of the defects clause and the purchaser is trying for what is quite a substantial concession. Our response must reflect that situation: 'I'm sorry if you misunderstood the position but we went over this clause carefully and it clearly states that the end of the defects period is the end of our obligations. This was the basis upon which we agreed the defects period and your other amendments to our clause. We really cannot go back over this now. If there is nothing else you wish to raise can I suggest that we get the fair copies printed off and then we meet at say 10.00 hours to initial them before the final signature tomorrow afternoon.' If we were to give in and start negotiating on the clause then, even assuming we could come to some compromise agreement, he would try the ploy again on a different issue.

Of course the concession asked for may not be nearly so substantial as this and we may perhaps for the sake of getting the signature quickly and retaining the goodwill that has been built up between us be inclined as the final 'sweetener', to agree. In that event our reply must be such as to make it clear that this is the last move we are going to make: 'All right, for the sake of bringing matters to an end and in view of your agreement on the extensions of time, we are prepared to accept that the manuals should be made available to you in draft form 56 days before the tests on completion and not 28 as at present with the final versions being supplied with the as-built drawings 14 days after the passing of the completion tests. I think that meets your point. But I must emphasize that this is it – no more discussions, no more last-minute points.' Then refer to the timing for the copies to be initialled and the contract signed.

Suppose now that as the negotiator you are faced with an ultimatum from the other side. They set out their terms for the bargain and tell you in so many words 'Take it or leave it'. Is it a bluff or for real? You should have anticipated this when you made your final review. At this stage in the negotiations it is more likely to be for real than a bluff. Your only guidance is in:

● The seniority of the person by whom it is made; the more senior the more likely it is for real.
● The way in which it was made, the firmness of expression, the completeness of terms and the lack of any fall-back position. All this will again point to it being genuine.
● Any external factors such as your knowledge of any real deadlines to which he is working, e.g. the programme requires that the contract is signed by the end of the week.

Assuming that you decide the ultimatum is real then you accept it, provided that it satisfies at least your minimum acceptable terms, your 'walk-away point', and if there is no better alternative available to you within the same time-scale. If you believe it to be a bluff then you seek to reopen the negotiations, and you will soon learn whether you were right or not! If you are wrong, you can certainly expect an emotional outburst and probably the person who delivered the ultimatum to march out of the room.

If he does, don't panic. They have put a lot into the negotiations as well and must have decided that you were the right party with whom to contract so are unlikely to want to start all over again with somebody else from whom it's doubtful that they will get a better deal. Keep the talking going and wait for the atmosphere to calm down. Recognize, however, that your mistake is going to cost you and that the very best you can hope for are the terms of their last ultimatum. More probably you will be offered rather less and if it meets your minimum negotiating objective then accept.

Returning to our example of the sales negotiation which we left in Chapter 27, p. 201, with the seller having to decide on his response to the buyer's ultimatum to give him his best offer, what's the seller to do? It is suggested that his reply should be on the following lines:

> Thank you for the opportunity to clarify the terms of contract.
> Provided it is agreed that:
> ● Our penalty liability is 0.5 per cent per week to a maximum of 10 per cent
> ● The terms of payment are 85 per cent on interim certificates, 10 per cent on takeover and 5 per cent at the end of the defects period,
> then we would agree to your request for a 24-month defects liability period and to a reduction in the contract price from £348,000 to £315,000.

This should be said simply, with maximum conviction and firmness, looking straight at the buyer's negotiator. The figure of £315,000 has been chosen deliberately because it achieves the seller's negotiating objective as identified in his brief and is a round number from which there is nowhere for the seller to move. It offers the buyer a substantial reduction and is a point on which the parties could coordinate. In practice, it is considered that the offer would be likely to be accepted. However, any attempt by the buyer to reduce the price further, must be totally rejected by the seller. He has made his pitch and must not concede further. Also what he has offered is a total bargain. Any suggestion of modifying the contract terms in the buyer's favour equally cannot be accepted.

29.2 *Ensuring that the agreement is genuine*

One of the difficulties in negotiation is to ensure that the two sides have an identical understanding of what is being said. Differences in terminology, the use of words which are terms of art to one side but not to the other and differences in language can all contribute to misunderstandings. It is vital when the bargain is being made that the two sides should have the same understanding of the terms to which they have agreed.

The following is a guide to some points which commonly cause difficulties and on which the negotiators should be especially careful.

PRICE

1 Is this fixed or can the contractor recover for increases in labour and material costs?
2 Does the price cover taxes, duties and other statutory charges? If so, and these are increased during the period of the contract, who pays the increase?
3 Is the currency fixed against exchange-rate fluctuations?
4 Is it clear what the contract price does *not* include?

COMPLETION

5 Is completion clearly defined? Does it include customer testing of the plant/system?
6 Can a completion/acceptance certificate be issued if minor items are missing which do not affect system/plant performance?
7 Can completion be by sections and is this clearly set out?
8 Are the maximum liquidated damages for delay in full satisfaction of the contractor's liability for delay or can the purchaser terminate once the maximum has been reached?

SPECIFICATION

9 Are the purchaser's obligations clearly defined for the issue of permits, licences and approvals of drawings, etc., with time periods for the performance of each?

10 If any general standards of national or international institutions are referred to, is it clear which issue of these applies and which parts are relevant to the contract?

11 Are the materials/equipment tests both in factory and on-site clearly defined with their tolerance limits and testing methods?

12 Is it clear who has the responsibility for customs clearance, delivery of goods to site, off-loading and storage?

13 Is it clear who has the design responsibility for both the permanent and any temporary works?

DEFECTS

14 Is the contractor's liability to make good defects in addition to or in substitution for the purchaser's rights at law?

15 Is the contractor still liable in damages for latent defects after the expiry of the defects liability period?

LAWS AND JURISDICTION

16 Does the contract define the applicable law?

17 Does the contract define how and by what tribunal(s) disputes are to be determined?

CLAIMS SETTLEMENT

18 What is the scope of the settlement?

19 Is the settlement a final bar to any future legal proceedings?

Points such as these, so far as they apply to any particular negotiation, and any others judged relevant, should be gone through thoroughly to ensure that there is a genuine meeting of minds between the two sides. It may be objected that this gives either side the opportunity to back-track and reopen a point already settled. It is admitted there is a risk of this, but it is judged to be a less serious risk than that of entering into a bargain which genuinely is interpreted quite differently by the two sides.

29.3 Recording the bargain

Depending on the nature of the negotiations, there are a number of ways in which the bargain may be recorded; the fundamental point is that it is recorded in writing and initialled by the two sides before they depart. The possible methods of recording are:

1 Notes or clauses are read over and agreed between the negotiators as each point is settled. Normally this method is used when the negotiations are concerned with the commercial clauses and specifications for a complete contract.

2 Notes of the day's discussions are prepared by one side in the evening and presented for agreement as the first item of the next day's agenda. Only when these have been agreed do

the negotiations proceed. This is laborious but recommended for prolonged negotiations particularly in certain overseas countries.

3 Notes of the discussions are prepared by one side and presented for agreement at the end of the negotiations. This is the easiest method provided that the negotiations only last two or three days.

The meetings should never be allowed to break up without an agreed written record. The practice of one side issuing minutes days or even weeks later has nothing to commend it, and only causes more argument as the minute writer is so easily tempted into recording what he would have liked to have been said and not what actually was said.

Note

1. G. Kennedy, *Kennedy on Negotiation* (Aldershot: Gower, 1998), p. 259.

PART 4

NEGOTIATION TACTICS

30 INTRODUCTION TO PART FOUR

Tactics are often thought of as negotiating ploys used in certain ways and in defined situations to obtain some advantage. Some books on negotiation, especially those originating in the USA, contain very little other than a description of such ploys, often with rather colourful names attached to them. Some ploys as described in such books are ethical while many others most certainly are not. Kennedy gives a number of examples of such non-ethical ploys in his book on negotiation, making clear his own dislike of them.[1] He also points out that the problem with these ploys is that they take no account of how the contract works out in the end or of what happens either when the two negotiators meet again or the reputation of the one using the ploy, in essence to cheat the other, gets known around the industry concerned.

It may be that US culture favours the individual who is sharp enough to put one over the other side, however ethically dubious the tactic may have been which was used. Importantly, the examples and illustrations used in the US books are very largely one-off deals and many take place in domestic situations, like selling a house or buying a car. Others are descriptive of management–union negotiations, selling/buying a business or even negotiating with your boss over a salary increase. Complex contractual negotiations involving organizations likely to do business with each other again are rarely discussed.

Interestingly, several US texts seem to find it difficult to distinguish between what is sound, practical and entirely ethical advice, and referring with admiration to tactics whose use is clearly unethical and an abomination. For example, Philip Sperber in *Fail-Safe Business Negotiating*[2] suggests that it is a good idea immediately after the deal has been reached to have it recorded in a jointly signed memorandum of understanding. I quite agree. However he then goes on in the next paragraph to state

> ... even after the signing of a formal contract many *skilled* tacticians continue to negotiate for better terms ... an example is when your vendor gives terms of net thirty days. You write saying it is your company's policy to pay cash in fifteen days and take a 2 per cent discount. You indicate it is your expectation that this is acceptable and that any objection should be received in writing in 10 days. When it comes to performing under the contract many *skilled* negotiators use the tactic of nibbling which involves minor breaches of the contract or other actions which are not technical breaches of the contract but which are not in the spirit of what the parties intended. Buyers nibble by paying bills late, taking unearned discounts, requesting special services, getting consulting and training

> assistance without payment and getting better quality than contracted for.

He goes on to give examples of the ways in which sellers 'nibble'. How one reconciles the statement that the negotiators are 'skilled' by adopting the practices which even he refers to as 'not in the spirit of what the parties intended' is not explained.

Such negotiators for either buyers or sellers are not 'skilled', they are cheats and their behaviour is nothing short of fraudulent. It is not a matter of genuine misinterpretation of the contract but of acting deliberately, certainly against the spirit if not the letter, of the contract in minor respects in the hope that the other side will not be bothered to take action to stop it.

The use of tactics such as 'nibbling' should have no place in the armoury of a skilled negotiator other than to use as a counter, say, to his having been forced to reduce his initial price below a reasonable level, or by the buyer's insistence, probably untrue, that there was no way in which he could possibly pay any more for the goods and services in question. That is of course the major problem with ploys of that nature. The success of the ploy of the 'bogey', that is, 'there's no more in the budget', in forcing the seller to bring his price lower than he should have done, is almost an invitation for the seller during the performance of the contract to 'nibble' in every way possible. No extra effort will be forthcoming to overcome difficulties unless paid for in full. Instead every opportunity provided by the contract will be taken to obtain additional payment. Not only will he be working to recover his lost margin but to satisfy his emotional resentment against the purchaser for the way in which he considers he has been treated.

To be found out playing tactical games, especially ones which involve deceit, is a sure way to end up with a substantial bill for extras.

Are there then legitimate tactics which can be used to assist the negotiator without being unethical and causing serious resentment to those acting for the other side? Yes, there are a few, and a few more which are borderline cases of which the negotiator should be aware. But essentially tactics should be directed towards obtaining a bargain which sufficiently satisfies both sides that they are wholehearted in their support for carrying it out in the terms in which it has been negotiated.

Notes

1. G. Kennedy, *Kennedy on Negotiation* (Aldershot: Gower, 1998), pp. 110, 208–15.
2 P. Sperber, *Fail-Safe Business Negotiating* (New Jersey: Prentice Hall, 1983), pp. 160 and 161.

31 ATTITUDINAL TACTICS

Tactics fall into two categories: attitudinal and situation. Attitudinal tactics are those which relate to the attitudes the negotiators for the two sides have towards each other.

In adopting such tactics, the negotiator is seeking to create the conditions under which the personal interactions between himself and his opposite number lead to a solution which is closer to his own viewpoint and at least satisfies his minimum negotiating objective. In a long-term relationship between the two sides a factor of almost equal importance is that the desired result is achieved without creating a feeling of resentment in the other negotiator.

In any negotiation, the negotiators for both sides are each playing a role in which their role characters are to a degree opposed to one another. The factors which will determine the extent of this opposition are:

- The way in which the negotiator 'sees' the role character – He may have been conditioned by the industry culture, and his own management and colleagues, into believing that he should behave in a 'macho' manner. This is the attitude traditionally associated with buyers and with site managers for construction contractors. It still prevails to some extent, particularly when times are difficult for the firm.
- The negotiator's own personality and the extent to which this is in sympathy with or opposed to his view of the role character – His role attachment will be that much stronger to the extent to which it is in line with his own personality.
- The negotiator's own level of aspiration relative to that of his opposite number – In general, the higher their levels of aspiration the greater the degree of opposition between them.
- The personality interaction between the two negotiators. This will be affected by the perception which each has of the other, which is of two kinds:

  1 Of what he expects of anyone in the role which that person is playing – If he is the buyer he may expect a sales manager to be silver-tongued and economical with the truth.
  2 How he perceives the actual person with whom he is negotiating – He may fit the negative stereotype which the negotiator has in mind or he may recognize him as someone for whom he can have respect and with whom he can do business.

For the success of the negotiations and long-term relationships between the parties it is important that negative stereotyping, unfortunately in some situations only too common, is combated as early as possible.

The tactics which are designed to modify these four factors, so as to improve the chances of reaching agreement on terms which are favourable to us, may be classified as *positive* and *negative*.

A positive tactic is one which is intended either to reinforce the other side's behaviour, which is already favourable to us, or to change their behaviour in the desired direction by emphasizing the rewards which they will obtain from so doing.

Negative tactics are those which are intended either to deter the other side from some foreseen course of action, which would be unfavourable to us, or to change their behavioural direction away from its present course, by actually penalizing them, or at least indicating the penalties they will suffer unless they do change.[1]

31.1 In the opening phase

At the commencement of any negotiation the initial attitudes of the negotiators for the two sides will range between reserved cordiality and concealed hostility depending on the extent to which:

1 The negotiators are already known to, and have respect for, each other
2 The results of the last negotiation and the outcome of the contract, if any, which followed from these, and how far the result satisfied the negotiator's personal motivation.

The manner in which the negotiator makes his first approach, and the tactic he selects, will be based upon his judgement as to the form which these attitudes take. The possible situations and the appropriate tactical choice are analysed as follows:

Situation	Class of tactical choice	Example of tactic to be employed
Negotiators known to, and respected by, each other. Last negotiation satisfied both sides.	Mild, positive	1 Questions designed to identify the sharing of common business interests: 'How are your plans going for . . .' 'I was interested to see the progress you have been making in . . . 2 Questions and/or statements intended to re-establish close personal relationships. 'How is the family? 'Have you been playing any (golf, tennis, etc.) lately?'
Negotiators known to and respected by each other. Last negotiation did not wholly satisfy our negotiator.	Mild, positive plus Mild, negative	1 As for the previous situation. 2 Use of statements to indicate negotiator would have a personal problem if he does not achieve a better result than he did last time:

Situation	Class of tactical choice	Example of tactic to be employed
		'I'd better say straight away John that I cannot afford a repeat of what happened on (name of last contract). If we are going to get anywhere, and I am sure we will, I hope you have come prepared to be a little more flexible.' Note this approach identifies the problem as one which is personal to the negotiator and he appeals to his opposite number on a personal basis, but with just the hint of a threat behind his words.
Negotiators known to each other but the negotiator does not respect his opposite number.	Strong, positive plus Strong, negative	Use of statements to emphasize benefits to be gained by not repeating the past coupled with with definite threats should the other side not respond. 'I am sure we both want to make progress so I suggest we ignore past negotiations and concentrate on the present and future. We have got some firm proposals to make which are intended to be constructive. I suggest we discuss these with an open mind and see how far we can reach. If, having done that, you still do not feel they can form the basis of an agreement, we shall have to decide where we go from there. Maybe we shall have to take the matter upstairs and call in (refer to managing director or other relevant person of superior authority) and get him to talk to your Mr. . . . I would prefer that not to happen and so, I am sure, would you so let us see if we can get there on our own.'

Situation	Class of tactical choice	Example of tactic to be employed
Negotiators not known to each other personally but the other side has had previous dealings with the negotiator's company.		
1 Previous dealings regarded by the negotiator as having been satisfactory.	Mild, positive	Use of statement to indicate that the negotiator is aware of the satisfactory nature of the previous dealings and to identify personal points of mutual contact. Use of questions to discover points of common interest and to bring the negotiator into the family of personal relationships which exist between the negotiator for the other side and the member of our firm.
2 Previous dealings not regarded by the negotiator as wholly satisfactory, so that he wishes to avoid these being treated by his opposite number as a precedent for all aspects of the current negotiation.	Mild, positive plus Mild, negative	Use of questions and/or statements which will lead to the establishment of a personal relationship, but which will also indicate to his opposite number that the negotiator has taken over from those with whom he dealt before, and does not necessarily accept as a precedent the terms of the earlier bargain. The selection by the negotiator of one or more issues upon which he takes a tough line to serve as a warning to the other side that the negotiations will not be so easy this time, and the sooner his attitude changes the better.
Negotiators not known to each other and no recent personal contacts between members of their respective firms.	Strong, positive	The use of questions aimed at discovering points of common interests and identifying any strongly held beliefs. Not all these questions would be asked at once but as the opportunity arose during initial

Situation	*Class of tactical choice*	*Example of tactic to be employed*
		periods of conversation, over drinks or during lunch/dinner. These questions might cover:

1 Length of time with company and area of responsibility.
2 Previous company and position held.
3 Professional background.
4 Outside interests, e.g. golf, tennis, sailing.
5 Family: children, education, etc.

Having asked the questions, the negotiator volunteers in reply information about himself and his own business/ social situation which emphasizes points of mutual interest or contact. Points upon which the negotiators differ or lack mutual interest are minimized.

31.2 In the later phases

It has already been suggested that one of the factors which will affect the other side's attitude towards the negotiator is their level of aspiration, and that they will select a level which maximizes the product of their personalistic utility function and the probability of achieving that level.

Since the higher their level of aspiration, the greater their opposition to us, it must be in our interest to reduce their aspiration level, and so develop in them an attitude more favourable towards our viewpoint. Therefore our attitudinal tactics will be those which the negotiator considers are the most appropriate for persuading them that the utility we would gain, and/or their chance of obtaining that outcome, are less than they thought.

Some possible means which we can use for this purpose are now considered.

CHANGING THE OTHER SIDE'S UTILITY VALUATION

One course of action would be to persuade the other negotiator that in the long term he personally will lose more than he will gain if he insists on demanding a particular outcome.

As an example, consider a contractor who is negotiating with a construction authority which is insisting on a more onerous penalty clause than the contractor wishes to accept. One argument against the authority could be that if the particular line on penalty is insisted upon and the contractor is forced to agree, then to protect himself, he would be compelled to apply strictly all the administrative procedures on variations, extensions of time, etc., during the course of the contract. That would increase the authority's administrative work and costs. It would also reduce flexibility and could affect the good relations which have existed between the site staffs in the past, which could be detrimental to the contract. The authority's negotiator should be asked if he really believes that this insistence is in his own interests and be reminded that he may soon have complaints from his local staff.

A second method is to offer him an alternative bargain with reasons which he can use to justify its acceptance both to himself and to others and, at the same time, making it clear that he has minimal chance of obtaining the outcome for which he has been pressing.

The following is based on my experience. An exporter had been arguing with an overseas buyer that acceptance of certain high-technology equipment should be at the exporter's works; the buyer had been arguing that he only ever accepts goods on delivery to site. There were three remote sites involved.

The exporter finally proposed provisional acceptance at his works and final acceptance at the buyer's central depot, with the buyer having the right only to repeat the exporter's factory tests according to the exporter's test procedures and specifications. If the tests were not carried out within 30 days of the equipment's arrival at the depot, acceptance would be deemed to have been given.

The proposal was accepted by the negotiator for the buyer although he knew that they had no intention of carrying out the tests, since to do so would have meant purchasing additional and expensive test equipment. However, the proposal satisfied the negotiator's aspiration level in that:

1 It appeared on paper to be an improvement on the exporter's original proposal.
2 It retained the principle of final acceptance only being given after the equipment had been delivered to the buyer's country.
3 It satisfied the objections of the buyer's legal department since it followed closely enough past precedents from other contracts. (They were, of course, unaware that the right existed only on paper and the negotiator for the buyer had no intention of telling them.)

Naturally the negotiator for the exporter emphasized the above points in presenting and discussing his proposal and, at the same time, made it clear that he had no intention of agreeing to acceptance at site with the delays and uncertainties which that would involve.

Success in using tactics which are intended to persuade the other side's negotiator to modify his utility function depends on selecting the right person in their organization to whom to present a particular line of argument. In the first example, it would have been little use presenting that argument to a lawyer who would probably believe that strict adherence to contractual procedures is a good idea. To an engineer or commercial negotiator acquainted with the way in which contracts are actually run in practice, the argument is highly persuasive.

A third course of action is to persuade them that their valuation conflicts with commercial equity. Already the view has been expressed that negotiators the world over do not like to be criticized by their opponent for being unfair (see Introduction). In companies which have established written purchasing procedures there is often to be found some phrase such as 'fair and reasonable' or 'fair and equitable' to describe the approach which the buyer should take in negotiation, for example, see the Ford Motor Company Policy guide extracts from which are set out in Appendix C to *The Industrial Buying Decision.*[2]

Despite the widespread use of such phrases it is difficult to arrive at a definition of what constitutes fair commercial conduct which would command universal acceptance. The moral basis upon which one human being should deal with another in a business sense has been, and still is, the subject of much ethical speculation. Where moral precepts have been derived from religion they appear too unrealistic to provide practical guidance, although it is interesting to note that the major religions of the world do not appear to differ significantly in their general attitudes. The suggestion which seems most nearly to approach enlightened commercial practice is that of Professor Stace: 'The proper degree of unselfishness in my dealings with you is that degree which will result in both you and I receiving a fair and equitable share of the available satisfaction.'[3]

Into the definition of what is fair, this imports the concept of sharing the benefits which are available in an equitable manner, but still leaves undefined the question of the proportions in which the sharing is to take place. Professor Stace's words are reminiscent of those used by Nash in describing his formulation of a fair division between two rational bargainers and certainly Nash has provided one answer to the problem.[4]

It can, however, be argued that the Nash solution is only fair in an ethical sense if there is economic symmetry between the negotiators. If their economic roles are asymmetrical then, as Luce and Raiffa have pointed out, this will be reflected in the shape of their utility functions.[5] If each then behaves rationally and adopts the Nash solution this must result in the negotiator whose economic position is weaker, and his need accordingly the greater, receiving the smaller share!

Contract price £'000s	Profit share Supplier	Profit share Buyer	Supplier's utility	Buyer's utility	Utility product
20	5	0	1	0	0
19	4	1	0.95	0.1	0.095
18	3	2	0.9	0.3	0.27
17	2	3	0.7	0.6	0.42
16	1	4	0.4	0.8	0.32
15	0	5	0	1	0

Figure 31.1   The Nash solution

This may be illustrated by the following example. It is agreed between a buyer and a seller that the shop cost for a contract is £15,000. The buyer's budget allows him to spend up to £20,000. The buyer is a large corporation and the supplier is a small firm desperately short of work. The respective utility functions for the two firms relative to the £5,000 to be split between them are set out in Figure 29.1 which also shows the product of these. The Nash solution would give a profit of £2,000 to the supplier and £3,000 to the buyer.

The form of the supplier's utility function (which shows that he is indifferent to a certainty of profit of 1 and a gamble with a 40 per cent chance of a profit of 5 and a 60 per cent chance of a zero profit) clearly reflects his urgent need for orders. Given that the buyer's utility function is more or less linear with money, or shows a slight risk preference in favour of taking the gamble, as in the example, the result of applying the Nash solution must be an outcome which favours the buyer.

Although it is not pretended that negotiators in the real world base their strategies on knowing the Nash solution, it is contended that their preference functions, if both behave rationally, and consider only their own interests, will lead them to an outcome which is very close to that proposed by Nash. Only if the economically stronger party includes the needs of the weaker when making the assessment of his preferences from which his utility function is derived, can the effect of asymmetry be corrected. He must consciously consider the results of his own preference choice on the other negotiator so that his reasoning would be on the lines: 'I know I would prefer a gain of 3 for myself but that would only leave 2 for him which hardly seems fair. After all, I can afford to pay the extra 1 more than he can afford to lose it.'

It is recognized that such reasoning implies an interpersonal comparison of utility values which previously have been regarded as inadmissible. Once ethical considerations are introduced which require the negotiator to have regard to the effect of his preference choice upon the other side, and to modify that choice if he feels that it would produce an unfair result, then it seems inevitable that such comparisons must be made.

Appealing to fairness is particularly appropriate in the negotiation of long-term contracts, especially those on a partnering basis. Such contracts must be based on trust between the parties and this will only be achieved if both take the interests of the other into account when formulating their negotiating objectives. The proposal would then be on the lines of the negotiator saying 'If we undertake to meet your requirements by doing X then it would only be fair if you were to do Y', where Y will be recognized by the other negotiator as a fair response.

In a contract dispute situation, the purchaser might say 'If we can get this resolved quickly and amicably then our little disagreement at the end of an otherwise successful contract will be no barrier to your going on our tender list for project Z which is planned for next month.' In a sales negotiation, the buyer might point out that whoever is successful in being awarded the contract would gain the benefit of being closely involved with the operation of the project and be in the pole position to obtain ongoing work such as equipment upgrades and plant modifications.

Statements such as these should only be made if they are true, otherwise their effect will be totally counter-productive in terms of future relationships between the parties. They should of course have been foreseen by the supplier when he made his original valuation of the worth to him of a particular bargain, but they may have been overlooked or not fully appreciated. They need, however, to be treated by the supplier with great caution. Neither is any guarantee as to the future and to commit oneself now to the certainty of an otherwise less than satisfactory bargain against the uncertain expectation of some future reward is a high-risk policy. One is reminded of the old fable of the carrot dangled in front of the donkey's nose but always just out of reach.

CHANGING THE OTHER NEGOTIATOR'S ASSESSMENT OF SUCCESS PROBABILITY

In an ego-orientated and commitment situation such as a commercial negotiation, a negotiator's subjective assessment of success probability will be related primarily to:

1 Past experience and precedent
2 Cues provided by the behaviour of the opposing negotiator
3 The degree of support provided to the negotiator by his own company.

Since the assessment is subjective it will be biased by the wishes and fears of the person concerned. More specifically this bias will be a function of:

1 The negotiator's motivation for success – The stronger his achievement orientation, the more optimistic his assessment; conversely the stronger his motivation towards avoidance of failure the lower his assessment.
2 The attractiveness of attainment – The more attractive the end objective, the more optimistic his assessment. Note that this end objective is the negotiator's personal one which may differ widely from that of his company.
3 The consequences of failure – The more serious these are, the lower will be the negotiator's assessment.

Clearly certain of these factors are wholly within the negotiator's own control or that of the company which employs him. In varying degrees, other factors can be manipulated by his opponent. These factors and the way in which such manipulation may occur are now considered.

Cues provided by the negotiator's behaviour

1 Apparent strength of commitment – The stronger the other's beliefs that the negotiator is totally committed to a specific position, the lower will be the other's estimate of his own success probability. Since he cannot know in any absolute sense the true strength of the negotiator's commitment, he must infer it from his behaviour. The signs which will guide him in making that inference are:

1 The choice of language – The simpler and more direct this is the stronger the commitment.
2 The degree of precision in the definition of his position – The less the ambiguity the stronger the commitment.
3 The openness of his statements – Statements made in front of colleagues are more binding than those made privately.
4 His willingness to state his position in writing – A written statement is always a stronger commitment than one made verbally.
5 Gestures which support his commitment, for example, putting his papers in order, sitting back with arms folded seemingly unmoved by any verbal attack.

6 Exhibiting patience and a willingness to wait, for example, not booking a return flight, not contacting the other side to arrange further meetings but leaving them to contact him.

7 Not leaving open any obvious line of retreat – He should have a fall-back position but he should not reveal it unless forced to by the strength of the other's position.

By giving these signals, the negotiator will seek to demonstrate the high degree of commitment which he feels toward the negotiating position he has adopted. At the same time he will recognize the other may be trying to do exactly the same. In his reaction to the other's words he would be wise to be guided by the advice of Bacon who wrote: 'The Sinews of Wisdom are slowness of belief and distrust; that more trust be given to countenances and deeds than to words; and in words rather to sudden passages and surprised than to set and purposed words.'[6]

2   Demonstrating a lack of anxiety – There is a distinction between indicating a firm commitment to a specific position through personal attachment and demonstrating anxiety. Some apparent personal involvement is necessary if a commitment is to appear credible. But the involvement should be supported by reasoned argument on the lines that if the other side could only understand the problem then they would agree with the proposition. The involvement is intellectual rather than emotional. In presenting an argument on this basis the negotiator also shows a certain indifference to whether the other side believe his argument or nor as it will make no difference to its validity or to his commitment which he has no intention of changing.

However, any indication by the negotiator that his commitment is based on fear of the consequences should he not be successful, and not on reasoned argument, must immediately expose the weakness of his case. I can argue against a high rate of delay penalty on the ground that it exceeds any probable loss that the buyer might suffer and is contrary to normal commercial dealing in that type of business. I cannot argue that it is too high because I am afraid I might have to pay it. If I do, the buyer will respond by saying that there is even more reason for having the penalty since, clearly, I am not confident on my delivery and only a penalty spur will compel me to complete on time.

In order to reduce the other's estimate of his chances of success the negotiator should blend commitment with a measure of indifference. Conversely, irrespective of his inner feelings, the negotiator should never reveal anxiety or use arguments which have as their base fear of his own or his company's inadequacy.

Adjusting the attractiveness of the bargain

Since the other will tend to overestimate his chances of securing any bargain which appears to him to be attractive, and conversely will tend to underestimate the success probability of one which appears to be unattractive, it is in the negotiator's interests to present the range of possible bargains in a way which will lead the other to regard as attractive the outcome which best satisfies the negotiator's objective.

He may do this in two ways.

1   Leading the other to propose a solution to a point of difficulty rather than the negotiator proposing it himself – This is an example of what is commonly referred to as the NIH factor (Not Invented Here). The other will value more highly a solution which he believes he has thought up for himself than one suggested by the negotiator.

He therefore guides the other in the right direction by narrowing the range of options but leaves the final choice to him

For example, an exporter is negotiating the delivery terms of the contract with an overseas buyer. His major negotiating objective in relation to this clause is to persuade the buyer to waive the requirements that the goods are shipped on the national shipping line of the buyer's country, which is notorious for the infrequency of its sailing and the unreliability of its service. His argument might be that hc appreciates the buyer's wish for delivery to site to be effected in twelve months, but the facts should be examined. It has been agreed that ten months is a reasonable period for manufacture, including one month's factory testing which the buyer wishes his engineers to observe. Buyer is insisting on the use of his shipping line, to which there are no objections, but his shipping agents say that realistically six weeks should be allowed for delivery to port of entry. In addition five weeks should be allowed for customs clearance and one week for onward delivery to site, giving a total of 13 months. This period will have to be adhered to unless buyer can suggest anything.

He has narrowed the options open to the buyer to the point at which he waives the factory test, removes the restriction on the shipping line or makes a special deal with the customs authorities. He knows that in practice the buyer is unlikely to do the first and has no power to do the last. Therefore he has really no alternative but to remove the shipping line requirement if the twelve-month delivery period is to be achieved. He does not ask for this directly but leaves it up to the buyer.

The buyer might reply that it looks as though the shipping question will have to be re-examined since nothing can be done about the time for customs and the month really is needed for testing and to familiarize the engineers with the equipment. If the exporter is allowed to use a line of his own choice, would he be willing to guarantee delivery in twelve months?

He should of course know the answer to this question but equally he should not admit it since to do so might lead to the buyer becoming suspicious. It is suggested that he should reply in a way which will strengthen the buyer's commitment to the idea and reinforce it as having been his suggestion. The reply could be that the idea had not been considered in any detail since until the other made the suggestion it was thought to be out of the question. Clearly it would help, and it looks as though the twelve months might be possible, but it will be looked at as a matter of urgency and the answer will be confirmed tomorrow. In the meantime discussions can proceed on the basis that the twelve months can be agreed upon under that condition.

2   Over-emphasizing the apparent importance to the negotiator of securing a particular point when his real objective is the direct opposite – Sometimes this is colloquially referred to as 'pulling the pig's tail' since the usual result of that activity is that the animal pulls as hard as it can in the opposite direction. The same result in intended here; namely that the other will become convinced that this is just the point he must secure and will direct all his efforts to doing so.

As an example, consider an issue that has arisen as to whether an installation activity should be paced as a firm lump sum or on a man-day basis. The contractor would prefer the lump sum as this would avoid the purchaser becoming involved in the details of the operation and allow the contractor greater flexibility.

Initially the contractor suggests, and argues, for the man-day basis, pointing out that the work involves risks which will be difficult to allow for in his pricing. The more the contractor points out the risks the more the purchaser becomes convinced that the contract should be on a firm lump sum, so that he knows his commitment in advance. Eventually the contractor 'concedes', leaving the negotiator for the purchaser pleased with his 'success', and convinced that he has obtained the better bargain.

Had the contractor argued for a lump sum in the first instance, the purchaser would have been suspicious that the price was too 'fat' and might well have proposed a man-day basis. Also by leaving it to the purchaser to suggest the lump sum, the contractor is in a better position to argue for the inclusion of a reasonable allowance for contingencies. The contractor might argue that he suggested a man-day basis but it was unacceptable for the very reason that risks are involved and the total commitment is difficult to calculate. This is understood and appreciated, but by the same token contractor's price must now include an allowance for those risks.

Notes

1. There is an obvious relationship between these tactics and the learning process of *operant conditioning*. This process is described briefly in E. R. Hilgard et al., *Introduction to Psychology* (New York: Harcourt, Brace and Jovanovich, 5th edition 1971), p. 196 ff. The application of the process to union–management negotiations is considered in R. E. Walton and R. E. McKersie, *Behavioral Theory of Labor Negotiations* (New York: McGraw-Hill, 1965), pp.185–270.
2. G. T. Brand, *The Industrial Buying Decision* (London: Cassell/Associated Business Programmes, 1972).
3. W. Stace, *Concept of Morals* (London: Macmillan, 1962), p. 134.
4. 'Now since our solution consist of rational expectations of gain by the two bargainers, these expectations should be realizable by an appropriate agreement between the two. Hence there should be an available anticipation which gives each the amount of satisfaction he should expect to get.' J. F. Nash, 'The bargaining problem', *Econometrica*, vol. 18 (April 1950) pp. 155–62.
5. R. D. Luce and H. Raiffa, *Games and Decisions* (New York: Wiley, 1957), p. 130.
6. Sir Francis Bacon, *The Advancement of Learning*, edited by D. W. Kitchen (London: Dent), p. 190.

32 SITUATION TACTICS

Situation tactics may be divided into two classes: offensive and defensive. Offensive tactics are those which are designed to take or retain the initiative. Defensive tactics are not merely the counter to these but the springboard from which a counter-offensive can be launched. Therefore, both are concerned with the initiative, i.e.:

1 The order in which items are taken
2 The points on which to exert pressure
3 The degree of pressure exerted
4 The basis upon which the issues are argued
5 The time over which the argument lasts.

Purely defensive tactics are ruled out since, if the negotiator were to adopt such an approach, this would leave it open to the other continually to switch his attack from one point to another in search of the weak point in the negotiator's defences. Given that no defence is ever perfect, ultimately a weak point will be found upon which the other can then concentrate his attack.

Students of military history/tactics will recognize the analogy which can be drawn between negotiation as a form of conflict and warfare, and indeed many of the principles governing the use of situational tactics and military tactics are similar.

32.1 Offensive tactics

ASKING QUESTIONS

Probing questions
The negotiator's first use of questions is as a means of probing the other's defences, a reconnaissance in military parlance. Having discovered what he believes may be a weak point in the propositions which the other has put forward, the negotiator wishes to be sure that it really is a weak point before he launches a major attack.

Such a question is deliberately phrased in general terms. Thus a buyer having reviewed a seller's quotation may start off the discussion by saying: 'We have had a look at your quotation but before we get down to details perhaps you could explain rather more fully the way in which you have arrived at the increase in price over the last contract.'

A question of this type asking for general clarification is most difficult to answer directly. The supplier does not know whether the buyer agrees generally with the item as stated in his tender or not. Any overall reply may merely provide the buyer with fresh points on which specifically to direct his attack. In fact this is the idea of the question.

The supplier's correct response is therefore the *counter-question*, designed to compel the buyer to limit the scope of his inquiry and to reveal more of the buyer's own position. The supplier's reply might therefore be on the following lines: 'I am sorry if there is a difficulty here; I thought we had stated the general position quite clearly in our offer. However we will be pleased to try to clarify any particular points about which you are unhappy. What in particular is worrying you?'

Notice that the supplier in addition to asking the buyer to be more specific has made the suggestion that the buyer must be dissatisfied with some aspects of the quotation. This is included in the counter-question in order to elicit from the buyer one of the following statements:

1 He is not really unhappy with the supplier's offer but just wants some more information.
2 He is unhappy with the offer and the reasons for this concern.

In this way the supplier seeks to regain the initiative. Counter-questions are really part of defensive tactics and their general use is discussed in Section 32.2.

Specific questions

A question is defined as specific when it can be answered only by supplying a piece of data, the nature of which is determined by the wording of the question itself, as in the following examples: 'What labour and material price indices did you use to calculate the escalation allowance in your price?' 'What is your programme for manufacture and testing?' 'How long will it take to produce the layout drawings?'

The rules for framing an attacking question are:

1 Keep it short and simple.
2 Do not disclose all the facts.
3 Never suggest an answer to the respondent.

Perhaps the most effective attacking question of all is the single word 'why?'

In the example just considered, the buyer does not refer to the ratio between the movement in the manufactured goods index and the movement in the price of semiconductors, nor the extent to which the weighting given to various elements in the construction of the index allows for semiconductors. The supplier is left to provide his own answers which can then form the subject matter of a further attack.

In the description of the use of the question as an offensive tactic, three consecutive stages have been identified:

1 The probing question: intended to gain information.
2 The specific question: based on the information gained from 1 and data already known; designed to force an admission.
3 The attacking question: based on the answers to 2 and other data; designed to force a concession.

It should also be clear that specific and attacking questions are never asked 'blind'. The questioner already knows in advance that the answer, at least in part, will support his line of attack.

The yes/no question

Some questions are so worded that the only answer to them can be a simple yes or no; others can be replied to in that way if the respondent wishes.

If the use of a question of this type gives the questioner the response for which he is looking then nothing can be more effective. He has obtained a direct admission without equivocation. However, if he obtains the reply he does not want, it is extremely difficult for him to reopen the issue and any opportunity that was available for compromise has been lost.

The reason is that a simple yes/no is the strongest commitment into which a negotiator can enter. In the example quoted at the end of Section 26.3, after I had said yes, there was no way in which the negotiator for the other side could proceed except to adjourn the discussions which was, in fact, what he did. On the side which I was representing there was total commitment in that word to the propositions which had been made. Fortunately, they came back 48 hours later, much to my relief, and agreed – they were a long 48 hours!

In another instance I was asked to break down a total price quoted for the staffing services and the hire of equipment into these two elements. The answer was a straightforward no without any reason being given. Faced with this answer the buyer let the matter drop and turned the discussion to another topic. He really had no alternative except to discontinue the negotiations.

A yes/no question should never be asked therefore unless the questioner has prepared the ground in advance and is satisfied that the answer he will obtain is the one which he wants to hear. Ideally it is an explicit confirmation of an understanding at which the two negotiators have already informally arrived.

Questions like these, to all of which there are factual answers, can run the questioner into a dead end unless he has already prepared supplementaries. If he cannot challenge the reply given, he is bound to accept it and that line of questioning is then exhausted. As a corollary, therefore, a specific question should be only asked in one of the following situations:

1 The questioner believes the subject area to be a weak spot and has already prepared follow-up questions with which to continue the attack.
2 The question is designed merely to confirm a position with which the questioner is generally satisfied.

For example, the question on labour and price indices might be asked by a buyer if, as a result of his initial probing, he believed that the seller had used indices which were more favourable to the seller than those which the buyer considered appropriate to the seller's type of business. If the seller's reply confirmed this, then the buyer's supplementary questions, which he had already prepared, would be directed at the inappropriateness of the indices selected. Continuing the example, the buyer's supplementary question after the seller's reply might be: 'You have chosen as the material index that for manufactured goods used generally in industry, whilst some 70 per cent of your material costs must be semiconductor devices. How can you possibly justify this?'

Note that the nature of the question has now changed from one which was purely designed to extract information to one which has set up a direct attack. This type of question is referred to as an attacking question.

Attacking questions

Any question which includes phrases such as: How can you justify that? How can that be valid? What justification can there be for that? is classified as an attacking question.

PRESSURIZING INDIVIDUALS

In the same way as there will be weak points in the other's arguments, there will be weak members in his negotiating team. Individual team members may be vulnerable to:

1 Flattery
2 Coercion
3 Blackmail.

Flattery

This is the weapon used against someone junior or inexperienced when the negotiator believes that the person concerned, rather than admit he does not know, will express an opinion or make a decision and that such an opinion/decision will be favourable to the negotiator. The opinion/decision is likely to favour the negotiator since, because of his junior status/inexperience, the team member involved will not want to be 'difficult'. This is especially true of junior professional advisers when faced with experienced commercial negotiators. In these circumstances there may even be a tendency for the commercial negotiators for the two sides to form a group against the professional adviser whom they may jointly regard as being outside of their 'club'.

The type of remark which may be made by the other would be: 'This is something on which we would value your advice Mr Jones. Do you see any problem here? We see no problem, but then we do not have your expertise in these matters.'

If this is Mr Jones's first experience of a major negotiation, he will need considerable moral courage to reply that he does see a problem. This is when he needs a great deal of help from his team leader who must firmly resist any temptation to align himself with the negotiator for the other side: he must act to protect his own colleague and provide him with cover. He could do this by replying for Mr Jones: 'It is hardly fair to expect Mr Jones to answer that off-the-cuff. I suggest we let him think about it and come back to the point after coffee/lunch.'

The team leader will then use the natural break to go over the point with Mr Jones in private.

Coercion

Coercion is the opposite to flattery and may be used against a junior team member who is standing in for his chief. He may be asked: 'We have always dealt with Mr Smith before, and he has never taken this line. Are you sure you have his backing over this, Mr Jones?'

Again the team leader must intervene and answer the question himself instead of leaving it to Mr Jones who may well be embarrassed. He could do this by saying: 'Let us leave Mr Smith out of it shall we? He is not here, so it is not very helpful to ask whether he would approve or not. Mr Jones is here and I have every confidence in him. As far as I can see, the line which he has taken is perfectly reasonable, but if you do have any specific points of criticism Mr Jones and I are willing to listen.'

By identifying himself with the argument which Mr Jones has used the team leader diverts the pressure onto himself and commits himself to the support of Mr Jones so integrating him more closely into the team. At the same time the commitment is not total; he leaves himself with a line of retreat by suggesting that both of them are willing to consider criticisms. But these have to be specific, which once more puts the ball back into the other side's court.

Blackmail

This is a tactic which may be used against the team leader himself and describes the situation in which the negotiator for the other side seeks to make use of some personal relationship which he alleges he has with the Chairman, Managing Director or other senior officer of the negotiator's firm, to threaten the negotiator that if he does not behave reasonably then he will be in trouble. In practice it is seldom put in quite those words but the inference is clear.

So, the seller when dealing with the professional buyer may take the line: 'You may not be aware that I had dinner with your Mr X last week and he made it clear he took a great interest in this project and expected that we would be participating in it. Indeed, he seemed surprised that we had not signed up already. I only mention that in order to let you know that your own top management are all in favour.'

The team leader must immediately call the other side's bluff if he is to retain credibility as a negotiator. One way would be for him to reply: 'If you would like me to arrange an appointment for us both to see Mr X, I would be pleased to do so, although I do not think it would be very helpful. However, in the meantime, I suggest we get ahead with our discussions.'

ARBITRARY BEHAVIOUR

Sweet reason is not necessarily the best form of argument. Sheer arbitrary behaviour can be more effective.[1] Once a negotiator's behaviour becomes in our terms 'irrational', he is outside the value system and untouchable by the arguments normally used.

If a buyer indicates that he does not care about whether costs have risen or not, he is just not going to pay more for the goods under this contract than he did last time, this may be a more effective tactic than arguing about changes in labour/material costs, allowances for increases in productivity and the other factors which are usually treated as forming an integral part of such negotiations. It will certainly present the negotiator for the supplier with a difficult form of challenge in which his statistical data on cost increases, so carefully compiled, are valueless.

The point about so-called 'irrational' behaviour is that it relies for its effectiveness on the other side continuing to behave rationally. General Amin was certainly, in the eyes of the countries who received the Asians expelled from Uganda, behaving irrationally. But his action was effective because he relied on our behaving rationally by our own standards, which we did both in meeting his deadline and in providing the refugees with a home.

If a man says: 'Give me a £100 or I will kill that child', and from the circumstances and his appearance it is judged that he will carry out the threat, then it is likely that he will be paid the £100. But suppose normal value standards are discarded and his adopted; suppose he is told 'Very well go ahead and kill the child', that at once alters the bargaining situation. Level terms are resumed again. No longer does the person uttering the threat possess any advantage because of his irrationality.

To return to the example of the 'irrational' buyer, if the supplier continues to try to argue on the rational grounds of unavoidable cost increases, he must lose. Either he will be forced to accept the buyer's terms or lose the bargain.

Supposing the supplier says 'Fine, I will take the contract at the old price, but if I find I cannot meet the costs then, unless you increase the price, do not expect me to deliver. Further at that stage you will have no chance of obtaining the goods from anyone else in time to meet your production schedule. It will do you no good to sue me; it will be too late and by the time you get an award of damages, if you do, there will not be any assets left in the company.

Both sides have now introduced irrationality into the bargaining game and the rules have been stretched to the point at which there are virtually no rules, and the uncertainty involved is too great for the continuation of normal business relationships.

The lesson is clear. Irrationality, short term and in small degrees, may pay; extended in time or extent and opposed in equal measure it must fail.

MAKING THE OTHER SIDE APPEAR UNREASONABLE

One method of challenging the validity of a proposition is to find a case in which application of the proposition would be manifestly absurd. The person advancing the proposition is then challenged to redefine it in more limited terms which will avoid the absurdity. It is closely related therefore to the method of logical argument known as the *dialectic* in which a *thesis* is stated, a contrary case known as the *antithesis* is then produced, and the reconciliation of the two produces the *synthesis*.

An example of the *dialectic* would be as follows:

> *Thesis:* The contractor is responsible for any delay to the contract work.
> *Antithesis:* Responsibility presupposes control; a contractor cannot therefore be responsible for events over which he has no control, e.g. war or riots.
> *Synthesis:* The contractor is responsible for delays to the contract work except when these are due to causes beyond his control.

One frequent application of the tactic is to circumstances in which it is proposed that liability should vary in degree with some defined scale or should change significantly when some particular point is reached.

For example, in negotiating a penalty clause for failure to meet guaranteed performance limits the buyer might propose a series of steps as shown:

1 £1,000 between 89 and 90% purity
2 £5,000 between 88 and 89% purity
3 £10,000 between 88 and 87% purity
4 £20,000 below 87% purity

The contractor in reply could point out that a change from 88.95 per cent to 89.05 per cent, i.e. a change of 0.1 per cent, could make a difference of £4,000 which he would claim was absurd and unfair, even assuming that one could measure to that degree of accuracy.

The outcome or synthesis in dialectical terms would probably be a much smoother relationship between percentage purity and penalty. Alternatively, after it has been demonstrated that the thesis as originally stated is too wide, the proposer may find great difficulty in justifying one particular synthesis redefining the proposition in narrower terms in preference to any other. If £4,000 is wrong for the change between 88.95 and 89.05 per cent, what is right? At what point does the proposition become fair?

To take another example: the buyer might claim the right to reject a whole consignment for a single defect. The antithesis argument would be that it would be unreasonable to reject a consignment, say, of 100 items value £10,000, all of which are usable, because, say, the paint on one was scratched.

The first synthesis might be to limit the right to reject the whole to where the number of defects exceeded say 5 per cent. Assuming this was acceptable to the supplier, it does not overcome the problem of what kind of defect entitles the buyer to reject. For example, does it include a paint scratch and, if so, how deep a scratch?

A second synthesis might be that the right to reject would apply only if the defect was one which affected the purpose for which the item was being supplied.

Because of its probing nature, and the use it makes of hypothetical assumptions, the adoption of the tactic frequently leads to an emotional outburst from the other side who may seek to dismiss the arguments as 'mere quibble'. If this can be avoided, or with patience overcome, the tactic is a valuable means of clarifying and delimiting broad propositions, or of causing them to be abandoned altogether if they are too difficult for precise definition.

FISHING

This describes the tactic of deliberately overstating a demand in order to discover the other's reaction. The negotiator's demand would be well beyond any level he considers the other likely to accept.

In discussing the level at which the negotiator should make his initial offer (see p. 317), it was concluded that, ignoring time costs, the level would be the upper limit of the bargaining zone increased by the amount of the concession which the negotiator anticipated being compelled to make in order to reach an outcome equal to the upper limit of the bargaining zone. So that the negotiator may follow this rule he must reasonably be aware of the other's concession function and the level at which he would just prefer a bargain to no bargain. When the two sides have negotiated before, or have information on the terms/prices which the other has agreed in contracts with third parties, it is not difficult for either to arrive at a reasonably accurate estimate of these values, at least for the major issues.

If the two sides are largely unknown to each other, then the only way for the negotiator to discover what the other might accept is to overstate his demands and see what happens. Before deciding to adopt this tactic, the negotiator must plan his next move, depending upon what sort of reaction he obtains. Broadly, there are three possibilities: violently anti, a reasoned reply or apparent acceptance.

Violently anti

The other side dismiss the demand with some statement such as: 'You cannot possibly be serious. Your suggestion is out of the question. If that is the line you intend to take it would be better to terminate discussions now.' The negotiator must have a position prepared against this type of response which will extricate him with a minimum loss of reputation for firmness (see Section 26.2). The simplest means of doing this is for the demand to have been made by the number two in the negotiating team and for the team leader now to reply: 'Mr Jones was being serious. We are concerned about two points. However, there are always two sides to every story: you have heard ours, perhaps we can now hear yours. I am sure that when we have listened we will be able to find a way to reach some understanding.'

The response is aimed at achieving two objectives: first, forcing the other to state his case in reasoned terms and so expose his position to further questioning and reveal more of his pre-ference function. Second, to prepare the way for a retreat with an alibi which protects the negotiator from being thought weak, if the other's reply indicates that he is totally firm on the point, and is supported by arguments which the negotiator cannot shift. If that does happen, then the next statement from the negotiator might be, addressing Mr Jones: 'Well John, you have heard their arguments, and I must say they seem to be fairly solid, I know how you feel but I think we must go over this point again and see what we can come up with.' Turning to the other side, the negotiator might continue: 'Thank you for spelling it out so clearly. I think there may have been some misunderstanding here on our side. Obviously we need to consider this further amongst ourselves so perhaps we could leave it there for the moment and return to the point later.'

Reasoned reply

The other treats the demand as a serious basis from which to proceed to negotiate. The negotiator immediately reassesses his estimate of the final outcome and of the strength of his negotiating position relative to the other's since this is obviously greater than he thought.

Apparent acceptance

This is in some ways for the negotiator the most difficult response of all. He finds it hard to believe from what he knows of the other that the demand should be acceptable to him. It is highly probable that he has either made a serious mistake or misunderstood what the negotiator meant. Alternatively it is just possible that the negotiator has misjudged the situation and the other's acceptance is genuine.

The negotiator's next move therefore should be to explore whether or not the other has misunderstood, or made a mistake, without revealing his anxiety in a way which, if the acceptance is genuine, would cause the other to reconsider.

The negotiator might use some words such as: 'This is a reasonably important point and I would just like to be certain that we are both clear on it. Perhaps it would help to do this if you were to state your own understanding of what we have just agreed. Then we can move on to the next point on the agenda.'

Asking the other to restate the argument should ensure that if there has been a misunderstanding this will be revealed. Also it leaves the initiative to the negotiator to comment on the other's statement.

It may be asked why, if the other has made a mistake, the negotiator should be concerned to have it corrected; why not simply take advantage of it and let the other suffer for his foolishness? The answer is that contracts are a continuing relationship, and when the other finds out his error his defence mechanism to internal criticism from within his own organization will be to claim that he was tricked by the negotiator. Accordingly he will seek retribution against the negotiator whom he considers to have been responsible. He may seek to have that negotiator personally blacklisted and to secure some concession by way of compensation.

PARTNERS AS OPPOSITES, OR 'GOOD GUY – BAD GUY'

It was suggested that one way in which a negotiator could be provided with a line of retreat from an extreme position was by his partner taking the responsibility. Frequently in negotiations the following kind of remarks may be heard between team members: 'You are being very difficult this morning, John. I would have thought we could have agreed to ... I think they have a point there. Should we agree to ... I know it is a problem for you, Bill, but perhaps you could see your way clear to ...'

In all these instances one team member is ostensibly taking the other side's part and suggesting to his partner that he should make a 'concession'. More often than not, the two are playing a game in which it was decided in advance that John or Bill would take the hard line, and that at the opportune moment his partner would propose the compromise to which, with a show of great reluctance, John or Bill would agree.

Naturally having obtained this 'concession' for the other, the partner would expect the other to return the favour on the next negotiating point.

Alternatively, the game may be played the other way round. John may make a few early concessions on points of little significance; then on the point which really does matter his partner Bill will provide the firm backing; 'I am sorry John, I know you are in a very generous mood this morning but you cannot give away this one. We have given away too much already.'

John turns to the other with a slightly pained expression as if to suggest that there is nothing more which he can do to help and that the other is on his own.

In cold print the game may appear obvious and even trivial; certainly not something likely to deceive an experienced negotiator. However, under the pressures generated by long and tense negotiating sessions, the trick is not nearly so easy to recognize, particularly if the two negotiators have worked together on a number of occasions, so that rehearsal becomes unnecessary, and the trick a matter of habit.

There is also always in the other's mind a measure of doubt. He can never be absolutely sure that it is a game; perhaps the words are genuine, so that the opportunity exists to divide the negotiator's team.

The other advantage of the tactic, if it is used on an apparently random basis, is that the other can never be certain just how strong the negotiator's feelings are on any individual point. He cannot therefore judge with any accuracy the true form of the negotiator's concession factor.

PULLING THE PIG'S TAIL

Reference was made earlier (see pp. 235–36) to the idea that one way of persuading the other to agree to X is to propose the converse of X. Some negotiators are suspicious of any proposal made by their opposite number. If the supplier offers to deliver cif (carriage, insurance and freight), he must be making a profit on the shipping charges; so the buyer insists on purchasing fob (freight on board). If the supplier had offered fob this must have been to reduce his liability; so the buyer insists on cif.

In this situation it is no use the negotiator attempting to negotiate by persuading the buyer of the honesty of his proposals. If the personality of the buyer is what Cattell refers to as *sizothymic,* at least when he is acting the role of Buyer within a commercial environment, the attachment to that personality characteristic will be too strong.[2,3] Scrooge may have changed in *A Christmas Carol,* but commercial negotiators do not have the advantage of possessing as allies ghosts which can portrary to the buyer past, present and future. So the negotiator, foreseeing the rejection of his proposal, demands the opposite to his preferred requirement.

ENTERING INTO A PRIOR COMMITMENT

Previously, the use of commitment has been discussed in terms of the negotiating framework and the need for the negotiator to persuade the other of the truth of the statements which he is making. Commitment also represents a major offensive negotiating tactic, the persuasive power of which varies with the degree to which visibly his hands are tied. The commitments may be listed in order of the strength of their persuasive power.

Commitment	*Example*
1 National law binding on the purchaser.	Under the law regulating public contract, the purchaser as a government department must insist that the contract is governed by the law of his country.
	The supplier has no alternative; he must either accept or withdraw from the negotiations.

Commitment	*Example*
2 Regulation which is legally binding on the purchaser unless and until amended by some administrative or legislative body.	Standard forms of contract and/or contracting procedures are established for public authorities which require the authority of some higher council to amend.
	The purchaser will clearly be reluctant to ask for amendment and the formalities will take a considerable time to complete if the request is made. The supplier will therefore be under significant pressure not to press for any amendment – to do so may cause him to lose the contract.
3 Standard procedures of the company/ authority which are binding on the unit which is negotiating the contract. Alternatively, instructions received from some third party whose involvement is necessary to the conclusion of the contract, e.g. a credit insurance bureau.	The purchaser's contract procedures require that the approval of some higher level, head office/Board of Directors, is required before they can agree to the supplier's proposals.
	The purchaser will be reluctant to ask for such approval and the head office/Board will equally be reluctant to grant it for fear of creating a precedent. The supplier may therefore have to be content with a *side letter*.[4]
4 Previous precedents.	On previous contracts either with the supplier or other contractors the purchaser has negotiated certain terms. To depart from these would show the negotiator for the purchaser as weaker or less competent than those who had negotiated the other bargains. Alternatively, if he had negotiated the other bargains hurriedly, he could be accused of having accepted a bribe in order to show favour to the supplier.
	The supplier must therefore provide the purchaser's negotiator with reasons which he can use to justify his acceptance of the supplier's arguments.
5 Instructions from a superior.	The negotiator for the purchaser, having consulted his immediate superior and obtained his agreement to the negotiating plan, is in some difficulty in going back and saying the plan cannot be achieved.

Commitment	*Example*
	Again the supplier's success will be dependent largely on providing the other negotiator with reasons with which to support his request for revised authority.
	Alternatively, the supplier may propose that he accompanies the other's negotiator to discuss directly with his superior.
6 Position adopted at the outset of the negotiation by the purchaser's negotiator on his own initiative.	The negotiator, for motives usually associated with earning esteem, takes a particular stand and makes it known within his own organization that he has done so.
	Later it becomes obvious that the line he has taken is incompatible with the achievement of a bargain, and the need to obtain agreement is of greater priority.
	The supplier must now find some way to 'get the other's negotiator off the hook' as gently as he can.

It is obvious that both sides will use commitment tactics. The supplier will refer to a commitment to his board; the purchaser to one to his higher authority. When the commitments are of different rank, the higher will normally prevail. So a commitment on a contractor to comply with a requirement of his head office must give way to a law or regulation which is binding on a purchaser. An example would be a procedural rule within the contractor's organization, that contracts should be entered into only on the basis of disputes being referred either to the courts of the supplier's country or the International Chamber of Commerce, as opposed to a regulation of the puchaser's country which provided that, for public contracts, disputes were to be determined by the courts of their territory. To continue the example, if the contractor could reinforce his argument by reference to the requirements of his credit insurance bureau, he might be able to secure that financial disputes are referred to the International Chamber of Commerce whilst only other disputes went to the national courts of the overseas territory. (This example is based on my own negotiating experience in the Middle East.)

So it becomes a battle to secure the stronger commitment for the supplier and to undermine that put forward by the purchaser, by showing that it is not as strong as he has maintained, e.g. that there is not a law on the subject concerned; that it is only a matter of convention which can be disregarded.

THE WELL IS DRY

Reference was made to this tactic earlier – see p. 173. It is quite simply the tactic of telling the other party that there's no more money or that the proposal is too expensive to be accepted and he will have to do better. Of course if it's true the tactic is quite legitimate. Unfortunately, only too often it's not true; there is more money available but the purchaser does not want to spend it.

If the supplier believes it to be true and modifies his demand, then the purchaser knows that he is onto a winner and will continue protesting about the non-availability of funds until he has forced the supplier down to his breaking-off point, even sometimes beyond it. He may try the same game with two or more suppliers, indicating to each that they will have to improve upon their last offer. Played like this, it is certainly not ethical and the purchaser has only himself to blame when the suppliers revolt or he is left with one who either cuts quality and delivers late, or goes out of business.

NIBBLING

This tactic was also referred to earlier. It's not ethical other than perhaps in response to the buyer who has been forced to drop his price by use of the 'well is dry' tactic. The supplier, having agreed to the basic terms of the bargain, then tries to recover some of his lost ground by suggesting extras which he recommends the purchaser to procure: 'It will only cost you £X if you buy it now and it will be a lot more if you have to purchase it later which I am sure you will want to do.' Of course, it probably will cost you more if you buy it later but do you want it at all. The answer is probably 'no' and if so, that's the reply to give.

Nibbling is also played the other way around by the purchaser: 'While you're on site I am sure you would not mind ——' (describing that little extra for which you don't want to pay), or I did mention that we would want ——' (another little service), which of course has previously never been referred to at all.

The tactic is insidious – the first time you are never quite sure whether they are really trying it on or if it's something to which perhaps you should agree as a gesture of goodwill. However, as soon as you suspect it's the tactic, it's the time to stop it: 'Yes, we would be delighted to provide that facility against a variation order and I will get my people to prepare a price for it' is the sort of answer you should make.

32.2 *Defensive tactics*

MINIMUM RESPONSE AND PRETENDED MISUNDERSTANDING

A well-known interrogation technique is to persuade the suspect to repeat his story a number of times in the expectation that sooner or later he will contradict himself and so reveal the truth. Conversely, the less a suspect says the less likely he is to give anything away to his interrogator. Many more people are convicted through the telling of their own stories than by the evidence of others.

It follows that amongst the most effective of defensive tactics in negotiation is to say only just enough to compel the other side to go on talking. The more they talk the more they will reveal; the more they will feel compelled to reveal in order to be persuasive, and the nearer they will come to exposing their genuine motives and the real level of their minimum negotiating objective. The association between minimum response and pretended misunderstanding, which is another useful defensive tactic, is that the easiest way to persuade the other to repeat his argument is to pretend that you have misunderstood it. As well as making him go over the same ground again, this has the added advantage of giving the negotiator more time to consider the merits of the other's argument, and to decide on his counter-argument. So one member of the negotiator's team may be listening to the repeat argument while the others are busy studying the implications of the argument as presented, and checking it against their prediction of what the other would demand and the arguments which he would advance. Therefore, having listened politely to the other's opening remarks, the negotiator may make some reply to the effect that he is probably being very slow but would the other mind going over that again.

Also, it can be an infuriating technique. The other has delivered a carefully rehearsed statement expecting some sort of positive response, only to be met with a bland smile and the polite request to start all over again. He is not likely to be pleased and for this reason the repetition made under conditions of emotional stress will be that much more unguarded.

The technique is particularly effective in dealing with technical experts from whatever discipline. Few experts can resist the temptation to show off their expertise to a captive audience. But in so doing, it is virtually certain that they will give away more of the real reasons why the proposition in question is being made than ever had been intended.

ANSWERING INACCURATELY

Another way of answering a question without giving the other the answer for which he is looking is to start the reply by some phrase such as 'As I understand your question you are asking...' and then go on to rephrase the question slightly before replying to your rephrased version. Not only does this avoid giving the direct answer but it also gives you and your colleagues time to think.

CHANGING THE LEVEL

Specific questions where the other is asking for detailed information can be answered by raising the level to that of greater generalization. Thus the question referred earlier of 'What labour and material indices did you use?' could be countered by your replying 'Obviously the possible effect of inflation is something we have had to consider. It is not something we are seeking to make a profit on but equally we don't want to lose.' The negotiator would hope then to turn the discussion into more a general one on the subject of escalation and establish that the other did agree that escalation should be fully reimbursed before any detailed discussion on indices took place.

SIDE-STEPPING

Rather than answer the other's question directly at the time it is asked, the negotiator may seek to sidestep the issue. So in answer to a question 'Can you guarantee completion by a specified date?' the negotiator might reply 'Here have a look at the programme, shall we, then I can show you how we have arrived at the end date and you can see for yourself the problems and the allowance we have made.'

ANSWERING INCOMPLETELY

There is no need for the negotiator to volunteer more information in answer to a specific question than necessary. If the other has limited his question to asking 'Have you included for customs duties?', there is no need in your reply, assuming it is 'yes', to go on referring to your having allowed for other taxes or charges related to importation. You might want later to be able to argue that those were extra.

THE 'YES – BUT' TECHNIQUE

The outright, negative *no* represents a definitive and uncompromising commitment and should be reserved for those occasions when such a commitment is really intended. Because of its inflexibility and the risk of giving offence, the use of the direct negative in certain cultures is almost unknown; there are just three versions of yes; one meaning 'no', one meaning 'maybe' and one meaning 'yes'. For example, the shopkeeper to whom a watch has been entrusted for repair will answer 'yes' to the question of whether the watch will be ready tomorrow. Of course, it will not be ready, and the shopkeeper knows that. But to reply 'no', which is clearly not the desired answer, would mean giving offence in a face-to-face situation. So the shop-keeper answers 'yes' and hopes that it will be recognized as a form of politeness.

Social behaviour is often similar, for instance, a pressing invitation to go to a party may be received from a friend. To avoid 'hurting feelings' by saying 'no', either an excuse is found or the reply is indirect by explaining that events of that date are uncertain or that someone else has to be consulted first. Again, like the shopkeeper, it is hoped that the reply will be recognized as a form of politeness and not taken at its face value.

So the negotiator faced with the direct question which he wishes to answer in the negative, but without giving offence, and without definitely committing himself, may use the technique of 'yes – but'. Asked, for example, to agree to a reduction in the period of delivery he may reply that *yes* he agrees that the delivery period looks rather long, *but* a number of factors have to be taken into account; for instance, the shortage of materials which is affecting the current level of output and also the fact that the design has not yet been finalized.

The affirmative part of the answer should appear to align the negotiator alongside his opponent and so establish the negotiator as someone who is cooperative and appreciative of the viewpoint of the other side.

The negative part of the answer is intended to identify some of the reasons which neverthe-less prevent the negotiator from doing what the other would like him to do; in the example, to shorten the delivery time. In choosing the reasons he puts forward, the negotiator should select those which are likely to appeal most to the other by reason of his background, personality or the position which he holds. Ideally the negotiator should use this part of the reply to lead the other into taking action which would overall favour the negotiator's case or at least present the other in the ultimate with the choice of acting in that manner or of withdrawing his request.

In the above example the negotiator, in the course of the discussion which followed his reply, might seek to persuade the other to settle the outstanding issues on the design and to authorize the negotiator to order the long-delivery materials on the basis that this would enable him to reduce the delivery time. Such action would clearly increase the other's commitment to the supplier and so improve his negotiating position. If the other were unwilling to take these actions then the longer delivery must stand.

THE COUNTER-QUESTION

Closely related to the 'yes – but' technique is that of replying to a question with a question. The classic from domestic life is that of the woman who replies to the invitation to attend some social engagement with the question: 'What am I going to wear?' In contract negotiation, for example, the other asks the negotiator: 'Why will you not accept that the period for installation should be 20 weeks and not 25?' The negotiator replies: 'Can we look at this another way. On what are you basing your estimate of 20 weeks? Can we have the breakdown of that and the assumptions which you have made?'

His real answer to the other's question may be bluntly that he knows more about it than the other does, but this is hardly the most tactful of replies. The negotiator therefore seeks to turn the discussion into an examination of the basis of the other's estimate of time, and from that to lead the other into admitting his own lack of experience.

A further use of the counter-question is to switch the direction of an argument and to prevent attention being concentrated on one area to the exclusion of others. In a price negotiation, for instance, the other may be attacking one small area of the negotiator's costs. At some point instead of replying to the other's questions the negotiator might say: 'Look, could we get away from this business of the transport costs as they are only minor. Surely it's the price as a whole in which you are interested. Are you saying that is unreasonable?'

STRAW ISSUES

In legal terminology, a *man of straw* is a person of no means and one from whom no compensation can be recovered. By transferring to a man of straw property which is a liability rather than an asset, the liabilities arising out of the ownership of the property may be avoided.

In negotiating terminology, a *straw issue* is one which is of no value to the negotiator in itself but which is raised with the intention that it should be lost and so provide the opportunity for the negotiator to secure a genuine concession from the other in return.

As stated earlier (see p. 188) the alternating of concessions although not necessarily the matching of their magnitude, is virtually a norm of negotiating behaviour. If the negotiator wishes to secure a particular concession from the other, he knows that he must be willing to allow the other something in exchange. By including one or more straw issues in his initial demands the negotiator ensures that he has 'something in the bank' to allow as compensation for the other abandoning or modifying his own initial demands.

The negotiator can add to the number of straw issues available to him as bargaining counters by declining in the opening phases of the negotiation to agree to any of the other's demands no matter how reasonable these may appear to be. A major difference between the approach of a 'true' bargainer and that of the average Western commercial or legal negotiator is to be seen in the different ways in which they respond to the other's initial demands. The typical Western negotiator will agree immediately to those demands which he considers reasonable or of little importance, and he will be impatient to move quickly to those which he regards as the real issues in dispute.[5]

A true exponent of bargaining will concede nothing during the initial stages. Each point on which he does intend to concede will be carefully reserved for later use as a means of extracting a concession from the other side. Obviously this lengthens the time spent in negotiation and increases the time costs, so in each instance the negotiator must decide on how far to follow the 'bargaining' approach in order to achieve the optimum outcome.[6] It is essential that this should be a conscious decision and not one taken in default.

In deciding on what to select as a 'straw issue', the negotiator must view the problem through the other's eyes and have regard to subjective as much as objective considerations. The achievement of some concession, however minor in an objective sense, may be of major importance to the other in terms of selling the bargain to his own management and enhancing his own prestige.

TACTICAL RECESS

A negotiation can gain momentum from the application of incessant pressure by, say, the other until it reaches the point at which the negotiator knows that his defences must break down unless relieving action is taken. The flow of the negotiations must be interrupted in an attempt to throw the other off balance and allow the negotiator the opportunity to recover. Some ways in which this may be done are as follows:

1 He finds some excuse to leave the room in the middle of the other's presentation of his case.
2 He arranges for the timely arrival of coffee, tea or drinks depending on the time of day.
3 He requests a short adjournment.

Although in case 3 the recess may be used to review the position reached in the negotiations, and to plan the next move, this is not the primary purpose of the recess. It is simply intended as a way of breaking up the other's attack. When the negotiations are resumed the negotiator may seek to continue the diversion by raising some new issue which he can pretend is related to those previously under discussion, but which he knows is likely to lead to a long and detailed argument between his own and the other's experts. By the time this argument is over the negotiator would have hoped to have thought up new lines of defence.

There are several means by which strategems 1 and 2 may be achieved. A junior member of the team leaves the room ostensibly to go to the cloakroom but in reality to tip off the team leader's secretary, so that five minutes later the leader is summoned to take a long-distance telephone call. The team leader may arrange with his secretary that if he calls her to perform some apparently innocent assignment, unconnected with the negotiations, this is in fact a signal to interrupt the meeting within the next few minutes either by calling him out or by bringing in refreshments.

WEARING OUT THE OTHER SIDE

Negotiation is a tiring business. It demands intense concentration, patience and the exercise of mental agility, very often under conditions which are totally unfavourable, for example, in rooms which are too hot and with inadequate ventilation. The negotiator may not be able to relax for long when the day's arguments are over; he may need to continue the discussion with his colleagues. If operating away from home base he will have the further problems of reporting back on progress and requesting further information and assistance, overcoming in the process any difficulties due to poor communications and time difference between his own country and the one in which the negotiations are taking place.

These natural hazards may be added to by tactics which artificially prolong the negotiations and/or deprive the negotiators of the limited opportunities which they do have for rest and relaxation. The apparently friendly evening hospitality extended to the visiting negotiator may be only a trap to keep him out of bed until well past midnight, and try to ensure that when he does get there it will be with the makings of a hangover. Naturally the leading negotiator for the other side will regret that he is unable to join the party and delegate the social task to a colleague not otherwise closely involved in the discussions.

So the days pass in interminable arguments and the nights are shortened, until it is exhaustion, rather than the other's skill in debate, which is the determining factor in shaping the final outcome.

The ethics of such tactics may seem dubious but their lineage is an ancient one. Bacon in his essay on cunning wrote: 'When you have anything to obtain of present dispatch, you entertain and amuse the party with whom you deal with some other discourse that he be not too much awake to make objections.'[7] It is important to be aware of such tactics and to guard against their employment by others.

LACK OF AUTHORITY

A tactic more often used in contract dispute situations than in buying or selling is that of deploying a negotiator with limited authority. After the parties have spent a considerable amount of time and effort in the negotiations and an offer has been made by the contractor in final settlement, the negotiator says 'Well, that seems a reasonable proposal to me but I don't have the final authority in this matter – I will have to refer it to my [Board] [Managing Director]. However that should only take a few days and we will let you know the answer by the end of the week.' Of course, the other side have no way then of knowing whether the assertion of lack of authority is genuine or not and there is little that they can do about it. If the negotiator later comes back and says 'I'm sorry I put it to them as strongly as I could but they insist that it's too much and the maximum to which they will agree is ——', that again leaves the contractor in a difficult position. Does he believe the negotiator and consider that he must either accept, go to the dispute resolution procedure under the contract, or take the risk that the negotiator is bluffing and demand a meeting with whoever is alleged to have made the decision?

He should never of course have allowed himself to be placed in this position. Before even commencing the negotiations, he should have insisted that the negotiator disclose whether he had the necessary authority or not. If the negotiator had then admitted his lack of authority, the contractor should have demanded that he be replaced with someone who did have the necessary authority to settle.

SILENCE

After the negotiator has made a full presentation of his case, his opposite number sits there in total silence. The negotiator feels that he must go on to say something more. Unfortunately for him he usually finishes up by going with an indication that his demand is not final, that he is willing to consider moderating his demand if the purchaser would have problems accepting it, anything to break the silence and get the purchaser's negotiator talking. All the purchaser is likely to say is 'Go on, I'd like to hear some more', and the negotiator obliges by digging himself into an even bigger hole.

The only safe response which the negotiator can make is to repeat his opening statement briefly and then ask his opposite number for his response.

FLINCHING, ALSO KNOWN AS 'THE WINCE'

The response from the purchaser to your request, say, for a variation order which would increase the price, is a sharp intake of breath with a little shake of the head. Nothing is said and it's left to you to continue. Again you are tempted to say something like 'If that's too much we could have another look at the costs but really we do need something'. Then the purchaser, without doing anything, has already forced you into a concession. Again the only safe response is to repeat your request unchanged.

TAKING THE OTHER INTO CONFIDENCE

The difficulty which a negotiator may have in persuading the other side that he is telling the truth has been pointed out several times. It is, however, only by doing so that the negotiator can enlist the support of the other in turning the issues which divide the two sides into an exercise in problem solving. If the negotiator is up against a genuine difficulty in complying with some requirement from the other, provided the negotiator can convince the other of the reality of that difficulty, and the efforts which he is making to resolve it, then this may be a far more effective tactic than trying to hide the truth and find excuses.

But when he does decide to adopt this approach he must be completely honest and hold nothing back from the other. To attempt to enlist the other's support, and then to be found out in some petty deception, must destroy the negotiator's credibility both for the negotiation in question and for a long time to come.

The tactic is essential in the type of negotiation which occurs during the course of the contract, and arises out of delays or the failure to meet some specification limit, by either side. The true interests of both sides in these circumstances are to ensure that the work is completed as soon as possible to whatever technical standards are necessarily required to meet the employer's essential needs. Only integrative bargaining can provide the basis upon which those objectives may be achieved.

It is recognized that frank disclosure may be prejudicial to the negotiator's contractual position and that agreement by the other to some action may constitute a waiver of his legal rights. But what are the rights of the two sides worth in relation to contract performance? In the nature of events there can be no single answer but the question must be answered by any who advocate, in such circumstances, the maintenance of an arm's-length distributive bargaining position.

IT WOULD HURT YOU MORE THAN IT WOULD HURT ME

A favourite defensive tactic with many negotiators is to seek to demonstrate that, on balance, agreeing to the other's demands would hurt them more than it would hurt the negotiator. In a typical example the negotiator might state that if he gives the other a discount, this must come out of the margin which means the business is less attractive for the negotiator and less money will be available for investment in research and development. Therefore the facilities which the supplier can provide for the purchaser today will not be available in the future. In the long run therefore the purchaser will be the loser.

The argument is often totally genuine, but the tactic can only be effective if the person to whom it is presented is both convinced of the honesty of the other negotiator and willing to take the long view. If not, then the negotiator is wasting his time. The purchaser will reply that he will judge what is best in his own interests, and will then ask the supplier what discount he is willing to offer.

Notes

1. See also T. C. Schelling, *The Strategy of Conflict* (London: Oxford University Press, 1963), p. 18 ff.
2. R. B. Cattell, *The Scientific Analysis of Personality* (Baltimore: Penguin Books, 1965).
3. An individual's personality may be described in terms of traits; a sizothemic personality would be described by R. B. Cattell (see note 2) in terms of being critical, grasping, cool, aloof and suspicious. But these traits may only be characteristic of that person when acting under certain environmental conditions, e.g. at work as a buyer, and his behaviour may be quite different under domestic conditions. The situation under which the individual is acting influences his traits and may either provide the outlet for their expression or modify them.
4. A *side letter* is the term used to describe a letter written at the time of signing the main contract, and signed by the persons who signed the main contract, which defines the way in

which some clause in the contract, is to be interpreted. To the extent that the side letter actually modifies the main contract, its legal validity may be doubtful and will depend on the legal system by which the contract is governed. However, commercially it is normally regarded as binding, and its value as a device is that if the contract document as such has to be approved by some third party or made public, the side letter can be kept private.

5. If the reader is not convinced, let him think how often he has been involved in a discussion which has taken a letter written by one side as the agenda and the other side has started off by saying something like: 'We have been through this and we have no problem with points one to four, but five to six do create some difficulty, so I suggest that we concentrate on these two and the others can be taken as agreed.' Four possible 'straw issues' which, following the norm of reciprocity, could have been used to create a sense of obligation to repay the favour have been thrown away and nothing gained in return. One at least of these issues could have been of importance to the letter writer who is now inwardly much relieved at having obtained something for nothing.

6. It may be suggested that time spent in haggling is normally regarded by the Westerner as a waste, and that his objective is often simply to reduce this time to a minimum. This is understandable in a society in which in domestic matters it is the custom to purchase requirements on standard terms and at fixed prices. As demonstrated in Section 15.1, if the other side has made their offer on the basis of bargaining, or at least a risk of bargaining, then a negotiator is compelled to bargain whether he likes it or not. Given that premise, then clearly he should do so in the most efficient manner.

7. Sir Francis Bacon, 'Cunning', in *Essays of Sir Francis Bacon* (London: Grant Richards, 1902), p. 62.

EPILOGUE

Negotiation has been examined as an exercise in micro-economic analysis and more so as a study of interpersonal human behaviour. Although the need has been stressed for building up long-term business relationships on the foundations of mutual respect for the other's legitimate interests, accusation may still be made for having at times been cynical and distrustful of the existence of honesty in human communications. Contract negotiation is not unique in the demands which it makes on human behaviour; the motives which lead to deception in business do not differ in nature from those which cause men to deceive their wives or politicians the electorate. Human nature does not change with the centuries, either as buyer or seller, as the following lines from *The Ship of Fools,* written in 1494, testify and serve as a conclusion:[1]

> They try to kill off competition;
> Then, bankrupt take an expedition,
> For, having slashed their prices downward,
> Their best direction's out of townward;
> If one of them won't cut the price
> His brothers won't be overnice,
> For if the customer is tight,
> The goods he gets will serve him right;
> The masters now make shoddy wares:
> If they can sell 'em then who cares?
> But such a business will not keep:
> To buy stuff dear and sell things cheap;
> Some tradesmen underestimate
> A deal, then take the city gate.
> Whoever loves a bargain, he
> Won't get much for a guarantee.
> They make so much at little cost;
> They sell it quick and nothing's lost;
> They profit from a slick veneer
> Now honest tradesmen disappear.

Note

1. S. Brant, *The Ship of Fools,* translated by William Gillis (London: The Folio Society, 1971).

APPENDICES

APPENDIX 1: DECISION TECHNIQUES

A1.1 Choice under risk[1] – the decision rules

One basic problem in contract negotiation is that of choosing between two or more alternative courses of action under circumstances in which:

1 It cannot be predicted with certainty whether the choice will lead to the desired outcome or not and, therefore, in making the choice one defined combination of value and risk must be preferred to another.
2 Generally the probability of reaching agreement can only be increased by selecting a course of action which is of lower value, and conversely by selecting a course of action of higher value that probability will be reduced.

In order to make the selection the following are required:

1 To define the objective in such terms that a value judgement can be placed on each alternative course of action.
2 A method whereby such value judgements can be made consistently, to weight them according to assessment of success or failure and finally to select that course which optimizes the achievement of the objective.

Consider this problem in relation to the submission of any offer. Traditional economic theory asserts that the rational decision maker will act so as to maximize some value, usually profit. It was seen in Section 13.3 that in most instances the value to Party of any offer cannot properly be expressed solely in monetary terms and certainly not in terms of profit which, in any event, has a different meaning to the economist and the businessperson.[2] The value to Party will be his assessment of the worth of a mixture of the immediate financial gains and other less tangible benefits, to be derived from the acceptance of his offer, with the contractual risks and asset utilization involved. The whole being expressed in relation to Party's needs at that time and his attitude towards risk taking. For the moment, reference is made to the worth of the offer to Party, the objective being to maximize this worth function.

The concept of the rational decision maker as a 'maximizer' has been challenged on the grounds that it does not accord with how people in business behave in practice, and it assumes a degree of knowledge and capacity for immediate calculation which no businessperson, even when supported by a computer, can hope to possess.

As an alternative it has been proposed, primarily by Simon, that the businessperson is a 'satisficer', that is to say, he limits himself to selecting some course of action which satisfies one or more minimum criteria and once he has done this he searches no further for any improvement.[3]

As a description of how many people and firms behave, the 'satisficing' theory is clearly correct. Observe how often a manager asked to approve the submission of a capital goods tender will simply ask whether or not the bid meets the profit contribution or other target set by his budget or business plan. If it does, then his approval is assured; if it does not, then he will require significant justification before giving his agreement, or else require that the bid is adjusted to comply with the target. He does not ask how far the price could be increased so as to provide a contribution in excess of the target without at the same time making a bid unacceptable to the recipient.

Also it is agreed that maximizing in its complete sense is in most circumstances impracticable; there is not time or knowledge to identify and evaluate every possible alternative.

However, as a normative 'theory, satisficing is conceptually unacceptable. Psychologically it provides no framework which allows for the exercise of that restless ambition which goads us ever forward; the need of the individual for what Maslow referred to as 'self-actualisation' – 'the doing well of the thing one wants to do' so that one never stops short of the fullest possible realization of one's potentialities.

Economically, the theory is equally unattractive. Any target established by a profit plan will be an average. Unless the manager is motivated to aim to exceed that average on every possible occasion the final result of the year's trading will be a below-target performance. Compare the case of the motorist who wishes to drive at an average of 40 mph. Unless he takes every chance of a clear road to travel at the legal maximum, he is most unlikely to reach his target, taking into account delays due to speed restrictions, traffic lights, roundabouts and road congestion. All businesses have their counterparts to these restrictions: factors which operate to depress the contribution actually earned on certain individual contracts well below those anticipated at tender stage. It is to compensate for this that the manager should never be content with any satisficing level but should always be aiming to maximize profit contribution on each and every occasion.

But the satisficing theory has brought out two valuable points; the existence of target levels, which it will be the first objective of the manager to achieve, and the need to limit the practice of maximizing by reference both to the state of knowledge and the cost/opportunity of improving it within the time-scale and computational facilities which are available. However, the latter are imposed operational restraints, the severity of which will vary according to circumstances, and not self-imposed norms limiting ambition.

Combining these features of satisficing with the basic concept of maximization of worth the following two rules emerge; these will be the objective for decision taking in relation to the submission of any offer:

1 The submission of an offer is preferred to no submission, provided only that the expected value of its worth satisfies some predetermined minimum requirement and no more favourable opportunity for the use of the assets involved can be identified within the limits of existing knowledge, computational ability and time available.

2 Subject to satisfying rule 1, the worth of the offer selected will have the maximum expected value determinable within the limits of existing knowledge and such further data as it may be decided to acquire, the time available and the capability for computation.

Expressed in operational terms it is proposed therefore to maximize the expected value of the worth of the offer subject to:

1 Satisfying the minimum requirement
2 The limits of the existing state of knowledge and any further data it may be decided to acquire
3 The time-scale within which the offer must be submitted
4 The ability for computation and comparison.

This defines the objective. The method for evaluating and comparing each course of action to be considered is now needed. The techniques for determining expected value and for assessing the worth of any given offer under conditions of risk are required for this purpose.

A1.2 Expected value

The beginning of Section A1.1 referred to the proposition that the more valuable the offer is then in general the lower the probability that it will be accepted by the person to whom it is made. Since the value which the offer has is realized only if it is accepted, and its rejection may cause a positive loss in expenses and unrecoverable overheads, for the purpose of comparison a single value is need for the offer which will take account of:

1 The value if the offer is accepted
2 The probability of acceptance
3 The loss suffered by rejection
4 The probability of rejection.

The standard procedure for arriving at such a value, known as the *expected value* of the offer is as follows:

1 Ascertain the value of the offer if it is accepted. This is referred to as the *conditional value* of the offer since it is conditional on the event 'offer accepted' occurring.
2 Estimate the probability that the other party will accept the offer.
3 Multiply the conditional value of the offer by the probability that it will be accepted.
4 Ascertain the loss to be suffered by the offer's rejection which becomes the conditional value of rejection.
5 Multiply the conditional value of the offer if rejected by the probability of its rejection. If no possibility of a counter-offer exists, and it will be assumed for the moment that it does not, then the two events 'offer accepted' and 'offer rejected' are mutually exclusive and collectively exhaustive. In accordance with the rules of the probability calculus the probability of rejection must therefore be equal to one minus the probability of acceptance.

6 Add the two values so obtained together, their sum being the expected value for the offer.

A simple example is given in Figure A1.1.

Event	Conditional value £	Probability	Expected value £
Offer accepted	10,000	0.6	6,000
Offer rejected	– 1,000	0.4	– 400
	Expected value of the offer		5,600

Figure A1.1   Expected value of an offer

In calculating the expected value of an act it is essential to ensure that *all* possible events have been included. It was assumed in the example in Figure A1.1 that a 'go' – 'no-go' situation existed and that the offer would be either accepted or rejected. If, however, there was reason to believe that the recipient would make a counter-offer then that event must be included in the example which might then become Figure A1.2.

Event	Conditional value £	Probability	Expected value £
Offer accepted	10,000	0.3	3,000
Counter offer	8,000	0.5	4,000
Offer rejected	–1,000	0.2	–200
	Expected value of the offer		6,800

Figure A1.2   Expected value of an offer may lead to a counter-offer

The procedure outlined above is based on the ability to measure two independent variables: the probability of the offer being accepted and the value of that offer conditional on either its acceptance or rejection. How this is to be done will be considered in the next two sections. First, comment is necessary on the independence condition of these two functions.

If consistency in making comparisons between the expected values of any two or more offers is to be maintained, then the conditional value placed on the acceptance or rejection of any offer A_1 must not be influenced by the assessment of the probability of that offer being accepted. Equally the estimate of the probability of offer A_1 being accepted must not be affected by that conditional value, and similarly for any other offer A_2.

Normatively the independence requirement is clear, but it is less clear whether it is satisfied by actual human behaviour to an extent which justifies the use of expected values as a guide for decision making.

Some evidence suggests that people put a higher estimate of success probability on gambles on which at worst they stand to break even than they do on gambles on which they could actually lose.[4] From this and other experiments it has been deduced that optimism in probability assessments tends to be associated with desirable outcomes and pessimism with undesirable ones.[5] (See also p. 78 for a discussion of this problem in relation to the negotiator's level of aspiration.) This is also supported by the observation that a manager whose objective is sales maximization will be more inclined to assign a lower success probability to a higher-priced bid than will a manager whose primary objective is the maximization of profit.

In practice, therefore, some interaction between conditional value and subjective probability appears likely. However, provided that the danger is recognized and positive action taken to minimize it by, for example, a cross-check of the manager's assessment by someone with a different motivation, it is not considered that such interaction is sufficient to invalidate the use of EV (expected value) techniques.

PROBABILITY ASSESSMENTS

The objective probability of a future event occurring is that which any rational individual would assign to that event if he had complete data available to him and perfect capability for assessment of such data. In all but the simplest cases it is an abstraction. Subjective probability is that which would be assessed by a rational individual on the basis of the data available to him, at the time of such assessment, and his own personal judgement and experience.

By definition, there can only be one objective probability for any given event but there can be more than one subjective probability according to the different data available to, and the judgement/experience of, the individual assessing the event's probability. In Laplace's well-known example of three urns, one containing black balls and the other two containing white balls, a rational individual would assess the probability that the third urn contains black balls as one-third, with no other knowledge available. If, however, it is known by another person that the second urn contains white balls then his subjective probability of the third urn containing black balls would be one-half.

The probabilities under consideration are those of the managers involved in any particular negotiation. They are subjective probabilities based on the judgement and experience of the managers concerned and of the information which they possess. It is permitted to use these probabilities for the purpose of decision making, and to assume that they comply with the normal mathematical laws relating to probabilities, provided only that:

1 When assigning a probability assessment to a given event the manager acts rationally, having regard to his experience and the evidence before him; specifically he does not act arbitrarily.
2 So far as is practical, probabilities are assigned to those events of which the manager has the most experience, and the theory of probability is then used to compute the probabilities of events of which he has lesser experience.
3 The manager is consistent in his assignment of probabilities.

It is the last requirement, of consistency, which causes the most problems. An individual's consistency of judgement would appear to be a function of:

1 His maturity – children have been shown to exhibit far more inconsistencies in the assessment of probabilities than adults.[6]
2 The degree of his business training and experience – the skilled negotiator will develop a 'feel' for the probability that his opponent will accept or reject an offer.
3 A built-in bias which is partly due to his intrinsic personality characteristics and partly derived from his own previous experiences. The ever-optimistic salesperson is an example.

Factors 1 and 2 will clearly respond to training and experience; factor 3 is more difficult. If, however, over a period of time the manager's bias remains more or less constant, i.e. he continually overestimates his changes of success by, say, 10 per cent, then provided this can be established by comparing his past forecasts with what actually happened, the bias can be allowed for and the appropriate correction factor applied. The need to do this in relation to estimating costs is amusingly if somewhat cynically described by Lock but experience would certainly support his general conclusions of wildly optimistic estimating by engineers.[7] He also refers to the bane of any manager's existence: the inconsistent estimator whose only reliably displayed characteristic is his inconsistency! Unfortunately Lock does not suggest a means of dealing with such individuals.

A1.3 *Utility under risk*

So far, in referring to the value of the offer, whether positive or negative, such value has been expressed in monetary terms. The purpose, however, is to compare the expected outcome of what is in effect a gamble, and for this purpose, where any significant sums of money are involved, monetary values themselves are not adequate.

Supposing that I am offered a choice between a certain gain of £1,000 and a 30 per cent chance of winning £10,000 and a 70 per cent chance of nothing. I would take the £1,000 certain, and so would very many other people. Some, for a variety of reasons, would prefer the gamble. Yet on an expected monetary basis the gamble is the mathematically 'correct' choice since the expected value of the gamble is £3,000.

Clearly in my judgement, and that of others who would act similarly, a certainty of £1,000 possesses a greater 'worth' than a gamble of securing £10,000 which has a 30 per cent chance of success. If, however, I already had £100,000 then I might decide to take the gamble; I would definitely want more than an offer of £1,000 certain to persuade me not to take the gamble.

What is true of individuals in their private lives is true of the same individuals as company managers and is followed, therefore, in the behaviour of their companies, or should be if the company's judgement is properly to reflect the worth to that company of an offer under conditions of risk. This worth function will clearly vary from one situation to another and is not linear with money. Factors which contribute to this variability and non-linearity are as follows:

1 The potential loss involved in the rejection of the offer in relation to the company's resources. If this is significant then the company will value each pound they stand to lose more highly than those which they might gain. An example would be a small company with low liquid assets which would not be able to afford the risk of high legal costs and an award of damages against them if they lost an action for breach of contract. To such a company, the negative value of losing, say, £5,000 would be higher than the positive value of a gain of a similar amount and a break-even point could be positive. This implies that our worth function takes into account what Pruitt has described as the *risk level* of the gamble and distinguishes between our preference for gambles of high and low risk.[8]

2 The setting of budget of planned targets of profitability which managers are expected to achieve, or alternatively, the acceptance within a firm that a certain contribution rate is 'normal'. Due to satisficing behavioural tendencies of the type already discussed there will be an increasing lack of interest at any point above the profit norm and at some point even a certain anxiety that the profit is perhaps unreasonable or may create a precedent which the manager would find embarrassing in the future.[9] Accordingly the marginal rate of increase in worth of each additional pound of contribution above the norm will progressively decline.[10]

3 The manager's attitude as a person towards risk taking. As previously suggested it seems probable that the manager carries with him into business the same attitudinal behavioural pattern towards risk taking as he has in his private life. The fact that if he is only a salaried employee without equity participation in the business the money is in no sense his own, does not appear to be sufficient to alter what is a very deep-rooted personal characteristic.[11]

4 The manager's need at any particular time to obtain business in order to fulfil other targets, e.g. maintenance of shop output, retention of key staff or conversely the lack of any such need.

It follows that where the monetary values are significant, for the purpose of comparing the expected value of one offer with another, or indeed of making any strategy comparison, a system of worth assessment which will take into account all the factors concerned is required:[12]

1 The actual cash gain or loss involved
2 Other benefits to be derived or lost
3 The strength of the ambition to secure the cash gain/other benefits and to avoid suffering loss
4 The risks involved in the venture
5 The attitude towards risk taking.

Any such assessment will be subjective to the individual who makes it and peculiar to the particular circumstances under which it is made. It will reflect at that time, and under those conditions, the individual's attitude towards the factors listed.

The construction of an index of preference, or scale of utility values as it is usually called, is carried out as follows:

1 Decide on the best and worst possible outcomes of the risk decision which has to be made. Assume, for example, that these are gain £1,000 and gain £0.

2 Assign to each of these two possible outcomes an arbitrary value. Any values may be selected provided only that the value assigned to the best is greater than that assigned to the worst. Conveniently for the best outcome in the example gain £1,000, the value 1 will be selected, and for the worst outcome 'gain £0', the value 0. These then are the two end points of our utility scale.

3 Assume that there is the choice between the receipt of a stated sum of some value between £1,000 and £0 and participating in the risk venture. On that basis decide for what probability of success in the risk venture 'gain £1,000–gain £0, the choice would be exactly balanced between receiving for certain the particular sum or taking the risk. For example, if the sum offered was £300 the choice might be balanced between that amount or a 50/50 chance of winning £1,000 or £0.

4 Because the choice is balanced between these two events, they can be said to possess the same utility. By substituting in the equation for expected value the two fixed reference points and the probabilities assessed, it is now possible to determine the utility of gain £300 as being $U(£300)= (1 \times 0.5) + (0 \times 0.5) = 0.5$.

5 By repeating this process for a number of possible values, a scale can be built up and a curve of the utility values plotted on a graph. This scale can then be used to predict the conditional utility values of differing gains without any further calculation. By applying the estimates of the probabilities of their being accepted to such conditional values, the offer, which on this occasion and under the defined risks possesses the maximum utility, can then be selected.

An example is set out in Figure A1.3.

Offer	Value £	Utility if accepted	Probability of acceptance	Utility if rejected	Probability of rejection
A	80,000	0.7	0.7	0	0.3
B	100,000	0.8	0.6	0	0.4

Figure A1.3 Comparison of the expected value of two offers

The expected values of the two offers are:

$$A (0.7 \times 0.7) + (0 \times 0.3) = 0.49$$
$$B (0.8 \times 0.6) + (0 \times 0.4) = 0.48$$

Offer A should therefore be selected. It will be noted that had the expected value of money been used the decision would have been different since the expected value of offer B in monetary terms (£60) is greater than £56 the monetary expected value of offer B.

The reason is that the utility scale has taken into account the preference for a lesser degree of risk taking and also the diminishing marginal value of money. To this extent it accords with the observed practice of managers and the intuitive feel for the correct solution.[13]

The validity, however, of the above calculation depends on the persons making it possessing certain basic attributes of rationality of which the most significant are:

1   Transitivity – If A is preferred to B and B to C, then A must be preferred to C.
2   Continuity of preference – If there is a preference to participate in the risk venture rather than to receive a sum certain when the probability of success is 1, and equally prefer the sum certain to participating in the risk venture when the probability of success is 0, then at some probability value, p, we will be indifferent between the risk venture and the receipt of the sum certain.
3   Preference for success probability – If a choice must be made between two outcomes of the risk venture which are of equal value, then the one which has a higher probability of success should be chosen. It is interesting to note that this means the challenge of overcoming the greater risk or the excitement of winning against the odds cannot be taken into account. At this point it is suspected that being rational also carries the penalty of being dull!

Utility values on the scale described represent a precise ordering of preferences over the length of the scale. Therefore it is possible to additionally interpret the results when shown graphically as indicating:

1   Through the shape of the curve the general attitude towards risk taking under the conditions defined for the particular exercise for which the curve was drawn. The three curves shown in Figure A1.4 illustrate three differing attitudes for the same risk venture. Curve X is typical of that of a cautious manager more concerned with the near certainty of a low profit than the lesser chance of a high one. Curve Z is that of the gambler who eschews low profits. Curve Y may be said to be that of the 'middle-of-the-road' manager.
2   By a comparison between the slope of the curve at different points how the attitude varies as the level of the offer changes. This will enable a comparison to be made of the relative strength of feelings for particular changes and a decision to be taken on the lines of resistance as part of the negotiating plan.

Before leaving the subject of utility under risk, of which the above is necessarily only a brief outline, a word of caution is necessary. The units of utility have been defined in terms of ordinary numbers which, although convenient, are also dangerous, since it may lead to the belief that they can be treated mathematically in all respects, as if they were ordinary numbers. But they cannot, since each unit of utility represents a separate value/risk assessment; the utility of gain £500 in the example is not twice that of gain £250.[14] The true nature of the utility unit has been well defined as 'an indecomposable mixture of attitude towards risk, profit and loss in a particular kind of situation'.[15]

Secondly it is stressed that this attitude is personal to the individual and to the circumstances existing at the time at which he makes his assessment. For the individual to reassess his utility value structure as circumstances or those of the company change does not pose any particular problem. What does raise difficulties, however, is that the individual manager does not neces-

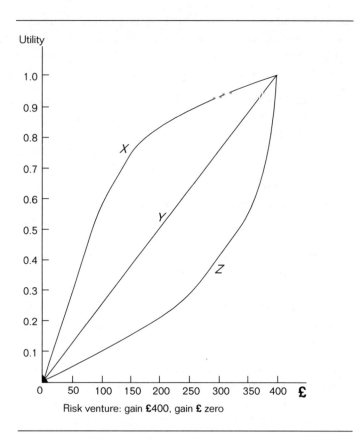

Figure A1.4 Typical utility curves under risk

sarily make the decision alone, for example, on which offer should be submitted. More likely he will be one of a group and it seems improbable that all members of the group will have the same utility function. Their preferences and the intensity with which these are held will vary.

The problem arises as to how the utility functions of the group are to be combined to provide a group utility. No formal mechanism on a theoretical basis for doing this has been developed, and it has been suggested that the problem in terms of defining a 'fair' method is insoluble.[16] Utility values are, however, only a means of giving expression to beliefs and values which will be held by the group members in any event. The problem of reconciling conflicting attitudes is still there, whether the members think and talk in utility terms or not. This problem exists in any management group and in practical terms two solutions are possible.

First, one of the members of the group by virtue of his standing or authority acts as a dictator and either imposes his will on the others or they each adopt his utility function in preference to their own.

Second, the group interact and through a process of adjustment modify their own value functions until a consensus emerges which is adopted by the group as a whole. This may happen through a majority of the group finding that their own functions are so similar that they can act as one and the minority accepting their view. Alternatively the group may be led by one or more of its members to coordinate one particular function where this is recognized as having some particular aptness to the decision in question.

A1.4 The theory of games

In selecting a decision rule which he believes will optimize the value to him of any strategy, Party must necessarily make assumptions as to the decision rule which will be chosen by Opponent and the same is true for Opponent in relation to Party. Both firms will therefore make their decisions according to their beliefs as to how the other will behave.

Coddington has drawn a useful distinction between two types of decision rule:[17]

1 A 'self-generating' decision rule: One which satisfies the condition that if Party expects Opponent to follow rule A then this also leads Party to adopting rule A. If the negotiation concerned the division of £100, and Party expected Opponent to follow the rule split 50/50 this could lead Party to follow suit.
2 A 'self-replacing' decision rule: One which satisfies the condition that if Party expects Opponent to follow one rule then this leads Party to adopt some different rule. In the above example of dividing £100, if Party believes that Opponent will adopt decision rule B: ask for 60/40, this will lead Party to choose some other decision rule, say, ask for 75/25.

It has been shown by Coddington that in relation to self-replacing rules one or both of the bargainers will be wrong in their judgement as to the other's expectations.[18] Party's judgement will only be correct if Opponent has made an error in assessing how Party will behave and conversely, if Opponent is right in assessing Party's intended behaviour, then his judgement of how Opponent will behave must be wrong. In rule 2, if Party was correct in his assessment of Opponent's demand then Opponent was wrong in his judgement of Party, since his choice of decision rule B could only have been based on an expectation that Party would choose some other decision rule A, say '55/45'.[19]

As an illustration of how this problem arises in regard to the submission of any offer, assume that Party is intending to quote at a price level of 96 based on his belief that Opponent will tender > 98. The position looked at from Opponent's viewpoint is shown in the first three columns of Figure A1.5, and, to complete the picture, column four shows the correctness of Party's judgement on Opponent.

Opponent's belief as to Party's action	Opponent's reaction	Opponent's view of Party	Party's view of Opponent
1 Party will bid <96	bid 94	wrong	wrong
2 Party will bid ≥96<99	bid 95	correct	wrong
3 Party will bid ≥99	bid 98	wrong	correct

Figure A1.5   Example of self-replacing decision rule

It will be seen that in no case are both parties right. In 2 when Opponent is correct in his judgement as to Party's action, Party is wrong, since his decision to bid at 96 was based on his belief that Opponent would tender at least 98.

This result is quite general and confirms the theory that in any instance where Party adopts a self-replacing decision rule then either he or Opponent or both will be mistaken in his expectations regarding the decision rule adopted by the other.[20]

Unfortunately for Party's marketing manager, he must still decide on the actual level at which to submit his bid, despite the uncertainty he feels as to Opponent's intentions. To assist him he prepares a bid pay-off table on the lines set out in Figure A1.6.

Price level	Probability (p) of bid being successful	Conditional utility of an award at that price	$p \times u$	Probability $(1-p)$ of bid being unsuccessful	Utility of losing the bid	$(1-p) \times u$	Bid EV
99	0.05	10	0.5	0.95	−1	−0.95	−0.45
98	0.25	9	2.25	0.75	−1	−0.75	1.50
97	0.60	8	4.80	0.40	−1	−0.40	4.40
96	0.80	7	5.60	0.20	−1	−0.20	5.40
95	0.95	5	4.75	0.05	−1	−0.05	4.70

Figure A1.6   Comparison of bid expected values

The strategy having the maximum expected value is bid at price level 96 and this is clearly best in the sense that it provides the optimum expected return against the manager's assumed probability distribution for Opponent. However, such a strategy is clearly not as safe as that of bid at price level 95. This is shown by Figure A1.7 which, using the same probabilities, compares the expected values of the two strategies conditional upon whether Opponent tenders above or below Party.

	Expected value to Party	
Price level	Opponent tenders above Party	Opponent tenders below Party
96	5.6	−0.2
95	4.75	−0.05

Figure A1.7   Comparison of two bid strategies

If, therefore, Party's marketing manager prefers to minimize risk, rather than maximize profit opportunity, he will prefer the strategy bid at price level 95, for which his expected loss is only 0.05.

The concept of a strategy choice which maximizes one's security against the worst which one's adversary can do is central to that branch of decision theory known as the *theory of games*.

This theory was first developed comprehensively by Neuman and Morgenstern in 1944 and has since been the subject of considerable study and elaboration.[21, 22] For present purposes the account of the theory is limited to its simplest form and attention, is concentrated on that part which has the most relevance to a two-party bargaining position.

The theory describes a conflict of interest situation referred at as a *game* in which strictly:

1 Each player has a finite number of possible courses of action, referred to as his strategies for the game.
2 Each player has complete information as to his own and his opponents' possible strategies, and the resulting pay-off values, depending on the strategies selected by each.
3 The players make their strategy choices simultaneously, i.e. neither knows the other's choice until he has made his own.
4 The pay-off values for each player are expressed in terms of utilities as described in Section A1.3 and represent, therefore, a strict ordering of preferences such that the player will always prefer the higher to the lower value. The player's objective is the maximization of utility and it is assumed that he will act at all times in the manner best calculated to achieve this, i.e. each player assumes that his opponent's choice will be optimal.

It will be appreciated that these conditions, if applied strictly, would severely limit the application of the theory to real-life situations. The extent to which they can be relaxed without destroying the essential spirit of the theory will now be considered.

Since two-party bargaining is the main interest, the games will be restricted to those with two players which conventionally are divided into two types. The first is *zero-sum games*, in which the gains of one party are the losses of the other. For this reason such games are strictly competitive and collusion between the parties would not bring them jointly any advantage. The second is *non-zero sum games*, in which, as might be expected, the gains of one party are not necessarily the losses of the other and very often it is only through collusion that the players can optimize their joint strategies.

The set of strategies for Party in any game is denoted by $a_1.. a_2.. a_i.. a_m$ and those for Opponent by $b_1.. b_2.. b_j.. b_n$. To the strategy choice $a_1 b_1$ there is an outcome O_{ij} The presentation of this is given in the form of a pay-off table as in Figure A1.8.

ZERO-SUM GAMES

The usual convention in zero-sum games is to draw only the pay-off function for Party since it is known that the pay-off function for Opponent is the negative of this. Considering the pay-off matrix given in Figure A1.9 which strategy should each party adopt, assuming that Party wishes to gain as much as possible and Opponent to lose as little as possible?

		Opponent			
		b_1	b_2	b_j	b_n
	a_1	O_{11}	O_{12}	O_{1j}	O_{1n}
Party	a_2	O_{21}	O_{22}	O_{2j}	O_{2n}
	a_1	O_{i1}	O_{i2}	O_{ij}	O_{in}
	a_m	O_{m1}	O_{m2}	O_{mj}	O_{mn}

Figure A1.8   Strategy pay-off table

		Opponent		
		b_1	b_2	b_3
	a_1	5	4	8
Party	a_2	12	3	2
	a_3	0	2	20

Figure A1.9 Example of zero-sum game with saddle point

Consistent with rule 4 for the game – 'assume that your opponent's choice will be optimal for him' – the greatest gain of which Party can be certain, *irrespective of Opponent's strategy choice*, is equal to the maximum of the minimum value in each row. It will be remembered that Opponent's losses are the reverse of Party's gains and therefore it must be expected that Opponent will select that strategy which minimizes Party's gains. The three minima values are 4, 2 and 0, so that the strategy which maximizes Party's certain return, in game-theory terms *his security level*, is a_1 which gives Party an assurance of a gain of at least 4. This strategy is known as Party's *maximin strategy*.

Similarly Opponent can guarantee his smallest loss by selecting that strategy which contains the minimum of the column maxima. Since these are 12, 4 and 20, Opponent's *minimax strategy* is b_2 which restricts his loss to 4.

The unique pair $a_1 b_2$, sometimes referred to as a *saddle-point*, is in equilibrium in the sense that neither party has any incentive to change his strategy provided that the other does not change his. Stated more formally, a strategy pair a_{io}, b_{jo} is in equilibrium if:

1 No outcome O_{ijo} is more preferred by Party than O_{iojo}.
2 No outcome O_{jio} is more preferred by Opponent than O_{iojo}.

It follows that the entry O_{iojo} will be the maximum of its column j_o and the minimum of its row i_o.

Do zero-sum games with equilibrium pairs exist in the real world or are they only theoretical abstractions? Luce and Raiffa suggest there could be an application in military decision making, and quote an example from Haywood drawn from World War 11.[23, 24] Other writers are more doubtful, the principal stumbling block being the requirement that the gains of one player are the losses of the other.[25]

		Vendor B	
		b_1 Raise price	b_2 Maintain price
Vendor A	a_1 Raise price	0	−1
	a_2 Maintain price	1	0

Figure A1.10 Commercial example of zero-sum game

One commercial situation which approximates to a zero-sum game with an equilibrium pair is that of a duopoly market in which the brand loyalty of each firm's products is low, the elasticity of demand relative to price is high, and the market is just saturated. For each vendor, his present price maximizes total revenue, given that the other does not change his price. The choice facing the duopolists is whether to raise the price 5 per cent, or leave it as it stands, and may be represented by the matrix given in Figure A1.10.

The strategy pair $a_2 b_2$ (maintain the price as its current level) is the unique equilibrium pair.[26]

ZERO-SUM GAMES – NO SADDLE POINT

		Opponent	
		b_1	b_2
	a_1	5	3
Party	a_2	4	6

Figure A1.11   Example of zero-sum game, no saddle point

Not all zero-sum games have an equilibrium pair. Which strategy, for example, should Party adopt in order to maximize his security in the game shown in Figure A1.11?

His reasoning when trying to make up his mind could go something like this:

> If I choose a_2, I guarantee myself at least 4. But if Opponent believes I will choose a_2 then he will take b_1, and if he is going to do that, then I would be better off with a_1. I must, however, regard Opponent as being clever enough to work that one out and if he does then he is bound to select b_2. In that event I am better off with a_2 which is where I started.[27]

Is there any way out of this circular reasoning? It can be shown that Party maximizes his security by playing $\frac{1}{2}a_1$ and $\frac{1}{2}a_2$ and similarly that Opponent maximizes his security by playing $\frac{3}{4}b_1$ and $\frac{1}{4}b_2$.[28] If the game were to be played only once it would be interpreted as saying that Party should make his choice by the use of some device which would select a_1 with a probability of 50 per cent and a^2 with the probability of 50 per cent. Party's strategy of $\frac{1}{2}a_1$ and $\frac{1}{2}a_2$ is described as a maximum mixed strategy and the two mixed strategies $(\frac{1}{2}a_1 : \frac{1}{2}a_2)$ and $(\frac{3}{4}B_1 : \frac{1}{4}b_2)$ are an equilibrium pair. It can further be shown that every two-person zero-sum game has an equilibrium pair when mixed strategies are permitted.[29]

Whilst mathematically elegant, does the concept of a mixed strategy have any relevance to real life? Clearly it is not suggested that a negotiator should select his strategy by tossing a coin or selecting a card!

The use of randomized strategy can be seen as a form of hedging, bluffing and concealment of intentions. For example, over the period of a long-term bargaining relationship, one negotiator will start to learn the type of strategy the other is likely to adopt.[30] To prevent this happening, one bargainer may at irregular intervals delegate the strategy choice to a colleague of known different views, having first bound himself to accept his colleague's decision. Schelling suggests something similar when he points out that by randomizing his choice of strategy, Party defeats any attempt by Opponent to coordinate their strategy choices based on deductive reasoning as to Party's probable intentions.[31] The act of randomization itself ensures that Opponent can have no better chance of being right than the odds involved in the random selection.

This is not theoretical. Firms manufacturing a standard product or providing a standard service with a limited number of known competitors, e.g. motorway construction, do maintain long-term records of their competitors' bidding behaviour from which they seek to predict what will be their competitors' price level on the next bid opportunity. If, for example, firm X is believed never to have bid at less than, say, total cost plus a margin of around 7 per cent then given that Party can reasonably estimate X's construction costs for the job in question he can arrive very closely at X's most likely lowest bid price. If, however, X now decides to bid without addition for profit not only will Party's predictions for that tender be upset but more importantly he can no longer be so certain as to how X will behave on *any* future occasion, which will make it that much more difficult for Party to assess his own success probability – see further p. 365.

NON-ZERO SUM GAMES

Most bargaining situations can only be represented by a theory which permits the respective gains and losses of the parties for any outcome to be different. This means that both parties can gain from a given outcome and therefore allows for the case in which the maximum joint gain is achieved by collusion between the parties as to the strategy each will adopt.

In the analysis of this type of game a distinction is made between those which permit collaboration and those which do not.

Non-collaborative non-zero games

Both players have a preferred strategy which would maximize their expected gain, but only if the other player is obliging enough to use his inferior strategy. If both players adopt their preferred strategies then both will lose.[32]

A suitable illustration of this game is a situation in which two bargainers have a single major issue, the contract price, to settle before an agreement can be concluded. Each has a preferred price level and each knows what he believes the other party might accept as a compromise. Therefore, each bargainer is aware generally of the value to himself and to his adversary of concluding a bargain at either the preferred or compromise level and of the value of no bargain. The time available for negotiation has almost expired and so the choices open to the parties are restricted to sticking to their present offer, which is the preferred level, or offering a compromise. The problem can be represented by a game matrix in the form shown in Figure A.12.

		Opponent	
		b_1 stick	b_2 compromise
Party	a_1 stick	0,0	6,1
	a_2 compromise	1,6	3,3

Figure A1.12   Example of non-zero sum game

The parties are assumed to make their strategy choices simultaneously and to be committed to them, i.e. they cannot change their minds after hearing the other's choice. The higher value shown for the strategy choice compromise in $a_2 b_2$ is based on the idea that the original concessions may not bring final agreement, but would bring it so close that the parties would then bridge the remaining gap between them by each making a further minor concession. If, on the other hand,

Opponent has chosen to stick and Party to concede, then Party will be compelled to continue to concede to the point of matching Opponent's preferred level, which must represent a worse bargain for Party, although one which he presumably prefers to no bargain.

Party's maximum strategy is clearly a_2 concede since this would guarantee him at least 1. If Opponent is also a maximiner and reasons in the same way, then Party would gain 3. It is at this point that Party is tempted to argue that if Opponent is a maximiner and is going to concede then why does he, Party, not stick out and so gain 6? On an expected value basis, at any probability > 25 per cent that Opponent will concede, strategy a_1 stick has a greater expected value (1.5) than strategy a_2. But it is not a guaranteed value and if Opponent adopts the same line of reasoning then both will finish up with gaining nothing. At this point, Party settles for a_2 concede, only again to think perhaps that his decision was cowardly and that he should have taken a chance.

Party is left still making up his mind because there is no one answer. The game has two equilibrium pairs, a_1b_2 and a_2b_1, but these are neither equivalent nor interchangeable and the game has therefore no solution.[33] Party can only judge on the importance to him of some bargain rather than no bargain and on his experience of Opponent. How will he reason? Leaving the realm of 'pure' game theory, that of judgement and psychology is now examined.

If a solution must be suggested, then on the utility values given in the matrix, if experience of Opponent showed that the chance of his conceding was greater than 25 per cent, strategy a_1 stick would be adopted. Alter the utility value for Party of no bargain to, say, −3 and for any subjective probability of Opponent adopting b_1 stick greater than, say, 20 per cent, a_2 concede would now be selected. This is so even though, on an expected value basis, a_1 would remain the apparent optimum choice up to a 40 per cent probability of Opponent choosing b_1 stick. The consequences of no bargain are now too serious; more formally the risk level of the gamble select a_1 has increased sharply to a point at which it would be regarded as unacceptable.[34] This argument is reinforced by the fact that, in accordance with game-theory convention, Opponent would be aware of the change in the utility to Party of no bargain, and this would strengthen his view that Party would not dare to choose a_1; therefore, Opponent was safe in choosing b_1 stick which would provide him with his maximum return.

It should be clear from the above analysis that the theory in relation to non-zero sum games is far less developed than it is for zero-sum games and can offer much less precise guidance to the course of action to be adopted. The trouble is that the maximin strategies need not form an equilibrium pair and there is always therefore the temptation to defect. For further discussion see Luce and Raiffa.[35]

Even when there is only one equilibrium pair, troubles still persist. In the classic non-zero sum non-cooperative game, the prisoner's dilemma, the outcome represented by the single equilibrium pair is one which both parties would prefer to avoid, if only they could find a rational way of doing so![36]

The game is of the form shown in Figure A1.13.

	Opponent	
	b_1	b_2
a_1	(4,4)	(–3,6)
Party		
a_2	(6, –3)	(–1, –1)

Figure A1.13 Commercial example of 'the prisoner's dilemma'

In terms of contract negotiations it would seem more appropriate to regard this game as representing the situation facing two duopolists who are submitting a tender to a monopoly buyer in a market in which demand for their product is declining, the product is homogenous, and the cost is highly volume-conscious.[37] The problem facing the two bidders is whether to maintain the current price level, their first strategy in Figure A1.13, or to reduce prices in an effort to obtain increased volume and maximize profit: strategy two.

Strictly their second strategy in each case dominates the first and the outcome a_2b_2 is the unique equilibrium pair. That pair would be selected therefore as the solution to the game, provided there was no opportunity for the parties to cooperate either openly or tacitly.

Open cooperation, to stand even a chance of being effective, would need to be supported by a binding agreement between the parties, the penalty for breach of which would be more severe than any likely gain.[38] This is so because neither a_1b_2 nor a_2b_1 are in equilibrium and so either party will always be tempted to defect if he believes that the other will not follow suit. The existence of an agreement, if it is loose or informally expressed, will support such belief despite the apparent irrationality in one player believing that the other will act differently from the way in which he intends to act himself.

Tacit coordination could arise simply from the competitive bidding being repeated a number of times. The suggestion made by Luce and Raiffa is outlined as follows:

> In most cases it is felt that an unarticulated collusion between the players will develop, much in the same way as a mature economic market often exhibits a marked degree of collusion without any communication among the participants. This arises from the knowledge that the situation will be repeated and that reprisals are possible.

The experimental results referred to by Lee and the bidding experiments carried out by Siegel and Fouraker do not appear to support this proposition.[39,40] Both found that the competitive choice a_2b_2 predominated over the collaborative choice a_1b_1.

The explanation may lie in the motivation of the players. Lee has suggested that the subjects playing the games to which he refers were largely motivated by the desire to 'outscore their opponents'.[41] Siegel and Fouraker identified simple profit maximization as the primary motive of the subjects. Significantly, however, although the games in these experiments were repeated a number of times, the bargaining relationship between the parties was essentially short term and little or no opportunity existed for the development of personal relationships between the players.[42] Conditions were therefore weighted against the parties establishing a maturity of understanding or of learning to control their aggressive tendencies in the interests of long-term stability.

It is also of significance that when Siegel and Fouraker increased the amount of data available to the bargainers at the end of each game, thus more accurately simulating real-life conditions, there was far more support for the collaborative choice.[43] In certain bargaining pairs, one player, by continually repeating the bid which maximized joint profit, 'taught' his opponent that he was prepared to coordinate on this choice. (Siegel and Fouraker allowed no communication between the bidders who did not even see each other, so that this can only be regarded as pure tacit coordination.)

The urge to win, even if the victory is pyrrhic, is a deep-rooted human emotion often originating in a basic feeling of insecurity. This theme was considered in Chapter 14 when ways of satisfying a negotiator's personal motivational drive were discussed.

COLLABORATIVE NON-ZERO SUM GAME

It has already been indicated several times that the difficulties facing the players in making their strategy choices would be eased if they were allowed to communicate with each other before doing so and to enter into collaborative agreements. Certainly it would enable them to agree on the outcome which maximizes joint profits, which otherwise they are unlikely to do.

In a static situation where the choices are limited, and once made irrevocable, prior communication and the ability to make binding agreements may enable the parties to identify and agree on their joint pareto-optimal choice.[44]

In a dynamic situation, however, problems still remain which may be illustrated with the aid of the matrix given in Figure A1.14.

		Opponent	
		b_1	b_1
Party	a_1	(u_1, u_5)	(u_1, u_1)
	a_2	(0.0)	(u_5, u_1)

Figure A1.14   Example of non-zero sum game – collaborative

Diagramatically this is shown in Figure A1.15, in which the line between the two maximin strategy outcomes u_{51} and u_{15} is known as the *negotiation set* and represents all undominated outcomes of the game. Since the players know each other's utility pay offs, it is assumed that they will not accept an outcome less than optimal and will therefore select some bargain on this line. It is inferred that the outcome u_{ij} is the choice of both parties, i.e. given that Opponent will select b_1 with a probability p_1, and b_2 with a probability p_2, $(p_1 + p_2 = 1)$, then for Party $U(p_1u_1 + p_2u_1 > U(p_2) + p_2O + p_2u_5)$.

However, what is the value for u_{ij}? Is it feasible to predict a single solution for this game?

Normatively it has been proposed by Nash that having set the utility functions for both players of no bargain at zero pay off, the solution is that point which maximizes the product of the player's utilities: in Figure A1.15 the point marked X.[45] Other suggestions have been made, based primarily on the principle that a bargainer will concede if his loss would be smaller than that of his opponent.[46] Mathematically this proposal will lead to the same answer as Nash's. These solutions have been reviewed by both Cross and Coddington.[47]

The difficulty with all these theories is that they are static; the outcome can be predicted

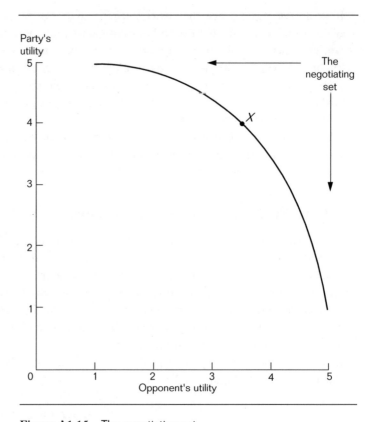

Figure A1.15   The negotiating set

without the players even being present. The static nature of game theory was no problem when dealing with the competitive bidding decision which is in itself static given that post tender negotiations are excluded. Each party has a single opportunity with no possibility of later adjustment.

Bargaining, however, is dynamic. There are a series of decisions to be made over a time-scale, each dependent on what has already occurred and on the bargainer's future expectations. According to past events, future predictions as to both his opponents and his own behaviour, and the factor of time, the bargainer will adjust his present offer accordingly.

This is not to suggest that the Nash point will never describe the outcome. If the structure of the negotiations and the anticipations of the parties are such that the Nash point is intuitively recognized as a landmark on which to coordinate, then it can be expected to be the outcome.[48] The simplest example would be bargaining over the division of £100 where utility for both parties was linear with money. The Nash theory would predict a 50/50 division as would the above theories, given no other points of equal convergence.

In dispute, however, is the claim that the Nash point or indeed that predicted by any other of the theories describes the *unique* outcome. That is dependent on a multitude of factors which it is the purpose of our present study to consider.

GAMES AGAINST NATURE

So far in this discussion of game theory it has been assumed that the Opponent is a deliberate adversary who will at all times adopt maximizing behaviour. Many situations can, however, be characterized in game-theory format in which the opponent is not an adversary but a state of nature; a circumstance over which no control can be exercised but the form of which will determine the extent of the benefit to be derived from the adoption of any given strategy.

Assume that Party is asked by Opponent to agree to a penalty clause for delay and believes that should he refuse Opponent will insist on a discount of 5 per cent. The situation can be represented by the matrix shown in Figure A1.16.

		State of nature (delay)	
		Delay does not occur	Delay does occur
Party	Agree to penalty	0	−1% up to 10% dependent on period of delay
	Do not agree to penalty	−5%	−5%

Figure A1.16   Commercial example of a game against nature

In a game against nature the maximin strategy can no longer be relied upon. Nature's acts are not deliberately against individuals. (For example, it will not rain tomorrow just because a picnic has been planned.) Equally, performance of the contract will not be delayed just because it has been decided to accept the penalty. Indeed the reverse can be argued; by accepting the penalty the danger will be minimized by taking all steps possible to ensure that the work is not delayed.

Clearly the maximin strategy would be too pessimistic to provide a realistic guide to action since, for any possibility of the penalty causing a loss in excess of 5 per cent, it would propose that the discount should be offered.

Given that the situation can be treated as being one of risk, the probabilities of the two events, no delay and delay, can be assessed and the strategy with the most favourable expected value selected.[49]

Assuming the utility is linear with money, in the above example for any probability of delay occurring for which $p \times$ (delay penalty) < 5 per cent of the contract price, the decision should be to accept the penalty clause.

It must, however, be recognized that adopting this approach of selecting the strategy which has the maximum expected value for all possible states of nature involves a certain gamble. The assessments of probability being subjective may be wrong; the outcome most disliked may occur. This is a chance which must be taken willingly, the alternative being to play safe and follow the conservative maximin rule.

A1.5 Riskless utility

The previous discussion of utility theory was concerned with the situation of risk. The decision maker may also be faced with the problem of choosing between two or more alternatives under conditions of certainty in which the choices open to him are multidimensional and the same choice is not best on all dimensions. The theory of riskless utility seeks to establish a method by which to explain and predict how that choice will be made. For this purpose it is necessary to construct an index for the decision maker which will accurately reflect his ordering of preferences.

It has been proposed that riskless utility can be measured only over an ordinal scale, i.e. the scale represents only a pure ordering of preferences and says nothing about the strength of one preference as compared with another.[50] Clearly such a scale could not be used to predict behaviour or to compare movements in relative worth. The difficulty is recognized of composing other than an ordinal scale when dealing with an individual's preferences for such items as books and pictures. In contract negotiations, however, provided the assumption is made that the decision maker is behaving rationally, then it is proposed that the choices open can be compared and evaluated in terms of their worth to the negotiator and that an index of cardinal utility can be constructed.

However, it will still not be a pure cardinal index in the sense that it will not be possible to subtract one utility value in the index from another and say that the difference between them represents the difference between the monetary values to which they relate. Referring to Figure A1.19 the utility of £120,000 cannot be subtracted from £100,000 (0.7–0.5) to give the utility of –£20,000 equals 0.2, but it can be said that under the conditions for which the scale was constructed, and for that particular decision maker, a change in the value of the offer from £100,000 to £120,000 represents a reduction in utility to the buyer of 0.2.

Further, this change can be compared with that which occurs between £120,000 and £140,000 and the conclusion drawn that the reduction in utility is 2.5 times greater over £120,000 than it is below £120,000.

Rate of change prior to £120,000 $= \dfrac{1 - 0.8}{1} = 0.2$

Rate of change over £120,000 $= \dfrac{0.8 - 0.4}{0.8} = 0.5$

CONSTRUCTION OF THE INDEX[51]

The basic assumption behind the construction of any such index is that riskless utility is additive, i.e. the utility of an offer is the sum of the utilities of its component parts: price, quality, delivery, etc. The particular case of riskless utility to be considered is a comparison of the strength of an individual's preferences for a defined combination of two or more factors with another combination of the same factors under conditions in which the best and worst possible factor combinations can be established in advance. Specifically this will be required (see Section 15.2) in order to:

1 Know the order in which a buyer would rank, say, three tenders each offering him different price/delivery combinations
2 Predict if the buyer were to be presented with a fourth tender how he would prefer this in relation to the other three.

The two components in each tender are regarded as ordered pairs where x_1 represents price and x_2 represents delivery. The first component x_1 will be a member of a set K_1 in which $x_1 > y_1 > z_1$ and the second component x_2 will be a member of a set K_2 in which $x_2 > y_2 > x_2$.

The utility of any pair of components to the buyer, U, represents the strength of the buyer's preference for that combination over any other. The value 1 is arbitrarily assigned to the combination $U(x_1x_2)$ which, by definition, is the most favourable to the buyer and which he believes he will receive, and the value 0 to any combination in which either component has a value below the minimum which is acceptable to the buyer. This is justified on the basis that the buyer would automatically reject any offer in which one of the components failed to meet a mandatory requirement, e.g. price in excess of his budget, *irrespective of the value of the other component.*[52]

The value U of any ordered pair of components is then equal to the utility of the one component added to the utility of the other, i.e. for all x^1 in K_1 and for all x_2 in K_2 $U(x_1x_2) = u(x_1) + u(x_2)$ provided that both components have a value above zero.

It is then crucial to decide the proportion of $U(x_1x_2)$, to which the value 1 has been given, to be assigned to $u(x_1)$ and the proportion to $u(x_2)$. This can only be done by asking the buyer how valuable he regards price relative to delivery. Having done this, through the additive assumption, a complete matrix of preference ordering can be determined for all tenders which the buyer anticipates he will receive by:

1 Establishing from the buyer his preference strength for y_1 compared to x_1 and z_1 compared to y_1. Note that this preference ordering in Figure A1.17 takes no account of the member of the set k_2 with which the component is paired; the two sets are ordered independently.
2 Similarly establishing from the buyer the strength of his preference for y_2 compared to x_2 and for z_2 compared to y_2, again ignoring the member of the other set.
3 Adding together the values so obtained for each combination.[53]

Component	Price in £	Utility
x_1	100,000	0.7
y_1	120,000	0.5
z_1	140,000	0.1
	Delivery in months	
x_2	12	0.3
y_2	13	0.25
z_1	14	0.1

Figure A1.17 Example of preference ordering: riskless utility of price and delivery

A simple matrix to illustrate the above formulation is given in Figure A1.18 based on the table of preference orderings (Figure A1.17).

			Delivery		
			x_2 12 months	y_2 13 months	z_2 14 months
	x_1	£100,000	1.0	0.95	0.8
Price	y_1	£120,000	0.8	0.7	0.6
	z_1	£140,000	0.4	0.35	0.2

Figure A1.18   Additive utility values for price and delivery

Assumptions

The additive model set out in Figure A1.18 is based on the following assumptions.

1 The ordering of preferences is transitive, i.e. if $x_1 > y_1$ and $y_1 > z_1$ then $x_1 > z_1$.
2 x_1 is only preferred to y_1 if $u(x_1)$ is greater than $u(y_1)$.
3 Each of the sets K_1 and K_2 can be ordered independently of the other. This means that since x_1 is preferred to y_1 then $(x_1x_2) > (y_1x_2)$ and similarly for any other values in set K_2. In the example the buyer will always prefer the lower price if the deliveries quoted are the same and equally he will always prefer the shorter delivery if the prices quoted are the same.
4 The strength of the buyer's preference for any component is not affected by the component in the other set with which it is paired. Thus the buyer's preference for x_2 over y_2 does not change as the price level alters. The value of one month saved is the same at a price of£100,000 as at £140,000.[54]

This can be inferred from assumption 3 but does not necessarily follow. Intuitively, however, there seems no reason why the worth of either price, quality or delivery taken on its own should be affected by the value of any two of the other three factors. Preference for, say, quality alone will not diminish as the price increases. The worth of the price/quality combination will diminish, relative to other offers, as the accelerated marginal reduction in the utility of the price component at the higher price levels takes effect.[55]

It must again be stressed that if the value of either component falls below that which is acceptable to the buyer then he must automatically assign to that combination the value zero, *regardless of the value of the other component*. Thus, if in the example in Figure A1.18 a delivery period exceeding 14 months was longer than the buyer could tolerate then an offer of £100,000/15 months must have the value zero.

DOMINATION AND CONFLICT

A pair in which both components are preferred to the other components in the alternative pair may be said to dominate that pair and creates no problem in the analysis of the buyer's preferences. If both price and delivery in offer A are better than those in offer B, then the buyer will obviously prefer offer A. Of more difficulty are the pairs in which one component is preferred from the first pair and the other component is preferred from the second pair, e.g. the pairs $(x_1 y_2)$ and $(y_1 x_2)$. How will the buyer resolve the conflict and will his answer stay constant over a range of offers?

It is proposed that:

1   The buyer will resolve the conflict by comparing the utility intervals between x_1 and y_1 and between y_2 and x_2 and choosing that offer with the maximum utility. Thus he will prefer the lower-priced longer-delivery offer to the higher-priced shorter-delivery offer, provided that the advantage in price outweighs the loss in utility due to extended delivery. In the above example, the buyer would have no hesitation in choosing $x_1 y_2$ from the two pairs since 0.95 > 0.8.

2   His preference will not necessarily stay constant. If in any matrix, as shown in Figure A1.18, at utility values of either component which approach the maximum, he consistently prefers any combination with the higher-valued price component then it is predicted that, as the value of the delivery component moves towards its limits of acceptability, at some point his preference will change. At that point he will prefer (or be indifferent to) a combination with a lower-valued price component, but higher-valued delivery to at least one combination with a higher-valued price but lower-valued delivery.

Whether or not such a point exists within the range of practical possibilities, and if it does at what point it will occur, depends on:

1   The weighting of the price to the delivery component in the combination $x_1 x_2$. The greater the value Of x_2 to x_1, i.e. delivery to price, the sooner the preference change point will occur.

2   The rate of change of the price component relative to the delivery component in all values lower than $x_1 x_2$. The slower the rate of change of the price component relative to delivery then again the sooner the change point will occur.

This is illustrated by redrawing the matrix shown in Figure A1.18 with the value of the delivery component relative to the price component increased, and the rate of the delivery component relative to that of the price component also increased. The revised values and the amended matrix of combined utilities are set out in Figure A1.19.

		x_2 (0.4)	y_2 (0.3)	z_2 (0.1)
x_1	(0.6)	1.0	0.9	0.7
y_1	(0.5)	0.9	0.8	0.6
z_1	(0.3)	0.7	0.6	0.4

Figure A1.19   Revised additive utility values for price and delivery

It will be seen that the following preference changes occur where the higher-priced shorter-delivery offer is preferred to the lower-priced longer-delivery offer:

$$y_1 x_2 \text{ and } y_1 y_2 \text{ are preferred to } x_1 x_2$$
$$z_1 x_2 \text{ is preferred to } y_1 z_2.$$

With the revised matrix it is most unlikely that an offer with a delivery of 14 months will be accepted even though it is at a lower price.

Supposing now that the buyer were offered a fourth tender at a price of £110,000 and a delivery of 13 months. It can be predicted from the matrix in Figure A1.19 that the utility value of such an offer would be:

$$u(x) + u(y) = 0.55 + 0.3 = 0.85.$$

(It is recognized that this makes the assumption that the utility interval between £100,000 and £120,000 is linear.)

The buyer could therefore be expected to prefer such an offer to any except x_1x_2, y_1x_2 and x_1y_2.

Notes

1. Risk is used here in Knight's sense of a situation in which the outcome is not certain but the probabilities of the alternative outcomes are either known or can be estimated. From the practical viewpoint it is considered that the decision maker in contract negotiations will always have some evidence on which to construct a subjective probability distribution. S. H. Knight, *Risk Uncertainty and Profit* (Boston: Houghton Mifflin, 1921); reprinted by The London School of Economics in *Scarce Tracts in Economics*, No.16, 1933.

2. For the nature of this distinction, see W. J. Baumol, *Economic Theory and Operations Analysis* (New Jersey: Prentice-Hall, 1965), pp. 315–16.

3. H. A. Simon, *Models of Man* (New York: Wiley, 1957) p. 204.

4. W. Edwards, 'The prediction of decisions amongst *bets*', *Journal of Experimental Psychology*, vol.51 (1955), pp. 201–14.

5. W. Lee, *Decision Theory and Human Behavior* (New York: Wiley, 1971), pp. 123–26.

6. Ibid., p. 65.

7. D. Lock, *Project Management* (Aldershot: Gower, 3rd edn, 1984), pp. 43-45.

8. D. G. Pruitt, 'Pattern and level of risk in gambling decisions', *Psychological Review*, vol. 69 (no.3, 1962), pp. 187–201.

9. Walton and McKersie in discussing the utility function of a labour negotiator suggest that the value to him of a high wage settlement could be negative in that it would make life difficult for him in the future. Having achieved so much that time he would be expected to achieve even more in the future. Some practical experience suggests that this could apply also to commercial negotiators. R. E. Walton and R. E. McKersie, *A Behavioral Theory of Labor Negotiations* (New York: McGraw Hill, 1965), p. 26.

10. The converse is equally true. Most company control systems are based on punishing managers for any deviations below the control level. A manager is likely to react strongly against any suggestion for risk taking which could lead him to being exposed in terms of achieving his performance 'norm'. See also R. O. Swalm, 'Utility theory – insights into risk taking', *Harvard Business Review* (November/ December 1966) quoted in J. S. Hammond,

'Better decisions with preference theory', *Harvard Business Review* (November/December 1967).

11. It is recognized that others have come to a different conclusion. R. O. Swalm and J. S. Hammond (see note 10) have suggested that because of the system by which managers are punished or rewarded, the manager in a large corporation will have a more conservative attitude towards risk taking than the corporation would consider desirable. Others have felt the opposite, that the manager will tend to take greater risks with the company's money then he would do with his own. Hence the slogan printed and distributed to all managers in one company: 'Would you do it if it were your own money?'

12. J. Forester, *Statistical Selection of Business Strategies* (Homewood, IL: Irwin, 1968), p. 71, suggests the following tests for determining whether or not there is a need to use utility values:

    1 Is the proposition merely one of many for which the possible losses and profits are similar?
    2 If a loss resulted, would this materially affect the company's working capital?
    3 If a loss resulted, would it affect the ownership of the company?
    4 If successful, would the proposition enable the company to expand into new fields?

    These tests have been thought of in relation to a small business. In a large corporation they should be applied to the division or other unit concerned.

13. R.O. Swalm, 'Utility theory-insights into risk taking', p. 123.

14. In the theory of utility under risk as developed here, there is no such thing as the 'utility of £100'. All that can be said is that for a particular individual, at a particular time and under stated conditions of risk, his preference for an offer of £100, as compared to his preference for any other offer, can be represented by a utility value. Utility values are only a representation of preferences. Offer X is preferred to offer Y; therefore a higher utility value is assigned to X than to Y and never the other way round.

15. R. Schlaifer, *Probability and Statistics for Business Decisions* (New York: McGraw-Hill, 1959), p. 42.

16. K. J. Arrow, *Social Choice and Individual Values* (New York: Wiley, 1951). See also the discussion on pp. 327-68 in R. D. Luce and H. Raiffa, *Games and Decisions* (New York: Wiley, 1957).

17. A. Coddington, *Theories of the Bargaining Process* (London: George Allen and Unwin, 1968), p. 60.

18. Ibid., p. 62.

19. In choosing a decision rule, Party selects that demand which is optimum against Opponent's anticipated choice. For the factors contributing to such optimality, particularly the effect of time, see Chapter 16.

20. There would seem to be one partial exception to this rule, in which although both parties are correctly aware of the other's intentions neither alters his decision rule. Thus, in the example, assume the parties were duopolists dealing with a monopoly buyer. Party could decide that although he believed Opponent would bid, say, 95, which was correct, he would not alter his decision of bidding at 96, and reduce the price to 94, since this would

lower the market price level. Party's strategy would then be based on securing the next order at a more favourable price and at a time when he anticipated Opponent's capacity would be taken up with the first order. His decision rule would then be to bid at 96 to maintain that as his price level on the basis that Opponent will secure the order at 95 but he will have a better chance of securing the next order at 96.

Opponent could also be correct in assessing that Party would bid at 96, and might even be shrewd enough to work out the remainder of Party's strategy. However, this would not cause him to change his decision rule to bid at 95 since he believes this will be a winning price and he needs the order.

Coddington has not dealt with this case which involves a difference in motivation between the parties, leading them both to retain their original decision rules even though they correctly recognized their limitations. It cannot be suggested that either party has acted in a manner inconsistent with the maximization of subjective expected utility but only that they differ in identifying the utility to them of an immediate order.

21. J. Neuman and O. Morgenstern, *Theory of Games and Economic Behavior* (Princeton: Princeton University Press, 1947).
22. R. D. Luce and H. Raiffa, *Games and Decisions;* R. Shubik, *Game Theory and Related Approaches to Social Behavior* (New York: Wiley, 1964).
23. R. D. Luce and H. Raiffa, *Games and Decisions*.
24. O. G. Haywood, 'Military decision and game theory', *Journal of the Operations Research Society of America,* vol. 2 (1954), pp. 365–85.
25. See W. Lee, *Decision Theory and Human Behavior*, p. 286. 'The zero-sum game does not appear to model real-life interactions very well.' See also J. Forester, *Statistical Selection of Business Strategies* (Homewood, IL: Irwin, 1968), p. 35, and W. J. Baumol, *Economic Theory and Operations Analysis* (New Jersey: Prentice-Hall, 1965), p. 542.
26. An interpretation of this game could be two ice-cream vendors at a fair on a cool evening. If either raises his price and the other follows suit, the revenue of each will stay constant, the increase in price being offset by a reduction in demand (the balance of demand being absorbed on other products). If either does not follow the other's lead then he increases his total revenue by gaining the other's customers, total demand in this case remaining static.
27. If the differences are regarded as too trivial to make a choice worth considering, then think of the numbers as representing an equivalent amount of pounds thousand.
28. If Opponent chooses the pure strategy b_1, then Party's expected return from playing a_1 with a probability of x and a_2 with a probability of y, would be given by $5x + 4y$, and similarly if Opponent selects b_2, Party's return would be $3x + 6y$. The security level is given by the values for x and y for which these two expected return functions are equal; $x + y = 1$. This is 5/2 and $x = \frac{1}{2}, y = \frac{1}{2}$.

    The same concepts apply for Opponent whose security level is given by $5p + 3Q = 4p + 6q$ where he selects b_1 with probability p, b_2 with probability q and $p + q = 1$. His expected return against either a_1 or a_2 is 5/2; $p = 3/4$, $q = 1/4$.
29. R. D. Luce and H. Raiffa, *Games and Decisions*, Appendix 2.
30. The following comment from a negotiator in an experimental negotiation is illustrative: 'One thing I noticed with certain strategy groups was you could begin to detect after a

while what their strategy was. They would concede the smaller issue and skip over the most important wages and then hopefully come back later and use the argument "oh since we gave you that, how about. . . ". ' B. M. Bass, 'Effects on the subsequent performance of negotiators of studying issues or planning strategies alone or in groups', *Psychological Monographs General and Applied* (no. 614, 1966), p. 20.

31. T. C. Schelling, *The Strategy of Conflict* (London: Oxford University Press, 1963).

32. A pay-off matrix similar to that given in Figure A1.12 has been used by Samuelson to illustrate the classical price-cutting war between two departmental stores. In the absence of a collusive agreement the two firms will end up with the pay-off $a_1 b_1$, since the solution at $a_2 b_2$ is not stable in the sense that both firms could gain more if only the other would adopt his weaker strategy. Samuelson also points out that the 'safeguard' against collusion is the existence of more than two competitors.

33. For a non-cooperative game to be soluble in any sense, the equilibrium pairs must be interchangeable; to be soluble in a strict sense the pairs must be both interchangeable and equivalent.

   The pairs $(a_1 b_2)$ and $(a_2 b_1)$ are equivalent if $v_1 (a_1 b_2) = v_1 (a_2 b_1)$ and $v2(a_1 b_2) = v2(a_2 b_1)$, where v_1 and v_2 are the pay offs to players 1 and 2 respectively. The pairs are interchangeable if $(a_1 b_1)$ and $(a_2 b_2)$ are also in equilibrium.

34. *Risk level* as defined by D. G. Pruitt (see p. 269 and note 8) is the sum of the negative outcomes of a gamble multiplied by the respective probabilities of their occurrence. Pruitt's suggestion is followed that as the risk level of a gamble increases so will the conflict between that function and the expectation of gain. At some point, no matter how favourable the anticipated gain may be, the risk involved will not be willingly accepted.

35. R. D. Luce and H. Raiffa, *Games and Decisions*, Chapter 5.

36. The interpretation which gave the game its name is that two prisoners interrogated separately have the alternative of confessing or not confessing. If neither confesses they will each receive a light sentence; if either confesses and the other does not, he receives a nominal sentence but the other is punished severely; if they both confess they will receive less than the maximum sentence. The first strategy is not confess and the second confess.

37. A similar formulation was suggested by L. E. Siegel and S. Fouraker in *Bargaining Behavior* (New York: McGraw-Hill, 1963), p.104, Table 7.2.

38. Any such agreement between firms carrying on business in the UK would be registrable under the 1956 Restrictive Trade Practices Act unless it related exclusively to export.

39. W. Lee, *Decision Theory and Human Behavior*, pp. 293–97.

40. L. E. Siegel and S. Fouraker, *Bargaining Behavior*, Chapter 10.

41. See W. Lee, *Decision Theory and Human Behavior*, p. 297: 'Perhaps subjects are largely motivated by a desire to outscore the opponent regardless of the absolute levels of the pay off.'

42. L. E. Siegel and S. Fouraker expressly disallowed any contact between the bargainers. W. Lee, *Decision Theory and Human Behaviour*, reports that in experiments by McLintock, Nuttin and McNeel (1970) friendship, or to a lesser degree prior acquaintanceship, decreased the percentage of competitive choice. The personal relationship between the marketing managers of the duopolists could therefore be of significance in this context. If

both prefer to live on friendly terms, neither is likely to opt for the competitive choice; in simpler terms 'dog does not eat dog'.

43. See L. E. Siegel and S. Fouraker, *Bargaining Behaviour*, p. 188, Table 10.11, which shows that under conditions of complete information 13.4 per cent of all transactions were negotiated at the pareto-optimal price as compared with 0.4 per cent under conditions of incomplete information.

44. A situation is described as *pareto-optimal* when it is impossible to effect a change which benefits one party without adversely affecting the other.

45. J. F. Nash, 'The bargaining problem', *Econometrica,* vol.18 (April 1950), pp. 155–62.

46. J. C. Harsanyi, 'Approaches to the Bargaining Problem', *Econometrica,* vol. 24 (April 1965), pp. 14–57.

47. A. Coddington, *Theories of the Bargaining Process*, Chapter II; J. G. Cross, *The Economics of Bargaining* (New York: Basic Books, 1969).

48. See the discussion in T. C. Schelling, *The Strategy of Conflict* , Appendix B.

49. Risk is used here in S. H. Knight's sense of a situation in which the outcome is not certain but the probabilities of the alternative outcomes are either known or can be estimated. See note 1.

50. R. D. Luce and H. Raiffa, *Games and Decisions*, p. 15.

51. The index proposed here is derived from the model described by E. W. Adams and R. Fagot in 'A model of riskless choice', *Behavioural Science,* vol. 4 (1959), pp. 1–10, but I devised the actual detail of the means of construction.

52. This is the equivalent of personnel selection decisions based on multiple criteria. As Stagner has pointed out, these should be based on minimum cutting scores on a number of variables rather than a single regression equation: 'The personnel manager will want to hire workers who will have good absentee records, will accept supervision and will produce at a high level of quality and quantity. There is a point on each of these beyond which the employee is unacceptable regardless of how good he is on other aspects of performance.' R. Stagner, 'Corporate decision making', *Journal of Applied Psychology*, vol. 53 (February 1969), Part 1.

53. Latane in his paper 'The rationality model in organizational decision making' delivered to the first seminar in the Social Science of Organization, Pittsburgh, June 1962, and published in *The Social Science of Organization* (New Jersey: Prentice-Hall, 1963) has described a similar model for selecting a secretary. I noted this paper after completion of my own model. The only difference of approach is that Latane initially valued the factors personality and efficiency on the same 0–1 scale and then applied a weighting factor when combining the two, which leads arithmetically to the same result as that given by method of construction used here. For interest of comparison, and in case the reader might find the method suggested by Latane easier, his secretary example is set out below:

Possible Actions	Value Measures		
	Personality	Efficiency	Combined
Ms C	0.9	0.5	0.8
Ms D	0.5	0.8	0.6

Combining
  weight   0.7   0.3   1.0

Value measure rating on a scale from 0–1.0 for each characteristic.

Combining weight: The weighted average of the two measures reflects the opinion of the decision maker as to their relative importance.

Decision Rule: Choose that strategy with the maximum combined value measure.

Choice: Ms C.

Note that it is complete coincidence that both Latane and I chose the same combining ratio!

54. The same assumption is made by K. Simmonds in 'Competitive bidding, non-price features', *Operational Research Quarterly* (March 1968), pp. 5–14.

55. Again, the same conclusion is reached by K. Simmonds in 'Competitive bidding, non-price features', pp. 5–14.

APPENDIX 2
THE LEVEL OF THE FIRST OFFER: COMPETITIVE BIDDING, PURCHASER'S STRATEGY, QUICK KILL

In choosing the decision rule by which a bidder should submit his first offer, one needs to distinguish between the situation where the bid represents a single opportunity and where there are multiple opportunities.

The expression *single opportunity* refers to the situation in which Party's sales forecast shows this opportunity as the only chance of utilizing the same resources within the same time-scale. Similarly the expression *multiple opportunities* refers to the case in which Party's sales forecast has predicted that there will be other such opportunities within the same time-scale.

The confidence which Party can possess in making any such forecast of other opportunities will depend largely on the flexibility with which he can use the resources concerned. In general building work, for example, it is possible to use the resources of men and plant over a wide variety of projects and customers and it would be exceptional for Party to have to treat any bid as a single opportunity. In manufacturing, however, particular machines and operator skills, or even whole manufacturing shops, may be tied to particular products which are themselves tied to particular customers. In the short term, and in the absence of any clearly identified alternative inquiry for that product, Party must treat the bid as a single opportunity.

In engineering designer – contractor type business, e.g. petrochemical plant or oil-refinery design and construction, the number of major bid opportunities is small and each one is usually significant in terms of the use which any resultant contract would make of Party's assets. Again Party would normally classify any such bid as a single opportunity.

A2.1 Competitive bidding, single opportunity, purchaser's strategy, quick kill

This is the classic case of bidding to a public authority or other corporation which follows the rules of strict competitive tendering, in circumstances in which Party cannot clearly identify any other opportunity for the use of the resources involved within the time period concerned. It is the only one which appears to have been treated extensively in the literature on the developing of bidding models.[1]

The essential feature of this situation is that Party has only one chance both in terms of winning the award and also of utilizing the resources. His decision rule should therefore be: *submit the bid at a level which will maximize its subjective expected utility value.*

The formula for determining expected value (see Appendix 1) requires Party to establish the following inputs:

1 The conditional utility value of the bid is successful.
2 The conditional utility value of the contribution loss and variable marketing expense which would be incurred were the bid to be unsuccessful.
3 The subjective probability of the bid being successful, taking into account any non-price bias for or against Party's bid.

CONDITIONAL UTILITY VALUE OF THE BID

Party is expected to have some idea from market research of the general level of prices ruling in the market in question. If the product or service is new then it is assumed that Party has already decided on his general pricing policy: whether he is aiming to skim the higher price segment of the market or to penetrate the market as a whole as deeply as possible. He knows, therefore, the possible range of price levels which can be considered.

The first influence on Party in determining the conditional utility value to him of a bid at any given price level will be the profit contribution given by that price level, taking into account as profit any over-recovery of fixed overheads which would result from the award of the contract. Unless, however, the assumption is made that Party's utility of money is linear with money and no other worth factor is involved, such profit contribution is only one factor in building up the bid utility value. Remembering the discussion on utility in Section A1.3, such an assumption is justified only in the very simplest case in which:

1 The award or loss of the bid would have no significant effect either on Party's business or the manager's achievement of any sales or profit target.
2 None of the factors referred to below regarding the effect of the bid on further marketing opportunities, contractual risks or asset utilization are present to any appreciable extent.
3 The manager has no positive bias for or against risk taking.

In any other case the view is taken that the use of the expected value criterion is only appropriate if utility rather than monetary values are used. The factors apart from profit contribution which will be of significance in establishing the manager's preference for one bid rather than another, and, therefore, in determining his utility value for a bid at that price level, are as follows:

1 The relationship of the profit contribution to any target level which the manager concerned has been set to achieve
2 Party's immediate need to obtain income to meet the fixed expenses of running the business
3 Party's need to obtain work in order to retain key staff
4 Party's need to obtain a sufficient volume of production to support the engineering,

marketing and other expenses incurred in maintaining a viable business for the product concerned

5 The creation of a particular market price level or the disturbance of an existing market price level

6 Longer-term marketing benefits which Party might derive from an award of the contract. These could include:

(a) Weakening a competitor's ability to stay in the market through depriving him of business or denying him the chance to enter the market

(b) Having the opportunity to obtain follow-on business on a negotiated basis, e.g. extensions to a plant or system

(c) Increased success probability on other business with the same customer because of the advantages of standardization or the compatability of other products with those being supplied under this contract

(d) Acquiring a base in the market from which to launch other bids. This may be particularly important if the market is overseas and the contracts concerned involve installation work

(e) Maintaining a presence in the market or with the particular customer in anticipation of more favourable opportunities in the future

(f) Obtaining entry to a new market in which there is judged to be the chance of securing future profitable business

(g) Securing recognition of Party as a competent contractor in the particular market through the prestige value of the contract and the reputation of the customer.

7 Contractual risks involved, particularly those relating to:

(a) Risk on non-payment or late payment

(b) Currency devaluation

(c) Escalation of costs over the contract period

(d) Abnormal warranty liabilities, e.g. for consequential damages

(e) Risk of incurring delay penalty

(f) Any clause allowing customer to terminate for convenience

(g) Standards of technical performance required in relation to Party's normal standards

(h) State of the development of the product

(i) Sub-contract work for which Party is contractually responsible but in which he has no expertise

(j) Non-recovery of extra costs incurred through *force majeure* or customer default

(k) Disputes not referable to truly independent arbitration or court of law

(l) On-demand tender, advance payment and performance bonds.

(m) Adverse cash flow.

8 Any capital expenditure which would be involved to the extent that it would not be recoverable within the minimum quantity of the product to which the customer would be committed

9 High tendering costs

10 Resources which would be required for contract implementation in relation to those available

11 The manager's attitude towards risk taking.

POSSIBLE FORM OF THE BID UTILITY VALUE

The utility value which Party will place on any given bid is an intimate blend of the monetary value of the profit contribution itself and each of the factors 1–10, to the extent of their relevance to the particular bid opportunity concerned. As stressed in Appendix 1, it is an assessment peculiar to the individual who makes it and to the time at which it is made. Further, it should always be remembered that the utility value is an expression only of a preference for one bid as against another; bid A is preferred to bid B and therefore bid A is assigned a higher utility value, not the other way round. It is important to avoid the trap of saying that A is preferred to B because bid A has the higher utility.

To attempt a generalization of the form to be expected of the bid utility function is difficult since circumstances, and therefore preferences, will vary so widely. However, three general guidelines are suggested.

1 It will be assumed that the upper limit of the utility scale (the most favourable bid Party could contemplate) is taken as 10 and the bottom of the scale (the loss which Party would suffer from a rejection of the bid) as 0. Then the suggestion would be that a bid at the manager's target profit level would have a value of approximately 8, provided that all other factors which could affect his preferences for or against bidding were neutral, i.e. no serious contractual risks, no significant marketing benefit, no urgent need to obtain the order.
2 On the same assumptions a bid at 75 per cent of the manager's target level would have a value of around 6. Thereafter any further reductions would cause the utility value to drop sharply so that a bid at 50 per cent might have a value of 2 and one at 25 per cent of the target level, a value of 0.5.

The general form of Party's utility function under the conditions stated in 1 and 2 is given in Figure A2.1 in which utility is plotted against profit contribution/loss expressed as a percentage of cost.

From the brief note on utility theory in Section A1.3, it will be remembered that the points on the curve represent indifference to the receipt of a sum certain and the taking of a gamble. If it is assumed that the costs are £100,000, then point A on the curve is based on being indifferent to a certainty of receiving a profit contribution of £16,000 and taking part in the risk venture with an 80 per cent chance of receiving a profit contribution of £24,000 and a 20 per cent chance of incurring a loss of £2,000. Similarly point B expresses indifference between the certain receipt of a profit contribution of £8,000 and a 20 per cent chance of £24,000 and an 80 per cent chance of losing £2,000.

At point A, which represents the manager's target level, the expected value of the gamble in monetary terms of £18,800 is slightly higher than the target profit contribution of £16,000, which reflects the manager's somewhat cautious approach to bidding when the profit contribution satisfies his aspiration level. However, at point B the expected value in monetary terms of £3,200 is well below the profit contribution of £8,000. This is clearly the result of not being interested in bids at this level of profit, a lack of interest, however, which the graph shows

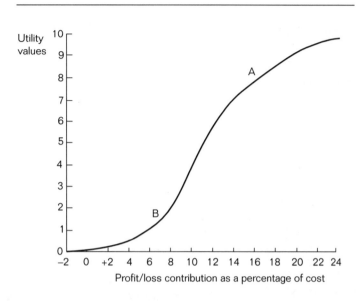

Figure A2.1   Bidder's normal utility curve

diminishes rapidly as the profit contribution climbs up to 12 per cent. Thereafter the rate of increase is much slower up to the manager's target level and even slower still as the target level is passed.

Under the neutral conditions assumed so far, it is believed that these results and the form of the curve derived from them are quite general and that their applicability would not be affected by the absolute values of either the costs or the profit contribution/loss. It will be appreciated that under neutral conditions the loss can never be appreciable. If it were, then either Party must really need the business in order to avoid an unrecovery of fixed overheads or the tendering costs are high both in absolute terms and relative to the anticipated profit, and therefore the situation is no longer neutral.

The inclusion of any of the factors previously referred to as having an influence on Party's utility function would not significantly affect the general shape of the curve but would displace it along the horizontal axis. Two out of the many possibilities will be considered and in order to illustrate the general proposition one at each end of the range will be selected.

In the first possibility, Party's order intake situation is such that he has a significant negative operating variance. Unless the position can be improved he will be compelled to discharge staff and close down a section of the business. An improvement in sales and margins is forecast longer term and Party is anxious therefore both to avoid losing key personnel and also to stay in the market. The bid being considered represents the one opportunity presently foreseen of bringing actual overhead recovery back in line with current expense. There are no significant contractual risks.

A suggested utility curve for Party under these conditions is shown in Figure A2.2.

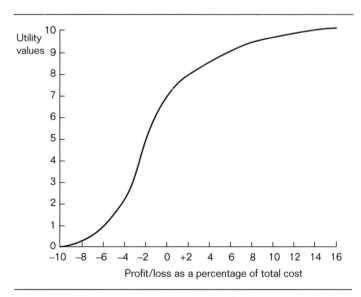

Figure A2.2 Bidder's utility curve: poor order book

Assuming again costs of £100,000, Party's attitude is clearly shown by the table of Figure A2.3 which shows selected outcomes between which he is indifferent.

	Probability of	
Certainty	gain £16000	lose £10000
£'000s	%	%
6	90	10
2	80	20
Break even	70	30
−2	50	50

Figure A2.3 Outcomes between which Party is indifferent

This is obviously an extreme case but unfortunately it does happen and, when it does, it is not difficult to imagine a rather unruly exchange of views between the marketing manager and the line manager. The marketing manager will state that, from what is known of the competition, the company have a 50/50 chance at a 10 per cent margin, and probably about a 70 per cent chance at a margin of 5 per cent; the line manager will retort that he is not at all interested in probabilities and margins but just the business, as long as money will not be lost.

In the second possibility, Party's situation is happily the reverse of that just examined. Orders on hand are slightly ahead of budget; sales prospects are buoyant. The bid opportunity being considered is for export and there are certain contractual risks on delay penalty and abnormal warranty costs.

The suggested utility curve is shown in A2.4. In comparison with that of the 'neutral' position shown in Figure A2.1, the worth to Party of a bid at a profit contribution of 16 per cent has declined from a utility value of 8 to one of 7. Party's preference under the changed circumstances is for the bid with the higher contribution. The loss should the bid be unsuccessful represents the variable marketing expense which would be incurred in overseas sales visits, etc.

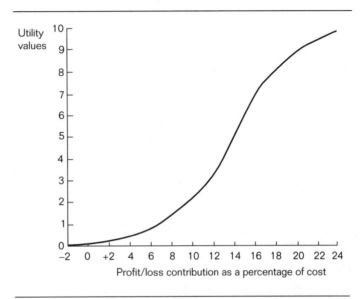

Figure A2.4   Bidder's utility curve: full order book

So far matters have been made easy by pointing all factors in the same direction. Unfortunately real life is not so simple; the bid opportunity which Party desperately needs to win in order to ensure full overhead recovery and maintenance of his position in the market is likely to be just the one which involves a substantial measure of contractual risk. How will Party react to this? It is suggested that Party will be acutely sensitive to the issue of contractual risk at the break-even point, and just either side of it, but that this sensitivity will decrease as the profit margin rises. The likely effect is shown in Figure A2.5 where the solid line reproduces the curve shown in Figure A2.3 in which Party was most anxious to secure the award but there was no serious contractual risk. The dotted line shows the effect on this curve of importing into the situation issues of contractual risk.

SUCCESS PROBABILITY

Party's assessment of his chances of success is a compound of:

1 Customer bias for or against Party's bid at any given price level due to non-price factors.
2 Party's subjective estimate of the probability distribution of competitor's prices.

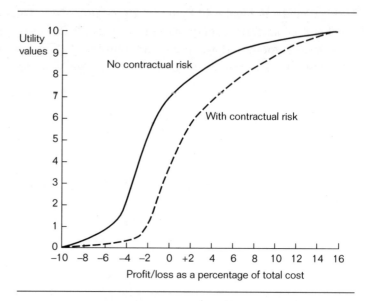

Figure A2.5   Bidder's utility curve: poor order book and contractual risk

Customer bias

In the discussion on riskless utility in Section A1.5, the following points were noted regarding the manner in which customer will value any offer:

1 That in determining the worth to him of any bid, customer will take into account non-price factors, e.g. delivery, supplier's reputation, etc.
2 That the worth to customer of each such factor and also the factor of price is determined independently of the other features of the bid, i.e. the worth to customer of a month's earlier delivery remains constant and does not vary with the price level.
3 That if any factor is below customer's minimum requirements he will reject the bid irrespective of the worth to him of the other factors.[2]
4 That any factor will be subject to decreasing marginal utility as it approaches its optimum value to customer, i.e. the value to customer of the sixth week saved will be less than that of the third week saved and at some point any further time saved would be of no value to customer at all. Conversely, as any factor approaches its level of minimum acceptability to customer the marginal reduction in utility will increase rapidly, i.e. if the maximum acceptable delivery period is 14 months and the minimum which is of interest to customer is 12 months, then the rate at which the utility value of delivery changes between 13 and 14 months will be much more rapid than between 13 and 12 months. This can be seen from Figure A1.18.

By preparing a product-comparison grid using the method outlined on pp. 88–9, but excluding the factor of price, it is possible to compare the non-price features of Party's offer with those of his competitors. This comparison must then be converted into a bias factor for or against Party which can be used to adjust the value to customer and, therefore, the success probability of any bid price.

The method adopted is to estimate the worth that customer will place on the non-price factors in Party's bid in comparison with those of his principal competitor(s). It is essential that this valuation is made strictly from customer's viewpoint. Party may justifiably be proud of the high quality of his products but if customer is only interested in whether or not they meet specification, Party cannot give himself any bonus points for being above specification.

For the unit of comparison either monetary or utility values could be used. Preference would be for utility values since this will enable the utility value of the non-price factor to be combined with price, and to give effect to the diminishing marginal utility of both as they approach their respective limits of acceptability. This is an important difference between the use of utility and monetary values.

If monetary values are used, the effect of the bias factor would be a constant over the contemplated range of bid prices. If the worth to customer of, say, two months saved were to be estimated at £20,000 as in the example shown in Figure A1.18, and it was believed that Party had a two-month delivery advantage over his principal competitor, then it could be said that a bid at £120,000 by Party was equal to a competitor's bid of £100,000. Equally a bid at £140,000 by Party would be equivalent in worth to the customer of a competitor's bid at £120,000.

Using utility values, however, it will be seen from Figure A1.18 that whilst the bids at £100,000/14 months and £120,000/12 months are equivalent, the bids at £120,000/14 months and £140,000/12 months are not. In the latter the lower-priced longer-delivery bid is strongly preferred, as shown by the sharp reduction in worth to the buyer of the higher-priced bid as the price level moves towards the maximum which he is willing to accept. Experience indicates that this represents far more realistically the way in which bids are valued in practice. The sensitivity of the buyer to the same absolute differential in price will increase sharply as the price level rises.

The method used will therefore be that described in Section A1.5 and it is suggested that the reader should refer again to that section. Briefly the proposed method is to first identify the non-price features which will be of significance to customer and then rate these relative to the estimate of the worth to customer of the anticipated minimum bid price. A scale representative of the assumed preference of customer for each such factor is then prepared, together with that of the factor of price, over the estimate of the range of possible factor values derived from the product comparison grid. This scale will take account of judgement of the variable diminution in customer preference for each such factor as it moves towards the limit which it is believed customer would accept.

These estimates can most conveniently be represented by a graph in the form illustrated in Figure A2.6 which is based on the same figures as those used in Figure A1.18. Reading the graph horizontally it is possible to determine the bids which are judged to possess the same value for customer and can therefore be regarded as equivalent in terms of success probability. By comparing the utility intervals between bids, Party's success probability can be estimated for any bid within the possible price range when combined with the bid of his principal competitor. Using the assumption that Party will bid with a delivery of twelve months and his

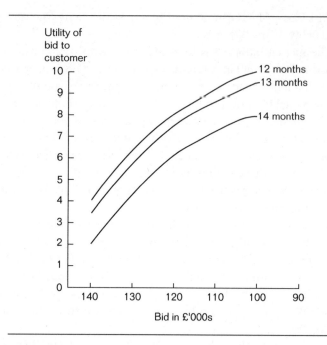

Figure A2.6   Graph of Party's success probability for a range of bids

principal competitor will offer a delivery of 14 months this comparison expressed in terms of Party's success probability is shown in Figure A2.7. It will be seen that the effect of the non-price bias in Party's favour diminishes rapidly at the higher price level but declines much more slowly at the lower level, again reflecting the customer's preference at the higher price levels for the lower price/ longer delivery bid.[3]

		Competitor's bid (14 months delivery)									
		140	135	130	125	120	115	110	105	100	
	140	1	0.7	0.4	0						
	135	1	1	0.8	0.5	0.3	0				
Party's	130	1	1	1	0.9	0.7	0.4	0.2	0		Party's
bid	125	1	1	1	1	0.95	0.7	0.5	0.4	0.2	success
(12	120	1	1	1	1	1	0.95	0.8	0.7	0.5	probability
months	115	1	1	1	1	1	1	0.95	0.9	0.8	
delivery)	110	1	1	1	1	1	1	1	1	0.95	
	105	1									
	100	1									

Figure A2.7   Party's conditional success probability

Obviously this is a very much simplified example which is intended only as a description of the principles to be applied. In a real-life situation it is likely that Party would have to take account of two or more competitors for each of whom the non-price bias would differ and there would be more than one factor contributing to such bias.

It is also appreciated that the use of this technique is dependent on the accuracy and completeness of the input data relating both to the customer's preference and to the non-price features of the competitor's bids relative to those of Party. However, the following statement by Simmonds would appear to be entirely appropriate:

> ... the difficulties in finding out what the customer's values are for different features is no argument for not attempting to find out. And again the need is paramount to plan the acquisition and flow of information so that what is wanted from those making customer contact is known by them and the data efficiently transmitted to the decision-making point.[4]

Subjective estimate of success probability

Figure A2.7 gives Party's estimate of his success probability for any selected bid price, conditional on the price level quoted by his principal competitor. Since in practice Party cannot be certain of the price which his competitor will quote, his expected success probability for any bid will be the sum of each of these conditional values multiplied by Party's estimate of the chance that his competitor will in fact bid at the level.

		Competitive bid £'000s								
	Party's bid at £125,000	140	135	130	125	120	115	110	105	100
Line 1	Party's estimate of conditional probability taken from Figure A2.7	1	1	1	1	0.95	0.7	0.5	0.4	0.2
Line 2	Party's estimate of the probability distribution of the competitive bid	0	0	0	0	0.15	0.50	0.25	0.1	0
Line 3	Party's expected success probability line 1 × line 2	0	0	0	0	0.14	0.35	0.125	0.014	0

Figure A2.8   Party's expected success probability

Let us assume that party wishes to determine his chance of success at a bid price of £125,000. Line 1 in Figure A2.8 shows Party's conditional success probabilities for a bid at this level taken from Figure A2.7. Putting himself in his competitor's position, and knowing he has a disadvantage on delivery, Party now estimates that his competitor is likely to go in at a lower price. However, on past experience of his competitor's pricing, Party does not believe that he will drop below £100,000 and that his most likely bid will be between £120,000 and £110,000. Line 2 in Figure A2.8 gives Party's estimate of the probability distribution for his competitor's bid. Line 3 is simply line 1 × line 2.

In round figures, Party's subjective estimate of his success probability at a bid of £125,000 is 65 per cent.

Repeating the process for the other possible bids given in Figure A1.7 the following values emerge:

Bid price (£'000s)	Party's subjective success probability (%)
140	0
135	5
130	30
125	65
120	90
115	95
110	100

So far only the case of one competitor has been considered. In practice Party will normally have more than one firm competing against him and in these circumstances it is suggested that the following procedure is adopted:

1 If the facts relating to the non-price bias and likely pricing policies of the other competitors are sufficiently similar they may be treated as an average competitor and the analysis, therefore, can be the same as if there were only one competitor.
2 If the facts are markedly dissimilar, and each firm represents a competitive threat, then the analysis must be completed separately for each firm to the point of arriving at a subjective estimate of Party's success probability against each considered individually. Party's success probability for any bid price against all the competitors taken together is then the product of these; so if the individual probabilities are 0.7 and 0.5 and 0.8, then Party's success probability for the bid is $0.7 \times 0.5 \times 0.8 = 29\%$.[5]

One problem here is that of the competitor whose behaviour is not predictable in the sense that sometimes he will submit an extremely low bid, at which he would be certain to obtain the contract award, and sometimes bid normally. Party could simply ignore the possibility of a very low bid on the grounds that having taken the decision to tender knowing this risk exists, and not being prepared to match, there is no point in trying to bring the problem into the analysis since it will have no effect on Party's actions. In terms of the calculations given in Figures A2.7, A2.8 and A2.9 if it is assumed that there is a 50/50 chance of competitor making a low bid i.e. of £105,000 or below, then it can be shown that the effect will be to reinforce Party's bid of £125,000 as maximizing Party's SEU. This is because of the reduction in Party's expected success probability at both the lower and higher bid values and the non-linear relationship of Party's utility function to money. The results would of course be totally different were Party using money values and seeking to maximize expected contribution.

Alternatively Party could amend his assumptions regarding competitor's behaviour to allow for this possibility.

COMPUTATION OF BID EXPECTED VALUE

The necessary input data is now available to quantify the expected value for Party of a series of possible bid prices and to select that which maximizes his subjective expected utility function.

To provide a simplified example the utility function for Party given in Figure A2.1 which represents a 'normal' bidding position will be used and applied to the estimates of his success probability given on p. 306. For this purpose costs will be taken as £110,000, i.e. the bid price at which party has a 100 per cent chance of success. The result is set out in Figure A2.9.

The bid at £125,000 should be Party's choice if he wishes to maximize his SEU function. The manager's target profit level of 15 per cent on cost which equates to a bid of approximately £126,500 should now be considered. Using the same method of calculation this would produce a bid expected utility value of 3.8 and it would not be surprising if in the end the manager was tempted to relax his perfect rationality and bid at this level. The calculations made have, however, given him a compelling alternative and the reasoned choice would certainly be for a bid at £125,000.

It is interesting to note that the same calculation if repeated for the other two situations where Party was anxious for business and where he was less so, would indicate in the first instance a bid of £120,000 as maximizing SEU and in the second case a bid of £130,000.

1	2	3	4	5
Bid price £'000s	Profit as % of cost	Conditional utility from Figure A2.1	Success probability from p. 306 %	Expected utility col 3 × col 4
140	27	10	0	0
135	23	9.8	0.05	0.49
130	18	8.7	0.30	2.6
125	13.5	6.8	0.65	4.4
120	9	3.2	0.9	2.9
115	5	0.7	0.95	0.67
110	0	0.1	1	0.1

Figure A2.9   Expected utility to Party of a series of bids

It is hoped that the principles of the method suggested have been clearly established but to conclude this section the steps needed in carrying out the calculation are set out in sequential order.

1 Determine Party's utility function over the range of possible profit and loss values for the particular tender.
2 Estimate the conditional success probability for Party against each anticipated competitive bid taking into account any bias for or against Party.

3 Estimate the probability distribution of the competitive bids.
4 Multiply the results of steps 2 and 3 together to obtain the expected success probability for Party of any bid.
5 Determine the subjective expected utility for Party for each bid by multiplying step 1 by step 4.

A2.2 Competitive bidding – multiple opportunities

Party's objective in this instance is to maximize his subjective expected utility over a series of bids in the knowledge that he can take the longer-term view. In arriving at the method for achieving this, two cases need to be distinguished.

Success probability remains constant
This implies two features in the bidding situation. First, that Party's own success or failure on the first bid will not affect his conditional success probability on the second or subsequent bids. Second, that the competitive bid probability distribution also remains constant, i.e. that the competition will also not alter their bidding tactics depending upon whether their initial bid is successful or not. It will be assumed for the present that Party's conditional utility function is also not affected. Given these assumptions the task is simple. All that is necessary is to bid at a level which will maximize the expected utility value per award. If it is assumed that the probability of any one award is p, at a bid level of x, with a conditional utility value of U, then the expected value of the utility of any one award is given by the expression:

$$1 - (1-p)^{\,n} U_x$$

where n is the number of bids under consideration. This is now applied to the significant bids in Figure A2.9 on the assumption that the number of bids in the series is three. It can be shown that the bid which now maximizes SEU over the three bids is that at £130,000, and this is the level at which the first bid should be submitted.[6]

Success probability does not remain constant
This is the more likely case. If the first bid is awarded to competitor X then Party must assume that competitor Y will be that much more eager to secure bid number two, and so the probability distribution of his bids will change. Party can expect, therefore, that the competition will be more severe on the second bid than the first. Equally it seems likely that Party's utility function will change. Not having secured the first award his anxiety for success on the second opportunity will be that much increased. The really interesting situation is reached on the third bid, if Party has again not been successful. On the one hand it can be assumed that his utility function has now changed dramatically to that of the contractor who desperately needs business as depicted in Figure A2.3; on the other hand he knows that both his competitors have secured orders and are therefore less likely to submit low bids so that his success probability for any given price level has increased.

The suggested strategy in these circumstances, given that the results of one bid are known before the next has to be submitted, would be:

1 Submit the first bid as if success probability was not going to change over the series, i.e. follow the rule just described.
2 If the first bid fails, submit the second bid as if it were an individual opportunity, adjusting as appropriate the probability distribution of the competitors' bids.
3 If the second bid also fails, then the third bid must obviously be treated as an individual opportunity but with both the probability distribution and Party's utility function adjusted accordingly.

MULTIPLE OPPORTUNITIES WHICH ARE INTERDEPENDENT

So far it has been assumed that having secured one order in the series, Party will have no great incentive, because of capacity limitations, to secure the second. That assumption will now be reversed to consider the case in which, not only would Party like to secure a further order, but success on the first would favourably influence his chances of success on the second. This could arise from standardization benefits to customer, contact between Party's and customer's engineers during execution of the first contract, etc.

If acceptance or rejection of the initial offer would have an impact on Party's future business opportunities, particularly if the potential profit contribution from the second bid would be higher because of Party's preferred position in the eyes of customer, then this is clearly a factor which Party must take into account in deciding which initial offer level would possess the maximum expected utility. The suggested method of doing this is as follows:

1 Party estimates the total maximum profit contribution which he anticipates could be earned by the two bids taken together. He then establishes a new utility scale on which the upper limit is represented by this combined maximum total profit contribution.
2 The conditional utility values of the two bids taken together are assessed by Party in the same way as he arrived at the value for the initial offer taken on its own.[7]
3 Party estimates the joint probabilities of the ultimate outcome. For each pair of bids taken together there are four possible outcomes:
    (a) Win first bid, win second bid
    (b) Win first bid, lose second bid
    (c) Lose first bid, win second bid
    (d) Lose first bid, lose second bid.
    The joint probability of event *(a)* is the probability of the first bid being won multiplied by the probability of winning the second bid *given that the first bid has been won.*
4 The conditional utility values for the combined outcome of each event are then converted into expected values by multiplying by the joint probability of that event occurring.
5 The expected ultimate value of the initial bid is then the sum of these four amounts.

The following simple example, based on a case in my own experience, illustrates the application of this method.

A tender was to be submitted for an overseas project valued at approximately £100,000. In twelve months' time a second tender would be issued by the same customer for a similar project estimated to be worth £500,000. Due to anticipated cost reductions then being engineered into the equipment which formed the subject matter of both tenders, it was considered that the profit contribution on the second tender could be about 15 per cent and the price still remain competitive. On the first tender, however, which would have to be submitted on the existing design of equipment, market intelligence suggested that the profit contribution and related success probability were as follows:

Profit contribution	Success probability
Break-even	80%
10% margin	40%

It was further considered that success on the first tender would increase the probability of success on the second tender from 40 per cent to 70 per cent.

There was obvious reluctance on the part of management to submit the first bid at break-even. However, a decision tree was drawn on the lines shown in Figure A2.10 from which was determined the joint probabilities associated with the combined outcome for each bid.

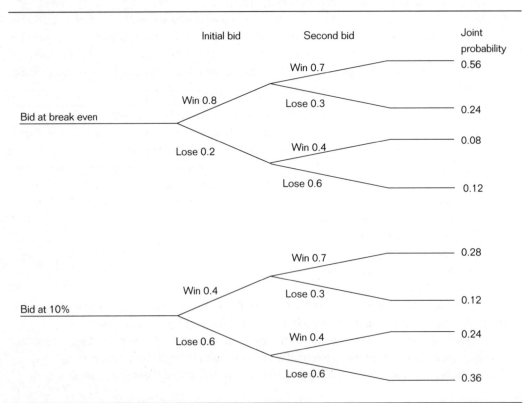

Figure A2.10 Decision tree of possible outcomes to multiple bids

At that time there was a definite need to obtain orders to maintain shop output at a level which would recover budgeted overheads, and it was believed this situation would continue until the time when the second tender was due to be submitted. No contractual risks were foreseen on either bid. The profit contribution/utility function curve was, therefore, of the form indicated in Figure A2.11. Failure to obtain the first award would lead to a loss of £5,000 and failure to obtain the second award to a loss of £20,000.

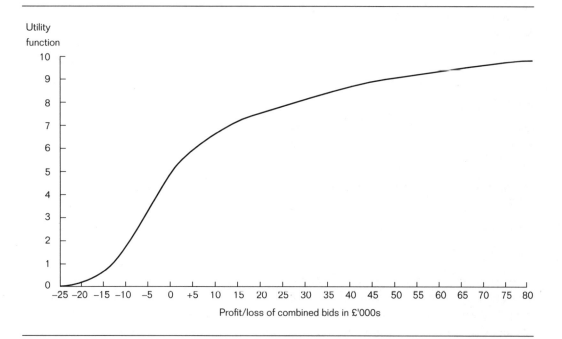

Figure A2.11   Utility curve: multiple bids

Using the data provided by Figures A2.10 and A2.11 the expected utility values for the alternative bids, taken together, were calculated as shown in Figure A2.12. Based on this the decision was made to submit the initial bid at the break-even level.

A COMMENT ON THE USE OF UTILITY SCALES IN COMPETITIVE BIDDING

In arriving at his own scale of utility values for differing profit contribution levels for any one bid in a particular risk situation, a manager is indicating:

1 His own personal approach to risk taking
2 His own degree of preference for one margin level as compared to another.

Such a scale does not represent for him the value of money, although, obviously, the worth which he places on defined amounts of money under stated risk conditions is one of the factors which enters his assessment of utility values. Rather, the scale depicts his attitude in that par-

Event	Conditional monetary value £'000s	Conditional utility value	Joint probability	Expected value
Bid at break-even				
Win:win	75	9.8	0.56	5.5
Win:lose	−20	0.2	0.24	0.048
Lose:win	70	9.5	0.08	0.76
Lose:lose	−25	0	0.12	0
			——	6.308
Bid at 10%				
Win:win	85	10	0.28	2.8
Win:lose	−10	1.5	0.12	0.18
Lose:win	70	9.5	0.24	2.28
Lose:lose	−25	0	0.36	0
			——	5.26

Figure A2.12   Expected utility value to Party of a combination of two bids

ticular situation towards a mixture of risk, profit and loss, from which it follows, as emphasized throughout, that his utility function will change as the factors relevant to his assessment change. Thus the extent to which he has assets under- or over-employed, and the availability or otherwise of other opportunities, will both influence him in the degree of risk which he is willing to accept.

It may be objected, however, that in practice business managers do not calculate utility values in this way and that the whole exercise though interesting is entirely theoretical. This objection seems unsustained as there is significant evidence that the observed conduct of managers responsible for profit centres is explicable only on the basis that they do use expected utility values, rather than expected monetary values, in arriving at bidding decisions, even though they may not be familiar with the term 'utility value' as such.

The following example, again taken from my own experience, is typical of such conduct.

Party was submitting a tender against known competitors A and B. Other firms might bid but their actions were classified as random and as such ignored. Firm A had a low cost structure and normally could be expected to under-bid Party by about 20 per cent. Firm B's cost structure was similar to that of Party's. In this particular case, because of the use of a certain component which Party manufactured himself, Party has an off-setting cost advantage of 5 per cent over firm A which reduced his overall deficit to around 15 per cent. As against firm B, Party had an advantage, which was difficult to quantify, of a far better performance record.

If therefore firm A were to bid seriously then Party knew he was wasting his time. However, Party considered that due to capacity problems there was at least a 50 per cent probability that firm A would either not bid at all or would deliberately bid in such a manner as not to be competitive.

On the basis of the above facts and estimates, Party's marketing manager drew up the following appraisal of the situation in the form of the decision tree shown in Figure A2.13.

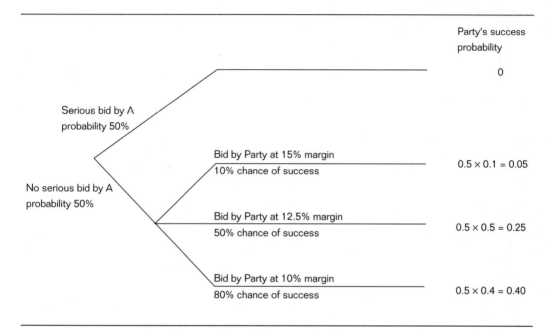

Figure A2.13   Decision tree – Party's bid against competitor A

Using the maximization of the expected value of money as the criterion by which to select the profit contribution then Party should submit the bid at a level of 10 per cent since 40 per cent of 10 per cent > 25 per cent of 12.5 per cent. In fact the marketing manager selected the bid with the 12.5 per cent margin. The total value of the bid was approximately £400,000 so that the difference in profit contribution was £10,000.

When questioned on his decision the manager justified his choice on the following grounds:

1 He did not need the order to sustain volume and he preferred to maintain his price level up, even although he was taking a serious risk of not securing the order.
2 He could foresee other business opportunities materializing in the near future with prospects at least as good.
3 His planned margin for that product line was 15 per cent and he had therefore already made a reduction.

Clearly in the judgement of that manager the existence of other prospects, the lack of any pressing need to obtain orders, and the benefit to be gained from the additional £10,000 margin, if the gamble came off, were worth more than the extra 15 per cent probability of securing £40,000 profit contribution. Assuming he was behaving rationally, and seeking to maximize expected value, this could only mean that he was using, even if unknowingly, utility values rather than money, and that his utility curve as against profit contribution in that particular situation was of the general form shown in Figure A2.14 from which the expected utility values for the two margin levels in question are as shown in Figure A2.15.[8]

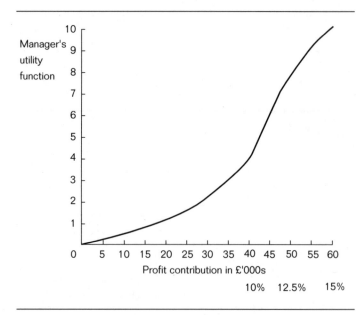

Figure A2.14 Utility curve for marketing manager

Profit contribution	Conditional utility	Success probability	Expected utility
10%	4	0.4	1.6
12.5%	8	0.25	2.0

Figure A2.15 Expected utility values

When the above analysis was discussed with him the manager's actual words were as follows:

> The existence of other prospects affected the degree of risk I was willing to accept at that time. I know that if the tender discussed was the sole and last chance of filling a production gap the importance of getting it would have been much different and so would therefore the acceptance of risk.

The manager accepted the analysis without reservation.

His comments, however, emphasize the point made already that an individual manager's utility function is not constant and is subject to significant change as business circumstances alter.

Notes

1. The line manager's intuitive judgement is supported by the expected utility analysis carried out using the marketing manager's subjective estimates of success probability:

Bid margin	Conditional utility	Success probability	Expected utility
10%	9.5	0.5	4.75
5%	8.8	0.7	6.16
Break-even	7.0	0.9	6.3

2. This assumes that the customer is behaving rationally and will not adjust the worth to him of a given factor, say delivery, so as to enable him to accept the lowest-priced bid. It also ignores factors of personal motivation.
3. It is in this respect that the method proposed here differs from that suggested by S. Edelmann in his paper 'Art and science of competitive bidding', *Harvard Business Review* (July/August 1965). The bias in his comparable table Exhibit VI to that shown in Figure A2.7 is a constant. This may be justified in the type of case he was considering but is not in my experience true for capital-goods contracting.
4. K. Simmonds, 'Competitive bidding – deciding the best combination of non-price features', *Operational Research Quarterly* (March 1968), pp. 5–14.
5. It is for this reason that the chances of success with long tender lists are so low and why bidding under such circumstances tends to produce very low initial prices and subsequent contract disputes over extras.
6. This is based on the assumption that once Party has secured one bid in the series that his capacity has been filled. If the first offer fails then we re-estimate for the second offer with $n = 2$ and if that again fails then for the third offer we are back to the individual bid situation.
7. Note that the monetary values of the two profit contributions must be added together first *before* converting to a utility function. As noted in Appendix 1 two utility values under risk cannot be added together.
8. No significant loss would have been suffered in the event of non-receipt of the award, and to simplify presentation of the calculations the effect of losing the bid has been omitted since it would have a nil value.

APPENDIX 3
MODEL OF THE BARGAINING
PROCESS: BOTH SIDES USING
HOLD-BACK STRATEGY

In submitting an offer which we believe that customer may use as a basis for subsequent negotiations, our objectives are to:

- Prevent outright rejection of our bid
- Avoid bidding to any significant extent below the level at which we believe that customer would be just willing to place an order, and
- Ensure that at least our own minimum negotiating objective is secured by the time that agreement is finally reached.

A3.1 The bargaining zone

The term 'bargaining zone' refers to the area which the parties have selected within which the negotiating is to take place. Prior to the submission of any offer, the upper level of the bargaining zone is formed, the point at which the customer would just prefer to accept an offer than for the negotiations to end in no bargain. It is a value derived solely from the customer's preferences, although it is to be expected that if he has had the opportunity the supplier would have earlier tried to influence those preferences in his favour, e.g. by making recommendations as to the specification which the customer should prepare. This upper limit is not a function of time but is the break-off point beyond which the customer is not expected to concede however long the negotiations take, unless some factor changes which was used in the build-up of that valuation.

After the submission of our first offer, the upper limit will be formed by the higher in value to customer (and therefore in all probability the lower in price) of the:

- Previous limit
- Our own offer
- Any competing offer the value of which to customer is higher than our own offer.

The lower limit of the bargaining zone after the submission of our first offer is our walk-away point. The minimum value which any competitor would accept does not affect the lower limit of the bargaining zone. Having decided as part of our negotiating plan on the offer which provides for us the minimum acceptable utility value, we are not expected to change unless there is a change in some factor which was used in the formulation of the utility value to us which that offer possesses, e.g. the sudden cancellation of an important existing order which causes us to reappraise our need for work. The lower limit is dictated by our preference function in the same way as before the submission of our initial offer was by customer's preference function.

It is recognized that emotionally the effect of a competitor's lower bid may be to encourage us to place a higher subjective value than previously on securing the order. This is only to be expected, since no one likes to lose and in business there are no prizes for coming second. However, normatively, this is not allowed for in the description of the bargaining zone.

It is essential to recognize the effect on the upper limit of the bargaining zone of the level of our first bid. The further our bid is below the level at which the customer would just prefer a bargain to no bargain, the more we have reduced the area for negotiation. It is appreciated that it may be difficult for us to determine this level but the question 'What is the most the customer will be prepared to pay and the least onerous terms to us on which he will contract?' is one we must try to answer to the very best of our ability. The table set out below illustrates the point.

Description	Monetary Terms £'000	Utility value to customer	Utility value to supplier
Maximum customer willing to pay pre-bid	100	6	10
Supplier's offer	80	7	8
Customer's negotiating objective	70	8	6.5
Supplier's negotiating objective	75	7	7
Supplier's walk-away point	65	10	6

Figure A3.1   The bargaining zone

By bidding well below the maximum level which the customer was prepared to pay, the seller has reduced the area of the bargaining zone.

A3.2 The effect of time on the initial offer level

When customer's strategy was quick kill, and Party responded accordingly by putting forward his final offer first, Party's influence on the time which would elapse before contract award was minimal. The period was determined solely by the time taken by customer to adjudicate the bids and obtain any financial or other authority necessary for contract signature. If that period was likely to be extended, then Party would, of course, have taken that into account in fixing his costs. However, there was no co-relation between Party's actions and customer's time-scale so that in deciding on the offer he would make, Party did not need to allow for the effect of that decision on the time which would be taken by customer to finalize the contract.

In the case under consideration Party has decided to adopt hold back either because he knows that customer has himself selected that strategy or because Party is uncertain as to which strategy customer will select. As a result Party will now have a direct influence on the time which will elapse between bid submission and contract signature (unless Party is eliminated from further participation because his bid so far exceeds that of his competitor(s) or the amount customer is willing to pay).

Party's influence on the time-scale for contract award arises first from the level at which he submits his initial offer. In general, the higher Party's original demand, provided that it is not so high as to be summarily rejected, or recognized as pure 'padding', the longer the negotiations will take.[1] The second way in which Party will influence the negotiating time is through his decisions on the rate at which he will concede and the minimum bargain which he is willing to accept. Again, it would be expected that the more favourable the bargain required by Party the longer will be the negotiating period.

Both these propositions which are intuitively appealing have received support from bargaining experiments. Pruitt and Drew found that when the negotiations were conducted under mild rather than acute time pressure there was both a higher initial demand and a higher minimal goal.[2] As they surmised, a tough negotiating strategy aimed at securing a highly favourable outcome takes time to produce the desired effect. Other experiments by Pruitt and Johnson found that Party's concessions were both greater and more frequent under extremes of time pressure.[3] One explanation could be that Opponent will regard any concessions by Party as less of a sign of weakness when he knows that Party is under severe time pressure than when he knows he is not, and because of this Party will be less concerned with appearing firm and saving his face by avoiding making concessions.

However, as Cross has pointed out: 'the more distant the agreement the less its present value'.[4] Since there are no benefits to be gained until final agreement is reached it is necessary to:

1 Discount the worth of any bargain, as valued at the time of agreement, back to its present value
2 Deduct from that value the costs incurred directly in achieving that bargain.

The extent to which it is necessary to be conscious of time costs will obviously depend on the period involved since, in general, such costs may be expected to be linear with time. However, in an age of inflation, even short periods of time can give rise to costs being incurred which will significantly erode the expected gains from further negotiation. These costs may be listed in five groups:

1 Negotiating costs – for example, hotel bills, air fares for the negotiators.
2 Resource costs – the negotiators if not involved on this bid could be employed on other activities.
3 Escalation costs – the longer it takes to finalize the contract the later in calendar time will be the period within which the work will be executed and therefore in times of inflation the higher the costs. Unless these are recoverable under a price escalation clause they must represent a straight reduction in margin.

4 Dislocation costs – the bid will have been made on the assumption that the work will be carried out within a certain period, during which the total activity has been forecast to be at a particular level. Any serious delay which places the contract work in a different calendar period, to which other conditions apply, may cause an increase in costs, e.g. the effect of winter, as opposed to summer, conditions on workers, or the need to work overtime.

5 Discounting costs – the later receipt of funds which will be generated by the contract as a contribution to margin means that these must be discounted to bring them to present values.

In deciding on the level of his initial demand Party must balance the gain to be derived from demanding more with the loss which he will suffer from delaying agreement. The offer which maximizes worth to Party is that for which any increase in utility value, because of a higher demand, would be exactly offset by the reduction in utility due to the greater time costs necessarily associated with the achievement of such demand:

$$\text{Marginal increase in demand utility} = \\ \text{marginal reduction in utility due to time costs}$$

This will be recognized as the bargaining equivalent of the optimal output of a profit maximizing firm at which marginal revenue equals marginal cost.

It is not suggested that in practice Party will have available input data of sufficient reliability to justify the use of sophisticated equations for ascertaining the level of demand which would exactly satisfy the above requirement. The study of the appropriate mathematical expression is, however, justified on the grounds that it will identify the factors which are relevant in determining such demand, and the manner in which they are interrelated. From the understanding so gained the negotiator can formulate his own initial demand which will be optimal in relation to the information available to him and the degree of reliability which he can attach to it.

A3.3 Model of the bargaining process in relation to the selection of the initial demand

Party's initial demand will be represented by q_1 and customer's initial offer by p_1 such that $q_1 p_1 = M$; $M > O$.

Party does not in general expect that he will be able to secure acceptance of his initial demand. His expectation is that at the end of the negotiating period he will have been able to secure a maximum concession from customer, at the price of having made some related minimum concession himself, and that these concessions when taken together will establish a bargain at some point $<q_1:> p_1$, which customer would accept. Note that such a bargain would not necessarily be acceptable to Party. It represents only the optimal outcome to Party of the two initial demands, the related bargaining period, Party's expectation of customer's maximum concessions, and Party's expectation of his own minimum concessions necessary to produce those he expects to obtain from customer.

If formally the concession factor is represented by F, then in relation to the initial offers $(q1 : p_1)$, Party expects that:

1 The maximum concession he can hope to secure from customer will be:

$F(p_1)$ $_{\text{limit } (q_1 F(q_1) T_{11})}$

2 In order to persuade customer into making that concession Party as a minimum will have to concede:

$F(q_1)$ $_{\max (F(p_1))}$

3 It will take time T_{11} to achieve the above concessions

4 $F(p_1)$ $_{\text{limit } (q_1 F(q_1) Tn)}$ + $F(q_1)$ $_{\max (F(p_1))}$ = M

The notation is intended to express the idea that the concession factor $F(p_1)$ represents the maximum concession which customer would ever be willing to make, given his initial offer p_1, i.e. $p_1 - F(p_1)$ equals the level at which customer would just prefer a bargain to no bargain. In practice, customer would first formulate his minimum settling figure and then add the negotiating margin, some or all of which he would hope to be able to retain, depending on how strongly Party presses his demands and the other pressures on customer to reach an agreement, which would be reflected in the form of his concession factor. This accords with the definition of hold-back strategy (see p. 87).

The true form of customer's concession factor $F(p_1)$ will be unknown to Party. He can only make his own subjective assessment of what form the factor will take and in practice he will probably tend to underestimate. The subscript $(q_1 F(q_1) T_{11})$ represents the variance effect on customer's true concession factor of Party's negotiating plan, based on Party's subjective assessment of what he believes customer's concession factor to be, expressed in terms of:

1 Party's initial demand
2 The intransigence Party plans to show and the concessions he intends to make in terms both of timing and amount, i.e. Party's own concession factor
3 The time-scale over which Party plans the bargaining to take place.

The expression 'limit' indicates that each of Party's factors has a limiting value in terms of the maximum concessions which Party can secure from customer. If Party does manage to select all three factors at their optimal limit, then his plan will be based on extracting the maximum concessions which customer is willing to make. If he selects a plan for which any one or more factors has a less than optimal value, i.e. he plans to concede more than customer would demand, then his ultimate return from that plan will be less than the maximum customer is willing to concede.

Equally, however, if Party goes beyond the limiting value of any one factor, e.g. by increasing his initial demand, then this will not increase customer's concession factor. Indeed any such action could have the reverse effect.

Associated with time T_{11} there are time costs C_1 which will be incurred by Party. Finally it is necessary to discount the value of any bargain reached by a discounting factor, r, which will convert it from the value at time T_{11} back to its present value.

The discounted outcome which Party anticipates from the above factors is represented by O_{11}.

In general form we can then state:

$$O_{ij} = [q_i - F q_{1\,(\text{max}\,Fp_j)}]\,(1 - r\,T_{ij}) - C\,T_{ij}$$

This expression is interpreted in the following way. For each initial demand which Party chooses to make $q_1, q_2 \ldots q_p$, related to the offer made by customer $p_1, p_2 \ldots p_j$, Party expects to be able to obtain a maximum concession from customer by offering some minimum concession $Fq_{1,2\ldots j(\text{maxFp1,2}\ldots j)}$ and that agreement will only be reached at time T_{ij}. Associated with time T_{ij} there are time costs $T_{ij}C$ and the value of the agreement reached at time T_{ij} must be discounted back to its present value.

A3.4 Relationship of the above model to that proposed by Cross

In deriving this model of the bargaining process, in so far as it relates to Party's choice of his initial demand, much credit is due to Cross and Coddington for their pioneering work in this field. However, it is believed that Cross's apparent wish to establish a theory which owed nothing to the behavioural aspects of bargaining has unduly restricted its further development. In particular, three of his major assumptions are disagreed with:

1 The demands of the parties are independent, i.e. in making his initial demand, Party does not consider the absolute level of customer's offer and Party's expectation of customer's concession factor is not affected by the level of Party's initial offer.
2 Party expects to remain totally intransigent and that all concessions will be made by customer. It is true that through Cross's adjustment process, Party would eventually concede if he found that customer was not conceding in the manner in which he had anticipated. However, this is made the only justification for Party making concessions. If customer does concede as expected by Party then Party remains intransigent and the same applies for customer. As Cross has stated: 'in terms of this model concessions are always a sign of weakness.'[5]
3 Customer's concession rate will be linear.

In the approach to negotiation, Party plans a strategy designed to achieve an end result. In making those plans he allows for what he anticipates is going to happen and he will realistically plan for making some concessions and also, at times, for being intransigent, although it is stressed that Party's concessions are made solely in order to achieve larger concessions from customer. Party's concession factor is therefore a total strategy plan for the whole bargaining period, whilst as Coddington has pointed out: 'a Cross-type bargainer is involved only with tactics and concerned with immediate expectations.'[6]

In the description of the initial expectations which Party has of the mutual concessions factors of both customer and himself, the F factor is allowed to take a wide form, the only restriction being that in relation to any pair of demands q_i: p_j the factor from Party's viewpoint is optimal, i.e. it represents the minimum concession which Party anticipates having to make in order to secure the maximum concessions from customer.

Specifically, and again departing from Cross, it is maintained that these expectations which the two sides have of each other's concession factors are themselves, in part, a function of their initial demands. There exists therefore in this model, unlike that of Cross, a direct relationship between the F factor and the initial demands such that a change in either q_i or p_j may lead to a change in any or all of:

1 Party's own concession factor
2 Party's expectation of customer's concession factor
3 Party's expectation of the time of agreement.

As regards the assumption of linearity of the rate of concession by customer (in Cross's model Party never expects to have to concede himself) Cross admits that this is only a convenient assumption made for the purpose of simplification. However, given the concept of the concession factor as representing Party's own plan and his expectation of Customer's plan over the negotiating period, it is an assumption which cannot be accepted. Rather a varying pattern of concessions would be expected, differing in amounts, with periods of intransigence in between, varying in length. In general it is proposed that:

1 The greater the total concession expected of customer the lower will be his average concession rate.
2 Customer's rate of concession will decrease the nearer the bargaining moves to his minimum acceptable level.

These propositions are based on the assumption of the increasing marginal utility of money the closer the negotiations approach to the limit at which customer would prefer 'no bargain'.

Cross recognizes this possibility but does not allow for it in his model, apparently on the grounds that Party cannot be expected to know customer's utility function. However, it is maintained that Party must attempt to assess this function and that it should be a primary objective of market intelligence activity to provide him with the necessary data to do so.

The less Party knows regarding customer's utility function the greater will be the gap between his belief as to the form of customer's concession function and the reality. Further, the interacting mechanism between Party's estimate of the worth to customer of the goods/services concerned, Party's behaviour and customer's concession factor, will operate to reinforce the effect of any such gap.

If Party underestimates customer's valuation of the goods/services, then Party will demand less, and the less Party demands, the less customer will believe he needs to concede. He will regard Party's initial offer as a sign of weakness and behave accordingly.[7]

Alternatively if Party overestimates customer's valuation then Party will submit an initial demand well above the upper level of the bargaining zone. Since customer as a rational bargainer knows that Party's demand is related to Party's expectations regarding customer's behaviour, he will recognize that Party has made a mistake and in consequence will not increase his own concession factor.[8] Eventually, when as a result of customer standing firm Party is taught to understand his error, he will be compelled either to reduce his demands substantially and lose his reputation for firmness, or break off the negotiations.

This is the variance effect of Party's negotiating plan on customer's concession factor, and indicates how critical it is for Party to gain the maximum understanding of customer's utility function and hence of his concession factor. A list of the principal factors likely to be involved in any such assessment is given on pp. 326 and 327.

A3.5 Selection of the optimal demand

Although the outcome has been defined in terms of Party's initial demand and his concession factor, together with the time at which Party expects agreement could be reached, it should be evident that both Party's demand and his concession factor are only a response to his expectations regarding customer's behaviour. If it is assumed that customer's initial offer is known with sufficient certainty by Party that it may be treated as a parameter, then Party's concern is with his judgement as to customer's maximum likely concessions from this offer, and the time which it would take to achieve these. for any given demand/concession factor which Party might select. Based on his judgement, Party can then derive a series of possible outcomes using the equation on p. 322 and select that demand which is optimal.

In exercising that judgement, the following are suggested as guide lines to the way in which the factors would be expected to interact:

1 When Party puts forward a demand initially he should do so with the expectation of a pattern of responsive concessions occurring over the bargaining period. In union–management negotiations alternative moves have become almost a convention so that failure to make some response, even if it is only minimal, will lead to an accusation of lack of good faith.[9] The alternating of the frequency of concessions (although Party's concessions may be smaller than those of the other side) has also been reported in the experimental work referred to by Baron and Liebert.[10] My own negotiating experience in various parts of the world, covering Latin America, Europe and the Middle and Far East, has again been that to obtain a concession from the other side, one is expected at some stage to offer him something in return. Moreover, the timing must be such that he will recognize your concession as a response to his. To behave otherwise would be regarded by him as an insult. Further, because he expects you to behave in this manner, the other side, will artificially create bargaining counters to be given away to you in return for a concession which he wishes to secure.

2 The rate at which concessions will be made will be dependent on the initial gap between the parties and whether or not:

   (a) Some particular bargain appeals as the unique outcome due to the manner in which the demands have been structured.[11]

   (b) The negotiators are concerned with their reputation and possible loss of face.

3 If the gap between the two initial demands is small, unless the marginal loss in utility of any concession would be significant, a high concession rate would be expected. With a small gap it should be easy for the two sides to identify a bargain with which both could be satisfied. Neither will wish to incur the time costs associated with a prolonged period of bargaining which could rapidly off-set any advantage gained by holding out for better terms. In practice the most likely bargain would be a 50/50 split.

Only if the identifiable bargain is at the outer limit at which both sides would only just prefer a bargain to no bargain, i.e. the marginal reduction in utility from any concession would be high, will the concession rate be low and the negotiations extended. This will most often happen when the outcome of the bargaining will establish a significant precedent for the future, even though its immediate impact may be small, and covers the case of bargaining on so-called 'points of principle'.

4 If Party increases his demands so that the gap widens, then no final bargain is likely to be immediately identifiable and customer cannot be expected to make any early concessions. Rather he will seek to test the strength of Party's resistance, establish trade-off factors and so formulate his ideas about the level and shape of the final agreement.

Equally Party is in no position to encourage customer into conceding by making any early concessions himself, since to do so too soon and at a stage remote from the final bargaining area would only be taken by customer as a sign of weakness. He too will wish to explore and test whether his expectations of customer's concession factor are likely to be justified.

By increasing his demand Party will therefore have altered his expectations of the timing and the size of the concessions to be expected from customer, and so also the shape of his own concession factor. He must now balance the need to communicate with customer (to invite a reciprocal response) with the need to show firmness. He may have to plan to move first immediately he senses that to do so will lead to a response. The position has been well stated by Peters in this quotation from advice given by a mediator to a union official in America:

> You have offered the employer no inducement, none whatever, to take another step. The employer has made it clear. He is not tipping his hand any further. Not until you show him where you are going. When you are up at 30 cents you are telling him nothing. When you come down to a point where he can guess roughly where you are going then he will reciprocate. It is possible to come out on the short end by dropping down too fast but you are so far away from the real bargaining area yet you have not even come to grips with the employer. The time to get cagey is when the dentist's drill is near the nerve. Then there is some advantage in forcing the other side to move before you do.

Having increased his demand Party must either accept a long drawn-out negotiation and retain his reputation for firmness, or concede more rapidly so reducing the negotiating time but lose face to customer by appearing weak.

This latter point will be of particular importance where the parties contemplate a long-term continuing relationship and the negotiators can expect to meet on numerous future occasions.

A high initial demand, if a reputation for firmness is to be retained, carries with it therefore the penalty of extending the negotiating period so that the delicate process of exploration and adjustment can be given time to work itself out in the manner suggested by Peters.[12]

5 By way of corollary to the last point, if the negotiating time is restricted by some factor which is external to the bargaining process, e.g. customer has a prior commitment to place the order by a definite date, then there is a limit on the initial demand for which Party should ask, unless his position is one of total dominance, and he can genuinely expect that customer will do all the conceding. In any other instance if he exceeds this limit then Party will find that he can only make a bargain if he concedes at a rate which would seriously prejudice his reputation for firmness. He will then be compelled to choose between the lesser of two evils: loss of face or failure to reach a bargain.

A3.6 Assessment of the concession factor

So far no attempt has been made to define how Party should assess customer's concession factor, although in the model such assessment is crucial to Party's choice of his own concession factor and his optimal demand. The following points are suggested as having the most relevance in making such assessment:

1 Party's knowledge of customer's budget and of the worth to customer of the contract. Is customer already committed to purchase? If not what are the alternatives open to him?
2 The existence of any competitive bid in which customer is seriously interested.
3 The importance to customer of time.
4 Past precedents which Party has established with customer, and Party's previous experience in dealing with the individual negotiators for customer and equally their experience of dealing with Party. The personality of the individual negotiators for each side and their knowledge of, and respect for, each other's skill and determination will have a significant effect on the expectations each side will form of each other's concession factor.
5 The manner in which the demand(s) are structured. An offer which is between round numbers usually implies that the person making it is willing to concede to the lower. Equally an offer in round numbers which has no obvious line of movement away from it may indicate a strong determination not to concede further.
6 The way in which customer will view his long-term relationship with Party and his expectation of Party's willingness to respect customer's viewpoint taking into account the prospects of future business.
7 The rationality of the concessions relative to the other factors in the total bargain and to customer's business. In relation to the conditions of contract and the associated risks the argument in favour of the concession is stronger, and therefore customer's acceptance of it

more likely, if it can be shown to be fair and reasonable, and if the terms of the final contract as amended by the concession would form a logical whole.

8 Party's ability to involve a third party whose wishes customer must respect, e.g. mandatory requirements of a bank or credit insurer if customer requires credit to finance the contract.

9 Precedents as to price level or terms of contract ruling generally in the industry.

10 The extent to which Party believes that customer has either studied the problem or developed a firm negotiating strategy. Problem study by customer but without definite commitment to a negotiating strategy is likely to lead to greater flexibility and therefore a higher concession factor. Development of a firm negotiating strategy, to which Customer's negotiating team are committed to their own management, is likely to lead to a lower concession factor and possibly to deadlock unless the negotiating objectives of Party and customer substantially overlap, i.e. there is a wide bargaining zone.[13]

11 The effect which the granting of concessions would have on customer's business with other firms, and the ratio which Party's business with customer bears to customer's business as a whole in this particular field. Customer is more likely to grant concessions if these can be isolated from the remainder of his business and if the proportion of his total business affected by such concessions is small.

12 Mandatory requirements imposed on customer either from the existence of rules internal to his organization, national laws or regulations with which he is obliged to comply or restrictions imposed by an external organization such as the World Bank. This factor applies most strongly to contracts placed by governments or government controlled agencies.

In this model, provided that a bargain at the upper limit of the bargaining zone would at least satisfy our minimum negotiating objectives, then the level of our first offer will not be related to that which we would find acceptable, but to the minimum Party believes would be acceptable to customer. Given a reasonable width to the bargaining zone, this will lead Party to adopt a hard rather than a soft approach; to pitch the initial demand at an extreme rather than a moderate level. Certainly the question of fairness will not enter into Party's calculations.

This approach is consistent with that of the rational bargainer of Harsanyi and with the experimental results obtained by Bartos, Cagguila, Siegal and Fouraker, and Chertkoff and Conley, all of which have shown that the hard-line negotiator who has made an extreme offer and conceded little, slowly, has obtained the best of the bargain.[14,15]

One word of caution, however; neither the time costs nor the cost of failing to reach agreement have been significant in these bargaining experiments. The participants have not been concerned with long-term bargaining relationships and the emotional disturbance to such a relationship which the adoption of a hard-line strategy may create. These psychological factors, within the context of a continuing relationship between the negotiators, may lead to a softening of approach. In commerce as in military matters it is the winning of the war, not the battle, which counts.

A3.7 Time and the limits of the bargaining zone

It has been previously established that the upper limit of the bargaining zone, prior to the submission of Party's initial offer, is the level at which customer would ultimately just prefer a bargain to no bargain. After submission of the initial offer, the upper limit of the bargaining zone is represented by the lower of Party's offer and the previous level (assuming there is no competitor).

Subsequently it has been shown that Party will expect customer, over varying negotiating periods, to be willing to reach agreement at some maximum level which is in part a function of the elapsed negotiating period. Further, there is some level beyond which customer would never concede, no matter how long the negotiations were to last. Does this mean that customer's preference function and therefore the upper limit of the bargaining zone will change over the negotiating period?

The answer in the model constructed is no; customer's preference for a bargain as opposed to no bargain does not change over time. However, as a result of Party's bargaining behaviour, there is a change in customer's belief as to the money which he needs to spend, and the terms to which he needs to agree, in order to acquire the goods/ services concerned. The assumption made regarding Party is now made regarding customer, namely that the final level beyond which he will never concede was formulated as part of his negotiating plan and therefore in his mind from the beginning of the negotiation. Any level less than this (i.e. more favourable to customer), which is the most to which he is prepared to agree at a point in time during the course of the negotiation, is merely an expectation of the concessions he considers necessary to make at that point in time in order to reach agreement. Customer only moves towards the upper limit of the bargaining zone as he becomes convinced of the necessity of so doing by the bargaining tactics adopted by Party. The approach is that of the man who says: 'I would be prepared, rather than lose the bargain, to pay £X but only if I am finally convinced that I cannot obtain what I want for less'.

The distinction between a change in preference and a change in belief is important to the choice which Party makes in selecting his negotiating tactics. In this model, that choice is directed towards tactics which will change customer's belief and persuade him that he can only obtain a bargain on the terms and at a price level which Party prefers.

In another model, in which customer's preference function did change, Party's tactics would be directed towards securing such a change by, for example, persuading customer that his offer was worth more than customer had thought and that he could afford to pay the extra. It is a model of this nature which would be required if customer's preference function were such that the point at which he would prefer no bargain was below the lowest level which Party was willing to accept, i.e. there was no bargaining zone. The lower limit of the bargaining zone has been defined as that at which Party would just prefer a bargain to no-bargain, and it has been stated that in so far as Party formulated this level as part of his original negotiating strategy, he is not expected to change it over time unless some factor which influenced his original decision changes, e.g. the state of his order book. Specifically, the model under discussion does not allow for it being changed simply as a result of time. This is in opposition to the conclusion reached by Stevens who states 'An approaching deadline does much more ... It brings pressure to bear which actually changes the least favourable terms upon which each party is willing to settle.'[16] Zubin and Brown in their review of the *Social Psychology of Bargaining and Negotiation* also refer to experiments which have demonstrated the same point.[17]

This divergence of view seems to be due to two factors. The first is the incorrect initial formulation of Party's minimum position. Rubin and Brown suggest that bargainers initially inflate their minimum level and then reduce it as more information becomes available to them as to the bargain which is actually obtainable. It is accepted that some negotiators do behave in this way, but normally in sales negotiations this must be wrong unless the information relates to some element which changes the worth of the bargain to Party at any particular level. If, for example, liability for consequential damages was unacceptable to Party when the tender was prepared, it should still be unacceptable if Party is told he will be awarded the contract provided only that he accepts such liability, assuming always that nothing else has changed which affects the worth to Party of the contract award. The evaluation at the break-even point between what is and what is not acceptable, should be made quite independently of success probability.

It is of course accepted that the two are interdependent. If Party judges the risk, say, of on-demand performance bonds as unacceptable, then this will deprive him of the opportunity of bidding into countries where they are mandatory. The same may apply to other issues such as law of the country, jurisdiction, or payment in local currency where non-acceptance of particular clauses may restrict Party's potential market or at least reduce his chance. What is argued is that, in deciding upon whether to accept the risk or not, Party is concerned with evaluating the bid as a whole in terms of its desirability and if the opinion is that the risk is unacceptable then the answer must be 'no bid', if acceptance is mandatory, or a qualified bid if Party is uncertain whether customer will insist on the point or not. If, however, a qualified bid is submitted, and the decision has been made that the risk is not acceptable, then Party must continue to maintain that position. He must knowingly recognize that he runs the risk of the bid being disqualified, or pressure brought both by customer and his own agent to remove the qualification if in other respects his bid is attractive. Indeed Party must ensure that his agent is fully aware of his intentions and accepts them.

Only too often, however, in practice Party does not make the evaluation in the manner suggested. His executives either engage in wishful thinking that customer does not really mean it, or console themselves with the thought that 'we will cross that bridge when we come to it'. In either case they are quite unprepared for the event when it happens and must then choose between either withdrawing, with the possible loss of a tender bond and certainly creating ill-feeling with customer and their agent, or continuing and being involved in a liability for which no provision has been made. There is also the alternative possibility that by inadequate initial risk evaluation the negotiator will be misled into believing that his management would refuse to accept a particular risk, as a result of which he continues to take that line and so loses the bargain, when in reality they would have been willing, if it was necessary for the purposes of securing the order, to accept it.

Strict definition of the minimum position is difficult and adherence to it when tempted by the prospects of contract award is even more so, but it is the corner stone of Party's negotiating behaviour.

The second factor is the structural difference between labour relations and sales negotiations. In the former a relationship already exists between the two sides from which neither normally contemplate permanent withdrawal. Strikes and lock-outs are seen primarily as phases within a negotiation. Some agreement is therefore virtually a necessity even if it is only a maintenance of the status quo which would only apply in sales negotiations to a case of strict duopoly. Although the union may try therefore to establish a minimum, which is usually the maintenance of their members' living standards, they may be quite unable to maintain this against complete intransigence from the employers' side which by their actions the employers show they are prepared to continue indefinitely, if the only alternative for their members is unemployment or taking other work on less favourable terms. The union's minimum is therefore accordingly interactive with the strength of the employer's resistance and so can vary over time.

A3.8 Level of Party's initial offer relative to the bargaining zone

From the discussion so far, two rules may be derived as to the level at which Party should submit his initial offer relative to the bargaining zone:

1 *The anticipated negotiating period is short enough for Party to ignore time costs and discount rates.* Party should submit an offer at a level which he anticipates will be equal to the maximum he believes customer would ever accept, i.e. an outcome equal to what Party believes is the upper limit of the bargaining zone. In order to believe that the negotiating period is short enough for Party to ignore time costs, he must have concluded that customer will be compelled to concede very rapidly and then can remain intransigent, e.g. customer must for some reason place the order immediately.

2 *The anticipated negotiating period is long enough for it to be necessary to take time costs into account.* Party should submit an offer which, when discounted to its present value and after deduction of time costs, maximizes the outcome to Party based on his belief as to customer's concession factor, and his own related concession factor, relative to time.

This offer will result in an outcome less than the upper limit of the bargaining zone, the degree to which it is less being a function of customer's expected resistance to Party's demands.

In the model, note that Party's initial demand only ever exceeds the upper limit of the bargaining zone by his expectation of the minimum concession he expects to be compelled to make to gain the maximum concessions from customer. Further, if the negotiating time is significant, his initial demand only exceeds the bargain producing the optimal outcome by the minimum concession he expects to have to make during the time taken to reach that bargain. If he were to demand more, then, assuming his expectations of customer's behaviour are correct, this must result in a less favourable outcome.

In the example Figure 16.1, if Party increases his demand to £190,000, his expectation is only an outcome of £153,500 at month 7, as compared to the optimum of £156,000 at month 4 from a demand of £180,000. This is due simply to the fact that the marginal gain between months 4 and 7, after application of the discount factor, is less than the marginal increase in time costs.

It may be suggested that Party should make the higher initial demand with the hope of obtaining the higher pay off but aim to complete the bargaining in four months thus avoiding the adverse effect of the extended time costs. He could only achieve this objective by securing a change in customer's concession factor since it has been predicted that by month 4 customer will only concede £25,000. To do this would require that Party remained intransigent for longer with the substantial risk that towards the end of the four-month negotiating period the gap between the two sides would be too wide to be easily bridged. Party would then have the choice of either conceding more rapidly in a desperate effort to reach agreement, thereby losing his credibility for the future, or facing up to the longer bargaining period and incurring the additional time costs and discount effect. Either way Party would lose.

Note also from the two rules the effect which Party's belief as to the form of customer's concession factor has on the initial demand made by Party. If Party anticipates that customer will resist strongly, so that the negotiating period is prolonged, the effect of the discount factor and the time costs will be to reduce Party's optimal demand. This will be so even if the higher initial demand pursued long enough would eventually produce a greater concession from customer.

This critical effect of Party's belief of customer's concession factor reinforces the importance of the negotiator for customer obtaining and retaining a reputation for firmness. Once established, such a reputation must, within the context of the model, result in a scaling-down of Party's initial demands. Equally a reputation for weakness would result in the demands being escalated.

So far the situation has been analysed from the viewpoint of a two-party negotiation – supplier and purchaser. In practice the situation is often complicated because there are two or more suppliers with whom the purchaser seeks to negotiate at the same time.

The presence of one or more competitors will primarily affect Party in his judgement as to the form of customer's concession factor. Party must recognize that customer will now believe in adding to the pressure through informing Party of the concessions, alleged or genuine, made by the other bidders. This applies of course both ways so that the process is interactive. Party is pressurized through the concessions, purported or real, made by bidders B,C, etc., and vice versa. The result in general is to lower customer's concession factor and increase the negotiating period (assuming customer does not have a fixed deadline by which agreement must be reached). The reduction in customer's concession factor and the extended negotiating period will suggest to Party (and all other bidders) that they should reduce their initial demands. However, it could also be suggested that to allow for the increased pressure from customer, Party (and all other bidders) should raise their initial demands and prolong the negotiations by only conceding slowly. That will bring time pressure on customer and result in a more favourable outcome for the successful bidder.

Figure A3.2 is an amended version of Figure 16.1 and represents the possible changes resulting from the presence of one or more competitors. Party cannot, however, now simply

200	12	30	170	0.06	160	1.5	18	142
190	10	25	165	0.05	157	1.5	15	142
180	8	25	155	0.04	149	1.5	12	137
170	6	20	150	0.03	146	1.5	9	137
160	4	15	145	0.02	142	1.5	6	136
150	2	10	140	0.01	139	1.5	3	136

Figure A3.2   Possible changes resulting from the presence of other competitors

choose the apparently optimal outcome of bidding at £200,000 since he has to take into account competitors' actions. Assuming that his competitors have approached the problem broadly in the same way as Party then each has two alternative strategies; bid high to gain the optimal outcome; bid low to maximize the chance of success. This is illustrated in the game-theory-type matrix in Figure A3.3.

		Competitors			
		High bid 200 – 190		Low bid 160 – 150	
Party	High bid 200 – 190	Possible gain 142	Possible gain 142	Certain loss	Certain gain 136
	Low bid	Certain gain 136	Certain loss	Possible gain 136	Possible gain 136

Figure A3.3   Game-theory matrix

Party's maximin strategy and competitor's minimax strategy (see p. 276) is to bid low since it gives each of them the possibility of obtaining the contract at a value to them of 136. Neither can take the risk of bidding high since this would expose them to a certain loss if the other bid low. This is based on the premise that customer is otherwise indifferent as to which firm he places the order with and having received at least one low bid will save himself the trouble and his own time costs by concentrating on the low bidder.

The bidding problem in this situation is a version of the prisoner's dilemma game (see p. 279) so that although the strategy choice low bid strictly dominates that of high bid and is the unique equilibrium pair, the bidders would stand to gain by a cooperative agreement between them to bid high. The chances, however, in practice of any such agreement being honoured are remote, and so, recognizing that at least one bidder may defect, all the others are bound to follow suit.

Notes

1. If Party deliberately inflates his demand by an excessive amount, and this is recognized by customer, then Party will be compelled to concede at a rapid rate to the true negotiating area or run the risk of losing the bargain entirely. Thus the length of the negotiating period will not be increased because of the additional padding and, indeed, may even be reduced, particularly if customer reacts emotionally against Party's behaviour.
2. D. G. Pruitt and J. L. Drew, 'Effect of time pressure, time elapsed and the opponent's concession rate on behaviour in negotiation', *Journal of Experimental Social Psychology*, vol. 5 (1969), pp. 50–52.
3. D. G. Pruitt and D. F. Johnson, 'Mediation as an aid to face saving in negotiation', *Journal of Personality and Social Psychology*, vol. 14 (no. 3, 1970) at p. 245.
4. J. G. Cross, *The Economics of Bargaining* (New York: Basic Books, 1969) p. 45.
5. Ibid., A. Coddington, *Theories of the Bargaining Process* (London: George Allen and Unwin, 1968).
6. Coddington, ibid., p. 78.
7. This is the attitude of the rational bargainer. If emotional factors are admitted then it seems more likely that customer will treat Party's bid as a cue to his own level of aspiration, and be content with the minimum bargaining necessary to satisfy his personalistic motivation. See Section 14.6 and R. M. Liebert, W. P. Smith, J. H. Hill and M. Keifer, 'The effect of information and magnitude of initial offer on interpersonal negotiation', *Journal of Experimental Psychology*, vol. 4(1968), pp. 431–41.
8. See J. C. Harsanyi, 'Bargaining in ignorance of opponent's utility function', *Journal of Conflict Resolution*, vol. 6 (no. 1, 1962), pp. 29–38.
9. R. E. Walton and R. E. McKersie, *Behavioral Theory of Labor Negotiations* (New York: McGraw-Hill, 1965), p. 88.
10. R. A. Baron and R. M. Liebert, *Human Social Behavior* (Homewood, IL: Dorsey Press, 1971), pp. 431–32. In particular, see D. G. Pruitt and D. F. Johnson, 'Mediation as an aid to face saving in negotiation', p. 246: 'People will be more reluctant to make concessions when the other has been unyielding than when he has been yielding, presumably because they feel it is the other's turn to concede.' The authors also point out that this matching of concessions in frequency was not found under low time pressure because as they suggest: 'There is not much incentive to concede under low time pressure regardless of the other's concession rate'.
11. See the examples quoted in T. C. Schelling, *The Strategy of Conflict* (London: Oxford University Press, 1963), p. 67.
12. E. Peters, *Strategy and Tactics in Labor Negotiations* (New London, CT: National Foreman's Institute, 1955).
13. See B. M. Bass, 'Effects on the subsequent performance of negotiators of studying issues

or planning strategies alone or in groups', *Psychological Monographs General and Applied* (no. 614, 1966).

14. J. C. Harsanyi, 'Bargaining in ignorance of the opponent's utility function', pp. 29–68.

15. O. J. Bartos, 'Concession making in experimental negotiations', Scientific report for the American Air Force Office of Scientific Research (November 16 1964); A. R. Caggiula, *The Reduction of Group Conflict: Group Goal Determinants* (Delaware: University of Delaware, 1964); L. E. Siegel and S. Fouraker, *Bargaining and Group Decision Making* (New York: McGraw-Hill, 1960); J. M. Chertkoff and M. Conley, 'Opening offer and frequency of concessions as bargaining strategies', *Journal of Personality and Social Psychology,* vol. 7 (no. 2, 1967), pp. 181–85.

16. C. M. Stevens, *Strategy and Collective Bargaining Negotiations* (New York: McGraw-Hill, 1963), p. 100.

17. J. Z. Rubin and B. R. Brown, *The Social Psychology of Bargaining and Negotiation* (New York: Academic Press, 1975), p. 122 ff.

INDEX

Energizing the Workplace:
A Strategic Response to Stress

Kim James and Tanya Arroba

If organizations want to make the most of their people's talents and skills, they need to address the growing phenomenon of stress in the workplace not only when it becomes apparent, but also before it emerges. Incidences of stress are rising rather than falling despite efforts to reduce it because approaches have been aimed solely at the individual and their problem without looking at the wider picture.

This book offers a totally new approach to the management of stress in organizations. It focuses on the organizational strategies and managerial actions required for reducing stress. It looks at how stress is created organizationally so that any response can deal with the problem at all levels in a targeted and tailored way to suit the culture and orientation of the business.

Straightforward and practical, the book outlines a new model which covers all the elements needed to manage organizational stress. Kim James and Tanya Arroba provide a step-by-step guide to exploring your needs and problems, and how to develop and implement a co-ordinated strategic package of measures that will create the best conditions for organizational performance.

Illustrated throughout with best practice examples and with pragmatic and salient key points, *Energizing the Workplace: A Strategic Response to Stress* is written for Chief Executives, Directors, Human Resource and Occupational Health professionals who recognize that, in order to thrive, they have to keep their people healthy and committed.

Gower

Gower Handbook of Management Skills

Third Edition

Edited by Dorothy M Stewart

'This is the book I wish I'd had in my desk drawer when I was first a manager. When you need the information, you'll find a chapter to help; no fancy models or useless theories. This is a practical book for real managers, aimed at helping you manage more effectively in the real world of business today. You'll find enough background information, but no overwhelming detail. This is material you can trust. It is tried and tested.'

So writes Dorothy Stewart, describing in the Preface the unifying theme behind the Third Edition of this bestselling *Handbook*. This puts at your disposal the expertise of 25 specialists, each a recognized authority in their particular field. Together, this adds up to an impressive 'one stop library' for the manager determined to make a mark.

Chapters are organized within three parts: Managing Yourself, Managing Other People, and Managing the Business. Part I deals with personal skills and includes chapters on self-development and information technology. Part II covers people skills such as listening, influencing and communication. Part III looks at finance, project management, decision-making, negotiating and creativity. A total of 12 chapters are completely new, and the rest have been rigorously updated to fully reflect the rapidly changing world in which we work.

Each chapter focuses on detailed practical guidance, and ends with a checklist of key points and suggestions for further reading.

Gower

Working in Partnership

Best Practice in Customer-Supplier Relations

Edited by Bernard Burnes and Barrie Dale

'Working in partnership' with customers and suppliers is a pivotal part of the cultural change from being shareholder focused to stakeholder focused which many organizations now see as essential in securing their future success.

This book draws directly on the experience of practising managers working in this developing area, providing sound advice on all the issues, for the benefit of any organization wanting to develop a closer working relationship with their customers or suppliers.

The recent research and examples of best practice collected here come from a variety of business environments, including the public sector, automotive and leisure industries. Investing time in partnerships is shown to lead to wide-ranging improvements in quality, time saving, decision making and cost, often resulting in demonstrably sharp turnarounds in overall performance.

Working in Partnership includes:

- the different types of partnership which can be established
- changes in attitude and behaviour required
- the typical barriers that need breaking down
- specific case studies written by managers who were personally involved.

This is a valuable book in best practice in a new area, which will give senior managers in all sectors the grounding they need to consider its importance to their organization.

Gower